# POLITICAL COMMUNICATION

# POLITICAL COMMUNICATION
## Rhetoric, Government, and Citizens

## DAN F. HAHN
*New York University*

STRATA PUBLISHING, INC.
State College, Pennsylvania

9 8 7 6 5 4 3 2 1

**Political Communication: Rhetoric, Government, and Citizens**

Copyright © 1998 by Dan F. Hahn
All rights reserved. Printed in the United States of America. No part of this publication may
be reproduced or distributed in any form or by any means, or stored in a data base or retrieval
system, without the prior written permission of the publisher.

Published by:

Strata Publishing, Inc.
P.O. 1303
State College, Pennsylvania 16804
Telephone: 814-234-8545
Fax: 814-238-7222

Library of Congress Cataloging-in-Publication Data

Hahn, Dan F.
    Political communication : rhetoric, government, and citizens / Dan F. Hahn.
        p. cm.
    Includes bibliographical references and index.
    ISBN 0-9634489-3-5
    1. Communication in politics.   2. Communication in politics—United States.   I. Title.
    JA85.H34    1998          97-34149
    324' .01'4—dc21          CIP

Text and cover design by Leon Bolognese & Associates, Inc.

Printed and bound by Data Reproductions Corporation.

Credits and acknowledgments appear on the following page, which is an extension of the
copyright page.

ISBN: 0-9634489-3-5

# Credits and Acknowledgments

Portions of Chapter 6 were presented as "Political Language, the Art of Saying Nothing," coauthored by Dan Hahn and Susan Drucker (paper presented at the convention of the New York State Speech Communication Association, Syracuse, NY, October 1986).

Other portions appeared as a chapter by Dan Hahn, titled "Political Language: The Art of Saying Nothing," in *Beyond Nineteen Eighty-Four: Doublespeak in a Post-Orwellian Age,* edited by William Lutz (Chicago: National Council of Teachers of English, 1989), 111–120. Copyright 1989 by the National Council of Teachers of English. Reprinted with permission.

An earlier version of a portion of Chapter 7 was published as "Myths, Metaphors, and American Politics," *Et Cetera* 35 (September 1978): 254–264.

Earlier versions of various portions of Chapter 8 were presented or published in the following venues:

"Romantic and Sexual Symbolism in Presidential Politics" (paper presented at the Speech Communication Association convention, Miami, November 1993).

"Thinking with the Body: Sexual Metaphors," *Communication Quarterly* 41 (Summer 1993): 253–260 (coauthored with Deborah Borisoff).

"Gender Power in Context: A Reevaluation of Communication in Professional Relationships," *New Dimensions in Communication: Proceedings of the 52nd Annual Conference* 8 (Fall 1995): 11–27 (coauthored with Deborah Borisoff).

"Gender and the Binary Discourse System," *The Speech Communication Annual* 9 (Spring 1995): 33–50 (coauthored with Deborah Borisoff).

"Sex' as Rhetorical Invitation to War," *Et Cetera* 45 (Spring 1988): 15–21 (coauthored with Robert L. Ivie).

"The Mirror in the Window: Displaying Our Gender Biases," in *Voices in the Street: Explorations in Gender, Media, and Public Space,* edited by S. J. Drucker and G. Gumpert (Creskill, NJ: Hampton Press, 1997), 101–117 (coauthored with Deborah Borisoff).

Earlier versions of various portions of Chapter 9 were presented in the following venues:

"The Passionless Honeymoon: Bush in the White House" (paper presented at the Eastern Communication Association convention, Philadelphia, April 1990), coauthored with Susan Mackey-Kallis.

"From Courtship to Date-Rape: False Intimacy in the White House" (paper presented at the Eastern Communication Association convention, Portland, ME, April 1992), coauthored with Mary Stuckey.

I also want to give my thanks to my good student, Alishia Urba, for her insights into seeing Nixon's resignation speech as a divorce document.

Most of the evaluative criteria in Chapter 14 are derived from LISTENING FOR A PRESIDENT, Ruth M. Gonchar Brennan and Dan F. Hahn. Copyright © 1990 by Ruth M. Gonchar Brennan and Dan F. Hahn. Reproduced with permission of GREENWOOD PUBLISHING GROUP, INC., Westport, CT.

# Contents

vii

# Preface

This book concerns the societal conversation that is politics. It discusses the major elements affecting the conversation—the liberal and conservative ideologies of politicians, the arguments on which those ideologies rely, the language in which the arguments are couched, the ways in which the conversation is undermined by government lies and secrecy, and the persuasive effects of media coverage. All these elements are sketched in a way that is intended to help students understand the political dialogue and enter it as active citizens.

Most of my students are intimidated by politics. They are not sure what the differences are between liberals and conservatives, where they themselves fit on the political continuum, or what criteria they might use to evaluate the political messages they receive. Many of them were born in the late '70s or early '80s; the only presidents they have "known" are Reagan, Bush, and Clinton. Thus, they vaguely believe conservatives are "hard-headed" and "practical," liberals "dreamy" and "ineffectual." Most are "turned off" by politics, yet idealistic about reforming everything.

This book begins by explaining the nature of the "ongoing argument" that is politics. I develop the thesis that the basic question in politics, hence in political argumentation and in the distinctions between liberals and conservatives, swirls around a single question: "how much freedom versus how much order?" I explain that conservatives favor freedom in economics and order in civil liberties while liberals opt for the opposite: order in economics and freedom in the sphere of rights.

After tracing the basic ideological arguments, I examine the language in which the arguments are framed, the importance of the power of definition, the significance of the forms in which arguments are cast, the major outlines of political semantics, the mythic beliefs that structure the language, the major metaphors of political discourse, and the importance of sexual language, not only in subjugating women but also in providing nearly subliminal persuasion about foreign policy, political candidates, and a myriad of other political issues.

I then consider how the societal argumentation can be undermined by overly suspicious government communication. The governmental uses of secrecy, surveillance, and lies are compared to similar practices in our interpersonal relationships. I also evaluate them in terms of how they are detrimental to the health of the public dialogue.

Finally, I examine the role of the media in the societal conversation. Specifically, I describe the enormous political effects of the media, beyond those normally attributed to them. That is, whereas the common view is that the ideological biases of the media shape the content of political communication, I describe how normal media practices affect public perceptions of issues. Hence, I examine how the media affect the structures of campaigns, how mediated campaigns affect both voters and politicians, and how individuals might go about protecting themselves from being unduly influenced by media representations of political phenomena.

Three central characteristics shape this book: (1) its concern with a broad scope of political communication, (2) its jargon-free consumer perspective, and (3) its rhetorical emphasis.

First, the book presents politics as an ongoing conversation about social issues, encompassing a broad scope of political communication without in any way denying the centrality of elections in our political system and the role of communication in electoral campaigns. I have tried to demonstrate the ubiquity of political communication in contemporary life, with the hope of demonstrating to students how central it is to their own existence.

Second, the book is written for readers who are intelligent but do not necessarily have much background in either politics or communication. I believe the level of sophistication will satisfy graduate students in both political science and communication, but I have avoided the jargon that would have made the material too difficult for undergraduates. I have tried to write clearly, using examples, quotations from the popular and scholarly discourse, and occasionally humor, addressing students not as idle spectators of politics and political communication, but as active consumers, i.e., as *citizens*.

Third, the book has a rhetorical emphasis that is manifested throughout the text, and particularly in the enormous amount of attention to the language of politics from the standpoint of the citizen. That is, I do not attempt to teach politicians how to use language; my goal, rather, is to give citizens some insight into how they can listen more critically to politicians' rhetoric. Throughout the book, whenever the words of politicians are considered, the central questions posed are rhetorical: Why is the politician using these words? What effects do they expect—and intend—these words to have on the audience? What do these words tell us about the speaker?

With this book, I have attempted to take students from where they are (confused, apathetic, yet idealistic) and give them the tools to get involved in the ongoing political debate.

## Acknowledgments

No book is the product of a single mind, though the singularity of the author's mind must put a distinctive stamp on it. This book is no exception. Many intellectual mentors, some of whom I never met, have led me through the thickets of rhetoric and politics. Most notably, the writings of Kenneth Burke and Murray Edelman have indelibly affected my own thinking about political communication. Indeed, without Burke and Edelman, the field of political communication *as I understand it* would not exist.

I also wish to credit contemporary colleagues whose encouragement and friendship contributed to this book (and vastly improved the quality of my life): Ted Windt, University of Pittsburgh; Judith Trent, University of Cincinnati; Jim Chesebro, Indiana State University; and Deborah Borisoff, New York University. Each in his and her own way has been instrumental in helping me see through the intellectual problematics of the field of political communication—and helping me stay sane long enough to do so.

I have been blessed with an excellent set of book reviewers, to whom I give thanks for their diligent work and insightful commentary: Dennis C. Alexander, The University of Utah; Moya Ann Ball, Trinity University; Dale A. Bertelsen, Bloomsburg University; Thomas A. Hollihan, University of Southern California; Kathleen E. Kendall, University at Albany, State University of New York; Darin Klein, Georgia State University; Sidney Kraus, Cleveland State University; Kathleen J. Turner, Tulane University; John W. Smith, Ohio University; and Theodore O. Windt, University of Pittsburgh.

Speaking of excellence, Kathleen M. Domenig, my editor (and publisher of Strata), has been a joy to work with. She is both incredibly supportive and intelligently critical. We have not always agreed, of course (what two people do?), but all disagreements have been resolved with compassion and good humor.

Finally, I must mention my parents, Joe and Irene Hahn, both now deceased. Although neither was in the field of communication, I learned much about the field from them. From my mother, whose middle name, appropriately, was "Mercy," I learned that criticism and meanness do not go together, indeed are anathema to each other. And from my father I learned that although people do not always say what they mean, they do always mean what they say. For these, and many other lessons about communication, and life, and love, I dedicate this volume to the memory of Joe and Irene Hahn. I wish they had lived to read it.

# Entering the Ongoing Argument

*The record of American public discourse is not just a record of old dead orators. It is the transcript of a continuing conversation*
— DAVID ZAREFSKY[1]

Anybody who has ever arrived late to a cocktail party knows how difficult it is to catch up. Every conversation you try to join is confusing. You don't know what has already been said, so you don't know what you should say. Sometimes you plunge in, only to have somebody say, "Yes, that was what Bill was saying a few minutes ago." After a few such embarrassing incidents, you learn either to keep your mouth shut or to change the subject as soon as you enter the group.

Unfortunately, those are also the two options most people take when becoming aware of politics. Nobody bothers to explain what the societal conversation has already covered (although history courses try to do so). Nobody brings you "up to snuff" on the nature of the controversies, what the various sides are, and why people on those sides take the positions they do. All too many people conclude that politics is too complicated and give up. Others try to change the conversation, suggesting new arenas for the societal dialogue, perhaps reflecting the truth of political communication expert David Swanson's assertion that "it is the conceit of each generation to imagine that their problems are without precedent."[2] Some few keep listening until they figure it out, then enter the ongoing dialogue. This last group includes those most likely to have an impact on the politics of the country.

## ▶ Bases of Political Communication

My purpose in this chapter is to help you enter the dialogue. The chapter will, first, demonstrate that political argumentation is not as complicated as it seems when you first encounter it. The chapter identifies liberal and conservative political positions—and the reasons for them—on some of the contemporary arguments that you may hear. It also discusses the argumentative language used by liberals and conservatives as they try to persuade you.

In my attempt to achieve this purpose I have intentionally eschewed the most common definition of politics—as a process concerning power (who has it, how they keep it, how they use it). One reason is that this definition, while valid, does not open up the subject in any particularly helpful way, probably because there are so many kinds of power—such as physical power, referential power, power stemming from authority, economic power, rhetorical power, and so forth. My other main reason for avoiding a power orientation is that, although most of us focus almost exclusively on physical or economic aspects when we hear the word "power," these may not be the most important aspects of politics. They certainly are not the most central aspects of political *communication*, though they do play a role.

A better approach, I think, is to see politics as a process that takes place through communication—from identifying a problem in society (perhaps through conversations with those suffering from it), through proposing a solution, debating the need for a solution (i.e., why this is a more "pressing" problem than a myriad of others), arguing the relative merits of this solution over others proposed, explaining the resulting law to the citizens and to those in the government whose job it is to enforce it, and so forth. At every step communication is involved. Thus, I conclude that politics is the process of solving public problems . . . and that the process takes place through communication. Power lurks in the background, of course, and plays a role in the decision-making. More analytic sophistication can be achieved, however, by focusing on the communication rather than on the power itself, especially if we can manage to keep our focus on why people want power and why they take the positions they do on the problems that face us.

The foregoing definition suggests politics is the process of solving *public* problems, but leaves open the question "what is public?" Whether any given concern is public or private depends on contemporary understandings of the key words "public" and "private." Many people today believe the two realms are absolutely separate—and should be. Further, some people seem to believe that private is superior to public; that it would be wonderful if there were no government, for then everything would be private. Unfortunately, the history of the world gives little comfort to that formulation.

In the Middle Ages (about the only period we know about in which there was hardly any state at all), according to Philippe Aries, in the most definitive work yet done on the history of private life, "the individual depended for protection upon a community or patron. A person had nothing that he or she could call his or her own—not even his or her own body. Everything was in jeopardy, and only willingness to accept dependency ensured survival. Under such conditions public and private were not clearly distinguished. No one had a private life, and anyone could play a public role, if only that of victim."[3]

What allowed the development of privacy, then, and the emergence of the private realm as we know it today, was the development of a more fully functioning state. Aries comments, "An important first step was the appearance of what Norbert Elias has called 'court government.' The king's court assumed responsibility for certain governmental functions that had previously been decentralized, such as maintaining law and order, courts of law, the army, and so on. Space and time thus became available for activities without public significance: private activities."[4]

Seen from this perspective, then, everything "private" depends on the government. On the one hand, it is private because the government has not claimed responsibility for it. On the other hand, it is private because the government has claimed responsibility for other areas, freeing us from concerning ourselves about them individually, thus giving us time to pursue areas we perhaps otherwise would not have time for.

Thus it certainly is not the case, at least historically, that some arenas are "naturally" public and others "naturally" private. Which activities are in which realm is determined by the people living in any era . . . and what could be more "political" than "determinations made by the people living in the era?" But those determinations are not static; they ebb and flow with each historic era. For instance, in feudal times, there was no clear delineation between the public and private realms, and that *social* fact was reflected in the architecture—the feudal estate and castle, protected with walls, moats, and drawbridges, architectural details that disappeared for a few hundred years. In our own era, however, we note the present popularity of walled and gated communities and are perfectly justified in wondering whether that popularity again reflects a perceived disappearance of differentiation between public and private . . . and whether that disappearance is related in any way to some not-yet-identified contemporary political phenomenon.

## The Basic Question

As amazing as it sounds, all political controversy swirls around one basic question: How much freedom versus how much order?

How much freedom should we have to spend our paychecks as we wish versus how much should the government withhold to pay for what kinds of order?

How much freedom should we have to talk in a college classroom versus how much order should be imposed to enable everybody to hear?

How much freedom should we have to identify others negatively, because of their ethnicity or gender or sexual predisposition, versus how much order should be imposed so that nobody is forced to live in a "hostile environment?"

How much freedom should we have to print whatever we desire versus how much order should be imposed in order to protect defense secrets?

How much freedom should we have to procreate at whatever rate we desire versus how much order should be imposed to limit family size so as to avoid worldwide starvation?

Every political question is, at base, a question of freedom and order. The "freedom" side of the question normally refers to something we think we would like to do or that we have a right to do; the "order" side usually refers to an alleged harm to which the exercise of the freedom might lead and suggests that therefore the government, the society, should limit the freedom in question in order to keep that harm from coming about.

Most political argumentation, then, deals with questions such as: Does the posited freedom really exist? Should it exist? What might be the results of everybody exercising that freedom? Are those results good or bad for the society? If bad, are they bad enough to justify interfering with the freedom? If that freedom were lost, would there be deleterious results? Even if that freedom has deleterious results, is interfering with that freedom within the legitimate province of the government? Ultimately, these questions (as well as the whole freedom-order paradigm) are related to our basic political documents: "order" comes from the Constitution itself, which outlines the basic rights and responsibilities of the different branches of government. "Freedom" comes from the Bill of Rights, which outlines the rights of citizens.

## The Basic Arguments

Because the basic question of freedom versus order concerns the *principle* of freedom juxtaposed against the *consequences* of exercising that freedom and whether those consequences justify the government stepping in to establish some limits (order), the basic arguments in politics are arguments from principle and arguments from consequences. For instance, the argument that everyone should be able to say whatever they want stems from the *principle* of freedom of speech, but limitations upon that freedom always are supported by arguments about *consequences*—to the national security, the morality of our kids, and so forth.

BUT (and here is where a lot of people get confused about political arguments) arguments from principle can support either freedom or order, and so can arguments from consequences. To demonstrate, let's look at several basic religious controversies with political ramifications. First, examine two arguments from principle:

A. Favoring freedom: God created us to be free; no lesser being should enslave us.
B. Favoring order: God provided us rules for living; no lesser being should tamper with those rules.

In both cases the argument is based on a principle, namely the principle of what God did and how His action impinges upon human action. One of the arguments, however, suggests that God's actions support the freedom principle, while the other holds that God's activity provides the basis for the order principle.

A second religious/political disagreement can be found in the following argument from consequences:

A. Favoring freedom: One can achieve the good consequence of a saved soul only by freely choosing between good and evil.
B. Favoring order: One can achieve the good consequence of a saved soul only within a society that follows God's rules.

This argument also has to do with what God wants and what humans should do, but it is based on asserted consequences.

I did not choose these two examples lightly, for if you look at them not as religious but as political arguments (which we can do in this country because our basic political orientation has, from the beginning, been firmly based in Judeo-Christian teachings) you see that these religious teachings provide the philosophical underpinnings of liberalism and conservatism.

Liberalism is basically concerned with freedom (liberty). Liberals think we are first of all free and should struggle to stay free. It takes an enormous consequence to convince liberals that people should give up any freedom to bow to governmental-induced order. The reason this basic principle of liberalism is not apparent from an examination of contemporary politics, where liberals seem more supportive of government programs than conservatives are, is that so much of government is aimed at the economy. Liberals see the economy as of secondary importance and so are more willing to impose governmental order on it.

Conservatism is basically concerned with order. Conservatives think that only in a well-ordered society can civilization be established and freedom be meaningful. Only in a few overriding situations can conservatives be convinced that individual freedom takes precedence over societal order. The Heritage Foundation, a conservative think tank, in a report prepared for the newly elected Reagan administration in 1980, reminded Reagan conservatives that "it is axiomatic that individual liberties are secondary to the requirement of national security and internal civil order."[5]

The foregoing does *not* mean, however, that liberals never favor order or that conservatives never favor freedom. It would be wonderfully simple if that were the case, for then we would have a formulaic politics in which liberal=freedom and conservative=order, but that is not how it is. The contemporary situation is not all that confusing, however, for while both sides favor both freedom and order, they are at least fairly consistent in the realms in which they apply their preferences. Thus, while there may be occasional minor exceptions to the rule, for the most part the following four-part division encompasses the liberal-conservative freedom-order belief system:

1. Liberals believe in freedom in the civil-rights arena.
2. Liberals believe in order in the economic arena.
3. Conservatives believe in order in the civil-rights arena.
4. Conservatives believe in freedom in the economic arena.

Visually, the beliefs can be depicted in a 2 x 2 box:

|  | Freedom | Order |
|---|---|---|
| **Economics** | Conservative | Liberal |
| **Rights** | Liberal | Conservative |

The reasons this seemingly simple paradigm is structured this way are somewhat complicated. We first must understand that, for both ideologies, rights are more important than economics, thus both sides hew to their basic concerns (freedom for liberals, order for conservatives) in terms of rights. The economic realm, the realm in which each deviates from its basic orientation, is more difficult to explain. But it helps if we try to see the economy through each perspective, because there is a sense in which neither ideology sees a contradiction between its own stands on rights and economics. For conservatives, economics should be free of government order because the economic system, capitalism, is a different kind of self-correcting order. In short, as conservatives see the issue, they still are supporting the idea of order, even if it is "enforced" by private powers rather than by government. For liberals—just as individuals need to be free of government order in the realm of civil rights, they need to be free from the constraints of capitalistic order in economics, even if it takes government-induced order to achieve that freedom.

## ▶ Major Contemporary Arguments

In order to enter the ongoing political dialogue it is helpful to know the major positions of the contending parties. While I obviously cannot cover all the controversies and all the arguments without expanding the present chapter into a complete book, I will identify a few major contemporary arguments. There are a lot of similarities in both the types of arguments and the major lines of reasoning, so with a little cogitation you should be able to extrapolate from these controversies to others. That is to say, there is enough consistency in political argumentation that you do not need to read all the literature on any particular subject to guess the major points liberals and conservatives would make on that subject.

### Military Defense

Arguing for freedom with an argument based on principle, liberals contend that the principle of self-government requires citizen debate to determine whether the U.S. should go to war, when and where to go to war, and how to conduct that war. And those citizen decisions, they argue, cannot be made intelligently unless citizens have all the available information on our military capabilities and the capabilities of any potential enemy.

Conservatives counter with an argument favoring order and based on consequences. They say that if the government releases sufficient defense information to have meaningful public debate on these issues, potential enemies will use that information and thereby gain an advantage. They conclude, therefore, that we should curtail our freedom and let the government make all military decisions in order to ensure our safety.

## Government Surveillance

Liberal and conservative arguments concerning government surveillance are nearly identical to those concerning military defense. Thus, liberals support freedom with an argument from principle. They say that the right of privacy precludes government from spying on citizens. Conservatives respond with an argument favoring order and based on consequences. They argue that the only way to protect society is to detect possible security threats. If that means some of us must be kept under surveillance, it is better to lose freedom and privacy in order to ensure national security.

## Academic Freedom

In the arguments concerning academic freedom we see a new twist in the argumentation. Now we encounter a topic on which both sides argue from both principle and consequences, although liberals still support freedom and conservatives still line up on the side of order.

Favoring freedom of academic pursuit of truth, liberals provide several arguments based on principle. First, they contend that professors are honor-bound to pursue the truth, no matter how repugnant others may find the fruits of their labors. And they add a second principle-based argument: to censor professors abrogates their right to speak and students' right to listen. But then liberals add an argument based on consequences when they ask, "if the professor is not the final arbiter of what is said in class, who is?" They suggest the consequence of giving that power to the dean or the president of the university or the board of regents or the state legislature would be intellectual uniformity and death of the pursuit of truth.

The conservative argument is for order based on principle. The first principle conservatives rely on is the idea that teaching is a responsibility, not a right, and that teachers' responsibility to the community that hired them is to teach what that community wants to have taught. The second principle-based argument favoring order is that students have the right to learn the *truth*, not some hare-brained ideas of some pointy-headed intellectual in the communication department. Conservatives also support order concerning academic freedom with an argument from consequences. They suggest that one result of academic freedom is that society is poisoned with falsehood.

As you may have noticed, at the center of this controversy is a disagreement about the nature of truth. Pro–academic freedom liberals think truth is unknown and should be pursued; anti–academic freedom conservatives think truth is known and should be disseminated. Liberals tend to think that the process of acculturation alienates people from their "true selves," whereas conservatives are convinced that the "true selves" of humans are driven by passion and given to sinning unless they are "civilized" by acculturation.[6] No wonder the two sides disagree on how education is best conducted!

## Welfare Programs

To this point, one side has supported freedom and the other has supported order, although liberals have not stuck completely to principle and conservatives have not relied exclusively upon consequences. Now we'll look at a more complicated case. In the debate over welfare both sides support both freedom and order and both sides use both kinds of argumentation.

Liberals support welfare programs with an argument favoring freedom and based on principle: that everybody should have the right to a minimum standard of living. But they do not stop there. They also make an argument favoring order based on consequences: They say that if we do not help the poor they may revolt against the system (i.e., against "public order").

Conservatives likewise support both freedom and order. They present this argument based on principle: freedom depends on independence from the state, but if you are reliant upon the state for your income you are not independent, thus not free. Conservatives also attack welfare programs with an argument supporting order that is based on consequences. They allege that if we give to the poor we will lessen their desire to strive and to excel, thereby undermining our economic system.

## Taxes

Nobody likes taxes. On the other hand, everybody recognizes that the government has to get money from *someplace* to pay for its workers' salaries; to buy guns, tanks, and planes; to fix the potholes in the roads; to build schools; and so forth. One possibility would be to designate a certain area of productivity—say, chicken farms—and let the government have a money-making monopoly in that area. But that would be government ownership of an arena of production, i.e., socialism, so we have rejected that approach. (Besides, many of us suspect that if the government owned all the chicken production there soon would be a law requiring each family to serve chicken at least once a day!) So instead of letting the government *earn* money, we have opted to keep all money-earning activities private and designate a portion of our earnings for the government to pay for its activities.

The problem is that we disagree on what the government should be doing and we resent being forced to pay for activities we don't want the government to engage in. And because nobody is perfectly happy with how the government spends our money, nobody is happy with taxes.

Given that nobody likes taxes, how did we end up in a situation where it *seems* as though liberals are always calling for new taxes and conservatives are resisting them? A lot of it has to do with what the government spends the money for. The biggest share of our tax monies goes to pay for the military, which everybody agrees we ought to have. Although liberals think we could get along with less and conservatives think we ought to have more, both camps are devoted to having a strong military. Liberals even have, by and large, given up on convincing the electorate that there is undue fat in the military budget, a large amount of money that would be better spent on other things.

Consequently, the hard-fought battles about government spending, hence about taxes, have to do with the smaller portion of the "pie" that concerns nonmilitary expenditures—such as monies for the poor, for children, for students and education, or for environmental protection. And since the major nonmilitary government programs were initiated between 1933 and 1968, by liberal presidents such as Franklin D. Roosevelt and Lyndon B. Johnson, most political controversy that seriously impinges on our taxes concerns whether to expand, supplement, decrease, or scrap these liberal programs. Clearly, liberals want to expand and supplement them, while conservatives want to decrease or eliminate them. Because these are the only portions of the national budget that get debated, the national political dialogue gives the impression that liberals *want* taxes and conservatives do not.

Saddled with the image of favoring some kind of "spend and spend, tax and tax" program, liberals have fallen on hard times in recent years while conservatives have gained popularity and power. With their ascendancy to power, first with Richard Nixon and Gerald Ford (1969–1977) and especially with Ronald Reagan and George Bush (1981–1993), conservatives have devoted much of the last third of the twentieth century to dismantling liberal programs put in place in the middle third. The big battle in the '90s between the Clinton White House and the Gingrich-led House of Representatives, advertised as a budget battle, was really a fight over cutting back and tearing down the structure of liberal programs for the poor, health support for the aged, protection for the environment, and so forth.

One measure of how successful conservatives have been is the annual report, "The Index of Social Health," from Fordham University. This report "grades" the country on how well it addresses social problems such as dispersal of food stamps, infant mortality, and out-of-pocket health costs for the elderly, i.e., problems where liberals want government involvement and conservatives do not. In 1970, at the beginning of the conservative resurgence, the "grade" given the country was 73.8; twenty-two years later (eighteen of conservative rule by Nixon, Ford, Reagan, and Bush, and four by a moderate Democrat, Jimmy Carter), in 1992, the "grade" Fordham assessed was 40.6.[7] Except in election years, when even conservative governments tend to spend more monies on social programs they know people want, the grades have marched steadily downhill throughout the recent conservative years. Nor is it likely that President Clinton, the most liberal president since Lyndon Johnson, will be able to do much to stem the tide, because the Reagan years put the country so far in debt to build up the military that no one can figure out how to pay to bring these social programs back to the level of funding and effectiveness they had in the Johnson years.

This brief history, then, explains why most contemporary debates about government programs disintegrate very quickly into debates about taxes and why liberals get tagged with the "Big Taxer" label. If the past thirty years had been devoted to dismantling the military rather than the social programs, the reverse situation probably would be at hand: conservatives would be calling for new military programs and liberals would be pointing at them and screaming, "Big Taxer."

## CONCLUSION

▶ I hope this short excursion through some basic controversies of modern politics—national defense, government surveillance, academic freedom, welfare, and taxes—helps you understand the debates swirling around you in newspapers, magazines, friends' houses, and classrooms; and on television and radio talk shows. As you understand the debates (which Kenneth Burke calls "the unending conversation")[8] better and better, seeing how they all are related to the single question of how much (personal) freedom versus how much (governmental) order, you will be in a position to take your stand in the various forums where you encounter the question, from the cocktail party to the voting booth. But this is not only a question of your comfort in various situations. As *Harper's* magazine editorialized over twenty years ago, "citizenship is not transferrable; neither is conscience. The state of America is the state of ourselves."[9]

## FOR FURTHER CONSIDERATION

**1.** In the United States politics is a voluntary activity. Those who practice politics choose to be participating members of the society. But many do not choose to participate, because of apathy, ignorance, anger, or any of a myriad other reasons.

Is this a reasonable way to organize ourselves for self-government? In many countries of the world a minimal level of participation is required; voting is compulsory. Should we adopt such a policy? Should we go even further and make voting a requisite for receiving governmental benefits (for example, students who do not vote could not receive student loans, farmers who do not vote could not receive crop subsidies, businessmen who do not vote could not receive help from the Small Business Administration)? Or would forcing participation unduly undermine our freedoms? Is it better to rely on persuasion to get people involved, even if it results in elections in which only about 50 percent of the people vote?

**2.** Test for yourself the freedom-order paradigm to see if any controversy about which you are concerned fits into the schema.

If you cannot think of one, try this: assume that the manufacturing industry supports a bill to limit product liability and the American Trial Lawyers Association is opposed to the bill. Who is fighting for order and who is fighting for freedom? Or might there be another paradigm that better encapsulates the two sides?

## NOTES

1. D. Zarefsky, "The Roots of American Community," The Carroll C. Arnold Distinguished Lecture, presented at the annual convention of the Speech Communication Association, San Antonio, November 17 [1996] (Boston: Allyn and Bacon, 1996), 10.

2. D. L. Swanson, "The Political-Media Complex," *Communication Monographs* 59 (December 1992): 397.

3. P. Aries, "Introduction," in *A History of Private Life, III: Passions of the Renaissance,* ed. Philippe Aries and Georges Duby (Cambridge: Belknap Press of Harvard University Press, 1989), 9.

4. *Ibid.*

5. J. S. Saloma III, *Ominous Politics* (New York: Hill and Wang, 1984), 16.

6. R. Rorty, "Education Without Dogma," *Dissent* (Spring 1989): 198.

7. "Report on U.S. Social Health Says It's Slightly on the Mend," *New York Times,* 24 October 1994, p. A6.

8. K. Burke, *The Philosophy of Literary Form: Studies in Symbolic Action,* 3rd ed. (Berkeley: University of California Press, 1973), 110.

9. "Countersigns: Notes on a Landslide," *Harper's,* January 1973, 51.

# Ideological Argumentation

*Democracy is . . . conversation . . .
meant to result in the consent of the
governed—an informed consent, a
persuaded consent, not just a sigh of
thanks that all that jabber is over.*
— JAMES D. BARBER[1]

**A**ll subjects are probably more complicated than they at first appear. Consider being asked to write an essay about "apples." Your first thought: "Ah, that'll be easy. Not as easy as 'what I did this summer,' perhaps, but relatively easy." So you start to work, and the first thing you discover is there are many more varieties of apples than you ever considered possible, and while some people may be able to distinguish among all of them, you can't. Then you realize you can't even describe clearly the differences between apples and pears . . . or explain why crab apples and Adam's apples are called "apples" but do not belong in your report.

Of all the myriad complicated subjects in the world, "ideology" is one of the most complex. At the purely definitional level there is the basic question, "what is it?" but that question is complicated by the need to distinguish between "ideology" and other words and processes that share many of the same features—such as "philosophy," "faith," and "belief." Even if we could define "ideology" so each of us would know what it is, we still only would have progressed to the point at which we started our thinking about "apples." That is, we knew what an apple is, but knowing that did not preclude complexities.

In the case of ideology, there is no general agreement on what it is. Some see it as a descriptive word, others view it pejoratively. Some approach it from a psychological perspective, asking, what is that person's ideology and how did (s)he come to believe that way? Others have more of a sociological bent, asking, what is the relation between ideology and society? What is the ideology of this particular society? Some assume the ideology of any given society is no more than a summary of the political and economic beliefs of its people; others focus on how the societal belief structure produces and reproduces the system of power relations (dominance and subordination) practices in that culture.

All these concerns are prior to the question of the variety of ideologies in the world and the differences within and among them.

To keep from getting too mired down and confused by conflicting perspectives, I am going to assume a very broad approach in which *ideology is defined as the belief structure of the society*. For instance, in our society there is a belief that "cleanliness is next to godliness." That belief fits into a belief structure (or ideology) about a whole approach to religion—the "immaculate" conception: the need to bathe and dress up to go to our place of worship; the neatness and cleanliness of our churches; the idea that God does not like anything "dirty" (physically dirty, morally dirty); the tendency of ministers, priests, and choirs to dress in white; and so forth.

Political ideology, then, is the political belief structure of the society. In United States society, there are two primary political ideologies (belief structures), liberalism and conservatism. We'll return our attention to them presently. For now, though, we need to identify the relationship between ideology and communication.

## ▶ Ideology and Communication

Ideologies cannot be developed, sustained, or challenged except through communication. And communication cannot occur without reflecting the ideology of the speaking individual and the society of which (s)he is a member.

Consider, for instance, the relatively simple example of a student going to a professor's office to talk about the grade received on the last test. The chances are good that the student will approach the professor with the degree of obeisance the student perceives is demanded by the ideology of the society. And the professor will respond with the degree of authority (s)he perceives to have been granted the professorial role by the societal ideology.

But realize that both participants are, in a sense, trapped. Neither student nor professor may step out of his/her role without risking his/her future in that role. The communication between people in any society, communication scholar Dennis Mumby tells us, regardless of the ideology of that society, "invokes a complex system of power structures that inscribe and position individuals in particular ways and with certain constraints and possibilities on their activities."[2]

That is to say, even if the professor believes the whole process of testing is so shot through with conceptual error and cultural biases as to be a time-consuming, worthless exercise; even if the student thinks the test probably was a fairly accurate gauge of how well (s)he understood the material covered on the test; the professor will feel constrained by the professorial role (and the requirement to produce a grade for the student at the end of the semester) to defend the test in general and this student's score in particular, just as the student will attempt to take advantage of the possibility that the test was flawed or that his/her score inadequately reflected the degree of information and expertise (s)he gained during this period of the semester.

But neither professor nor student is likely to perceive self as "playing a role," as being constrained by the way power is structured by the society. They will, of course, recognize the professorial prerogative/duty to grade students, but they will see it as *natural*, not as an expression of the ideology of the society. Further, neither is likely to notice the discontinuity between the educational and economic systems. The assumption that the buyer of goods is superior to the seller ("the customer's always right") is accepted in economics, yet in academia the seller of intellectual "goods" is superior to the buyer; the seller (the professor) determines whether the customer (the student) is right or wrong.

The relationship of such discontinuities to societal communication is relatively simple. In the first place, dialogues about economics and education tend to be separated, so it is a rare person who combines the two realms and discovers the "flip-flop" on the "the customer's always right" formulation. Secondly, we are taught (communicated to) that the institutions of society are permanent; that, moreover, they have been tested by ancestors wiser than we are and found to be good and moral and right and efficacious and a hundred other wonderful things.

Yet, despite all this societal communication about the excellence of our received formulations and institutions, we encounter the anomalies and discontinuities of our societal ideology every day. But, interestingly, we seldom perceive them as discontinuities, thus seldom consider the debilitating contradictions in our societal ideology. Another rather parallel example is the way in which youngsters are raised in hierarchically organized and autocratically governed structures called families for eighteen to twenty-one years, then expected to embrace the superiority of equality and democracy while at the same time taking a job in a hierarchically organized company and starting their own autocratically governed family.

It would be difficult to overestimate the harm such discontinuities do to the possibility of an individual developing a consistent ideology. When the social lives of individuals communicate so much variance from the political ideology of the society, something has to "give." Most of us are more likely to loosen our grip on the political ideology than to conclude that our own lives are flawed.

Because the only way we can receive ideology is through words (we cannot taste it or touch it), and because the words that carry ideological meaning tend to come from trusted sources (such as parents, schools, and presidents), we are in a sense "conditioned" to accept ideology as it is "fed" to us in our schools, churches, and media. The ideological words provide what rhetorical critic Michael McGee calls a "vocabulary of concepts"[3] that controls us by controlling how we can think about any phenomenon: the language predisposes us to analyze events the way anyone with that vocabulary would analyze them. Thus, if we are taught that every situation involves manipulators and victims, when we examine a new event we will, of necessity, find manipulators and victims—even if the new event really is a cooperative venture where "everybody wins."

To complicate the matter further, any concept in a "vocabulary of concepts" may be understood differently by any participant in a policy debate. The understandings, claims McGee, may be based on either vertical (down through time) or horizontal (across topics) comparisons. "Freedom," for instance, could be examined in regard to what slavery meant in 1860 as compared with what it means in the 1990s in terms of the average housewife. That would be a vertical comparison. Alternatively, "freedom" could be compared across topics in the same time frame. A comparison of the "freedom" of a contemporary small business owner with the "freedom" of a contemporary high school superintendent, for instance, would be a horizontal comparison. In both cases, a vertical comparison focuses on the history of the concept and how it has expanded and contracted from its original usage to today, whereas a horizontal comparison is based on how the concept is accommodated to the specific circumstances of today's situations.[4]

Because of differences in their vocabularies of concepts, both sides to any controversy might use and rely upon the same culturally significant concept, yet be in complete disagreement with each other. Consider, for instance, the way both sides in the abortion debate rely upon the concept of "freedom." Pro-choice activists want "freedom" for the woman to "control her own body" without interference from the state. Pro-life activists want the state to interfere by giving the fetus the "freedom" to be born.

At one level this difference might seem to be merely different applications of "freedom"—one side applying it to the mother, the other to the child. But it is more complicated than that, for one side is asking for freedom *from* governmental control, while the other is arguing for freedom *through* governmental control. Yet each side, in using the concept "freedom," is relying upon the totality of the history of that word (the vertically based meanings) to come to the defense of the present application.

Most of us in the audience for this debate are unable to determine which history of "freedom" is accurate, which side legitimately is using the concept to which we all subscribe. Both sides are giving us vertical understandings, but we want more contemporary, horizontal interpretations so we can see whether the "freedom" of either side parallels our understanding of freedom in other contemporary realms. Lacking that parallel, we tend to make our decision on the case at hand definitionally, i.e., by deciding whether what is being aborted is a "fetus" or a "child." If we decide to call it a fetus, we have thereby decided it does not deserve our empathy or sympathy; we sympathize with the beleaguered woman and believe that it is her freedom that should concern us. But if we decide that the fetus is a child, we sympathize with that wee human and believe that it, like any human, should share in the protection we all rely on—"*life*, liberty and the pursuit of happiness." Both sides believe they have correctly applied the cultural idea of freedom; in reality, however, both have sidestepped the "freedom" question by deflecting our attention to the definitional argument, "child" versus "fetus." (We will examine the power of definition in more detail in Chapter 4.)

But note that throughout the whole abortion debate nobody (not the pro-choicers, not the pro-lifers, not the audience) gives up any devotion to the societal concept "freedom." All of us are "freedom-loving" Americans.

Indeed, expressing support for freedom is so important in this country that most who would infringe upon freedom first endorse it. A typical declaration is "Of course I believe in freedom, but we're not talking about freedom here. We're talking about responsibility." Such formulations are interesting because it is clear that the speaker is experiencing a degree of cognitive conflict, i.e., some internal conflict between beliefs that inherently are in opposition. What we in the audience are hearing are conflicting ideologies, which communicologist

Teun van Dijk describes as "a more humane and tolerant one" versus "the more authoritarian and intolerant one."[5]

This form of argument is familiar to us. Who has not heard someone start a denunciation of some group with "I have nothing personal against _____, *but* . . . " or "Some of my best friends are _____, *but* . . . ?" For whatever reasons, the speaker finds it necessary to mitigate the "harsher implications" of the ideology being expressed, and so includes the more humane disclaimer as a strategy in "presenting oneself as flexible, humane or altruistic, and as a person who is not prone to rigid generalizations."[6] But we never are fooled by this construction; as soon as we hear the "but" we know that the first part of the sentence says less about what the speaker believes and more about what the speaker thinks *we* believe, thinks *must* be said in order to persuade us to listen to the material after the "but." We will examine this disclaimer process more fully in Chapter 5 under the label "affirmation by denial."

Communication scholar J. Michael Sproule reminds us that the ancient Greek society, where the idea of self-government and the corresponding necessity of rhetoric first were promulgated and celebrated, was quite different from the modern world. The geographical area was small, often only as big as a city (hence, we talk of Greek "city-states"). Political participation was limited to what today we would call the "upper classes," who were an informed and politically active elite. Modern rhetoric is different because modern society is different. Whereas ancient Greek orators tended to speak for themselves, modern rhetors function more as "spokespersons" for an ideology or geographical section of the country or some other "interest." Whereas the Greek speaker addressed an elite and could ignore the effects of proposed legislation on the nonenfranchised masses, today's modern speaker is more likely to try to mobilize the masses as a part of the process of persuading the other elites.[7] Modern rhetoric, therefore, is dependent largely upon mass media, especially television and radio, and must be supportive of the societal ideology.

## ▶ The American Ideology

While on most issues citizens line up generally along liberal or conservative lines, there are overarching beliefs to which both groups subscribe. These beliefs contain the elements of American democratic ideology and comprise, says political scientist Herbert McClosky, broad-based concepts that stress the valuation of tolerance, individualism, the presumption of equal opportunity and equal treatment in both the public and private domains. This ideology, moreover, embraces the seemingly contradictory notions of "majority rule" and "minority rights."[8] Most of these concepts are such vague abstractions, yet so commonly accepted as "right," that most of the time we are not even aware that belief in them constitutes an ideology, much less that they provide the bases of our societal belief system.

To say that these concepts are the major outlines of the American ideology is not to say that everybody in this country favors every one of them. Indeed, one classic study demonstrated that these tenets are endorsed much more by political elites than by ordinary citizens.[9]

Does this disappointing finding demonstrate that the average person is stupid, selfish, thoughtless or morally deficient? No. Other explanations are more compelling, such as the fact that most people are more concerned with what is happening in their own lives than in events taking place in the state capitol or in Washington, D.C. (or, for that matter, in the lives of their neighbors). Additionally, of course, most of us feel we are far removed from the centers of political power; we are confused about what is going on in those centers; we have trouble deciding which of the contending forces we believe; and—except for tax matters—we do not see the effects of any of these "great debates" and "momentous decisions" on our own lives.[10]

Thus, although there is an American ideology, it is supported much more wholeheartedly by the elites than by the average citizen, at least partly because most citizens are not particularly interested in politics, do not pay much attention to it, and are too involved in their everyday lives to spend much time "tuning into" the world of politics *except* when a topic comes along that seems to impinge directly on their lives. At that point they become involved and, as indicated in Chapter 1, opt to support one of two solutions for the problem at hand: freedom from government control or increased government control, i.e., either a liberal or a conservative solution.

## ▶ Liberalism and Conservatism

Chapter 1 identifies liberals as those who believed in freedom in the sphere of rights and order in the sphere of economics, and conservatives as those taking the opposite tack: order in civil rights and freedom in economics. That is a good shorthand way of identifying the two sides, but says nothing about why they are aligned in this manner. To get at that question is somewhat more difficult, but not impossible.

The keys to the two sides were identified in Chapter 1 also, but—interestingly—in the arguments about religious controversies rather than in the tracing of political arguments. Two of those religious arguments provide the foundation for liberalism: (1) God created us to be free; no lesser being should enslave us and (2) one can achieve the good consequence of a saved soul only by choosing freely between good and evil. Believing these religious positions, liberals opt for freedom, but freedom of a certain kind. According to C.U.N.Y. English Professor Louis Menand, such freedom implies "freedom *from* coercion by others" and reflects an outlook of "negative liberty."[11]

The liberal kind of freedom—freedom from—was most clearly identified and purely legislated in the Civil Rights Act of 1964, which said that whatever qualitative differences there might (or might not) be between men and women, between the dominant white culture and the various subcultures, among people of varying races, religions, and customs, those differences are to be ignored when counting votes, serving customers at lunch counters, admitting applicants to educational institutions, interviewing candidates for jobs, selling houses, and generally passing around social resources.[12]

Conservatives, on the other hand, believe in what might be called "positive freedom," i.e., freedom *to*, which I have called "order." Conservatives believe in the other two "religious" propositions identified in Chapter 1: (1) God provided us rules for living; no lesser being should tamper with those rules and (2) one can achieve the good consequence of a saved soul only within a society that follows God's rules.

It is hardly a stretch to see how these religious ideas lead conservatives to support the idea of "positive freedom." Professor Menand points out that these supporters believe that freedom emanates "from directing one's actions toward some articulated conception of the good life. A certain, preferably benign, degree of coercion is therefore appropriate . . . "[13]

Conservatives' idea of order, or positive freedom, is based upon their view of human nature. Edmund Burke, the great eighteenth-century conservative English political theorist, wrote that "History consists for the greater part of the miseries brought upon the world by pride, ambition, avarice, revenge, lust, sedition, hypocrisy and all the trains of disorderly appetites which shake the public." Clearly this is a negative view of humans. So it is not surprising that someone who holds this view would think that people need to be "brought to moral order" by the government. Indeed, Queens College political scientist Andrew Hacker has argued that this basic assumption about human nature has fueled conservatives' attitudes on topics ranging from capitalism, to capital punishment, to welfare. According to such a perspective, those on welfare view government assistance as a preferred option rather than as an interim necessity.[14]

If the foregoing descriptions of liberalism and conservatism strike you as being fairly far removed from the rhetoric and action of politicians who today call themselves liberals and conservatives, you are right. Each side has gotten fairly far off base. It is instructive, I think, to try to identify the ways in which contemporary wearers of the liberal and conservative badges have "gone wrong," have strayed from the original conceptions.

Liberals, I suggest, have made the mistake of abandoning the neutral idea of equal opportunity for an idea of equal results. Equality of opportunity requires only that everybody should be equal at the start of the race; equality of results posits that all should finish the race together. What happened to liberals, I think, was that they discovered that, soon after the race had started, some people were well ahead of others. That returned us to the original problem: inequality. So liberals jumped in again, trying to help those who were losing. While that was a humane gesture, it was philosophically unwise, for the original measuring rod was not the terribleness of inequality but the unfairness of the imbalance of opportunity.

There have been practical consequences of their change in concern from opportunity to results: liberals have come to be seen as people who care only for the downtrodden and unfortunate. That perception that has soured the middle class on the liberalism.

Further, as liberals attempted to meliorate inequalities, to buoy up devastated individuals, families, and communities through governmental acts, their remedies sometimes turned out to be worse than the original disease. As journalist J. B. Judis of the *Washington Post* has stated, liberal governmental intervention intent on helping individuals sometimes has meant that "State bureaucracies replace the family and community and nourish an idea of passivity and victimization."[15]

A second major mistake of contemporary liberals has stemmed from overstressing rights at the expense of community. Clearly, "negative freedom" requires a focus on rights, but there is a big difference between individual rights *within* a community and individual rights versus the community. At any rate, as liberals took the short step from defending individual rights to defending the rights of *groups* of individuals, a "politics of group identity" was spawned. According to John Gray of Oxford University, group identity had two ramifications. The first was to weaken "civic ties." Those weakened ties, in turn, had a deleterious effect on public discourse because public argument was no longer regarded as a conversation between disagreeing citizens who share a common heritage. Instead, according to Gray, public argument became a clash of "warring identities," and, by extension, of "opposing views, values, and interests."[16]

At some point in the twentieth century, perhaps starting in the 1960s—and almost certainly culminating then—liberals came to see attachment to community (i.e., patriotism) as somehow too bourgeois for them. In protesting governmental actions by burning the American flag, they seemed to divorce themselves from more than just contemporary policies. Perhaps in order to protest so avidly they *had* to divest themselves of a degree of patriotism, too. In any case, their contempt for patriotism, for the civic community, came to intersect with the overprivileging of individual rights, so that, by now, says Gray, both "communal attachments" and "civic engagement" are regarded as "optional extras on a fixed menu of individual choice and market exchange" by the prevailing "American culture of liberal individualism."[17]

It is no surprise, then, that contemporary liberalism, having lost its bearings, has fallen on hard times. But conservatism, too, has wandered away from its original formulations. Having for so many years been accused of "pandering" to the rich, and having been supported through those lean years by prosperous companies, conservatives became shills for big business and cheerleaders for economic growth.

Yet, as political scientist Andrew Hacker points out, corporate capitalism is not necessarily compatible with the small town, small farm, and local community values that conservatives normally and traditionally endorse. Hacker argues, "Boeing Company is not a blacksmith's shop, and the 747 is not a horse-drawn surrey. . . . America's love affair with the marketplace has become a Trojan horse its conservatives cannot handle."[18] That is, in supporting the small business owners who provided the core of their support, conservatives gave unflagging endorsement to capitalism, but that left them unable to attack those aspects of capitalism that allowed big businesses to buy out and drive out the smaller, community-oriented businesses that conservatives originally had intended their support of capitalism to sustain.

One problem with the conservative–big business connection is that multinational corporations are not bound to the triad of conservative geographical concerns—neighborhood, community, and nation. The orientation of the multinational corporation was evident in a 1989 statement from Gilbert Williamson, president of the NCR Corporation. When questioned about competitiveness in the United States, Williamson responded: "I don't think about it at all. We at NCR think of ourselves as a globally competitive company that happens to be headquartered in the United States."[19] That is not a statement that any conservative would utter or endorse.

Nor is it only the attitudes of the leaders of the multinationals that should make true conservatives shudder; so, too, should the lives led by their employees and the employees of most big business. While conservatives have been prescient in noting the effects of government dependency upon welfare recipients, they have been less observant of the evils of capitalist dependency, which, as journalist Suzanne Lessard has pointed out, occurs when an individual becomes trapped in a meaningless, but high-paying job that is accompanied by "fringe benefits, including a pension, and nowhere else to go."[20] How, in such a situation of perpetual dependency, can individuals learn the conservative value of self-sufficiency or "the importance of building individual and communal life around the enduring values of the civilization?"[21]

The second major problem of contemporary conservatism is somewhat more natural—we have outgrown and out-learned the conservative orientation. Andrew Hacker claims we have outgrown traditional conservatism by our rejection of hierarchy: "The conservative community assumes a deferential citizenry, one willing to accept prevailing arrangements and obey those administering them. . . ."[22] We no longer revere hierarchical leaders sufficiently for traditional conservatism to work. Continues Hacker, "A proclivity for questioning authority undermines traditional controls, weakening the legitimacy of what were once accepted standards."[23]

"Outlearning" traditional conservatism has been a natural result of social science research since World War II, research that shows that most criminals come from unhappy or dysfunctional homes, that most people on welfare are not too lazy to work but rather are too old or too young or too sick to hold down jobs, that viewing pornography is no more likely to lead to child molestation than is viewing certain sexually suggestive advertising. As the results of such research become known, claims Hacker, we become more likely "to excuse behavior once considered anti-social or immoral. Comprehension breeds compassion. . . . Hence the conservative conviction that science, when applied to human affairs, becomes a substitute for moral responsibility."[24] Faced with a choice between social science research and moral responsibility, the conservative chooses morality every time, but the average American, imbued (perhaps wrongly) with a love of facts and a near-idolatrous devotion to science, opts for the research.

It is the "wrongheadedness" of modern liberalism and conservatism, the tendency of modern liberals to support the lower classes and of modern conservatives to align with the rich—tendencies that in both cases are at variance with their traditions—that have allowed contemporary liberal-conservative oppositions to "slide into" a kind of class warfare. For most of the latter two-thirds of the twentieth century, liberals enjoyed the advantage of seeming to be aligned with the average person. They pressed that advantage by accusing conservatives of caring only for the rich, of being "economic royalists," of sacrificing the middle class on the altar of the upper classes. There was just enough truth in the allegation that conservatives were hard pressed to develop a reasonable response. Finally, in the last years of the century, they hit upon one: the unacceptability of "class warfare" in a democratic society. From that point on, whenever a liberal accused a conservative of favoring the rich over the poor, the response was "isn't it too bad that these liberals engage in class warfare this way, trying to drive a wedge between Americans on the basis of class?"

The truth, of course, is that both sides engage in class warfare, but neither side admits it. Conservatives today *do* favor the rich over the poor; contemporary liberals do favor the poor over the rich. And both sides try to get the vast middle class to align with them. In recent years conservatives have been more successful in achieving that alignment. We can see why if we employ the rights/economics (freedom/order) duality from Chapter 1.

In terms of rights (freedom), liberals believe each person should live life as (s)he prefers. This belief has led them to support some fairly unpopular causes—such as the rights of homosexuals, teenage unmarried mothers, marching K.K.K. members, and people accused of crimes. Conservatives have responded by depicting all these people as dangerous and accusing liberals of abandoning average citizens in favor of malcontents, of abandoning "family values" to support "wild-eyed radicals."

Because the term "family values" has a much more comfortable, everyday, ordinary ring to it than does "individual rights," it *seems* more in tune with the average middle-class citizen. Riding this seemingly common-person set of values, conservatives have engaged in what might be called cultural class warfare. That is, whereas traditional liberal class warfare was based on *economic* class, contemporary conservative class warfare is based on *cultural* class. Journalist Michael Kinsley has commented on a corresponding conservative achievement that shifted the target of "populist resentment" from Wall Street executives to "Chardonnay-sipping" Washington bureaucrats.[25]

A second portion of conservative resurgence has arisen from argumentation in the realm of economics. Here conservatives have been able to argue that the major liberal orientation has been designed to benefit the poor at the expense of the middle class, but that all it has accomplished, despite all the monies expended, has been the creation of a permanently dependent lower class. In short, the argument ultimately says the middle class has been "had" by the liberals—they've taken your money to help others, but the only beneficiaries are the bureaucrats who run these expensive, wasteful programs.

It is useful to notice that although the conservative argument here *seems* to concern economics, it relies largely on class resentment and on the fact that the middle class sees the poor as undeserving of its largess.

The argument also relies on what A. O. Hirschman, in his brilliant book on *The Rhetoric of Reaction*, has called "The Perversity Thesis": "Attempts to reach for liberty will make society sink into slavery, the quest for democracy will produce oligarchy and tyranny, and social welfare programs will create more, rather than less, poverty. *Everything backfires.*"[26]

Paralleling the conservative thesis about liberal programs not being helpful in eliminating poverty, the Perversity Thesis explanation posits that welfare "acts as an irresistible incentive to those working or potentially working at low wages or salaries . . . to flock to the welfare roles and stay there—to become forever 'trapped' in sloth and poverty."[27]

The Perversity Thesis assumes, rightly, that every governmental program has unintended effects. That is undoubtedly true. But what it overlooks is that those unintended effects divide fairly evenly between good effects and bad effects, and that some are mixed—both good and bad. As an example, consider what conservatives often point to as a bad effect of welfare—that, in order to receive Aid to Families with Dependent Children (AFDC), some families break up so there will be a "single mother" who is eligible for the money. That *seems* like an unadulterated bad effect, yet Hirschman points out that the effect is not so clearly bad, in that "the availability of AFDC makes it possible for poor women to escape from marriages in which they are being brutalized or otherwise mistreated. In this manner welfare assistance and the much-vilified 'dependency' on it can counteract another kind of dependency and vulnerability: that resulting from oppressive family arrangements."[28] I suppose it might be argued that if one cannot afford to get divorced one ought not get married, but to date nobody has proposed a "means test" as a requirement for obtaining a marriage license.

It is difficult to know what to conclude from this excursion into the politics of class. Clearly there are class differences in our society; clearly the various classes should be represented in the national legislature and have nationally-recognized voices speaking on their behalf; clearly which voices we listen to and which classes we align with must be free choices for each of us. There is nothing I can say to deny the presence or importance of class.

But I can definitively say that the political communication about class has been bogus. Liberal commentator Michael Kinsley asks why it is thought illegitimate for liberals to engage in *economic* class warfare but okay for conservatives to engage in *cultural* class warfare, especially inasmuch as much of cultural warfare is really based on economics. Ultimately, then, Kinsley asks, "If the Republicans feel free to exploit resentment of the poor, why shouldn't the Democrats feel free to exploit resentment of the rich?"[29] Kinsley has a point—each side should feel free to exploit whatever resentments and alignments it wants and neither side should have the gall to argue that it is not engaging in class warfare when it is so clear that both sides are doing so. And neither side should assume that "exploiting resentments" is a particularly healthy way to engage in political debate.

## CONCLUSION

▶ I assume you have noticed that I am not particularly happy with contemporary liberal and conservative rhetoric, but I hope you also noticed that I did not exactly take a "pox on both their houses" position. That is because I have a great respect for both ideologies *in their original formulations*. I see the need for both freedom and order—negative liberty and positive liberty. I recognize, as contemporary thinker A. L. Chickering has said, that "each is incomplete without the other, for freedom without order (community) is license or greed, and order without freedom is authoritarianism."[30] Our societal rhetoric needs *both* formulations.

▶ Additionally, I perceive that many flaws in our society stem from our failure to perceive ideologically: among them, contradictions between the educational system and the economic system, and between how we are raised and treated and what we are asked to believe. The overarching societal ideology would be improved by solid liberal and conservative critiques of it.

▶ I also am disturbed that so many of us claim to believe in the American ideology when we merely ascribe to the abstract concepts but are unwilling to apply the ideology. Thus, while most people say they think democratic procedures should be followed, Berkeley political scientist Herbert McClosky found that 42 percent say that they do not mind politicians' methods if they manage to get the right things done.[31] While nearly everybody believes in freedom of expression, over 50 percent believe "A book that contains wrong political views . . . does not deserve to be published."[32] While most of us believe everybody should have an equal vote, over 60 percent of us believe "'Issues' and 'arguments' are beyond the understanding of most voters."[33] And while most of us claim to think racism is wrong, 46 percent of us believe that certain races are inherently superior.[34]

▶ But mostly, as a person whose field is political communication, I am disappointed that American political communication has gotten all screwed up by ideological considerations and, more importantly, ideological mistakes and misunderstandings. Specifically, I am unhappy that:

1. The "disclaimer process" allows people to claim to prize freedom even as they attack it.
2. The mass media allow the elites to persuade us without our having very good instruments either for talking with each other or for responding back to the elites.
3. The complexity of contemporary problems and the vocabularies in which the elites discuss those problems preclude participation of most citizens in decisions that have profound impacts on their lives.
4. Opposition to some causes of liberalism has led too many of us to oppose the whole philosophy, with debilitating effects on our rights—rights that would be safer if liberalism had a stronger voice.
5. The seduction of conservatism by big business has undermined the important role of a vibrant conservatism in speaking out intelligently for community values.
6. Liberal abandonment of the neutral equality of opportunity means there is nobody left to talk about equality in a way that most of us might find persuasive.

7. The current debates about family values, political correctness, welfare, and many other issues, all potentially useful and necessary debates, have devolved into name-calling and grandstanding because both liberals and conservatives are more interested in making points and winning converts and votes than they are in solving problems. Ironically, in a sense political communication suffers because there is too much attention to the communication aspects and not enough to the problem-solving.

8. Class warfare has broken out because both liberalism and conservatism have abandoned their ideological roots in order to "stand with" specific groups in the society. It is poisoning both our political communication and our politics, filling them with hatred and spite. The concept of "honorable opposition" has been replaced with demonized enemies. Opponents could continue a societal conversation, but enemies do not engage in dialogue.

▶ Finally, I'm unhappy because I'm not sure what should be done about any of this. I do know that it would help if a lot more people could overcome their apathy and get involved. But it also would help if those now staffing the various ideological forts would lighten up—learn to laugh with the opposition and at themselves. As a start—and as something of a test—consider these differences between the political parties that comics have offered over the last few years:

▶ Democrats buy most of the books that have been banned somewhere. Republicans form censorship committees and read them as a group.

▶ Republicans employ exterminators. Democrats step on the bugs.

▶ Republicans tend to keep their shades drawn, although there is seldom any reason why they should. Democrats ought to, but don't.

▶ Democrats eat the fish they catch. Republicans hang them on the wall.

▶ Democrats watch TV crime and Western shows that make them clench their fists and become red in the face. Republicans get the same effect from a presidential press conference.

▶ Republicans sleep in twin beds, sometimes even in separate rooms. That is why there are more Democrats.

▶ And now the test: did you laugh at all of them? If any of them made you angry rather than tickled, you are in danger of becoming too attached to your ideology and ripe for an infusion of hatred that will make you distrust your neighbors, treat political opponents as enemies, and be unwelcome at community gatherings and office parties. It's your life, of course, and it's your right to live it as you wish (that's the liberal in me speaking), but you'll be much happier if you can see that others *might* have something worthwhile to offer . . . and if you treat them in a civil manner even if, after listening openly, you decide they are spouting rubbish (says the conservative in me). Good luck.

## FOR FURTHER CONSIDERATION

**1.** The two-party system normally is perceived as swirling around the question of where power is located, with Republicans wanting more power located at the state level and Democrats preferring power to be centralized at the national level. This chapter argues that the major difference concerns what the power is to be used *for*, with Democrats wanting to use it to protect individual freedoms and Republicans wanting to use it to enforce a moral order. Is one of these positions more accurate than the other? Are they naturally incompatible (i.e., could they exchange positions on where power should be located without switching positions on what the power should be used to accomplish)?

**2.** It often is said that the militias of the 1990s and the antiwar protesters of the 1960s shared many political positions. Both were anti-government, or at least were trying to force the government to change directions. Both were willing—under certain circumstances—to use violence in support of their aims. Both assumed a politicized military, that is, they assumed soldiers should be citizens as well as soldiers, and refuse orders counter to their individual political positions.

Given all these similarities, and others you may identify, why is it that the '60s movement was considered leftist and the '90s movement is seen as rightist?

## NOTES

1. J. D. Barber, "The Oval Office Aesop," *New York Times,* 7 November 1982, p. E17.

2. D. K. Mumby, "Ideology and the Social Construction of Meaning: A Communication Perspective," *Communication Quarterly* 37 (Fall 1989): 303.

3. M. C. McGee, "The 'Ideograph': A Link between Rhetoric and Ideology," *Quarterly Journal of Speech* 66 (February 1980): 5.

4. *Ibid.*, 14.

5. T. A. van Dijk, "Discourse Semantics and Ideology," *Discourse & Society* 6 (April 1995): 281.

6. *Ibid.*, 281.

7. J. M. Sproule, "Propaganda: The Ideological Rhetoric" paper presented at the conference of the Rhetoric Society of America, University of Texas at Arlington, 26–29 May 1988: 1–5.

8. H. McClosky, "Consensus and Ideology in American Politics," *The American Political Science Review* 58 (June 1964): 363.

9. *Ibid.*, 362.

10. *Ibid.*, 374.

11. L. Menand, "Mixed Paint," *Mother Jones,* March–April 1995, 31.

12. *Ibid.*, 32.

13. *Ibid.*, 31.

14. A. Hacker, "On Original Sin and Conservatives," *New York Times Magazine,* 25 February 1973, p. 13.

15. J. B. Judis, "The Divided States of America," *Washington Post National Weekly Edition,* 23–29 January 1995, p. 28.

16. J. Gray, "Does Democracy Have a Future?" *New York Times Book Review,* 22 January 1995, p. 24.

17. *Ibid.,* p. 25.

18. Hacker, *op. cit.,* 70.

19. Quoted in Judis, *op. cit.,* 28.

20. S. Lessard, "Civility, Community, and Humor: The Conservatism We Need," *Washington Monthly,* July–August 1973, 32.

21. *Ibid.,* 32.

22. Hacker, *op. cit.,* 70.

23. *Ibid.,* 70.

24. *Ibid.,* 72.

25. M. Kinsley, "Class Warfare? Tell Me About It," *Time,* 6 February 1995, 80.

26. A.O. Hirschman, *The Rhetoric of Reaction: Perversity, Futility, Jeopardy* (Cambridge, MA: Belknap Press of Harvard University Press, 1991), 12.

27. *Ibid.,* 34–35.

28. *Ibid.,* 41.

29. Kinsley, *op. cit..,* 80.

30. A. L. Chickering, "A 'Conservative's' View of the Politics of Meaning," *Tikkun,* November/December 1993, 27.

31. McClosky, *op. cit.,* 365.

32. *Ibid.,* 367.

33. *Ibid.,* 369.

34. *Ibid.,* 369.

# Ideology and Media

*It is ... the creative tension between conservatism and liberalism that is the genius of American democracy. The nation suffers when either of those traditions is denigrated or undefended.*
— GEORGE MCGOVERN[1]

If we assume that *everybody* has an ideology, that growing up in any culture provides an ideology, that ideology is implanted in the language and hidden in the cultural assumptions, then it is only common sense that the members of the culture who work in the information industries—in the various media—also have ideologies. But that means only that those people have a national or social or cultural ideology; it does not establish that media personnel are predominantly liberal or conservative.

Many people think there is an ideological bias in the U.S. media, but there is no agreement on which way the media lean. Conservatives perceive a pro-liberal bias; liberals think there is a pro-conservative bias. And each side can make a fairly good case for its position.

## ▶ Conservative Perceptions of Bias

The centerpiece of the conservative case is the undisputed fact that more reporters are Democrats than Republicans. A recent survey by David Weaver and G. Cleveland Wilhoit of the Indiana University School of Journalism found that 44 percent of reporters identify themselves as Democrats, 16 percent as Republicans, and 34 percent as Independents.[2] Obviously, these numbers are "out of whack" with the national figures on the American public, which show an almost even distribution between Republicans and Democrats in the general population. If these pro-Democrat reporters allow their political biases to be reflected in their reporting, the media are obviously "out of step" with the public, presumably in the liberal direction.

To prove these media biases shape political stories, conservatives turn to analyses of campaign coverage. Looking at the election of 1992, for example, they discover that coverage of President Bush was more negative than was the coverage of his rivals. A study by the nonpartisan (but conservative-leaning) Center for Media and Public Affairs found that in 1992 the commentaries aired on network news shows by voters, party officials, and policy experts cast Bush in a negative light: "Only 31 percent were positive about Mr. Bush; 69 percent were negative. For President-elect Bill Clinton, the results were not much better: 37 percent were positive."[3] The independent candidate, Ross Perot, received 46 percent positive coverage, better than either Bush or Clinton, which perhaps shows that reporters are at least open to other views. (It also shows that good coverage does not necessarily translate into votes.) These findings were more or less collaborated by a more liberal group, the Joan Shorenstein Barone Center on the Press, Politics, and Public Policy at Harvard's Kennedy School of Government, in its study of coverage during the 1992 primaries. Using a five-point scale, from one (very positive) to five (very negative), this group found that between February 1 and June 4 Bush's coverage scored 3.3, Clinton's 2.4, and Perot's 1.8.[4] In other words, the Bush coverage leaned toward the negative, Clinton's leaned toward the positive, and Perot's was the most positive.

Several points, however, should be made about these materials. First, the fact that there are more Democrats than Republicans among reporters does not, by itself, prove there are more liberals than conservatives. Republicans are not all conservative; Democrats are not all liberal. It is entirely possible that a Jackson, Mississippi, Democrat reporter is more conservative than a New York City Republican reporter, that a Los Angeles Republican reporter is more liberal than a Salt Lake City Democrat reporter. Additionally, if reporters are allowing their party preferences to affect their reporting, the differences in negativity in coverage should be greater than that discovered in the 1992 Bush-Clinton-Perot race.

But the conservative position does not rely only on the party labels of reporters and their presumed bias during presidential campaigns. It also holds that a liberal bias can be found in news coverage. Here conservatives point to the unremitting criticism of American officials as opposed to the relative lack of coverage of the leaders of countries that might be considered our enemies. Consider, for instance, these excerpts from letters sent to the White House Press Room during 1987, when Reagan was president: "please leave the president and Ollie North alone and go back to your caves"; "It is obvious your ranks are infiltrated by a great many Communist sympathizers"; "You dirty bunch of scunks [sic] support every Marxist dictator throughout the world."[5] It would be hard to argue with the conservative position that there are many criticisms of the president in the media (although conservatives *don't* complain about negative coverage of President Clinton like they did about coverage of Reagan and Bush) and many fewer criticisms of the leaders of other countries. Whether that is proof of a leftist bias or merely proof that U.S. media largely ignore the rest of the world, though, is problematic.

Likewise, it is difficult to disagree with the conservative position that the majority of documentaries on public television favor the left, though to say that they favor "left-wing ideology," as Senator Bob Dole has claimed,[6] may be over-stating the case. Nor is it entirely clear that the bias reflects some leftist intention of documentary makers or merely the natural bent of the genre. That is, given that what a documentary maker does is search for a problem that is not being solved by the society, dramatize that problem, and call for action, it is not surprising that most documentaries make the supporters of the status quo uneasy. But perhaps now *I* am overstating the case. That is, maybe the approach is not "natural" to the genre, but more a matter of the tradition within the genre, a tradition that has grown up *because* documentary makers *have been* liberal. The point is that *why* documentaries seem to be leftist is an open question, but *that* they are is not in doubt.

Another piece of the conservative case that the media are liberal concerns the ways in which the media cover social issues. Columnist Walter Goodman, for example, provides evidence of liberal bias in how homelessness is covered. (Notice that the "evidence" here is only anecdotal; but notice, also, that most evidence of both sides is of this type!) Having read in a newspaper report the "news" that two-thirds of homeless single men and one-third of adults in homeless families are addicted to either drugs or alcohol, he accused the (liberal) media of overlooking that truth, saying "Reports on the homeless often tend to imitate depression-movie scripts: hard-working folks in heart-wrenching situations. If only jobs and housing were provided, they would be like you and me."[7]

When I first read that analysis I found it persuasive, but the more I thought about it the less I was persuaded. For as I considered it here's what I discovered: I found it persuasive *not* because I had been brainwashed by a liberal media to think that the homeless had "run into a spell of bad luck," but because I had *assumed* that they probably had contributed to their own "fall" in some way, perhaps via drugs or alcohol. And how had I arrived at that assumption? Since I do not personally know *any* homeless people, it could be an assumption I had picked up from the media. If it was, Goodman must be wrong in his contention that a left-leaning media had misrepresented reality by feeding me sympathetic pictures of the homeless as "hard-working folks in heart-wrenching situations," a position which it turns out *may* actually be true for one-third of the single men and two-thirds of the adult families, but which I do not recall *ever* having seen in the media.

So, can we conclude, with conservatives, that the media have a liberal bias? At best, it strikes me that the charge is *partially* true: there *are* more Democrats than Republicans among reporters; campaign coverage (at least in 1992 and 1996) does seem to be hard on the Republican candidate; there are more criticisms of U.S. leaders than of foreign leaders; and documentaries do seem to favor the left end of the political spectrum. But what about the counter-charge from the left?

## ▶ Liberal Perceptions of Bias

Like conservatives, liberals make the people involved in media a centerpiece of their argument. The people to whom they point, however, are not reporters but owners, editors, talk-show hosts, and experts interviewed.

First, the owners. The networks always have been big businesses, but in the 1980s all three were bought by giant corporations: ABC by Capital Cities, NBC by General Electric, and CBS by real-estate operator Laurence Tisch.[8] Of course, not only the TV networks are big business; most newspapers and magazines in the country are also owned by large corporate entities.

But ownership by corporations does not, of itself, prove that the media have a conservative bias. In the first place, corporations tend to be conservative, they are not 100 percent so. Additionally, just because a newspaper, magazine, TV station or network is corporate-owned does not prove that any conservative influence is being wielded; the corporation may be more interested in profits than propaganda.

The second group of media people that liberals point to is editors. Editors are important because, as journalism professor Ben H. Bagdikian points out, it is the editor who determines which stories merit coverage, which reporters and camera personnel are assigned, and ultimately which stories and footage will be used.[9] Editors who want to infect the news with a conservative bias, then, have the power to do so. But is it reasonable to think that any significant portion of them have this desire? Consider Bagdikian's argument that in the 1980s many top editors were viewed as upper management. Often they were required to enroll in business schools, presumably to instill in them an understanding of fiscal responsibility.[10] Again, however, there is not a one-to-one correlation between "corporate thinking" and conservatism. Absent more direct proof of editorial interference, the argument is mostly circumstantial. Is there more direct proof? Bagdikian offers this example: "If, in the field, a correspondent showed the White House to be lying . . . that reporter was pulled back in favor of more congenial correspondents."[11] Under these conditions, suggests Bagdikian, reporters begin to engage in self-censorship. But that soon may be unnecessary, given the hiring practices now prevalent in the print media. According to Bagdikian, many news agencies have instituted "systematic screenings" to assure that only journalists who are likely to "comply with corporate wishes" will be hired.[12]

Additional evidence of editorial interference comes from a respected source in television news, Dan Rather, who has testified that one news director (the TV equivalent of a newspaper editor) announced he planned to subject all his hires to review by political groups he favored. More generally, Rather argues that television news has been "Hollywoodized": "Thoughtfully written analysis is out, 'live pops' are in. . . . Hire lookers, not writers. Do powder-puff, not probing, interviews. Stay away from controversial subjects. . . . Make nice, not news."[13]

The argument about editors and owners thus far seems to have a ring of truth. But even if we grant everything liberals say about owners and editors, we still have no idea how big the problem is. Quantification is missing. The lack of it doesn't mean managerial bias isn't a big problem, obviously; but it also doesn't mean it is.

The third group that liberals claim are indicative of a conservative media bias are talk show hosts. In terms of radio talk shows, the liberal argument here is not only correct (there are many more conservative hosts), but quantifiable—the most popular conservative host, Rush Limbaugh, is carried on 659 stations, while the most popular liberal, Texas populist Jim Hightower, appears on 130 stations.[14] The situation on television is even more skewed. Noting that conservatives William F. Buckley, Jr., Patrick Buchanan, Rowland Evans, Robert Novak, and John McLaughlin host television talk shows, Cohen points out that "Many right-wing partisans . . . have their own nationally telecast talk shows. Yet no partisan of the left has his own political talk show."[15] I see no way to escape this argument—conservative radio and television talk show hosts far outnumber liberals, are carried on more stations, and reach more listeners and viewers.

The final category of media "personnel" to whom liberals point in building their "the media are conservative" case are the experts who are called on for commentary. The group of experts the networks use, argue two journalists in a recent article, are "remarkably homogeneous in composition": "They tend to be . . . Republicans . . . rather than critics of the political establishment . . . ex–government officials (mostly from Republican administrations), and 'scholars' from conservative Washington think tanks . . . "[16]

Again, this argument seems unassailable. The experts are more representative of the right than of the left. Janet Kersten, a business-travel writer and self-proclaimed "news junkie," recently decided to try to answer the question of media influence for herself. She wrote down the name and point of view of every quoted expert for a period of two months. She discovered that during that period she had heard or read three liberals, twelve moderates and fifty-eight conservatives.[17] Perhaps we all should follow her lead and see what figures we come up with.

Another piece of evidence to which liberals point is the nature of news coverage; specifically, they argue that protests are either not covered or treated with contempt. For instance, in one week in March 1995 there was a protest in Boston against slashing the State's welfare system; a march in Washington, D.C., against the anti-children components of the Republican Contract With America; and a march from New York City to Albany protesting New York Governor Pataki's dropping programs for the poor, children, elderly, and mentally ill from his budget. The Boston protest received a four-second mention on one Boston station; the Washington, D.C., and New York protests were completely ignored by the mainstream media.[18] In that same week, a New York City rally of ten thousand people protesting proposed educational budget cuts was described as "Flower Power meets Generation X," and the *New York Times* suggested that most of the fourteen thousand students who boycotted school that day were interested only in having the day off.[19]

I have no doubt that protest coverage is weak these days, but that does not necessarily prove the media have a conservative bias. Consider, for example, that during the week in question the media covered the House of Representatives' passage of welfare reform and the Senate's passage of the line-item veto; there was a new C.I.A. scandal to be examined; and the big news of the week was the nerve gas attack on the Japanese subway. That some local demonstrations "fell through the cracks" is, under the circumstances, quite understandable—regrettable, perhaps, but hardly proof of a politically induced media conspiracy.

## ▶ Perceiving Bias Where None Exists

In evaluating the various charges of liberals and conservatives, I have suggested that some of what they see as biases may in fact be something else. Specifically, I have argued that

> ▶ the fact that there are more Democrat reporters than Republican reporters does not prove there are more liberal than conservative reporters;

> ▶ although the 1992 coverage did seem to favor Clinton slightly over Bush, the difference was not nearly as great as the difference in party preference of reporters would have created if reporters indeed allowed their own preferences to dominate their evaluations;

> ▶ the number of criticisms of U.S. leaders as compared to criticisms of "enemy" leaders is explained more by the fact that the media give short shrift to foreign news than to any anti-American bias;

> ▶ documentaries may be predominantly leftist because of the nature of the genre;

> ▶ just because media are corporately owned does not prove they are conservative;

> ▶ the conservative influence of editors has yet to be quantified; and

> ▶ the lack of coverage of any particular topic at any particular time may be as easily explained by the glut of events and issues to be covered as by political bias.

Beyond these arguments, other points help explain why people may perceive political bias where none exists.

One facet of contemporary journalism that seems to lead to charges of bias is that in the last thirty years there has been an increase in "advocacy" journalism. Commentator W. Goodman complains that when reporters become advocates, they subvert their primary responsibility, which is to report, and not to comment on, the news.[20] This increase in journalistic advocacy apparently galls conservatives more than liberals. Conservative reactions do not necessarily mean the positions taken by journalist-advocates are primarily liberal; the objection in this case is less to the content than to the change in form. It may just be that conservatives are as opposed to changes in form as they are to other deviations from the "old ways."

A second arena in which it sometimes looks as though there is political bias when something else is actually going on is presidential campaigns. I suggest that the media usually favor the challenger for reasons of pure ambition. The reporters following the challenger throughout the campaign tend to be younger and less established. They hope to follow "their guy" into the presidential mansion as a part of the White House Press Corps. Those who already have had that duty usually are assigned to cover the incumbent during campaigns. They aren't quite as "hungry" as the newer reporters; they are looking forward to being reassigned to editing or columnizing.[21] To the degree this difference explains why challengers get better coverage, it also sheds light on the conservative argument about campaign coverage favoring the Democrat, for in the last seven presidential elections, Democrats have been the challenger in five.

Third, it is possible that at least some instances of alleged media bias are really cases of reading or hearing biases. That is, as journalist W. A. Henry comments, at times "news consumers object fiercely to a story not because it is inaccurate but because the truth it tells is unhelpful to their side."[22]

Finally, we must wonder whether there are so many more conservative radio and television hosts only because of political bias, or whether there might be other explanations. Journalist David Shenk points out that Michael Kinsley, once the liberal voice on CNN's "Crossfire," is an eloquent writer but "just plain awful on television." Shenk suggests that "his civility, his affection for the finer points of policy and his lawyerly interrogative style are the antithesis of compelling television."[23] Another journalist suggests that liberals are "so serious and self-righteous you want to run in the other direction."[24]

Are liberals too civil for talk shows, too serious, too self-righteous? It's a difficult call. I cannot see that they have cornered the market on any of these characteristics. It has long been assumed that conservatives are the experts on civil discourse; liberals and conservatives seem to me equally serious (and, actually, I think most humorists and comedians are liberal rather than conservative); and liberals certainly are not more sanctimonious than conservatives.

Still, there does seem to be a difference between liberal and conservative attitudes. If I had to describe it I'd say that liberals lack the "killer instinct." And that *does* seem to be a personality characteristic that rather perfectly corresponds to a major feature of liberal philosophy: compassion, especially for the underdog. A liberal just never would subscribe to the philosophy outlined by a conservative comedian of the late 1950s, "Brother Dave," who said, "If a man's down, kick him. That gives him some incentive to get up and get with it." And as long as talk radio and talk television remain genres that thrive on conflict, put-downs, and anger, liberals will probably remain poorly represented in the ranks of talk-show hosts.

## ▶ Not Perceiving Bias

To this point I've acted as though everybody sees political bias in the media and the only disagreement is over the direction and extent of the bias. But that overstates the case. In fact, fewer people see media bias than perceive the media to be unbiased. Despite years of complaint from the right about PBS documentaries and from the left about the number of conservative talk shows on public television, *Time* reports that "A 1990 survey commissioned by PBS found that 79% of viewers see no political bias in public TV fare; the remainder were divided between whether it leans left or right."[25] Likewise, despite complaints from all the 1992 candidates, *Time* found that "71% of respondents thought Bush had been treated fairly by the press, and 74% thought Clinton had."[26]

Despite the documented numerical advantage of Democrats amongst reporters and a more naturally conservative ownership and corps of editors, according to W. A. Henry of *Time*, the news media reflect "the concerns of average Americans"[27] on most issues, partly because they "go to great lengths to appear neutral,"[28] partly because although media personnel may have political preferences, they are not loyal ideologues. Some of the toughest criticism of President Clinton can be found in the (supposedly liberal) *New York Times*; some of the sharpest criticism of President Bush came from fellow Republicans George Will and William Safire.

Additionally, of course, some techniques that journalists use either camouflage or obliterate the effects of any biases they might harbor. When writing "in the center," suggests journalist J. Cohen, reporters are seen as nonideological, as though being a centrist "is somehow not having an ideology at all. Somehow centrism is not an 'ism,' carrying with it values, beliefs, or opinions."[29] In election coverage especially, but also in covering issues, many journalists make their own ideologies irrelevant by steering the discussion into nonideological, politically technical questions—who's ahead, what staffing problems the politicians are experiencing, what interest groups are supporting which side, and what other countries think about the controversy. Additionally, says communication professor D. C. Hallin, the journalistic style, "with its attributions, passive-voice constructions, and its substitution of technical for moral or political judgments, is largely designed to conceal the voice of the journalist."[30]

For all these reasons, then, I do not think there is much of an ideological bias problem in U.S. media. The case for a liberal bias is overstated; the case for a conservative bias is overstated; there are reasons why it may sometimes look like a bias is exhibited when it isn't, and, anyway, most people do not even see a bias. If ideology leads to any consistently identifiable media bias, that "truth" is yet to be proven.

## ▶ The Real Media Biases

Although I have gone to great pains to demonstrate that the biases liberals and conservatives claim either do not exist or have been badly overstated, I do not mean to say no biases exist. Indeed, I perceive a number of them; I just do not think the more significant ones are *political*. It remains, then, for me to identify and demonstrate those more important, more real, biases.

### The Media Are Biased toward What Makes Money

The commercial media exist to make money for the owners. Like any business, they do what they must to make money. Political ideologues who assume media personnel are in the business of "selling" political positions misunderstand the business in which media owners and practitioners are engaged. What media really do is sell their readers and viewers to their advertisers. The more readers or viewers they have, the more they can charge for an ad. That means they have to keep the public happy, which they cannot do if they are too obviously political.

Their commercial nature favors whatever will make money and leads to at least two deleterious effects that have political consequences—trivialization and a conflict orientation.

Peter J. Boyer, author of *Who Killed CBS*, a book about the history of the CBS News Division, attributes the trivialization of the news to the money-seeking nature of television. He argues that when the big corporations took over the television networks, one of the first changes was to order that the news divisions, which always had been partially subsidized by the entertainment divisions, henceforth would have to pay for themselves. To meet that demand the news divisions "watered down" their reports, replacing coverage of important issues with trivia; coverage of "weapons agreements gave way to coverage of Zsa Zsa's misdemeanor assault trial."[31]

Another major effect of the moneymaking demand on media is a focus on conflict to the detriment of the search for truth. Deborah Tannen, professor of linguistics at Georgetown University and author of *You Just Don't Understand*, explains this thesis in a recent article. She claims that in our society there is a fundamental belief that truth emerges from opposition.[32] That may explain why we place so much faith in debate. But, as Tannen points out, the media—as moneymaking institutions—do not seek out the most reasonable and informed partisans to represent the two sides. Rather, they often choose and air extreme views to satisfy the audience's predilection for "watching a fight."[33] Two problems, then: (1) the truth *may* not emerge from the clash of the two sides, because there may actually be four or five or twenty sides, and (2) even if the truth is there someplace, in what Tannen calls the "complex middle" rather than in the "simplified extremes," it will not *necessarily* emerge from a clash between extremists who were brought together to produce steam for ratings rather than light for decision-making.

Additionally, Tannen takes the media to task for their tendency to confrontation, as when they quote a criticism to the person criticized and ask for a response. There are several problems with the technique. First, it plants the accusation in the minds of the audience, even if it is frivolous or has been made by an opponent for purely political reasons. Second, although some few people may be moved by the provocation to eloquence and brilliant repartee, many others are unable to find the appropriate words when they are hurt or "when their sense of fairness is outraged. In those cases, opposition is not the path to truth."[34]

Tannen's explanation, it seems to me, gives us some insight into the domination of radio and television talk shows by those willing to engage in hate-mongering and scurrilous charges against government officials. Such conflict-ridden discussions are good theatre; they may not lead us toward the truth and may indeed lead us away from it, but they are exciting and they build audiences, i.e., enhance revenue.

Another result of the media's moneymaking orientation has been a diminution of government coverage. The position of the business-oriented media controllers is that "incremental" news coverage (coverage of long-term news stories) turns off the audience. The problem with this position, as the editor of the *Washington Spectator* has commented, is "that governmental news develops incrementally. And if you don't cover it incrementally, you don't really cover it at all. Incremental is what it is all about."[35]

## Television Is Biased toward the Visual

Political correspondent W. D. Shannon notes that "TV is pictorial and puts a premium on vivid action."[36] The advantage of television over radio, and to a degree over newspapers and magazines, is that TV can show what is happening or has happened. Of course, the advantage can also be a drawback—if the camera crew doesn't get there, there is no story. Or if the essence of the story is not visual, it may not get covered, as political communication scholars Jamieson and Campbell have documented: "Some important issues, such as the economy, are not easily reduced to concrete, dramatic 2-minute-and-35-second bites of information. Hobart Rowen, chief economic analyst and columnist for the *Washington Post* reports, for example, that 'at the London economic summit in 1977, the chief correspondent for one of the major networks came to me with the final communique in hand and said: 'My God, what can we do with this?' Forget that Jimmy Carter and six other heads of state had agreed on several significant things relating to jobs, energy and inflation—there were no visuals quickly at hand, just words.'"[37]

Politicians have learned to take advantage of the visual bias of television—none better than those in the Ronald Reagan administration. For instance, political commentator A. Hochschild reports that when U.S. planes shot down two Libyan jets, Reagan was flown to the deck of an aircraft carrier for a "photo-op" that gave the impression that the President, the "commander-in-chief," was actually "commanding." The command, however, was illusory because the carrier was stationed in California, not in Libya.[38]

For whatever reason, TV reporters were slow to realize the political effects of their visual orientation. In one classic example during the 1984 presidential campaign, CBS correspondent Lesley Stahl aired a long piece critical of President Reagan. As the public watched clips of Reagan visiting a senior-citizens center, Ms. Stahl talked about how Reagan had cut federal programs for the elderly; as the audience watched Reagan mingling with African-American children, Ms. Stahl talked about the weakness of Reagan's civil-rights stances, and so forth. At the end of the program she was told she had a call from the White House. With some degree of trepidation, she took the call . . . and was surprised to hear a senior administration official compliment her on the story. When Stahl asked whether the official had actually listened to her report, she was told that viewers focus on the pictures and essentially ignore the message: "They didn't even hear what you said. So, in our minds, it was a four-and-a-half minute free ad for the Ronald Reagan campaign for re-election."[39]

What reporters did not realize, say Jamieson and Campbell, but could have learned from any film buff, was that "[t]he camera has a point of view; it becomes a viewer. Rules governing the shooting of news footage recognize the biases involved in camera angles and shots. For example, slow motion footage is considered tender, even romantic; jumpy images are considered dramatic; extreme close-ups are considered intense and dramatic."[40] Consider the political implications of how presidential press conferences are shot by TV. The president is shot close up, thus is given the opportunity to appear intimate with the viewing audience. Intimacy communicates involvement. But the reporter asking questions and the post-interview responses by anchors and others are shown in the medium close-up and medium shot. "These distances are considered impartial and detached, the visual counterpart of journalistic objectivity."[41] Hence, the media workers are not depicted as intimate, caring, involved. In short, the conventions covering film footage preclude media critics from being as persuasive as the president.

Thus does the visual bias of television have political consequences. And depending on your assessment of the politician in question, you may see the visual bias as a political bias.

## The Media Are Biased in Favor of the Contemporary and Immediate

*"Television news is like a lightning flash. It makes a loud noise, lights up everything around it, leaves everything else in darkness and then is suddenly gone."*
—HODDING CARTER

In addition to having a bias toward the visual, television also is biased in favor of the immediate. Its advantage over print is that it can show us what is happening any place in the world instantaneously. But that advantage, says journalist W. I. Thompson, contains a fatal flaw: as it *shows* us the world, "it has to contract intellectually from explanations to presentations. And so, every night on the news, television presents everything and explains nothing."[42]

Just as television producers favor putting on what is happening *now*, so the viewer is constrained to respond immediately. Television does not have the time, says M. Frankel of the *New York Times*, "to let the news breathe, to explain events and expose the arguments and purposes of newsmakers." In contrast, he says, a newspaper gives the reader time to reflect, "to stop, think, reread and maybe get it."[43]

But in order to "get it" in any really comprehensive way, the reader must see the immediate event in context, and context normally requires some understanding of history. TV supplies almost no history, newspapers some, magazines even more, books most of all. That is, the slower the medium in question the more it supplies the historical context. But note that the public favors the slower media much less than the faster; that is, more people watch television than read newspapers; more read newspapers than magazines; more read magazines than books. The result is that although many people know what happened today, few understand why it happened and how it relates to other events today and yesterday, or that there may be systemic causes rather than unreasoned and unreasonable random causes. Ultimately, the tendency to rely upon the immediate gratification of instant news ("give us twenty-two minutes and we'll give you the world") may be related to the equally debilitating tendency to consume "instant food" ("aren't you hungry for a Burger King *now?*") rather than taking the time to savor a slowly simmering roast, breathing in the mouth-watering odors as it cooks, and so forth. In both news and food consumption we have become oriented toward instant gratification, "grazing" rather than "dining." The dangers to our minds and our stomachs—to our lives—are incalculable.

## Media Are Biased in Support of the Status Quo

*"News is something someone wants to suppress. Everything else is advertising."*
—LORD NORTHCLIFFE

There is a sense in which what passes for news can be said to be advertisements for the status quo. Jamieson and Campbell note that "[t]elevision routinely covers the rituals of government, such as swearing-in ceremonies, inaugurals, welcoming addresses, and press conferences, that reinforce our sense of governmental process."[44] Not only do the media cover governmental processes, they go out of their way to try to prove that those processes work. Thus, when "Irangate" broke in the news, and President Reagan was asked what happened and replied "I don't know. I only know that's why I've said repeatedly that I want to find out," his admission of ignorance was greeted as somehow proving something positive. Journalist Alexander Cockburn demonstrates that how the conference was covered in the *Washington Post* is instructive. The senior political correspondent of the *Post* wrote that the conference was evidence that the president "has regained a good measure of his emotional balance"; a *Post* editorial applauded Reagan's "doggedness and apparent conviction," and the *Style* section used the terms "'Brisk and Reassuring' in the headline and 'masterful' and 'reassuring' in Tom Shayle's text."[45] A few years later Reagan testified in connection with the trial of one of the Irangate principals. It was obvious that he still did not know what had happened, nor, notes columnist J. Cohen of the *Washington Post*, did he know "his chairman of the Joint Chiefs of Staff, dates, places, origins of the Iran-contra affair, what happened to the money and even what the various investigations had revealed."[46]

Yet, throughout Irangate—and other governmental internal investigations such as Watergate—the media took the position that "the system works." Further, according to Jamieson and Campbell, "we are told not only that the system works, but that those who 'disrupt' it in strikes or social protest are wrong—a bias that will always favor the status quo."[47]

A part of the bias favoring the status quo, according to J. Cohen of *Z Magazine*, can be seen in coverage of foreign policy, where the U.S. is always depicted as "overseas making peace, trying to bring opposing parties together, constantly trying to negotiate and expand human rights."[48] Because it is assumed that the U.S. is peace-loving, the media ignore the violence done by America's client states and focus on how our enemies mistreat their victims.

Ignoring our victims and highlighting "their" victims, complain leftist advocates Edward Herman and Noam Chomsky, helps convince the public "that the enemy is evil, while setting the stage for intervention, subversion, support for terrorist regimes; an endless arms race, and constant military conflict—all in a noble cause."[49] Has it ever struck you that it is unlikely that our government is *always* right?

According to *Utne Reader*, part of the reason the media always seem to side with the government and support the status quo has to do with how news is "gathered." "The overwhelming majority of stories are based on official sources—on information provided by members of Congress, presidential aides, and other political insiders."[50] Investigative reporting, after a mini-resurgence in the wake of Watergate, has largely disappeared from American journalism. To the degree it still exists it is to be found in magazines and books, the slower media, rather than in television, radio, and newspaper coverage.

Additionally, the pro–status quo stance of news production is reinforced by the entertainment divisions. In the "cop shows," although there are occasional "dirty" cops, the assumption is always that those with authority and power—cops, judges, governors, and so forth—hold positive values that ultimately will prevail. Thus entertainment television, communication professor G. W. Selnow says, helps "perpetuate the cultural norm that associates goodness and positive values with the state, power, and recognized authority." Therefore, it "reinforces the association of such values with mainstream authority institutions."[51]

Thus, in both news and entertainment the status quo is favored. This bias has political ramifications, obviously, but it is not a liberal or conservative bias because it continues regardless of who is in control of the government. The media presumption always favors the rulers.

## Media Are Biased in Favor of the Assumptions of American Society

Such assumptions as that the United States is good, her enemies and potential enemies are bad, capitalism is good, socialism and communism are bad, and the "Third World" is irrelevant except as a pawn of the East-West struggle are almost never questioned by the mainstream media. Nor are these and many other assumptions denied in our popular entertainment.

A few years ago I was watching a "Matlock" movie on a Friday night and was startled to hear one of the characters say, "I lost my husband and don't even have any kids. I'm a failure." That got me to wondering whether these pro-marriage, pro-kids, pro–traditional housewife assumptions are common in the media. So the following week I took off a whole day and planted myself in front of the TV set to check it out—realizing, of course, that a few hours of "impression checking" does not qualify as formal research. It was a disturbing and eye-opening experience, especially with what I learned from watching the "soaps." (I recognize that "the soaps" may not be representative of the media in general, may be directed at people who are not representative of "American Society" as a whole; still, judging from the number of my students who are addicted to them as well as the ratings and longevity of such programs, I suspect there are few discrepancies between what is found in soaps and what is in other portions of television.)

I watched three soap operas, "All My Children," "One Life to Live," and "General Hospital," not because they were the most popular, or the best, or the most representative, but merely because they were at different times and thus could be watched as a "set."

The societal assumptions concerning the desirability of marriage, the "naturalness" of being parents, and the traditional role of "housewife" for women were all embedded in the programs. On each show at least one major character was pregnant. On "All My Children" the pro-natal bias was stated this way: "one of the few real joys left in life is watching your children." On "One Life to Live" the prospective father asked, "Are you trying to punish me because I got you pregnant and you weren't ready?" to which the mother-to-be responded, "No, I want this baby." Another character, who already had a baby, but a bad marriage, argued, "I'm staying with him. My baby has to come first. . . . I grew up without a father and always felt there was something missing. I want my baby to have a daddy."

Not only did I find these assumptions embedded in the programs, but also rampant in the commercials. On the 3 shows there were an average of 35 commercials. An average of 17 of the 35 featured mothers, but only 2 on average featured women at work outside the home. Of the 35, 15 had children in them.

The lessons these commercials taught about the roles of women were ubiquitous. Clearly, women purchase or prepare a lot of food (Wesson Oil, Hershey's, Hillshire Farms, Kraft Salad Dressing, I Can't Believe It's Not Butter, Carnation Instant Breakfast, Kraft Cheese, Nutri-Grain Breakfast Bars, Hellman's Mayonnaise, Today's Recipe Pasta Sauce, Oscar Mayer Foods, Bon Bons, Almond Joy, Pork, V-8 Juice, and Squirt). If they do not cook, they go out to Kentucky Fried Chicken.

Given all the food featured, it is no surprise that women need to diet (Jennie Craigs, Nutrisystem, Herbal Balance, and Weight Watchers).

Women also are involved in purchasing for and doing housework (Liquid Dial, Dow Bathroom Cleaner, Airwick, Raid, Clorox 2, Tarkett Floors, J. C. Penney Draperies, Dash Laundry Detergent, Dirt Devil Vacuums, Liquid Safe-Guard Soap, Dawn Dishwasher Liquid, Formula 409, Stanley Steamer Rug Cleaner, Spirit Soap, Lubriderm Facial Cleanser, and Shower to Shower).

They take care of the kids (Carnation Baby Formula, Huggies, Compound W for warts, and Playskool Toys) and the pets (Friskies Cat Food and Mighty Dog dog food).

But, of course, they must take care of themselves, too (Centrum Vitamins, Aqua Fresh toothpaste, Chlor-Trimeton Allergy Product, Oragel, Tylenol, Ogilvie Home Perm, Plenitude Anti-Wrinkle Cream, Tribe Perfume, Motrin IB, Gyne-Lotrimin, Alpha-Hydrox Skin Cleaner, Bufferin, Mylanta, Advil and Band-aids) and make sure they don't smell bad (Ban Deodorant, Soft-and-Dry, Masengill Douche) and check to see whether they're pregnant (Clear Blue Easy Pregnancy Test).

That's about it. Oh, they can talk on the phone (MCI) or go to the Holiday Inn, but what they wear in addition to their deodorant is unclear. The only clothing advertised was Haynes Underwear.

Given all of this support for the traditional roles of women as housewives, mothers, and wives, it is amazing that so many women have entered the workforce—and entirely understandable that those who haven't, those who watch the soaps, perceive them as unfeminine, bad wives, and bad mothers, creatures to be pitied and opposed.

Please note that I am *not* saying that I captured all the tendencies of television in one day, or even that daytime soaps are representative of all of television. That is not my point. Rather, the point is that the bias of television is to favor the assumptions held by the audience. If the program is designed for some subset of the society, it will appeal to the values and assumptions of that subset. If it is designed for a cross section of the citizenry, it will be biased in favor of the broad, abstract societal values. It will not be biased in favor of the political beliefs of the writers, producers, and owners, except when those beliefs are "in step" with the broader societal values.

## The Media Are Biased toward Fairness and Balance

That would not, at first blush, seem to be a *bias*, but it can be, especially if how fairness and balance are achieved introduces bias into the media. For instance, if the desire to provide balance *creates* controversy where none exists, a bias has been introduced. Yet this often happens. Communication researcher David Swanson points out that "to achieve fairness, news programs balance coverage between major candidates, even when one of the candidates has done little that is 'newsworthy.'"[52] One effect of that "balance" is that it makes *everything* a president does during the reelection season seem to be for political advantage. So in late 1995, every time Senator Dole, the Republican front-runner, gave a speech in an early primary state, the television coverage paired that speech with whatever President Clinton did that day. And if Clinton had sent a proposed bill to Congress, that pairing provided the implication that the legislation was being proposed as a political ploy to counter Senator Dole rather than as a serious attempt to solve a pressing public problem.

Further, because we have a two-party rather than multiparty system, the desire for balance leads the media to focus on just two sides. Jamieson and Campbell explain that "many problems have more than two solutions, and many issues generate more than two opposing viewpoints. News stories almost never reflect such complexity; instead, they tend to present issues in terms of pros and cons, to look at social movements as made up of moderates and militants, to divide reaction into support for or resistance to administration policy."[53] What we get, therefore, is not a search for truth but a search for impartiality, with the media devoted more to proving their own nonpartisanship than to seeking answers for the problems we face.

Additionally, say Jamieson and Campbell, "reporters rarely speak in the first person, refer to their own actions in observing events and finding facts, or reveal their perceptions of the sources' motives; nor do they ordinarily indicate the validity of quoted statements."[54] In other words, in adapting to the demand for fairness and balance, reporters obliterate their own viewpoints and avoid making judgments. That gives us a kind of fairness, a political fairness vis-à-vis the two political parties. But it introduces a kind of prejudice, too, for it means reporters can't say "that's a lie" even if they know it is, nor "that politician is in the back pocket" of a particular corporation or interest group, even if they know (s)he is. In short, detachment may be politically balanced and politically fair, and still create bias.

In fact, a *New York Times* reporter has argued that the popularity of the assumption of a liberal media bias has led—through reportorial fear of being labeled "liberal"—to a more conservative media bias than would otherwise exist, "as reporters bend over backwards not to seem at all critical of Republicans . . . the edgy liberal reporter ends up just as useful to the right as any ultra-rightist hack."[55]

Clearly, the desire to appear objective affects campaign coverage. In 1988 one executive turned down a tough piece on Bush, saying, "We don't want to look like we're going after George Bush."[56]

Thus, although "balance" and "fairness" *seem* not to be biases, the ways media personnel handle the news so as to accomplish the appearance of neutrality have the effect of introducing bias.

## The Media Are Biased in Favor of Bad News

This is a natural bias. That is, the fact that you didn't kill anybody today is not news; most of us didn't. We should actually be happy that news concerns the bad, for it means the norm is good. If we ever get to the place where the norm is bad, where news concerns what somebody did today that was good, then we'll be in *real* trouble. In the meantime, we can take some solace in the fact that news concerns the bad because news, by definition, concerns the unusual.

That does not mean there is no place in the news for positive reports. For instance, if we citizens are going to make intelligent determinations of whether our elected representatives should be re-elected, we need to know what good works they have done as well as where they have screwed up. That is especially true in terms of the economy. Consequently, it is important to realize that the "news is what is bad" definition leads to misunderstanding. For instance, in one study it was shown that "reports about increases in the unemployment rate were, on average, 48 percent longer and 106 percent more likely to lead the evening newscasts than reports about decreases in unemployment."[57]

Besides needing to know about the effects of public policy, we are interested in evaluating candidates by their personality characteristics. Yet, again, the presumptions about newsworthiness betray us. As a *Newsweek* reporter pointed out, "You can write about a candidate who is being sneaky and bumbling: that's objective reporting. But you can't write about a candidate . . . being kind and forgiving: that's editorializing."[58]

So, although it is true that news *should* be about the bad, because that is the unusual, there also must be arenas where the good is covered if citizens are going to arrive at accurate evaluations of public policy, the actions of public servants, the nature of the world, and the status of ongoing attempts to improve the lot of humanity. If the only thing we hear about politicians concerns the bad, how are we to judge; we must hear the good *and* the bad in order to make a balanced judgment.

## Media Are Biased toward Certain Ways of Covering "Stories"

The fact that news events are covered in "stories" tells us a great deal about this bias. The who, what, where, when, why, and how of any event are woven into a story, a narrative. Thus, the news is "framed" in a presentational form with which we are familiar; we are comforted by the form even when discomfited by the content. That is a kind of bias, then, because the familiar form in a sense "soft-pedals" the ugliness of the content.

We have seen enough "stories" in entertainment that we understand automatically, unconsciously, that when a dilapidated house on a hill is shown in the opening scene amidst the lightning and thunder of a terrible storm, the setting is evil and only evil can be expected. In like manner, report political communication specialists W. Lance Bennett and Murray Edelman, the setting of a news story "determines who are virtuous, who are threats to the good life."[59] If the setting is an achingly devastated village, you can bet the story will concern who is responsible for the desperate situation.

Set up by the way it is introduced, the story may follow any of a small number of plots. Nobody seems to know exactly how many plot lines there are. Jamieson and Campbell list five: appearance versus reality, little guys versus big guys, good against evil, efficiency versus inefficiency, and the unique versus the routine.[60] A slightly different set of story lines was presented by NBC commentator Sander Vanocur, who "observed that 'network news is a continuous loop: there are only a limited number of plots—'Black vs. White,' 'War is hell,' 'America is falling apart,' 'man against the elements,' 'the generation gap,' etc.—which we seem to be constantly redoing with different casts of characters."[61] Running through many of these story lines is an assumption that the government is doing the best that it can, the best that can be expected, against enormous odds: "deceitfulness . . . immorality . . . aversion to honest work."[62] Thus, the media imply, it is entirely understandable that the government makes so little headway against our problems.

Regardless of the specific story line the reporter chooses to carry today's story, the major outline of the plot moves from ambiguity to two-sided simplicity. The political result, Bennett and Edelman explain, is that "the contested issues in politics are quickly simplified and cast in mutually exclusive ideological terms."[63] That is to say, the plot line of the traditional news "story" very quickly sheds complexity and describes the situation in a way that invites the audience members to line up in their traditional liberal and conservative positions. A liberal mayor may propose a program to help the poor in an inner city *because* of a fear that if nothing is done the middle class will move to the suburbs and that the city, minus that tax base, will go broke. And conservatives may oppose the proposal *because* their analysis is that only a direct infusion of capital into the middle-class neighborhoods will keep people from fleeing. But you can bet that the way the media will tell the story will have the liberal kowtowing to the poor and conservatives draining public resources into the pockets of their rich friends. The story as told may not favor either side, but it does favor a bifocal rather than multifocal lens, encouraging the public to see the new phenomenon in the same old ways.

The conventional structure of the news story, according to Jamieson and Campbell, makes new forms of thought, new approaches to solving problems unlikely: "a news item is likely to begin with an action identified as a problem, develop through a narrative of increasing tension or conflict (including the iden-tification of opposing forces, often interviewed and quoted), and close with a suggested or predicted resolution. This structure . . . is ideally suited to reporting single, dramatic events, to presenting characters . . . , to focusing on action, and to covering novel, exciting events. Conversely, it is ill suited to coverage of an idea, concept, or process."[64]

The "predicted resolution" of a news story, they continue, is of particular interest. "Because the audience wants to know what impact the legislation will have and what it will cost, and because the press knows that unforeseen effects often are significant and newsworthy, reporters are particularly interested in gathering information about the specific effects of proposed action."[65] If we combine their interest in outcome with the reporters' tendency to rely upon "official" sources, we can begin to understand why presidents' assertions about the effects of their own actions get so much play in the media, and why other possible outcomes envisioned by those outside the "official expert" list get ignored so completely.

Political scientist M. B. Cornfield suggests that there are two highly popular "lines" for ending news narratives, each of which provide narrative closure in a way congenial to the reporter: "only one thing is certain" and "only time will tell."[66] A popular song of a few years ago suggested that we have fifty ways to leave our lovers; reporters apparently have many fewer ways to end a story. The two proffered endings both have political ramifications. If "only one thing is certain," the debate must have been exhausted and one side must have won. If "only time will tell," there is nothing to do but wait. In short, both endings lead away from politics, implying that what the citizen should do now is line up quiescently behind the one certain thing or wait for the passage of time to sort things out.

The final point to be made about the "stories" in the news is that they are written in a dwindling drama sort of way. James David Barber, a well-known political scientist, compares stories in the media to an inverted pyramid. The reader or viewer is provided first with the lead and then the story "dribbles away," eventually fading into "nothingness in the end."[67] Is that any way to write a "story?" Would any novelist or film writer compose it that way? Barber suggests that if a television journalist had covered the story of Little Red Riding

Hood, it would have gone this way: "Good evening. Last night a wolf ate a grandmother. Now here's Connie Chung on the steps of the Pentagon to fill you in."[68]

What is to be noted about the "dwindling drama" format is that the faster the medium, the less of the story is presented. Television and radio give you the first several paragraphs, newspapers give you those plus twelve to fifteen more, magazines supply even more and books the most of all. That explains why television and radio news stories are "more dramatic" than those in the longer and slower media. The form packs all the drama in the beginning. What follows is more complicated, requiring increasingly added measures of cogitation. In short, for most people nonelectronic news is boring.

## CONCLUSION

▶ There are undoubtedly other biases in the media beyond those few canvassed here—the large amount of sex depicted on television, for example, must indicate some kind of bias, as must the high incidence of violence—but these phenomena are so intertwined with our cultural biases that it is difficult to know where culture leaves off and the media begin, at least in terms of causality. That is, it is unclear whether the cultural obsession with sex and violence leads to the media obsession, or vice versa.

▶ What makes all this discussion about media bias important is an assumption that modern media control citizen responses. This assumption often relies on what has been called the "hypodermic needle theory." That is, just as a needle can be used to inject a substance into a person's arm—which will have an effect on that person—so do the media "inject" intellectual substances into a person's brain, with corresponding (usually negative) effects.

▶ Although the hypodermic needle theory seems to animate liberals' and conservatives' complaints, it has been disproved and discarded by mass communication researchers. I know of no academic in media studies who still subscribes to this position. This decidedly does not mean that such researchers assume there are no effects; if they assumed that they would probably move to a different line of inquiry. Rather, what researchers are finding now is that, as communication professor L. M. Bartels puts it, "the persuasive effects of the mass media may be more fugitive than minimal."[69]

▶ That is, the effects may be both cumulative and highly sophisticated, resistant to the methodological techniques available to most researchers. For instance, campaign research may find relatively little in the way of media effects because those effects can not be observed in an eight-to-twelve-month study. What if the effects of the media on George Bush's election in 1988 and defeat in 1992 were caused cumulatively by everything individual voters heard and read about Bush (and about government) from 1979 to 1988 and from 1979 to

1992? How could any researcher, or army of them, hope to encompass all that media consumption for any significant number of people over that time span? After all, researchers, too, have lives to lead.

▶ But the impossibility of such research does not obviate the possibility that those years of consuming this or that medium, watching news "shows," being entertained by politically relevant movies and seemingly irrelevant situation comedies, and listening to popular and not-so-popular music have "created" certain kinds of political responses.

▶ Ultimately, of course, the charge that the media are biased is related to a certain amount of distrust of "the people." Liberals think *they themselves* can resist conservative media, but that "the people" cannot; conservatives assume *they* can consume liberal media without losing their political orientation, but that "the public" cannot. Neither side trusts the electorate with the channel-changers and the radio knobs.

▶ Perhaps that *partly* explains why people were so immersed in the coverage of the O. J. Simpson trial in 1995, when television assumed that viewers not only would be interested in the arcane details of the case, but would be capable of following them over a long period of time. That, as political correspondent E. J. Dionne, Jr. has commented, "is almost exactly the opposite of what is assumed in coverage of political issues."[70] It would be interesting to see what would happen to politics, and political coverage, if politicians and the media started trusting the public with the facts. While I'm not completely sanguine that the O. J. case proved the public can become politically educated and involved, and am not sure I want to entrust my future to people who found that case exciting in any way (I lost interest in it sometime during the low-speed "chase" on the L.A. freeway), I also realize that we have little choice. We must choose either to trust the people or to trust the media and those they cover. If that is the choice, I cast my lot with the people.

## FOR FURTHER CONSIDERATION

**1.** Compare the "real" media biases Robert Entman identifies (favoring simplicity over complexity, persons over institutional processes, emotion over facts, and game over substance) with the "real" biases described in this chapter. Are there any inconsistencies between the two descriptions? Are they incompatible?[71]

**2.** Examine the stories on the front page of today's paper. Identify the plots of the stories, using the Jamieson and Campbell or Vanocur "plot lines." Do they all fit? If not, should the lists be expanded (or does the article in question seem so far out of the mainstream as to be idiosyncratic)?

## NOTES

1. G. McGovern, "A Word From the Original McGovernik," *Washington Post National Weekly Edition,* 2–8 January 1995, p. 25.

2. W. Glaberson, "More Reporters Leaning Democratic, Study Says," *New York Times,* 18 November 1992, p. A13.

3. E. Kolbert, "Maybe the Media Did Treat Bush a Bit Harshly," *New York Times,* 22 November 1992, p. E3.

4. *Ibid.,* E3.

5. I. R. Allen, "Dere Press Corps: Drop Dead," *Washington Journalism Review* 9 (March 1987): 14.

6. S. Tolan, "Dial 1-800-Censor," *New York Times,* 7 May 1993, p. A15.

7. W. Goodman, "TV Journalists' Urge to Prettify the News," *New York Times,* 19 February 1992, p. B3.

8. B. H. Bagdikian, "Journalism," *Mother Jones,* May/June 1992, 48.

9. *Ibid.,* 50.

10. *Ibid.,* 50.

11. *Ibid.,* 50.

12. *Ibid.,* 51.

13. D. Rather, "Call It Courage" (speech delivered at Radio and Television News Directors Association Annual Convention, Miami, 29 September 1993), 5.

14. R. Reynolds, "Take Back the Airwaves," *Mother Jones,* January/February 1995, 18.

15. J. Cohen, "TV Talk Is Stacked Against Liberals," *New York Times,* 30 November 1990, A30.

16. M. Cooper and L. C. Soley, "All the Right Sources," *Mother Jones,* February/March 1990, 20.

17. J. Kersten, "Liberal Media? It's Only a Myth Aimed to Scare," (Palm Beach) *Sun-Sentinel,* 21 November 1993, p. G1.

18. S. Douglas, "The Erasure of Revolt," *Progressive,* May 1995, 17.

19. *Ibid.,* 17.

20. Goodman, *op. cit.,* B3.

21. W. A. Henry, III, "Are the Media Too Liberal?" *Time,* 19 October 1992, 46.

22. *Ibid.,* 47.

23. D. Shenk, "On the Right, There's Pat Buchanan. On the Left . . . There's Blah," *Washington Post National Weekly Edition,* 23–29 August 1993, p. 24.

24. Reynolds, *op. cit.,* 18.

25. R. Zoglin, "Public TV Under Assault," *Time,* 30 March 1992, 58.

26. Henry, *op. cit.,* 47.

27. *Ibid.,* 47.

28. *Ibid.,* 47.

29. J. Cohen, "The Centrist Bias of the U.S. Media," *Utne Reader,* September/October 1990, 113.

30. D. C. Hallin, "The Passing of the High Modernism of American Journalism," *Journal of Communication* 42 (Summer 1992): 14–25.

31. P. J. Boyer, "When News Must Pay Its Way, Expect Trivia," *New York Times,* 2 October 1989, p. A19.

32. D. Tannen, "The Triumph of the Yell," *New York Times,* 14 January 1994, p. A15.

33. *Ibid.,* A15.

34. *Ibid.,* A15.

35. B. A. Franklin, "The Local Press is a Tragedy Waiting to Happen," *Washington Spectator* 22 (1 July 1996): 1–3.

36. W. Shannon, "The Network Circus," *New York Times,* 3 September 1975, p. 37.

37. K. H. Jamieson and K. K. Campbell, *The Interplay of Influence: Mass Media & Their Publics in News, Advertising, Politics* (Belmont, CA: Wadsworth, 1992), 32.

38. A. Hochschild, "All the President's Patsies," *Mother Jones,* July/August 1988, 52.

39. *Ibid.,* 53.

40. Jamieson and Campbell, *op. cit.,* 46.

41. *Ibid.,* 46.

42. W. I. Thompson, "The Past is Prologue. The Past—What's That?" *New York Times,* 10 June 1976, p. 37.

43. M. Frankel, "Full-Text TV," *New York Times Magazine,* 5 February 1995, p. 32.

44. Jamieson and Campbell, *op. cit.,* 65.

45. A. Cockburn, "Afterglow: All the President's Men," *Nation,* 4 April 1987, 422.

46. Cohen, September/October 1990, *op. cit.,* 113.

47. Jamieson and Campbell, *op. cit.,* 65.

48. J. Cohen, "Media Madness," *Z Magazine,* April 1990, 75–78.

49. E. S. Herman and N. Chomsky, "Propaganda Mill," *Progressive,* June 1988, 15.

50. W. Karp, "Who Decides What is News?" *Utne Reader,* November/December 1989, 61.

51. G. W. Selnow, "Values in Prime-time Television," *Journal of Communication* 40 (Spring 1990): 64–74.

52. D. L. Swanson, "And That's the Way It Was? Television Covers the 1976 Presidential Campaign," *Quarterly Journal of Speech* 63 (October 1977): 241.

53. Jamieson and Campbell, *op. cit.,* 36.

54. *Ibid.,* 39.

55. M. C. Miller, "TV's Anti-liberal Bias," *New York Times,* 16 November 1988, p. A31.

56. M. Hertsgaard, "Electoral Journalism: Not Yellow, but Yellow-bellied," *New York Times,* 21 September 1988, p. A23.

57. D. E. Harrington, "The Bad News Bias," *Wilson Quarterly* 13 (Summer 1989): 20.

58. R. Dougherty, "The Sneaky Bumbler," *Newsweek,* 8 January 1973, 7.

59. W. L. Bennett and M. Edelman, "Toward a New Political Narrative," *Journal of Communication* 35 (Autumn 1985): 159.

60. Jamieson and Campbell, *op. cit.,* 24.

61. E. J. Epstein, *News from Nowhere* (New York: Random House, 1973).

62. Bennett and Edelman, *op. cit.,* 156.

63. *Ibid.,* 158.

64. Jamieson and Campbell, *op. cit.,* 39.

65. *Ibid.,* 56.

66. M. B. Cornfield, "The Press and Political Controversy: The Case for Narrative Analysis" (paper presented at convention of the American Political Science Association, Washington, DC, April 1991), 6.

67. J. D. Barber, "The Journalist's Responsibility: Make Reality Interesting," *Center Magazine* 18 (May/June 1985): 13.

68. *Ibid.,* 13.

69. L. M. Bartels, "Messages Received: The Political Impact of Media Exposure," *American Political Science Review* 87 (June 1993): 267.

70. E. J. Dionne, Jr., "Trusting People with the Facts," *Washington Post National Weekly Edition,* 18–24 July 1994, p. 29.

71. Robert M. Entman, "Reporting Environmental Policy Debate: The Real Media Biases," *Press/Politics* 1 (Summer 1996): 77–92.

# The Power of Definition

*The powerful enjoy the prerogative of labeling and defining everything.*
— J. LIPMAN-BLUMEN[1]

**W**e are all sophisticated enough with language usage to have found ourselves saying, "Well, that depends on what *you* mean by . . . patriotism . . . excellence" or whatever the topic in question was.

Unfortunately, too few of us take our semantic skills with us when we leave the realm of interpersonal relations and begin to focus on governmental pronouncements. So maybe it is time, in one of Lyndon Johnson's favorite phrases, to "take the bull by the tail and look it straight in the eye."

In the first chapter I took the position that governmental power is based more on persuasion than on the vast physical force it has to (en)force decisions. In this chapter I turn to the question of the centrality of definitional power in the processes of persuasion, for both the government and for contending political groups.

We will attempt to discover how the government is able to convince so many of us so often to follow docilely along the path it has enunciated, as well as how contending sides come to believe so completely that *all* truth is on their side and *all* error is located in the opposition. The answer provided will, of course, be partial, for in addition to the influences of language there are contributions based on personality; on demographic factors such as age, gender, and relative wealth; on educational and familial inputs; and so forth.

But the power of language and the centrality of that power in the political milieu must be neither overlooked nor underemphasized. For language *is* powerful—it soothes us when we're upset, but can ruffle us out of a calmness. It can persuade us to admire a person or idea, or hold them up to contempt. One of the major ways in which language accomplishes these various feats is through definitions.

## ▶ On Defining "Definition"

Kenneth Burke reminds us that most of us carry around a rather commonsense notion about definitions and the process by which we decide what is the proper name by which to call entities, processes, and ideas. According to Burke, "The commonsense view favors the idea that 'words are the signs of things.'"[2] But what we too often forget is that the word-thing relationship is entirely arbitrary, invented by humans. Burke goes on to suggest that it would help to think of the decision about what to call anything as an act of "entitling," analogous to how a novelist entitles a book.[3]

As complicated as the relationship might be between the novel's title and the story it "entitles," at least there is an extant entity in this example; that is, the book exists. We can read the book, then come back to the title to see whether we agree that the title is an appropriate "summary" of the book. But in the realm of political communication, such "reality checking" is less possible. As Burke comments, with abstract words like "democracy" "there is no clear 'natural' counterpart to the word."[4]

Thus, the question of definitions, of which words do or ought "stand for" things or ideas, can become quite complicated if we let it. But there is no reason for us to get bogged down unduly with the definition of definitions. For our purposes, we need make only one basic distinction: between "defining" and "naming." Most simply stated, the distinction we will make is this: "defining" provides at least one reason for applying a term to a concept, while "naming" provides no reasons. Thus, when somebody says "Clinton's health care plan is socialistic because it provides for government control," we will call that a definition, but when a person refers to "Clinton's socialistic health care proposal" we will identify that as a naming.

In practice, however, the two processes are even more nearly identical than the above distinction indicates. The examples given are based upon single sentences, whereas we normally deal with larger entities—news stories, essays, books, speeches, and so forth—and the reasons for using a term may be separated from the first use of it by many paragraphs or many pages. Thus, an essayist might mention "Clinton's socialist health care proposal," then a few paragraphs later talk about the dangers of "government-controlled medicine," thereby providing a reason for the original "naming" and converting it to a "defining." Semanticists might want to debate whether the person "really" had *defined* "socialistic" or merely had *named* the proposal as socialistic; that is not a stupid debate, but it is not one in which we need to get involved. For our purposes, the two processes function essentially alike—to get the audience to see, discuss, and/or evaluate the health proposal as an example of socialism. Thus, whatever differences there are between "defining" and "naming" need not slow us down in our quest to see how the language used affects the ensuing public dialogue.

For all the foregoing reasons, I tend to see "naming" as a subset of "defining." Therefore, although at times I distinguish between the two, when I am talking of both processes I tend to use the word "definition" as a summational term. If that is confusing, I apologize. On the other hand, because both naming and defining *function* in the same way (telling us how to see something), and because it is the functioning that we are interested in, you needn't worry too much about any minor naming/defining confusion you might experience. In fact, I have mentioned the distinction between "naming" and "defining" not because it is inherently important to your reading of this text, but because you will run into the distinction in some of your other reading and will want to understand how those sources reinforce or contradict what you read here. To the degree the distinction is at all important to my analyses it is because rhetors who offer definitions also simultaneously are offering to debate, while those who only provide names often are masking or denying the fact that they are involved in a definitional process. "Clinton's proposal is socialistic" is an assertion, an opening for debate; "Clinton's socialistic proposal" is a description, closing off debate.

The point on which to keep focused is that the major political questions debated at any given time often are definitional. The opposing sides of the controversy may be actively struggling to persuade the public to adopt their definitions, or "camouflaging" the fact that a definitional struggle is taking place by "hiding" their definitions in the names they apply to the things, events, processes, or people under consideration. Either way, though, both sides want to make sure the societal dialogue adopts their language, for to accomplish that feat is to win half the battle.

## ▶ Functions of Definitions

As I already have indicated, the overall function of definitions is to control the societal dialogue. That is, all rhetors attempt to control the public dialogue by persuading others to see the world as they see it—to know as they know, to value as they value. It would not seem, at first blush, that definitions could accomplish all that, but they can—and do.

More specifically, definitions are like blinders on a horse: they focus attention on some aspects while blinding us to others. They identify what the societal problem is (i.e., what should be done); and that, in turn, helps identify who should act. They help to focus and thereby limit debates and, if successful, even entirely eliminate the need to debate.

Because most of us, most of the time, prefer to believe that the societal dialogues in which we are involved are about "truth" and "justice" rather than merely definitions, it may be helpful to take a historic example rather than a contemporary one. Let's consider a nineteenth-century controversy that has by now been solved: slavery in the United States.

What was the nature of the question? For some, it was defined as a moral question: slavery was morally wrong. For others it was an economic question: slaves were needed to work the land. (There were other positions, other definitions of the "problem," but these two will be sufficient for our purposes.)

We can look back today and see that the contending sides were caught up in a definitional battle, one side defining the question as one of morality, the other as a question of economics. And because those who saw it (defined it) as a morality question won, and their definition thus became a societal truth, today we are sure that it *was* a morality question.

But what if the South had won the war? How would we today define that nineteenth-century "problem"? I suppose the answer might be determined by whether we were brought up as citizens of the country called U.U.S. (Union of United States) or as citizens of the C.S.A. (Confederate States of America).

Please note that the definition of the question inherently carries with it the function of identifying whether the government should be involved. That is, to the North defining slavery as a moral issue meant the government should intervene. To the South, defining slavery as an economic issue meant the government should not get involved.

It is interesting—as a by-note—that we do not agree today that these definitional categories *necessarily* determine the necessity or nonnecessity of governmental action. That is, contemporary conservatives tend to believe that issues defined as moral may require government involvement while those defined as economic probably do not; contemporary liberals tend to believe that government should stay out of moral questions but get involved in economic ones. Yet both conservatives and liberals believe government should have abolished slavery *because it is immoral* . . . and both believe it should have done so *even if* such abolishment had deleterious economic effects in the South.

A third function of definition (beyond identifying the problem and specifying the appropriate actors) is to focus or limit the debate. That is to say, to define slavery as a moral question is to attempt to eliminate other questions (such as economics) from the public dialogue, to make them irrelevant or even illegitimate. This function helps explain why, in so many public "debates," the two (usually two) sides ignore each other rather than engaging each other's arguments. Each is trying to limit the debate to what it wants to talk about. To respond to the specific arguments of the other side would be to accept that side's focus.

The ultimate in limiting debate can be said to be a fourth function of definitions: eliminating debate completely. The hope of each side is always that its definitions will be so compelling, so persuasive, that people on the other side will see the "error of their ways," "come to their senses," and accept the opposing definitions. The North dearly hoped Southerners would hear the North's position and say, "Oh, my goodness, you're right . . . it *is* a moral question . . . and, of course, morality *must* take precedence over mere economics. Okay, let's abolish slavery." That, of course, is not what happened. That rarely happens.

Indeed, it more often is the case that we do not even notice that we are debating definitions. Probably neither the North nor the South realized it was debating the definitional question, "what kind of problem are we facing?" Rather, each side was debating truth: slavery is immoral; slavery is necessary. Each was debating justice: the government should not allow immorality to continue; the government has no right to interfere in my economic arrangements.

Further, we are so accustomed to thinking of "definitions" as a matter of "splitting hairs" that when we are involved in a definitional debate we deny that that is what is happening. We may think the "other side" is engaged in a definitional battle, but our side, we think, is involved in a much loftier pursuit—establishing justice, defending freedom, and so forth.

However, the truth probably is that most political debates are definitional; they are debates about what the nature of the problem is, and thus about who should act, what aspect of the problem we should focus on, and how to define the problem so that everyone will see it as we see it, thereby eliminating the necessity of debating it.

Thus, because we do not believe we are engaged in a definitional debate, we often do not bother to define terms but rather just provide names. And while it is *generally* true that two groups of citizens debating a political problem may either define their terms or merely provide names, the government almost never presents definitions. It relies almost totally on the naming process to accomplish its definitional purpose, perhaps hoping nobody will notice that the names provided carry with them definitional assumptions. Nowhere is this tendency more clearly seen than in the names the government applies to foreign affairs, especially to military endeavors.

## ▶ Government Defining via Naming

The general process of government defining via naming can be seen in a classic instance from 1971–72. In the summer of 1971, according to the United States government, Henry Kissinger flew to Peking to "explore the possibilities" of the U.S. gaining in some way from the Sino-Soviet rift of that period. In January of 1972, again according to official U.S. sources, Mr. Gromyko of the Soviet Union flew to Tokyo to "exploit the coldness" between the United States and Japan.[5] Note that in each case an antagonist flew in to take advantage of a strain in relations between allies. But look again at the language of the U.S. government communiques and you find the underlying assumptions clearly delineated: the good guys "explore," the baddies "exploit."

This example demonstrates something of the subtlety of the definition-by-naming process, for it shows that naming is not merely a matter of nouns but can be accomplished by other language, in this case verbs. Thus it is not necessary directly to name other countries "the enemy"; the same result can be accomplished by characterizing their actions. They "exploit," "ambush," "interfere," "violate," and so forth.

The government's definitional power is perhaps most clearly seen in the names it applies to military equipment and activities. A nuclear war is discussed in government circles as a "nuclear exchange," but it is in no way an "exchange" like any with which we are familiar—exchanging Christmas presents, for instance. Political scientist Murray Edelman points out that "to speak of deterrence and strike capacity is to perceive war as a game" while "to speak of legalized murder is to perceive war as a slaughter of human beings."[6] In order to study this phenomenon more closely, let us examine some of the governmental terminology of the Vietnam "War" (which was not even called a war for many years, although the attractive alternative phrase, "police action," was taboo from its debasement during the Korean War).

Government communiques, especially President Nixon's, seldom spoke of the Vietcong or the North Vietnamese, but rather of "The Enemy." Even newspapers that took editorial positions against the war, such as the *New York Times*, used the governmental phrase "the enemy" in their news columns—and *they* did not enclose the words in quotation marks.

Not only did government "naming" define the sides, it controlled the terms of the battle. The Enemy engaged in "sneak attacks" and "ambushes." The good guys went on "incursions" (military picnics?) and were sent on "protective reaction" strikes; that is, they "were authorized to seek out and attack enemy troops or planes that threatened them."[7] All this, of course, was for home consumption. The combatants, says Friedrich Heer, knew what they were doing by more realistic terms. Helicopter pilots flying over Laos said it plainly: "Killing is our business, and business is good."[8]

But the end was always near, the light at the end of the tunnel was sighted often. While most of us came to agree with Russell Baker's judgment that "There is a tunnel at the end of the tunnel,"[9] the president refused to approach the light until he could be assured that it was a light that would not cast a shadow on the Number One nation's national honor (the definition of which he kept to himself).

And so, inexorably, "The War" against "The Enemy" ground slowly toward a "Peace With Honor" over the bodies of many brave men from numerous countries (important only as numbers in the daily "body count" taken to prove we were winning a war we claimed we did not want to win). And practically no one in a position to counter the official definitions stepped forward to translate the Pentagonese into English. Senator McGovern tried, but he was perceived as using the war for his own political profit—so was not believed. Senator Birch Baye tried, too late, when he cut through the definitions to point out that the United States "is bombing four countries, and has invaded two, in order to withdraw from one."[10] If such bluntness had arisen in 1966 rather than 1972, the '60s might have been radically different. As poet Norman Rosten has said, "We have only a handful of crucial words standing between light and the darkness. To blur the meaning of even one is to hasten the darkness."[11]

But we did not learn from the Vietnam War to reject the government terms. So when the Gulf War came in the '90s we were still subject to how the government named the battles. Critic George Cheney identified how the term "collateral damage" for enemy civilian deaths had the effect of distancing the citizens from the brutal and bloody effects of American "firepower": "Terms such as 'collateral damage' . . . dehumanize the war, making it seem less real and less horrific."[12] "Peel the onion" was the innocent gardening phrase employed to refer to the process of "stripping" the multilayered Iraqi defense one layer at a time via U.S. Air Force bombing raids. Obviously, the missiles of each side (our "patriots" versus their "scuds") were named for psychological advantage.

If you think the military only uses obfuscating language in wartime, a few recent peacetime examples, provided by William Lutz, Chair of the Committee on Public Doublespeak of the National Council of Teachers of English, should disabuse you of that thought. In the summer of 1988 the Air Force renamed "cockpits"; they are now "Missionized Crew Stations." The Army renamed the "C-ration" as the "MRE," meaning "meal ready to eat." As the Army purchased Soviet combat-vehicle replicas in October of 1988, it assured us the replicas would have the "same visual signatures" as the actual Soviet vehicles. What does that mean? It means "they'll look like the real thing." Really? Is there any other way for a "replica" to look?[13]

Not having been privy to the discussions that led to these peacetime changes, it is difficult to know what the namings and renamings were intended to accomplish. What was wrong with "cockpit?" What did Army officials think was superior about "missionized crew station?" Had there been complaints that "cockpit" was sexist language? Did they merely want to underline the idea that everybody has a "work station" during any "mission"? As "cockpits" grew in size and complexity so that they no longer could be controlled by a single pilot, did the Army want to give more visibility to the "crew" now required? We do not know. But we do know that there *was* an intended effect; people do not change the names of things just for the sake of change.

Perhaps nothing is more under the spell of definitional debate than the move from peacetime to wartime. When, indeed, is a "war" a "war"—or an "invasion" or a "military action" or a "police action" or something else? In 1994, as President Clinton appeared to be inching toward a decision to invade Haiti, that old definitional debate broke out once again. The president and the members of his administration, following in the footsteps of nearly all twentieth-century presidents, asserted that they could take this step on their own, without congressional approval. Many others, in Congress and academia, denied their assertion.

Clinton's ambassador to the United Nations, Madeleine K. Albright, claimed that congressional action was unnecessary because what was being contemplated was not a "war" but a "police action."[14] The head of the Justice Department's Office of Legal Counsel, Assistant Attorney General Walter Dellinger, argued that the Haiti invasion would be "far different from a 'major military action' like the 1991 Persian Gulf War" and more like "the invasions of Grenada in 1983 and Panama in 1989, as well as 'interventions' in countries like Haiti and the Dominican Republic earlier in the century,"[15] all of which were initiated by presidents without a congressional declaration of war.

On the other side of the definitional debate, Duke University law professor William Van Alstyne said the Administration was making a "nonexistent distinction" and argued that "a planned landed invasion by a substantial force of combatant troops under the authority of the president of the United States" had to be considered a war.[16] Yale Law School Professor Harold H. Koh suggested "If [the president] needs congressional approval to get assault weapons off the streets of the United States," it makes sense that he would need that same congressional approval "to put assault weapons with American soldiers carrying them onto the streets of Port-au-Prince."[17]

So the military, whether at war, at peace, or during a debate about making the transition between the two, is as involved in semantics as it is in guns, planes, tanks, and soldiers. But the military is not an isolated case. The United Nations, that instrument by which nations are supposed to talk each other out of war, also is hampered by definitional difficulties. Hans Koning argues that the interminable debate on admitting China to the United Nations would have been exhausted much sooner "if the question had been phrased: 'Should the seat of China in the U.N. be occupied by China or by the representatives of its former rulers now on Taiwan?'"[18]

Or consider that U.N. Security Council mechanism that has caused so much trouble down through the years, the veto. Where did this "veto" come from? The U.N. Charter does not mention the word, although, as Max Black has commented, it talks of a similar process: "Consider the difference made to the procedure described in the United Nations Charter as 'the concurring votes of the permanent members,' when it is referred to by Americans as the 'veto' or by the Russians as 'the rule of unanimity.' A 'distinction without a difference?' Hardly. The reference is the same in all three cases, but the emotive force differs appreciably."[19] For one thing, the American phrase places the blame for inaction upon one party. When the explanation is "Russia vetoed it," we place all blame upon that one government. But when the explanation is "we failed to achieve unanimity," the blame is spread to all participants. The two phrases are more than different terms for the same process. One concentrates blame, the other spreads it. One announces the end of dialogue, the other encourages a continuation. One beckons impatience, the other gestures caution. Unquestionably, the American and Russian phrases were chosen at a time when all the single negative votes were being cast by Russia. The United States chose its phrase, "veto," to place blame on the Soviet Union, while Russia chose "lack of unanimity" to take some of the heat off. But as the power structure of the U.N. swung away from United States dominance, our government became caught in its own semantics. Now that the United States often casts the single negative vote, we are reaping the political rewards (the blame) of our own politically determined terminology.

Or take another United States–Soviet Union example. English professor B. Evans reminds us that in 1962, as the world anxiously approached the brink of nuclear confrontation in the Cuban missile crisis, "the use of the word *quarantine* instead of *blockade* was extremely important."[20] In international law, a "blockade" is an act of war, thus to have called our blockade a "blockade" would have been, in effect, to declare war on Russia. And the Russians, then, would have been honor-bound to respond by reciprocating, i.e., by declaring war on us. Obviously, we did not want that result.

The exact thought processes of our governmental decision-makers in settling on "quarantine" as the chosen locution have never been divulged, but we can identify some of the results of the decision. First, the word signaled the Russians that we did not want a war. Second, "quarantine" gave the Russians the possibility of honoring our blockade without losing any respect. That is, they would have "lost face" if they had backed down from a "blockade," but they could turn their ships around and go home because of the "quarantine" with no loss to their pride or their international standing.

Third, a "quarantine" is a public health measure that is legitimate for any government, so the word implied that the U.S. government was engaged in a lawful action. Finally, the word implied that stationing Russian missiles on

Cuban soil would have been analogous to the importation of a disease—i.e., it would be dangerous to the host and would threaten to spread to other countries in the vicinity. In other words, the selection of "quarantine" gave Cuba less reason to be upset and suggested to other Caribbean countries that the U.S. was protecting them from disease rather than endangering them with a reckless military adventure near their shores.

Effectively, then, selecting to label our action a "quarantine" rather than a "blockade" blunted the possibility of war and eliminated much of the controversy that is normally aroused when a blockade is initiated. Seldom in the annals of history has a government's naming power had such a positive effect on the resolution of a dangerous situation.

The power of governmental definitions via naming to affect issues and policy is not isolated to the military and foreign affairs spheres. It is also active on the domestic scene. Consider the current economic situation. Are we "enjoying" a "recession," a "depression," or just "bad times"? How much inflation is "too much"? How much unemployment is "acceptable"? Murray Edelman has noted that in many countries when three percent of the citizens are unemployed it is thought "intolerable," yet the "U.S. Government has succeeded within the last few years in instilling the belief that when only four percent of the work force is unemployed we are enjoying 'full employment.'"[21] By what mechanism is four percent unemployment "full employment" in the United States when just three percent is "intolerable" in England? By the power of definitional naming!

## ▶ Defining and Naming the Issues

Just as the government attempts to control the societal debate via language, so too do opposing groups of citizens, opposing politicians, and opposing political movements. Indeed, a brief history of the last few decades will demonstrate the ubiquity of definitional disagreements down through the years.

Every decade provides its own examples of the power of defining and naming in the world of politics. In the 1950s the central concerns of the so-called "McCarthy era" swirled around the seemingly simple questions, "What is communism?" and "Who is a communist?" The trouble was that the elastic definitions of McCarthy and his supporters allowed them to call anybody who ever had a communist friend a "pinko" or "dupe" or "communist sympathizer," and anybody who ever attacked any belief of McCarthy and friends was thereby assumed to be in league with the communists.

In the 1960s a good deal of public debate time was taken up with the attempt of certain Far Right groups, such as the John Birch Society, to determine the issues for public debate. Rather than questioning the proper role of government in the area of mental health, they wanted to debate whether psychoanalysis was a communist plot to incarcerate all conservatives. Rather than questioning the extent to which civil rights might be obtained through governmental action, they wanted to debate whether the civil-rights movement had been infiltrated by communists.

But the Right was not alone; the Far Left of the '60s also tried to control public debate through definitional power. As *Harper's* commentator J. Corry wrote at the time, as the Left stated the question, the bothersome issue of whether one Black Panther had killed another was never raised; the only question was "Do you or do you not support the Panthers?"[22] Raising the question this way had the effect of boxing in the audience, for it implied that if one did not support the Black Panthers one was a racist. Yet there were many Whites in the civil-rights movement who sincerely supported expanded rights but saw the Panthers as dangerous. But the Left provided little "wriggle room"; it tended to take the old aphorism, "A man shall be known by the company he keeps," and convert it into that ageless popular fallacy: "If you're not for us, you're against us." That is, the Left attempt to define the question in such a way that the "battle" would be on home turf was a classic example of what all definers try to do. In this case, the attempt was to define the sides so that any opponent would be seen as a racist. That definition changed the rules of the game, for now the debate could not be about whether the Panthers were legitimate players in the civil-rights struggle. We were now on the Left's turf, playing by their rules, and their rules said the question was merely "are you or are you not a racist?"

In the 1970s one big definitional debate came during the 1976 presidential campaign. Jimmy Carter was pressured from the Left to promise amnesty to those who had resisted service in Vietnam, many of whom had moved to Canada to escape the draft. Yet there was also pressure from the Right to do no such thing. So Carter adopted a novel definitional position, in which he said that he opposed amnesty because "amnesty says that what you did was right." But he added that, in his first week in office, he would issue a "blanket pardon" to "defectors" because "a pardon says that you are forgiven for what you did, whether it was right or wrong."[23] No one has ever located a dictionary that makes such a distinction; in fact, in most dictionaries "amnesty" is defined as "a general pardon."

In the 1980s "liberalism" was nearly defined out of existence by Ronald Reagan and his supporters. To understand how that happened you have to know that many liberal ideas were voted into law in the 1960s under the tutelege of President Lyndon Johnson—but were either not funded at all or were inadequately funded because the monies were appropriated for the war in Vietnam. Then Nixon became president and, although the war was nearly ended, funding these programs was not one of his priorities. Nor were they funded in the Ford and Carter years. By the time Reagan became president these struggling underfunded programs were in great trouble; President Reagan killed them with the argument that "We've tried liberalism, and it doesn't work." Of course, by then people had forgotten that the programs were underfunded, i.e., that they had not really been "tried" at all. They looked at the programs and saw that, indeed, they were not working, so they concluded that Reagan was right, that liberalism doesn't work. Goodbye liberalism!

In the 1990s one major definitional debate concerned governmental actions for the "middle class." The question debated is two-pronged: (1) who is the middle class? and (2) do they need help? Obviously, however, the answer to the second question depends largely on how the first is answered.

And that first question, who is middle class? is nearly unanswerable. Even the criteria are debated, though perhaps a majority of the definers focus on income. Many, including a large number of economists, suggest that "middle class" is the 60 percent of Americans whose incomes range about the $37,000 median annual income, which would define "middle class" as those who bring in from $17,000 to $64,000 per year.[24] Other economists identify "middle class" as those "between the 50th and 80th income percentiles,"[25] which sounds like a different set of numbers but is actually almost exactly the same group of people.

But if you ask the citizens, you get quite a different picture, for 93 percent of Americans consider themselves to be members of the middle class.[26] How can that be? Consider: 44 percent of Americans believe one does not escape from middle- to upper-class status until one is making over $100,000 per year; 12 percent think the escape point is above $200,000 per annum, and 3 percent believe $500,000 is the cut off point. Only 1 percent of Americans perceive themselves as "upper-class."[27]

Since only 5.8 percent of Americans actually make over $100,000 per year,[28] if 44 percent think it takes more than $100,000 to put one in the upper class that means an awfully lot of people think those richer than themselves are still middle-class, which probably means that a significant number of those below $100,000 see themselves as having the possibility of breaking that barrier in their lifetimes (but assume that doing so will not automatically propel them into another class). And indeed, in 1994 over 90 percent of Americans felt good about their own personal financial prospects,[29] although they also felt some anxiety because they feared that no matter how much more money they made the "upper-class" boundary would keep expanding upward and thereby keep them permanently anchored in the "middle class."[30]

Income alone, however, is not necessarily the best way to determine class standing. Another measuring rod sometimes used is status. Relying on this criterion, C. Chandler says, "the upper classes favor Proust, wine and the symphony; the middle class sticks to John Grisham, beer and Madonna."[31] The problem with this standard is that it is as elastic as the income criterion. There is as much difference between a fine French wine and a bottle of Ripple as there is between a mansion and a hovel, and a paperback edition of Proust being read by a lower-middle-class college student is exponentially different from a leather-bound and autographed limited edition residing in an étagère in an exclusive part of town.

So, whatever it is, how is the "middle class" faring? Again, that depends on whom you listen to. On the one hand, M. Levinson says the situation can be seen as pretty grim because "the median income of U.S. households is down 7 percent since 1989."[32] And if we look at some specific examples of some subsets of the 80 percent of Americans who have lost ground since incomes peaked in 1973, H. Hawkins points out, the grimness seems dire: "The manufacturing wage is back to its 1965 level and the retail clerk's wage is back to its 1952 level."[33]

But others, looking at different economic indicators, believe the gloom is overstated. M. Levington argues that "a sharp drop in family size leaves more money for everyone"[34] and conservative economist R. J. Samuelson concludes that "job security is better than it seems; studies show little decline in average job tenure."[35]

Those with the more "upbeat" approach think there has been an intentional skewing of the facts. Samuelson, for instance, argues that President Clinton and his supporters foster feelings of anxiety in the middle class for ideological advantage, making "people feel sorry for themselves so that government can rescue them and win thanks."[36] Others point in the other ideological direction, as when Levinson says the Republican claim that a middle-income family spends more on taxes than it spends on food, clothing and shelter combined "is flatly untrue": the $6,000 such a family pays in taxes is less than half of the $13,000 it pays for "the basics of life."[37]

I will not try to solve this definitional debate for you. For one thing, it is complicated almost beyond comprehension. To take a simple example of the complexities, I note that my own economic situation has suffered in recent years if you examine only gross-income questions—I make approximately $5,000 less per year now than I did five years ago, so I am included in the "falling income" statistics. Yet my change was intentional—I left a higher-paying job to make a geographical move that I thought would, despite the lower pay, improve the quality of my life. So am I "worse off" today? In terms of income, yes. On the other hand, I'm happier. Isn't that the idea?

The second reason I do not want to try to solve the "who's middle class and how are they doing?" conundrum is that I believe all citizens have the right to identify any issue they want to debate, and to try to define the issue to their own satisfaction. They have the right to have their positions stated . . . and to have them refuted. What should be recognized in all this is merely that if we enter a debate along the lines proposed by others we have given them a debating advantage. Their position can not be ignored . . . but if you meet them on their definitional grounds you find yourself fighting on their field according to their rules.

One arena of definitional debate that has spanned the decades is the ongoing debate about abortion. Semanticist Mary Alexander writes, "one of the most heated, angry, and irreconcilable instances of definition tyranny is in the abortion debate. As a nation, we seem to be locked into the stupid and simplistic expressions of each side. As the pro-choice faction screams accusations of backward thinking, religious fanaticism, and male domination, the pro-life group counters with cries of baby killers, satan-worshipers, and inhumanity. . . . Neither side is willing to stop yelling and consider the perspective of their opposition. Each group is trapped by a definition of life that leaves no room for compromise."[38]

The problem appears to be that the opposing definitions are intimately related to opposing views of life and opposing lifestyles, both religious and political. Religiously, says Alexander, the pro-life side tends to be drawn from fundamentalists with a "future orientation"; that is, "it asks that we wait for a better world, that we give up our self-control and trust that God knows best. To abort an unwanted pregnancy is to fly in the face of God's plan. From this point of view, it is vanity to believe that we can control our fate. We should wait and see what tomorrow will bring."[39] Pro-choice advocates, on the other hand, are more concerned with the present than with the future, with the suffering of the pregnant woman than with the not-yet-existing life in the womb. In Alexander's summary, "It is a movement focused on controlling fate and viewing the accidents of nature, not as God's will, but as things that must be fixed."[40]

These religious viewpoints, Alexander argues, are rather naturally aligned with political positions. Pro-lifers align with the Republican Party because "the 'ideology' of the Republican party is focused on the future. Their version of progress and the American dream has to do with waiting for things to get better. The poor should wait for the wealth of the rich and powerful to 'trickle down.' Rather than giving money to the 'underprivileged,' those in need should wait for jobs to be created, for entrepreneurs to improve our schools, and for the economy to get better."[41] Likewise, she says, there is a "natural" alignment between pro-choicers and the Democratic Party, because Democrats want "to fix the world as it exists now. They cannot wait for the money to 'trickle down' from the rich, they want to take it now. Jobs need to be created, schools need to be repaired, the poor and downtrodden must be repaid and remolded into happy citizens. The Democrats don't have time to wait for the future, things must be fixed now."[42]

Given the basic division between these positions and the extent to which their differing definitions are embedded in their political and religious outlooks, it is no surprise that neither side is willing to accede to the definitions of the other. To do so would be to accede to a whole different way of seeing the world and living one's life. Consequently, while the debate appears to be stymied by opposing definitions, it is not merely a definitional debate. It is much deeper than that. The definitional difficulties, while real, are not causal; rather, the opposing definitions are merely symptomatic of basic differences in religious and political outlooks.

So, whether opposing definitions have been reflective of deep-seated beliefs or only chosen for political advantage, down through the decades both the political Right and the political Left have tried to define the issues and the terms of the issues, and each has occasionally been successful. But individual citizens, or even groups of citizens, rarely win a definitional battle with the government—the government is successful *most* of the time, partly because it tends to get there first, partly because the presumption is almost always on the side of the government.

## ▶ Defining and Naming People

Not only issues are affected by the power of definition—people are, too. What people think of themselves and how they consider others can be determined by descriptions. For instance, people we today label "mental patients" were once called "heretics" or "witches," and we feel morally superior at our humane progress in now "correctly" labeling them "sick" rather than criminal. But are we so sure of our correctness? What will people exhibiting their strange behaviors be called a hundred years from now? According to psychologist T. S. Szasz, "these behaviors are incomprehensible only because those who ostensibly try to understand them define them as incomprehensible."[43]

In examining the attacks upon President Clinton in the 1996 campaign, it is instructive to see how one of those attacks, centering on some prepresidential business dealings, came to be named "Whitewater-gate." This term, obviously, was an implied reference to Nixon's "Watergate" scandal; it was a highly connotative symbol through which the American people were to provide a "schemata" into which what was known, as well as what was unknown but might soon be revealed, could fit.

"Whitewater-gate" brought to mind the events of 1973 that absolutely rocked the foundation of the Nixon presidency. More important, they strained American belief in the presidency as a symbol and repository of faith in the nation's destiny. "Whitewater-gate," in the context of our history since 1973, and in consideration of the promises of every presidential campaign since then (especially promises to restore faith in the office and in the government), was a term that "compelled" us to see Clinton in a dark "Nixonian" light.

Like Watergate, "Whitewater-gate" (the Republicans hoped) might reveal once again the corruption, abuses, duplicity, and dirty politics that we have assumed, since Nixon, inheres in all presidents. Juxtaposing one term with the other produced a sense of inevitability, perhaps even *deja vu*, and seemed to imply that one situation was like the other and would lead to similar results.

Likewise, the reference to Watergate recalled the form by which the 1973 events unfolded. Specifically, the day-to-day revelations of the congressional hearings were recalled. Americans, whatever their political persuasion, followed the Watergate hearings much as they follow a melodrama to its denouement. Characters were named, invested with personality, and aligned in relationship to each other. The crisis and its ramifications were pieced together. The events were assembled into a good-versus-evil narrative. Simply by virtue of its phonetic association with Watergate, "Whitewater-gate" promised to hold a nation's attention.

But journalist J. Corry reminds us that not all labeling is done by others. Sometimes we label ourselves. One of the most popular self-labels is "oppressed," and the oppressed "will fight hard to keep their way of life."[44]

And just as it is true that if you call others sick you have to expect them to respond as though they are sick, so if you call yourself "oppressed" you must expect others to respond to you as though you are oppressed. It is a fact of life, sometimes fortunate, sometimes not, that other people tend to believe our self-labels. And, rightly or wrongly, it is difficult for an audience to act with respect toward people who characterize themselves as oppressed. For one thing, there is always a lingering feeling that the oppression *may* have been created by some deficiency in the oppressed. It may not be true, but the propensity to think it is seems to be cued automatically by the use of the word.

Since people's perceptions are determined, at least partially, by language, and since perceptions of the people involved in politics affect perceptions of issues, it is no surprise that some issues, and the positions taken on them, are determined by the definitions of the people associated with them.

Murray Edelman says that bureaucrats convert people into abstractions by calling them "personnel" or "clients."[45] In wartime enemies are reduced to "Japs" or "Huns" or "gooks" or "slants" to make it easier for our soldiers to kill them. In peacetime our opponents are reduced to "commies" or "baby killers" or "Feminazis" to make it easier for our supporters to defy them. Thus, we get a basic rule of political language: if the opposing position is unassailable, attack its proponents. But that is not always possible. Sometimes verbalizing a characterization can do your side harm. At that point, you can avoid labeling the people by redefining the issue.

## ▶ Redefining and Renaming

Consider how some politicians have adopted the anti-welfare position of their most conservative supporters: Russell Baker of the *New York Times* says politicians "could scarcely go along with the more passionate welfare-haters' complaints that the recipients of the state's dole were 'bums'" because "the language was awkward."[46] The solution was to concentrate on the threat of welfare to "the work ethic."

But notice what happens when, in order to avoid negatively labeling those on welfare as "shiftless bums" or "lazy good-for-nothings," we redefine the problem in terms of an abstract principle called "the work ethic." First, the new language implies that anybody who is not working at a paying job is somehow a threat to society, including not only those on welfare but housewives (who work, but not for pay), retirees, and the disabled. If hard work has an *ethical* value above and beyond the utilitarian function, then those who do not work *for whatever reason* are unethical. Second, and more important, the concern for the poor, the downtrodden, the person who cannot find a job, and for the children of such individuals, gets replaced, by definition, with concern for an abstract principle—the work ethic.

And many *human* concerns, says J. Cogley of the Center for the Study of Democratic Institutions, are so converted—sometimes intentionally, sometimes innocently—by the simple expedient of defining issues abstractly rather than in terms of the humans involved. "With abstractions the favored language, the victims of poverty and racism can be transformed. The family struggling for existence . . . can be turned into something called the Welfare Problem."[47] The "rural problem," "inflation," "juvenile delinquency," "crime in the streets," and "the drug problem" are other examples of abstractly defined problems that omit any concern for the victims and thus overlook any appeal to our consciences to which such victims might otherwise be entitled.

## CONCLUSION

▶ The power of definition is the power to create—or to destroy. Definitions determine issues . . . and personalities. They help us to personalize issues—"The Truman Doctrine," "Nixon's War," "Reaganomics," "Clinton's health care plan"—or to depersonalize humans—"wops," "niggers," "kikes," "chicks." Through them, we inject people into issues in order to confuse the issues. Or we subtract people from issues, so our bloodthirsty acts can seem bloodless.

▶ In short, the language of politics is simply language. It can be used to tell a truth or a lie. The only inherent difference between the language of politics and ordinary language is that the government holds the central position in the process of solving public problems, and thus is able to determine the issues to be debated and the terms with which the debate proceeds. By controlling our language the government controls the people, and thus does not need to rely on physical force except at those times when the dialogue has escaped its control and the people have accepted a different set of definitions. In fact, the best way to predict revolutions is to compare the language of the government with the language of the people. If their definitions are too disparate the situation is desperate—one is holding the bull by the tail and the other is looking him straight in the eye.

## FOR FURTHER CONSIDERATION

**1.** One phrase that is often used in contemporary political argumentation, but that was not examined in this chapter, is "family" (as in "family values"). Trace the history of the "family" to see whether contemporary usage corresponds to the historic meanings of the word. Have families always been connected emotionally, or have there been times when practical considerations were more important? Has "family" always meant father, mother and children, or were other configurations more common in other eras? When a politician today says we should return to "family values," is the call for a return to the values of 1750, 1850, or 1950?

**2.** It is common these days for critics of contemporary political campaigns to decry the shrinkage of the "sound bite" (the length of time a candidate is seen on the airwaves speaking in his or her own voice). Yet it is possible that something about the phrase "sound bite" gives such a negative connotation that the critics are misled. For instance, are the direct quotations of the candidates in print media any longer than in the electronic media? If not, why are they not decried and called "ink bites?" Is there something about the nature of the computerized world that leads us to apply the word "bite" (or "byte") only to electronic media and not to the print media? Is this a case where the language chosen provides a negative evaluation to which another piece of language would not lead us?

## NOTES

1. J. Lipman-Blumen, "The Existential Bases of Power Relationships: The Gender Role Case," in *Power/Gender: Social Relations in Theory and Practice,* eds. H. L. Radtke and H. J. Stam (Thousand Oaks, CA: Sage, 1994), 127.

2. K. Burke, "What Are the Signs of What? A Theory of 'Entitlement,'" in *Language as Symbolic Action: Essays on Life, Literature, and Method* (Berkeley: University of California Press, 1966), 362.

3. *Ibid.*, 361.

4. *Ibid.*, 375.

5. H. Koning, "The Semantics of War," *New York Times,* 26 February 1972, p. 29.

6. M. Edelman, "Myths, Metaphors and Political Conformity," *Psychiatry* (August 1967): 218.

7. "Terminology in Air War," *New York Times,* 16 June 1972, p. 3.

8. F. Heer, "Man's Three Languages," *Center Magazine* 4 (November/December 1971): 69.

9. R. Baker, "Once More, With Numbness," *New York Times,* 17 December 1972, p. 11E.

10. P. Dickson, "Demeaning of Meaning," *New York Times,* 15 April 1972, p. 31.

11. N. Rosten, "Playing Games with Words," *New York Times,* 29 March 1971, p. 33.

12. G. Cheney, "'Talking War': Symbols, Strategies, and Images," *Studies on the Left* 14 (1990–91): 14.

13. W. Lutz, "Doublespeak Here and There," *Quarterly Review of Doublespeak* 15 (January 1989): 9.

14. R. Marcus, "A War Without a Mandate?" *Boca Raton* (FL) *News,* 14 September 1994, p. 2A.

15. *Ibid.*, 2A.

16. *Ibid.*, 2A.

17. *Ibid.*, 2A.

18. Koning, *op. cit.*, 29.

19. M. Black, *The Labyrinth of Language* (New York: Frederick A. Praeger, 1968), 104.

20. B. Evans, "Words: Our Most Important Tools," in *Language Awareness,* eds. P. A. Eschholz, A. F. Rosa, and V. P. Clark (New York: St. Martin's Press, 1974), 5.

21. M. Edelman, "On Policies that Fail," *Progressive,* May 1975, 23.

22. J. Corry, "The Politics of Style," *Harper's,* November 1970, 62.

23. David E. Rosenbaum, "Carter's Positions on Issues Designed for Wide Appeal," *New York Times,* 11 June 1976, A16.

24. C. Chandler, "And While We're on the Subject . . . ," *Washington Post National Weekly Edition,* 26 December 1994–1 January 1995, 14.

25. H. Hawkins, "Greens and the Election," *Z Magazine,* February 1995, 16.

26. Chandler, *op. cit.*, 14.

27. *Ibid.*, 14.

28. M. Levinson, "Hey, You're Doing Great," *Newsweek,* 30 January 1995, 42.

29. *Ibid.*, 42B.

30. J. Solomon, "Are You Anxious? You're Not Alone," *Newsweek,* 30 January 1995, 42B.

31. Chandler, *op. cit.*, 14.

32. Levinson, *op. cit.*, 42.

33. Hawkins, *op. cit.*, 16.

34. Levinson, *op. cit.*, 42–42B.

35. R. J. Samuelson, "The Nadir of His Presidency," *Washington Post National Weekly Edition,* 26 December 1994–1 January 1995, 29.

36. *Ibid.*, 29.

37. Levinson, *op. cit.*, 42.

38. M. S. Alexander, "Defining the Abortion Debate," *ETC., A Review of General Semantics* 50 (Fall 1993): 272.

39. *Ibid.*, 273.

40. *Ibid.*, 273.

41. *Ibid.*, 273.

42. *Ibid.*, 274.

43. T. S. Szasz, "Language and Humanism," *Humanist,* January/February 1974, 28.

44. Corry, *op. cit.*, 60.

45. Edelman, "Myths," *op. cit,* 222.

46. R. Baker, "Work Ethic or Idleness Envy?" *New York Times,* 8 February 1973, p. 43.

47. J. Cogley, "Person, Place, Thing—or Abstraction," *Center Magazine,* March/April 1973, 3.

# The Power of Form

*. . . the necessary symbolism of politics should not be allowed to govern the perception of political realities.*

— P. STARR[1]

People who have never studied art often say, "I may not know very much about art, but I know what I like." The art of rhetoric is, in a sense, similar to other arts in that the average person may say, "I don't know why I like that speech, but I do."

Faced with a painting, some people will like the subject—the flowers, the landscape, or the people. Others will be attracted by the craftsmanship—the brushstrokes, the texture, the colors. Likewise with rhetoric. Some will be attracted to what is said, to the position taken by the rhetor. Others will be impressed by the rhetor's crafting of the speech—the organization, the word choice, or how the language is combined.

Language, like paints, can be combined in many different ways. Just as there are many forms in which the sentiment "I love you" can be conveyed, there are multiple means of saying "I'm the best person for the office." These "means" include, but are not limited to, the elements of rhetorical form to be considered here.

The elements of what I've been labeling "craftsmanship" make up "form." Form concerns how the elements of the art are combined, the way they are put together, the pattern, the style of presentation. The rhetor's words are analogous to the painter's colors; how those words are combined corresponds to how the painter mixes the paint on the palette; how the speaker delivers the speech can be likened to the artist's brushstrokes. The totality of these elements makes up the form.

Just as most of us may not know much about what artists are trying to accomplish with their color combinations and brushstrokes, we also know little about what rhetorical forms communicate, that is, how they work upon auditors or how they provide insight into speakers. Nor is our lack of knowledge surprising. Except for art critics, viewers do not focus on artistic form; except for rhetorical critics, auditors do not concentrate on rhetorical form. Auditors

An earlier version of this chapter was originally published as "Persuasive Form in Presidential Rhetoric," in PRESIDENTIAL COMMUNICATION, Robert E. Denton, Jr., and Dan F. Hahn. Copyright © 1986 by Praeger Publishers. Reproduced with permission of GREENWOOD PUBLISHING GROUP, INC., Westport, CT.

listen for content, to see whether they agree with the speaker. How the speaker couches the points to be made, how the language is structured to win the audience's assent, is not a part of the audience's awareness any more than the mechanics of brushstrokes attract the attention of the nonartist art-museum patron. Yet, as students of political language we must attempt to understand how discourses work, how rhetors attempt to persuade us.

It is not enough to be "up" on all the current political issues so that we will know whether the speaker is depicting reality accurately. Politics, by its very nature, seldom deals in certainties; rather, it deals with actions today that will produce reactions tomorrow. It deals with hypotheses, speculations, and arguments about which actions among those possible for today will produce which reactions, desirable and undesirable, that are possible for tomorrow. Thus politics, inherently, is involved with rhetoric about the unknowable. How, then, do people come to believe so fervently that they do know? How do they become so positive that the newest influx of illegal immigrants will hurt the economy or that failure to build a certain weapon system will doom us to another war? And how do they go about convincing us to agree with them?

Obviously, decision-making and persuasion depend on many elements. One such element that is often overlooked is rhetorical form. As rhetorical critic C. L. Johnstone has commented, political discourse "seeks from its auditors commitments that are implicit in its formal characteristics; in the way it argues, in addition to the substance of its argument; in the ways of coming to judgment that it implicitly recommends, in addition to the judgment that it actually advocates; in the way it uses language, in addition to the proposition expressed by that language. The form of the discourse— . . . the way it uses evidence, the forms of reasoning it employs—solicits from the auditor commitments to certain ways of thinking, of viewing the world, of making decisions, that are not necessarily implied in the substance of the discourse."[2]

When the Far Right, in the 1964 campaign, said of Barry Goldwater, "In your heart you know he's right" and the Far Left countered with, "In your guts you know he's nuts," both were doing more than stating positions. At the content level, each side was giving an assessment of Barry Goldwater. Had the form been "He's right" and "He's nuts," no more than the evaluation would have been involved, but the way in which the assessments were stated connected the evaluations to intuitive processes for evaluating. That is, each side was recommending an intuitive path to knowledge: you know with your heart; you know with your gut. These forms of knowing were being recommended; by implication, then, knowing with your brain was being denigrated.

We understand, somewhat implicitly, that form accomplishes these things. We do not know how or why it does so. My purpose here, then, is to engage in some speculation about the hows and whys of form.

## ▶ Perspective and Form

In the same commonsense mode in which most of us think people's clothing tells us something about them, it is reasonable to assume their language "gives something away." But, given the imponderables in the relation between people's language and their way of knowing, what is it that is being "given away" and how do or should we react to those language clues? Rhetorical theorist Richard Weaver contended that a sure "index" to a person's political position could be found in the speaker's "characteristic way of thinking, inevitably expressed in the type of argument" presented.[3]

While Weaver the political conservative probably would have applauded former President Reagan's conservatism, I think it is possible that Weaver the rhetorical theorist would have abhorred Reagan's "characteristic way of thinking," for Reagan's thinking did not rely on logic, according to political critic J. Beatty. Rather, Beatty said, Reagan's thinking "work[ed] in an essentially imagistic way. Its most characteristic device [was] the figure of speech known as synecdoche: the use of a part to stand for a whole."[4] The function of President Reagan's anecdotes—the narratives about particular instances—was to "stand for" whole classes of people in similar circumstances.

One problem with such thinking is that a single example proves nothing, but in Reagan's case there was an additional problem: very often his example or narrative anecdote was a fictional story, not a true example. To the degree we believed and acted on the basis of such examples, we had been misled; to the degree Reagan himself believed and acted on his own false anecdotes, he had misled himself. While it is not important for us to determine whether Richard Weaver would have applauded or abhorred Reagan's rhetorical form, we should at least realize that his evaluation would have been determined by the perspective (political conservative or rhetorical critic) from which he made the evaluation.

The question of perspective, in turn, can be controlled somewhat by the form into which the rhetor casts the remarks. Ronald Carpenter, for instance, has noted that presidential discourse often is designed more to reflect citizen attitudes than to change them: "The audience renders a decision for the present, and the focus of approval or disapproval is how well the President articulates values with which listeners *already* agree."[5]

Even when a president does seem to be talking about policy-making, presenting information for the consideration of the citizenry—for example, in a crisis—the form of the address need not be perceived as an example of deliberative oratory in the Aristotelian sense, i.e., of a rhetor laying out the arguments of a position in an attempt to win the agreement of the audience. It may be that the president just needed a pretext to appear "presidential." Political rhetoric scholar Gary Woodward contends that "crisis is sometimes most profitably studied as an act of presidential *labeling*."[6]

Chapter 4 discusses "naming" (or labeling) as a subset of "definition." It is no contradiction now to discuss naming and labeling under the category of "form." Just because a painter *defines*, with several brushstrokes, where a hand ends and the flowers in the hand begin does not mean that how those brushstrokes are made cannot productively be considered as part of the painter's *form*.

Consider, for instance, how a good deal of controversy swirled around President Clinton's 1994 "invasion" of Haiti precisely because of this labeling/naming issue. One major argument Clinton set forth was that to allow the Haitian dictatorship to remain "would be to acquiesce in brutal violations of human rights, to endanger fragile democracies elsewhere in the hemisphere . . . "[7] Opponents of the invasion doubted Clinton's labeling and asked, "Why invade Haiti in an effort to implant democracy in soil where it has never flourished, any more than invade Cuba in an attempt to cultivate democracy there?"[8] That is, if an undemocratic government in Haiti is labeled a threat, why isn't the undemocratic government in Cuba tarred with the same brush? In short, the opponent tried to ignore the artistry with which Clinton juxtaposed "brutal violations" against "fragile democracies," and merely presented an opposing argument.

But President Clinton was able to "carry the day" on this labeling controversy, perhaps in part because of the artistic way he couched his argument. Thus, the ability to define the issues, not just by naming but also by artistic characterization, should be considered one of the foremost powers of rhetorical form. Yet it is also one of the simplest, for much of the power derives merely from the nouns employed, although the artistry also requires carefully selected adjectives. Politicians' nouns should tell you which portions of the world they find relevant. They will, in a sense, show you arenas of consciousness, and thus the arenas in which you can expect concern and activity. From 1976 to 1980 the country focused on energy because President Carter focused on it. Since 1980, the "energy crisis" has disappeared—not so much because objective conditions have changed but because "energy" has not been a field of interest to subsequent presidents.

Nouns function, then, to direct attention. And looking in one direction sometimes precludes looking in another. Thus, President Reagan's emphasis on individualism implicitly denied our relatedness, making easier his task of dismantling the welfare programs of Johnson's "Great Society." Similarly, President Clinton's concern for the unemployed, underemployed, and financially strapped lower middle class led him to focus on health care, one of the more expensive necessities of contemporary life.

As we are all aware, a major goal of all politicians is to prove they are on "our" side. My argument in this chapter is that the language forms they use help them do so. In presenting the argument I will start with the characteristics that politicians want us to attribute to them, then examine their language forms to see what contributions these forms make to politicians' attempts to persuade us to perceive them as they want to be perceived.

We've already seen that one way politicians try to get us to identify with them is by articulating values with which we agree and by "namings" that fit our perceptions, but more clearly form-related aspects of their language also contribute to their attempts to achieve that identification. We will examine those aspects first, as identification is probably the most important goal politicians seek. After that, we will investigate the contributions of form to other characteristics politicians try to persuade us to impute to them: activeness, emotional involvement, logicality and rationality, strength, honesty, grandeur, and ideological correctness. I will conclude the chapter with a short examination of the dangers that stem from using these forms.

## ▶ Identification

The concept of identification is central to political rhetoric, for an important job of leadership is to persuade the citizens that the leader identifies with their interests and thus it is in the citizens' interests to identify with the leader. When a leader says "I believe in X," all citizens who likewise believe in X have been given a reason to identify with that leader. Kenneth Burke, the rhetorical theorist who has made identification the basic thrust of his analytic framework, contends that identification concerns "one's ways of sharing vicariously in the role of leader or spokesman . . . allegiance and change of allegiance . . . one's way of seeing one's reflection in the social mirror . . . positive and negative responses to authority."[9] While the most obvious way for politicians to identify with the electorate is through agreeing with them at the content level, identification can also be accomplished through form.

To examine a politician's modes of identification through form, one can isolate words such as "and," "too," and "also." Such connectives establish relationships and tell you what the politician thinks goes with what. Critic Carol Berthold, for instance, found that in John F. Kennedy's rhetoric the words "freedom" and "peace" were usually linked.[10] In short, via the connectives Kennedy was able to identify with those citizens who thought that freedom is always threatened by war.

Pronouns also can tell us a good deal about identifications. For instance, Nixon's use of pronouns reflected his "benevolent dictator" approach. He tended to follow the pronoun "I" with action verbs, while using "we" and "us" in the receiving position. The Nixonian formula, or argumentative form, then, was "I, President Nixon, have acted . . . and we, the citizens, reap the benefits of the action." Voters who favored a president-citizen relationship in which presidential actions lead to citizen benefits were, therefore, given a reason to identify with President Nixon.

Pronoun frequency also may be perceived as revealing. Consider, for example, the implications of the fact that Nixon used the personal pronoun "I" 10 times as often in foreign policy as in domestic policy speeches, or that in the White House "Watergate" tapes he utilized "I" 16 times as often as most of us do in normal conversation.

There are numerous possible implications for each of these phenomena, and the implications people "read into" either phenomenon would have affected their identification or nonidentification with Nixon. For instance, if the implication of Nixon's high incidence of personal pronouns when discussing foreign policy was perceived to be that he saw foreign policy as more important than domestic policy, the voter who agreed with that assessment would have identified with Nixon, while the citizen who disagreed would not have identified positively with him. If you perceived the even higher incidence of Nixon's use of "I" in the tapes as nothing more than an indication of the centrality of the president in the governmental structure, it might have encouraged you to identify with Nixon, but if you saw it as indicative of some kind of egomania it undoubtedly would have discouraged identification.

Jimmy Carter's references to the populace also are instructive. He ran for the presidency as a repository of *our* goodness. In line with this theme, in his inaugural address he used "we" 43 times and "our" 36 times, while employing the personal pronoun "I" only 6 times. Of the 35 paragraphs of the speech, 25 began with "we," "our," or "let us." Yet by the 1980 reelection campaign, President Carter had taken a new orientation. The change was from Carter the commoner, the man of the people, who by relying on us would accomplish things *with* us, to Carter the president, who was above us, who relied on himself and his appointees and who did things *for* us.

Carter was unable to shake off his new orientation and return to his 1976 emphasis. For instance, rhetorical critic S. R. Brydon found that in the three 1976 debates with Ford, Carter had employed the phrase "the people" over 70 times,[11] on the average of 23 times per debate. In the 1980 debate with Reagan, however, he "referred to 'the people' only 9 times . . . while invoking references to the presidency 27 times."[12] Furthermore, when he did mention "the people" in 1980, it was clear that his perception of their role had changed: "Rather than providing the source of wisdom and knowledge for his presidency, the people had become subjects, to be commanded by the president. For example, in discussing energy, Carter said, 'We have demanded that the American people sacrifice and they've done very well.'"[13]

In short, Carter still was concerned with identification but the *form* had changed. In 1976 he clearly was saying that he identified with the people (who could passively agree or disagree); in 1980 he was asking the people to identify with him (which required much more active involvement on the part of the voters). Put that way, it does not sound like much of a change, but it is; when somebody extends his/her hand to you, it makes a big difference whether (s)he is offering to shake your hand (requiring little of you) or begging for a hand-out (which asks much more).

Most contemporary presidents have experienced identification problems. George Bush, partially because of his continued insistence on reducing the capital-gains tax (most middle-class citizens do not pay this tax, thus would not benefit if it were reduced), came to be perceived as identifying with the wealthy, as "out of touch" with the ordinary voter. Clinton's identification problems came from the other direction. Although he tried to sell his health-care proposals as necessary for the middle class, it was obvious that, to whatever degree those proposals might benefit that class, the people whose lot would be improved most were the lower classes. Thus he was perceived as wanting to "milk" the middle class to provide for those less fortunate. And the label "less fortunate" was particularly galling to the middle class, for they did not feel "fortunate"; they felt they were just barely scraping by; further, they felt that whatever advantages they might have over those lower on the economic totem pole were the result of hard work, not "fortunateness." And they resented the "unfortunate" below them because they perceived they were poor because they were unwilling to work, not because they were victims of the economic system. Ultimately, then, the linkage middle-class people made between their resentment of the lower classes and Clinton's attempt to improve the lives of lower-class people led them to perceive Clinton as identifying with these "others" rather than with them.

## ▶ Action

It is axiomatic that we elect politicians to act for us. Obviously, then, a central component in the rhetoric of officeholders is to demonstrate that they have been taking the right actions. As Gary Woodward has commented, presidents "use the imagery of movement . . . to transpose calculated *in*action [into] significant *action*."[14]

President Reagan's favorite metaphor, for instance, was a metaphor that implied action—the path metaphor. It is difficult to locate a Reagan speech that did not refer to "choosing the right road," taking the "first step," or "staying the course." And when the Democrats won back the White House in 1992 after twelve years of Republican rule, they did so not just with metaphors of motion, but with the path metaphor. Bill Clinton, in his standard stump speech in that campaign, said, "we're *going downhill* as a nation. The middle class is collapsing. Poverty is exploding. Even the wealthiest people know that we're *on the wrong track*."[15] (emphases added)

While metaphors imply action, politicians' verbs and adverbs also contain action messages. The verbs and adverbs employed explain politicians' behavior patterns and give insight into their attitudes toward leadership. Active politicians use active verbs and adverbs; passive ones employ more passivity. Let's examine, again, the "active" approach that allowed Clinton to win in 1992. Looking at just a few paragraphs of his standard speech, we find this sequence of action verbs and adverbs: "work," "create," "beating," "work," "beat," "start," "start," "start," "invest," "invest," "work," "retraining," "manufacturing," "vote," "invest."[16]

The politician who perceives life as controllable will be more likely to use strong verbs. The weak, passive verbs Jimmy Carter employed in his inaugural, "to help shape" and "a step forward," should have forewarned us of his approach to the presidency. Meanwhile, it should be noted that when a politician calls an invasion an "incursion," as Nixon did when he invaded Cambodia, the fact that there is no verb form for "incursion" (one would not say "to incurse") means no one is responsible for the action. An "incursion" apparently just happens.

It also should be noted that some judgments of political importance are built into our language. For instance, action normally is assumed to be good. Thus, locutions such as "stern action," "resolute action," or "immediate action" are presumed to be positive. Inaction is assumed to be bad. One wonders, therefore, if our language doesn't push us toward action for action's sake. I find it suggestive that in earlier ages, when the mind was more highly valued, people wrote "confessions," whereas in our time, when actions are more highly valued, we write "autobiographies."

Politicians' adverbs suggest salience and intensity, and will tend to show you not only what they plan to do, but how they plan to do it. Thus, those who expected Jimmy Carter to be an active president in the F.D.R. mold obviously overlooked his heavy campaign reliance on adverbs such as "gradually," "modestly," "accurately," and "slowly." Compare Carter's tentative language with Clinton's more assured language: "If you vote for me, I'll," "The answer is," "Here's what I think ought to be done," "We ought to," "We can," "And I'm telling you," "I hate it."[17]

## ▶ Emotional Involvement

Not only do politicians want to indicate what actions they favor, they also want to communicate how deeply they are committed to their actions. One way they do so is through the adjectives they choose. In the adjectives are lodged opinions about the world and judgments about what is worth saving or developing. And if you examine the adjective clusters you should be able to discover the criteria used to make judgments—moral, practical, or aesthetic. Military attitudes toward death, for instance, are evident in the fact that in the military language of war there are only two kinds of death—"prompt" death and "dilatory" death. Compare the attitudes expressed toward life in those adjective choices of the military with George McGovern's 1972 tendency toward an excessive use of modifiers. He would not say "American blood," nor "young American blood," but "precious young American blood."

Or consider the judgmental categories in the adjectives Bill Clinton used as he accepted the Democratic Party presidential nomination in July 1992. Notice how he did not address "the Americans who make up our middle class"; rather, he spoke to "the *hard-working* Americans who make up our *forgotten* middle class"[18] (emphases added). Likewise, he did not just talk of "the battles for opportunity and justice," but of "the battles for *economic* opportunity and *social* justice"[19] (emphases added). Think, for instance, of the differences if the emphases had been reversed, if he had talked of *forgotten Americans* of the *hard-working middle class*, or about *social opportunity* and *economic justice!* Changing the first set probably would have made little difference, but switching the second set would have signaled a completely different ideology, one more compatible with the Republican than the Democratic Party.

However, because citizens are not unified in their commitments, politicians sometimes want to speak in such a way that those who favor an action will perceive them as being supportive, while those opposed to the action can hope that action will not necessarily follow the words. A common method of accomplishing this purpose is to speak on one side of an issue but to act on the other, thus giving the rhetoric to one group and the policy to the other. President Reagan was a master of this ploy. In 1980, 1982, 1984, and 1986 (election years), he talked about the need to outlaw abortion and institute prayer in schools (the so-called social issues) in order to activate the votes of the Far Right, yet as president he never pushed these issues very much. In short, he gave the rhetoric to the Right, but the policy to the moderates. And the method was nearly foolproof (i.e., did not cost him votes) because people in each group could focus on the portion of the formula that pleased them and ignore everything else.

Closely related is politicians' penchant for protecting themselves by couching their promises in the subjunctive mood. For example, the *New York Times* attacked President Carter for hedging when he promised, "I would never give up full control of the Panama Canal as long as it had any contribution to make to our national security." The *Times* complained that the "conditional note . . . opens a wide realm of judgmental freedom."[20]

We will never know, of course, whether Carter really was hedging on the Panama Canal, saying what his audience wanted to hear, or whether his "conditional note" was the careful language of a realistic politician who understood that the political world is a probabilistic world, best dealt with through hypotheses, contingencies, and possibilities—that is, with the subjunctive. As George Will has noted, a president tends to talk in the subjunctive mood because "he can do little alone. A President's principal power is the highly contingent power to persuade Congress. And Congress hears a discordant clamor of other voices."[21] From this perspective, the subjunctive brings the rhetoric into realistic alignment with the political world.

Another form useful in avoiding overcommitment, employed in politics as well as in the rest of life, is what I call *affirmation by denial*. It is the same form Ralph Waldo Emerson had in mind when he said, "The louder he talked of his honor, the faster we counted our spoons." As literary theorist J. Hillis Miller points out, if a person says "I shall not compare thee to a summer's day, a rose, a running brook,'" the person has made the comparison even while denying the intent to do so.[22] When politicians say, "I wouldn't think of doing . . . X," we know only one thing for sure—that they did think of doing it; that is, it did cross their minds. When Henry Kissinger, after the *Mayaguez* affair, said, "We are not going around looking for opportunities to prove our manhood," one critic responded that the "curious comment . . . made it clear that at a level very close to his consciousness, Secretary Kissinger knew that this was precisely what America's reaction had been all about."[23] Of course, you understand, I wouldn't think of saying that the good secretary lied.

A favorite Nixonian variant of "affirmation by denial" was the "I would never have said that myself" form, in which Nixon reported the attacks the Silent Majority had made against his critics: "When I say I inherited this war, I want to point out that I am actually quoting what others say. I'm not going to cast blame for the war in Vietnam on either of my predecessors." Nixon disassociated himself from the statement by indicating that he did not personally hold with this view, but the jury was not instructed to disregard the testimony. The variant allowed Nixon to vindicate his action without having to specify blame. We just knew that the blame lay elsewhere.

An interesting attack mode used to suggest the opposition is insufficiently involved emotionally might be named after an old action injunction: "push, pull, or get out of the way." Here is how Bill Clinton, leaning heavily on the example of the revered Abraham Lincoln, phrased this attack during the 1992 presidential campaign: "right now I know how President Lincoln felt when General McClellan wouldn't attack in the Civil War. He asked him, 'If you're not going to use your army, may I borrow it?' George Bush, if you won't use your power to help people, step aside. I will."[24]

## ▶ Logical/Rational

We expect our politicians to be logical and rational (as we understand logicality and rationality). And the audience's expectations are a part of the milieu in which form operates. Consider, for example, foreign policies. Do we want our presidents to be logical and rational, or childish and emotional? Assuming we agree on the audience preference, does it give us any insight into the popularity of Lyndon Johnson and Richard Nixon versus that of the anti-war protesters in the late 1960s and early 1970s?

Consider, for a moment, Nixon's second inaugural in 1973. He demonstrated his own "logical" approach through what I call the *law of semantic equality*. That is, in presenting two dissimilar things as being equal, his grammatical structure and word choices seemed to say, "look how calm and logical I am being." For instance (and this is just one of many possible examples from that speech), Nixon said, "Just as America's role is indispensable in preserving the world's peace, so is each nation's role indispensable in preserving its own peace."[25] The parallel structure of the sentence argued rationality. The parallel word choices argued rationality.

But the argument was highly irrational. The given, the indispensability of America in preserving peace, was based on the "fact" that other nations were too weak to preserve peace. Therefore, the conclusion that other nations must preserve their own peace flew in the face of the weakness posited about them in the premise. Or, stated the other way, if the other nations had been capable of preserving their own peace, America would not have had an "indispensable" role in preserving peace. Regardless, the point remains that Nixon's structure and word choices suggested a rationality that his content belied. The form (or structure) was persuasive in much the same way that many men find 36-24-36 persuasive, that is, regardless of the unrevealed and unexamined content. Richard Nixon, through the form of the discourse, demonstrated his rationality, even though the content was irrational, even nonsensical.

Compare, now, one of the major rhetorical forms employed by the protesters, the slogans of demonstrators: "Hey, hey, L.B.J./ How many kids did you kill today?" or "One, two, three, four/ We don't want your fucking war." The form of the slogans suggested childishness: the simple rhymes of nurseryland, the cadences of high school cheerleaders, the directness of the naive child. Although the protesters undoubtedly selected the slogan form primarily because massed demonstrators could shout them, the form was childish. According to political scientist F. D. McConnell, though, this form was "misleadingly childish,"[26] for there is nothing less childish, more the province of grown-ups, than killing and war. But more, "Hey, hey, L.B.J./How many kids did you kill today?" asserted something serious about who should be blamed for the war and who was taking the brunt of it. (The assertions of responsibility and victimization may have been right or wrong; regardless, they were serious assertions.) Likewise, the phrase "fucking war" was a serious phrase. It was not merely an obscenity designed to shock; more important, it implicitly argued that war is obscene—a serious argument.

No matter. The political opponents' forms carried the day. President Nixon's form was rational, misleadingly so. The protesters' form was irrational, misleadingly so. And the American people chose the form their expectations led them to prefer, despite the fact that public opinion polls suggested that more people favored the anti-war content of the protesters than favored Nixon's pro-war arguments.

Rationality, of course, concerns the "real world," not the illusory world of fiction. This difference was used fairly often to attack Ronald Reagan, who came to politics after a lifetime spent in the world of Hollywood, a tinsel-town that thrives on illusion. Because of his long apprenticeship in the movies, he was attacked as living in a "fantasy world." For example, Jimmy Carter sneered, "It is a make-believe world of good guys and bad guys, where some politicians shoot first and ask questions later."[27]

## ▶ Strength

Ronald Reagan became president, at least in part, because people perceived him as having a toughness that they perceived President Carter lacked. Yet that perception of toughness arose almost exclusively from the content of Reagan's rhetoric rather than from the form. Indeed, I would argue that an examination of rhetorical form would yield the conclusion that President Reagan was not a particularly tough president. For instance, he often used phrases such as "let me say" and "let me repeat," which politely ask for permission to speak, instead of the more aggressive "I say" and "I repeat." If these were the only facets of Reagan's form to which we could point, it might be argued that he was just being polite, which can be indicative of power. However, additional characteristics of his form further the analytic point. For instance, his vocabulary was not as vivid or exciting as one might expect from an aggressive person. Instead, he used words like "well" and "now" and "I might add," creating a sort of archetypically Californian laid-back, almost sedated, language. Even in describing events that are in no way colorless, such as nuclear war, Reagan employed colorless words. In fact, his lexicon was never so bland and dull as when depicting the weapons of nuclear war.

Which was the real Ronald Reagan, the president with the "strong" policies or the one with the "weak" rhetorical form? We do not know for sure, but the relative softness of his actions against the Soviet Union following the "massacre" of the Korean airliner, the withdrawal of the Marines from Beirut, and his uninvolved leadership style suggest the rhetorical form may have provided the more accurate gauge of the man.

During the 1988 presidential campaign, George Bush had to go to unusual lengths to respond to the image that he was a "wimp." The Bush campaign even went so far as to divulge some information that, were it not designed to counter the question of "wimpiness," would have been considered too negative to release—such as the information that Bush "eats pork rinds and listens to country music,"[28] or that, in private, he likes "to throw around smutty language and locker-room jokes,"[29] that he is a "total C.E.O., cold, calculating, steel-jawed,"[30] or that he is a boss who is "perfectly capable of . . . saying, 'That's it for you. Boom. You're gone. History.'"[31] The message in all these snippets of information is the same: don't be misled by his soft wimplike public persona; in private he's one tough son of a bitch.

## ▶ Honesty

At least since Watergate, it has become mandatory for politicians to demonstrate their honesty. Fortunately for them, there are rhetorical forms available for that purpose. But unfortunately for them, overuse of the major form has undermined its power.

In our capitalistic society we all are familiar with the Latin phrase *caveat emptor*, the notion that the buyer should beware. Yet, we have all had the experience of having a salesperson tell us, almost conspiratorially, that it is a good thing we came in today because tomorrow the item we are interested in will be $10 more. The form of the dialogue says, "I'm on your side. I'll level with you and sell it to you today, even though my commission would be better if you delayed your purchase twenty-four hours." Maybe we believe him. Maybe we buy the item. And just maybe . . . we end up in the same store the next day shopping for another item. How do we now act toward our salesperson? Yesterday, his form told us, "Today I'm looking out for you; tomorrow I'll be lining my own pocket." If we are smart, we will take him at his word. (Of course, if we were *that* smart we probably would not have believed him yesterday, but that's another story.) The present point is that his *manner* of telling us of his trustworthiness yesterday makes him suspect today.

Politics has its own version of the personal *caveat emptor*. It is the senator asking, "Can I speak frankly?" or the president averring, "I'll be honest with you." This form may enjoy temporary success, but implicitly it conveys to us that these moments are exceptions to the nonfrank, dishonest norm. And, misused often enough, they can turn into liabilities, just as Nixon's phrase, "Let me make one thing perfectly clear," came to signal us to watch for the obfuscation, the muddying phrase, the escape clause in what he was about to say.

And practically any piece of metacommunication (that is, communication about the communication) underlines in about the same way. When a professor says, "Listen carefully, this point is important," (s)he underlines that point, but also, implicitly, says, "the rest of my presentation is not important, you do not need to listen to it."

## ▶ Grandeur

One goal of all politicians is to depict themselves as wonderful, perhaps grander than they are. Their language helps them do so. Take, for instance, the line from John Kennedy's inaugural that so caught the imagination of America, "Ask not what your country can do for you, but what you can do for your country." Think about the meaning here. What *can* most of us do for our country? Pay taxes. Die in a war. Work, thereby avoid welfare. Be law-abiding. Pretty grue-some or pedestrian behaviors he asked of us. So why the positive response? One part of the answer, suggests political scientist Murray Edelman, relates to the form. Kennedy's "Ask not what" formulation is unusual. The hearer associates "the unusual deployment of verb, adverb, and accusative pronoun with biblical language and with eloquent oratory of the past," responding "to the poetry of those associations."[32] That is, the form recalls other deployments of the same form and we react to the speaker as though (s)he were of the other genre—a poet, or maybe a minor prophet—rather than a politician. The form deflects our thought from the content of the line to the image of the speaker, simultaneously transforming the speaker from a grubby politician to a poet or prophet.

Another president, Jimmy Carter, was more obvious in deflecting our eval-uation of him from the political arena to the religious sphere. James Reston referred to Carter's inaugural as a "revival meeting,"[33] Frederick Smith said it was "less rallying cry than sermon,"[34] and Anthony Hillbruner entitled his analysis of it, "Born Again: Carter's Inaugural Sermon."[35] Certainly these commentators noted the most obvious subject in the speech.

In defining the world as two distinct parts, physical and spiritual, and then emphasizing the latter, President Carter set a religious mood in his inaugural address. In the very first sentence, when Carter thanked President Ford for "all he has done to heal our land," he implied that one of the presidential responsi-bilities is that of "healing," a job that can be seen either as medical or, metaphorically, as a divine responsibility.

Carter specifically referred to his faith by talking of the two Bibles before him and by quoting the prophet Micah. And, throughout, the speech was sprin-kled with religious language. He declared that the inauguration attested to the "spiritual" strength of the nation, that there was "a new spirit among us all," that "ours was the first society openly to define itself in terms of . . . spiritu-ality," and so forth. He used the word "spirit" seven times and other clearly religious words—such as "pray," "moral," and "religious"—an additional twenty-seven times.

In addition, Carter asserted his faith in the nation and in the American people. He seemed to ask the citizens to have that same faith in him. In this manner he became a missionary with his own church of political believers. He had made a commitment to America; in return, he sought a commitment from the people. Again, the religious overtones drowned out the political ones.

Clearly, Carter was deflecting our attention from the political to the reli-gious world, identifying himself with the religious, borrowing some of the grandeur of that world. Yet he may have overdone it. We Americans do not like to be sermonized; the descriptive phrase for somebody who does so is the negatively toned "preachy." While we expect a little religion to be interspersed in our political addresses, when the religious references become overbearing we get nervous about unbending fanaticism.

It should be noted, of course, that it is perfectly normal for speakers to weave their own experiences into their rhetoric. We all do it. But it is also true that *which* experiences we choose to use have enormous consequences to and repercussions on audiences and how they evaluate us. Indeed, we choose carefully which experiences to relate on an implicit understanding that audience evaluations will be determined, in part, by those choices. It is no stretch of the imagination, then, to suppose that politicians are saying something about how they perceive us and how they want us to perceive them in their selections, especially if we assume that they want to be perceived as possessing grandeur.

Thus, while Carter made his "bid" for grandeur by talking about religion and in religious language, Ronald Reagan's "bid" was grounded in the secular world and accomplished through a two-step process. Step one was to identify his audience as possessing grandeur by calling them heroes: "Those who say that we're in a time when there are no heroes—they just don't know where to look. You can see heroes every day going in and out of factory gates. Others, a handful in number, produce enough food to feed all of us and then the world beyond. You meet heroes across a counter—and they're on both sides of that counter. There are entrepreneurs with faith in themselves and faith in an idea who create new jobs, new wealth and opportunity. There are individuals and families whose taxes support the Government and whose voluntary gifts support church, charity, culture, art and education. Their patriotism is quiet but deep. Their values sustain our national life. Now, I have used the words "they" and "their" in speaking of these heroes. I could say 'you' and 'your' because I'm addressing the heroes of whom I speak—you, the citizens of this blessed land."[36] Step two was by implication: if you are all heroes and I am your leader, I must be some kind of superhero. What could be grander?

Bill Clinton and his wife, on the other hand, were attacked mercilessly for lacking grandeur. His weight problems, especially obvious in his jogging outfits, made him a butt of jokes, and Hillary's "off the rack" outfits were continually ridiculed by the cognoscenti of fashion. While both Clintons were recognized to possess some intellectual grandeur, especially in comparison with Ronnie and Nancy Reagan, that is not a form of grandeur politicians seeking to impress average citizens normally demonstrate. There is too much of a tendency for any of us who feel we are being intellectually bested to conclude that the other person is not so much smart as a smart aleck. Obviously, that is not a judgment any politician would wish to evoke among the voters.

## ▶ Ideological Correctness

The forms into which politicians choose or are internally forced to place their arguments, then, obviously are important, but are they purely idiosyncratic?

That is, are the forms determined solely by reference to unknown, highly personal characteristics, or are they determined in part by political ideology? Do liberals and conservatives tend to gravitate to certain predict able forms? The evidence is not all in yet; in fact, it has hardly begun to be collected.

For instance, some of the most commonsense notions about metaphors and ideology have not even been tested yet: Do conservatives use more rural metaphors than liberals? Do conservatives use more Biblical metaphors than liberals? Since sports metaphors are basically competitive, are they more useful in supporting *laissez faire* positions than welfare state formulations? Do liberals rely on metaphors of becoming (what humans can become) while conservatives rely on metaphors of being (what humans are) or of heritage (what humans were)? Do conservatives use more familial metaphors than liberals do? Do the land and property metaphors in our national tradition predispose us to conservatism? If metaphors are grounded in culture, it seems obvious that conservatives are likely to use "older" metaphors, while liberals would opt for newly invented ones. Thus, as economic, political, and social conditions change, the metaphors of the two groups likewise would change.

While very little research along these lines has been reported, minor preliminary work on sloganeering seems to indicate political differences in rhetorical form. Compare, for instance, these four slogans of the 1960s Right, "If guns are outlawed, only outlaws will have guns," "Support your local police," "America—love it or leave it," and "Honor America," with four from the Left of the same era, "Free the Soledad Brothers," "Right on," "Up the revolution," and "Power to the people." Beyond the obvious ideological content, are there differences?

A leading political scientist, F. D. McConnell, has made the comparison. He concludes that while the liberal slogans all were incomplete sentences that were unintelligible if taken out of context, the more conservative slogans were all complete sentences. This meant, says McConnell, that the audience of the rightists felt "the force of prepared and authoritative pronouncements," while the audience of the leftists had "the impression of having entered into an ongoing and not always verbalized conversation."[37]

It will be noted that the characteristics McConnell found in the opposing slogans nicely parallel known differences between Right and Left. For instance, we know that the Right tends to be more authoritarian than the Left, thus the penchant for "authoritative pronouncements" is "of a piece" with Right philosophy. Likewise, the Left's "openness" seems perfectly mirrored by its sloganeering tendency to leave more room for involvement and interpretation.

Perhaps there are other differences; perhaps the ones identified here are superfluous and could not be duplicated with other, more randomly drawn, samples of Right and Left discourse. But the idea of such differences appears a promising avenue. If there are correlations between preferred language forms and ideological positions, and if we want to understand the language of politics, we must continue this kind of minute examination.

## CONCLUSION

▶ As I suppose is obvious from everything I've covered in this chapter, we should be careful when analyzing form, for it is not always clear what the relation between form and content is in any piece of rhetoric. Sometimes politicians get so caught up in their own form that they substitute it for content; at other times the listener can react to the form and ignore the content. We need to analyze both, observing their interaction, rather than relying on one to the exclusion of the other.

▶ We should realize that one bizarre effect of language is that speakers come to believe their own language. Undoubtedly, Ronald Reagan believed he placed a "safety net" under the poor, despite the fact that poverty increased dramatically during his eight years in the presidency; undoubtedly he believed he slammed shut the "window of vulnerability," despite the fact that the Russian lead in missiles over the U.S. increased during his two terms. In short, language that ostensibly is descriptive can shade into self-fulfilling prophecies, blinding either the speaker or the audience to reality.

▶ President Carter's use of supposedly descriptive language as self-fulfilling prophecies is a case in point, probably created by his desire for and promise of trust. In the Carter lexicon, we are what we think we are; our feelings capture reality; our programs are as we describe them. We must trust ourselves, our feelings, our solutions. Then, as we see how well everything works, we will be able to trust each other and, eventually, even trust our government. Somehow, the key to this whole political approach was revealed and reflected in his language. It was, in a sense, the politics of biofeedback wherein trust and confidence flowed from actions, but successful actions flowed from trust and confidence. So the most logical, because the easiest, point at which to begin repairing the damage to public confidence was the rhetorical point. Hence the "trust me" campaign of 1976, the symbolism of his first year, the 1978 presentation of the liberation of the Panama Canal as an act of atonement, the malaise speech of 1979, and perhaps even his overall preference for the straightforward and banal rather than the eloquent.

▶ Unfortunately for Carter, the result was merely that he was seen as lacking eloquence, and his "plain" style was heard by William Safire, the resident conservative at the *New York Times*, as one that reduced "great phrases into banalities. Lincoln's 'we must think anew and act anew. We must disenthrall ourselves' degenerated into Carter's 'we must change our attitudes as well as our policies.'"[38] So Carter was defeated in 1980 and Ronald Reagan read his overwhelming victory as a mandate for his announced programs. Yet I would argue that the Carter-Reagan-(Anderson) 1980 race was determined largely on the basis of images constructed from their differing rhetorical forms, and said very little about what kind of policies the American people preferred.

▶ Likewise, the 1992 election seemed to hinge on matters of form as much as on substance. In the presidential debates among Bush, Clinton, and Perot, form dominated. Bush seemed out of it, unresponsive, bored. (He was even caught once sneaking a peek at his watch, an action that was interpreted, perhaps unfairly, as "I'm too busy to fool with this talking-with-the-citizens nonsense.") Perot was a big hit in the first debate with his pithy one-line zingers of the other two, but his novelty wore off fairly soon as people came to think he had no substantive proposals, that his rhetorical form was all he had, that he was, in the vernacular of his home state, "all hat and no horse." Clinton, by comparison, had the right rhetorical form for the time. Unlike Perot, he was substantive; unlike Bush, he obviously relished talking with the voters. His policies might not have been any more popular, or any wiser, than those of Perot and Bush, but his "involved" form, his seeming earnestness, and his enthusiasm carried the day.

▶ While it is a banality to say that form and content are wedded, I hope I have been able to demonstrate that the old truism is not *necessarily* true. But beyond the question of the truth of the form=content equation, a greater problem is that rhetorical critics have tended to mouth the truism—then go on to examine the content without considering the form.

▶ It should be obvious by now that much more research must be conducted before we can know for sure what forms communicate and how to avoid the dangers. We know little of the hows and whys of form, which is free to work its magic unbeknownst to us. Like the citizen standing in front of the painting in the museum, we may know what we like without knowing what the artist did that captured our positive assessment.

## FOR FURTHER CONSIDERATION

1. In the 1996 presidential election, the metaphor of the "bridge" was used for identification purposes. Clinton talked of a bridge to the future, trying to identify with those who are future-oriented. Dole talked of himself as a bridge to the past, trying to identify with those who yearned for the "good old days." As you examine the 1996 campaign, can you find other realms in which the rhetoric of the two candidates was designed to "reflect in the social mirror" other attributes of the voting public?

2. In this chapter I argued that Ronald Reagan, while generally perceived as a tough president, nonetheless had a relatively weak rhetorical form. Perhaps that was nothing more than the typical political "ploy" of "playing both sides." As a check on this possibility, examine the rhetoric of Bill Clinton, who was often perceived as somewhat "soft" in foreign policy, to see whether that softness was offset by a toughness in his rhetorical form.

## NOTES

1. P. Starr, "The Subversion of Hope," *Intellectual Digest,* June 1974, 40.

2. C. L. Johnstone, "Thoreau and Civil Disobedience: A Rhetorical Paradox," *Quarterly Journal of Speech* 60 (October 1974): 313–314.

3. R. M. Weaver, *The Ethics of Rhetoric* (Chicago: Regnery 1953), 112.

4. J. Beatty, "The President's Mind," *New Republic,* 7 April 1982, 12.

5. R. H. Carpenter, "The Symbolic Substance of Style in Presidential Discourse," *Style* 16 (Winter 1982): 39.

6. G. C. Woodward, "Toward a Model of Recurring Form in Presidential Rhetoric: An Overview" (paper presented at Central States Speech Association convention, Lincoln, NE, April 1983).

7. D. Jehl, "Clinton Addresses Nation on Threat to Invade Haiti; Tells Dictators to 'Get Out,'" *New York Times,* 16 September 1994, p. A5.

8. R. W. Apple, Jr., "Preaching to Skeptics," *New York Times,* 16 September 1994, p. A1.

9. K. Burke, *The Philosophy of Literary Form: Studies in Symbolic Action,* 3rd ed. (Berkeley: University of California Press, 1973), 227.

10. C. Berthold, "Kenneth Burke's Cluster-agon Method: Its Development and Application," *Central States Speech Journal* 27 (Winter 1976): 302–309.

11. S. R. Brydon, "Outsider vs. Insider: The Two Faces of Jimmy Carter" (paper presented at Central States Speech Association convention, Chicago, February 1981), 3.

12. *Ibid.,* 8.

13. *Ibid.,* 16.

14. Woodward, *op. cit.,* 7.

15. G. Ifill, "Clinton's Standard Campaign Speech: A Call for Responsibility," *New York Times,* 26 April 1992, p. 14.

16. *Ibid.,* 14.

17. *Ibid.,* 14.

18. B. Clinton, "Text of Address by Clinton Accepting the Democratic Nomination," *New York Times,* 17 July 1992, p. A12.

19. *Ibid.,* A12.

20. "Mr. Carter's World . . . Under Scrutiny," *New York Times,* 25 June 1976, p. A26.

21. G. F. Will, "Jimmy Draws His Sword," *New York Post,* 27 April 1977, p. 35.

22. J. H. Miller, "The Still Heart: Poetic Form in Wordsworth," *New Literary History* 2 (Winter 1971): 305.

23. L. Komisar, "You Won't Have Uncle Sam to Kick Around Any More," *New York Times,* 30 June 1975, p. 29.

24. Clinton, *op. cit.,* A12.

25. R. Nixon, "A Transcript of President Nixon's Second Inaugural Address to the Nation,"*New York Times,* 21 January 1973, p. 32B.

26. F. D. McConnell, "Toward a Lexicon of Slogans," *Midwest Quarterly* 13 (October 1971): 80.

27. J. Carter, "Text of President Carter's Convention Address," *Chicago Tribune,*15 August 1980, p. 2.

28. R. Toner, "Dukakis Works at Warmth, Yet Tries to Keep His Cool," *New York Times,* 8 August 1988, p. B5.

29. G. Sheehy, "Beating Around Bush," *Vanity Fair,* September 1988, 207.

30. *Ibid.,* 207.

31. *Ibid.,* 208.

32. M. Edelman, "Myths, Metaphors, and Political Conformity," *Psychiatry* 30 (August 1967): 226.

33. J. Reston, "Revival Meeting," *New York Times,* 21 January 1977, p. A23.

34. H. Smith, "A Call to the American Spirit," *New York Times,* 21 January 1977, p. A1.

35. A. Hillbruner, "Born Again: Carter's Inaugural Sermon" (paper presented at Speech Communication Association convention, Washington, DC, December 1977).

36. R. Reagan, "Let Us Begin an Era of National Renewal," *New York Times,* 21 January 1981, p. A20.

37. McConnell, *op. cit.*, p. 82.

38. W. Safire, "The New Foundation," *New York Times,* 25 January 1979, p. E21.

# From Euphemisms to Lies

*If welfare is not really about five million families with five million different stories, but about "the underclass" or "teen mothers," then the reality isn't so complex.*
— M. J. STERN[1]

**P**olitical language depends upon ambiguity because politicians need the ability to place their own interpretations on what they have said, to deny others' interpretations, to change their emphases without changing their words, to allow their audience members to hold different interpretations simultaneously without offending those who hold any one interpretation, and perhaps for other reasons yet to be identified.

Even when talking with each other, politicians employ such ambiguous phrases as "I'm all right on that one," "You can count on me," "Don't get me started on that one," and "A lot of people have been asking me about that." The "beauty" of such phrases, according to M. Tolchin of the *New York Times*, is that they allow the politician to imply agreement without making a commitment, leaving open the possibility of later voting some other way without "being accused of changing position or being inconsistent, both political sins."[2] This chapter explains the mechanisms that allow this needed ambiguity when speaking with the public—lies, euphemisms, simplifications, generalizations, and the art of saying nothing.

Although I will treat the various language mechanisms in isolation from each other, the truth is they are inescapably interwoven. Euphemisms generalize and simplify. Generalizations are simplifications, and vice versa. The various tactics of the art of saying nothing partake of the functions of other mechanisms; for example, "memorable phrases" simplify, "grand vision" generalizes, and "nice words" are often euphemisms. To demonstrate these interactions, I end the chapter by weaving the elements together in a partial analysis of the 1994 Republican "Contract with America."

## ▶ Lies

This opening section on lies will be relatively short, but not because public lies are in short supply. On the contrary, lies are so widespread and important that I will take them up again in a later chapter. In the current chapter, I present not a disquisition on the nature and amount of official lying, but the opposite: a defense of politicians via a demonstration that a fair proportion of what we call political lies are not that at all.

**Lots of "political lies" are not lies at all #1**    Some are language choices with which we disagree. Perhaps a personal example will demonstrate. In 1970 I presented a paper at the International Communication Association convention in which I said that the rate of American murder of Vietnamese was on the rise. During the question period, my statement was challenged by a member of the audience, who called me a liar. He did not deny my statistics; rather, his position was that Vietnam was a war, thus any killing could not be called murder, thus I was a liar. Question: was I a liar or were we having a semantic quibble? Clearly the argument stemmed more from my language choice, and his reaction to it, than from whatever it was that was going on in Vietnam.

**Lots of "political lies" are not lies at all #2**    Some are simplifications that we are in a position to recognize; that is, we see them as *over*simplifications, so we call them lies. One of the more common occurrences on a college campus is the firing of a member of the faculty. Often, such an event is accompanied by a student protest in which students claim, often with good reason, that the person was a good teacher. But to define a good *professor* as a good *teacher* is a simplification of the position. In addition to teaching, a professor is expected to publish—in fact, is normally given a reduced teaching load in order to publish. The students are usually not in a position to know whether the professor is a productive scholar. And there are other professorial duties: committees to sit on or chair, meetings to attend, forms to complete, and so forth. Again, students are seldom in a position to know whether the fired professor performed these duties well—or, indeed, performed them at all. Often other members of the faculty will try to explain to the students that the fired person, while perhaps a good teacher, was not a good *professor*. Inevitably, at least one student will miss the "lesson" and respond, "that's a lie—I learned more from that *teacher* than from all my other professors combined."

Likewise in politics. It is almost axiomatic that the more you know about a situation the less you believe governmental pronouncements about it. The anti-war movement of the '60s and '70s complained, justifiably, about how it was characterized by the government. But the government probably did very little more injustice to that movement than it does daily in its characterizations of poverty in the cities, the farm problem, or the Middle East crisis. In order to deal with any complex situation, the government first simplifies it. And a simplification is, by definition, a distortion. If that makes it a lie then there is no truth in government . . . but also no truth anyplace else.

**All "political lies" are not lies at all #3**    Some are policies based on generalizations, or abstractions that look like lies because we read different policies into them during the campaign. When Clinton in 1992 promised to "end welfare as we know it," what, exactly, was his proposal? Was he lying about his intention, or was his idea of how to "end" welfare just different from ours? Is it possible that the fault may have been in us—that we lied to ourselves when we said we knew what the abstraction or generalization meant? Of course, Clinton may have employed language precisely so we would do that. But that does not make him a liar—a very clever person, perhaps, but not a liar. Alternatively, of course, it is possible that he did not employ the language that he did to deceive, but only because of some fuzziness in his own thoughts. In that case we obviously would not suggest he had lied, for lies require intentionality.

**All "political lies" are not lies at all #4**    Some are pragmatic language. That is a new term, so let me explain. *Pragmatic language* is language that is used "in order to bring about its truth."[3]

You may have been on a dark, deserted street late at night, afraid of what might be lurking ahead of you. In that situation you might start whistling, to indicate that you are not frightened. And at least some of the time that whistling makes you less afraid. The whistling, then, has functioned as a self-fulfilling prophecy.

Pragmatic language is rather like that, only instead of self-fulfilling it is other-fulfilling. For instance, suppose a candidate for office tells supporters the night before the election, "I'm going to win tomorrow." Unless the election is rigged, the candidate cannot *know* that a win is in the offing. That knowledge is available to nobody. Is the politician a liar? No, the statement "I'm going to win" should not be evaluated on a true–false continuum any more than your whistling in the dark should be. Both are examples of the pragmatic use of symbols. In the case of the politician, the language is used to build the confidence of the followers, for they are the ones who can make the statement come true. At a minimum, they must at least believe the candidate has enough of a chance of winning that they go to the polls and vote.

While perhaps most of us would not bother to call "I'm going to win tomorrow" a lie, the real difficulty is determining where self-fulfilling prophecies leave off and lies begin. For instance, what is the difference between "I'm going to win tomorrow" and "I'm going to overhaul the welfare system?" Both indicate the speaker's *intent*; both are statements about the future that cannot be accomplished without the cooperation of a lot of other people. That is, they are "other-fulfilling" assertions made in order to get people to come out to vote. Are they both "pragmatic?" Well . . . it's not clear, is it?

So, not all "political lies" are clearly lies. Some are language choices with which we disagree, some are recognizable simplifications, some are abstractions which we previously misunderstood, and some are pragmatic language.

Then, of course, there are those that really are lies. And, just like the non-lies, they can mislead us. All too often the real lies come packaged in a nice box labeled "national security." My favorite of my adult life was when the Nixon Administration falsely claimed we were not bombing Cambodia. When the truth came out, the administration officials claimed they had lied for reasons of national security. I guess they were afraid somebody would tell the Cambodians we were bombing them!

## ▶ Euphemisms

What is a euphemism? My dictionary defines it as "the substitution of an agreeable or inoffensive word or expression for one that is harsh, indelicate, or otherwise unpleasant or taboo; allusion to an offensive thing by an inoffensive expression; a polite, tactful, or less explicit term used to avoid the direct naming of an unpleasant, painful, or frightening reality." In other words, euphemisms are words we use to make things sound better than they are.

We all use euphemisms. Complaining to a friend about a weekend, I might say "I didn't have much fun," when the truth is more like "It was the worst party I ever attended." Airlines instruct each flight on emergency procedures—where the life belts are, the location of the emergency doors with slides. In case you crash into the ocean? No, in the event of a "water landing."

There is a sense, of course, in which all language is necessarily euphemistic. English professor W. Gibson says that is because the world that we attempt to capture with our words is chaotic and ambiguous while our language is systematic and orderly.[4] Thus our language, by its very nature, makes the world seem more rational, thus controllable, than it really is. (Notice that in this sense there is very little difference between euphemisms and oversimplifications.)

In the 1992 election, candidate Bill Clinton had a sign hanging in his headquarters that read, "It's the economy, stupid." That sign, suggesting that all he needed to do to get elected was to keep talking about economic issues, was an oversimplifying euphemism because, of course, the world of voters is neither as simple nor as controllable as that. Some voters do base their votes on economic issues; some vote moral issues; some vote as their best friends vote; some vote a straight party line because their families always have voted for that party; and so forth.

Clinton's sign supposedly "captured" the sentiment of voters, but it missed enormous numbers because the many millions of voters can not be reduced to automatons, blindly pulling the voting lever for whoever stresses even as important and relevant a topic as economics. The sign (which may have been adopted merely as a strategy) gave Clinton the illusion that he could control the outcome of the election with a single topic, but (though he *did* win) the outcome *may* have been as much affected by Ross Perot's withdrawal and reentry or George Bush's supposed elitism as by Clinton's rhetoric.

Not only is our language by nature a distorting factor, so is our humanness. We have a desire to bathe ourselves and our activities in a more glorious light than we probably deserve. We don't like to consider ourselves ugly or mean or any of the hundreds of other negative things that we doubtlessly are at times. The Rambo syndrome notwithstanding, most people seem to want to be sensitive (or at least be perceived as being sensitive). You can prove this to yourself by reading the dating ads. The people who advertise always sound so nice: "Sensitive married man, 26, seeks young, vibrant, sensitive woman, 18–24, for loving, sensitive, supplemental relationship." Obviously, what this "sensitive" man wants is a mistress. One wonders how sensitive he is to the needs and desires of his wife . . . and how the slob would react if one of the letters of response were to come from his wife!

But the point has been made—all of us engage in euphemisms. And we do so at least partly because our language necessarily is euphemistic; that is, because we cannot possibly encompass all of reality in words, and partly because we want to "put our best face forward."

Why, then, be concerned about euphemisms in the language of politics? If they are inevitable, why not relax and enjoy them? In order to answer that question, another distinction must be made—a value judgment. Our choice is not between euphemistic language and noneuphemistic language; it is between what we consider to be good euphemisms and bad euphemisms. We will all make that value judgement, for any given euphemism, according to our personalities, ideologies, systems of morality, and backgrounds. The best I can do is indicate the kinds of euphemisms I applaud, the kinds I abhor, and the reasons that lead me to these judgments. As I do so, I will strive to give some insight into opposing evaluations, but those descriptions will necessarily be biased by my perceptual screens.

As nearly as I have been able to analyze my own behavior, I applaud euphemisms that uplift humanity and improve society. But I expect everybody could say the same thing—the stumbling block is that decisions about what uplifts humanity and improves society are moral and ideological decisions. An innocuous example of an euphemism that uplifts humanity without creating any obvious deleterious effects is calling garbage collectors "sanitation engineers." While the term strikes me as rather strange semantics, I have no moral or ideological objections.

But not all euphemisms are so innocuous. English professor W. Gibson provides this example: When prisons started being called reformatories, "the emphasis shifted from physical detention to social rehabilitation."[5] Few inhabitants may have been rehabilitated, but the reformers had good intentions. However, notice that the evaluation "good intention" is based on liberal ideology. Someone who endorses a more conservative viewpoint, say a position that prisons are the secular answers to the "eye for an eye" biblical injunction or that a major source of crime is the undue coddling of criminals in our society, undoubtedly would react to those euphemisms quite differently.

The clearest examples of bad euphemisms, for me, relate to the specific brand of killing to which we refer by the euphemism "war." But if "war" can be considered a euphemism for "organized national killing," it also can be considered too strong a word and itself get replaced by tamer euphemisms. Thus, the old "War Department" was replaced by tamer language when it was renamed the "Department of Defense." The Korean War was not known officially as a "war" but as a "police action." And other euphemisms—such as conflagration, skirmish, disturbance, "Operation Desert Storm"—occasionally are employed to camouflage the fact that we are engaged in a war.

While euphemisms make things sound better than they are, there are also words and phrases that make things sound worse—"dyseuphemisms," if you will. They are significant in defining the people and actions of the other side (which are dyseuphemized into "the enemy"). Thus, columnist G. Cheney notes that in preparing us for the Gulf War (euphemistically called "Operation Desert Storm"), President George Bush identified the leader of Iraq, Saddam Hussein, as "brutal, dictatorial, merciless, savage, evil, desperate, threatening, 'another Hitler.'"[6] Condemning the enemy as savage is a normal part of American war rhetoric, says communication professor Robert Ivie, who points out that "the usual strategy is to construct the image indirectly through contrasting references to the adversary's coercive, irrational, and aggressive attempts to subjugate a freedom-loving, rational, and pacific victim."[7] Such dyseuphemisms help prepare the populace for war.

In turn, the coming war is made to seem inevitable by the ways in which American actions are compared to those of "The Enemy." Essentially, the ploy is to suggest linguistically that "the enemy" is *choosing* war and that therefore we are being *forced* into the conflict. In terms of the Gulf War, Cheney points out that President Bush repeatedly claimed he had "no choice" but to go to war because Saddam was "forcing" him in that direction.[8]

Once the war starts, of course, the euphemisms and dyseuphemisms escalate right along with the fighting. In the Vietnam War the Pentagon came up with this euphemism: "routine, limited-duration, reinforced, protective reaction air strike." What in the devil did that mean? Try taking it apart: "routine"—we do it every day, "limited duration"—we don't do it all day long, "reinforced"—supported by Navy shelling and/or ground troops, "protective reaction"—we seek out the enemy and attack them before they can attack us, "air strike"—bombing. In short, "routine, limited duration, reinforced, protective reaction air strike" meant searching out and bombing the enemy, in concert with Army and Navy maneuvers, before they had the chance to attack us. So "attacking" was euphemized into "protecting."

Another kind of euphemism used to describe the fighting in Vietnam relied on what might be called "suburban metaphors." Air Force spokespersons, according to Professor Gibson, were particularly liable to use such euphemisms: Bombers concentrating their attacks on one small area were engaged in a *"carpet raid."* If they used cluster bombs they were said to *"lawnmower."* "Vietnamese huts were *barbecued* by American firepower. To shoot people from a helicopter was to '*hose*' them."[9] Barbecues, mowing the lawn, and using the garden hose sound more like weekend life in suburbia than death in wartime.

The weapons used in wars are also described in euphemistic and dyseuphemistic ways. The phrase "surgical strike" as a euphemism for a "bombing raid," according to conservative *New York Times* writer William Safire, makes a bombing sound "precise, quiet, clean, incisive," thus giving "a humane coloration to a military exercise."[10] In the Gulf War the comparative descriptions of U.S. and Iraqi missiles seemed to parallel the comparative qualities we assumed characterized the two sides. Thus, says Professor Cheney, U.S. missiles were identified as "smart," "accurate," and "precise," while Iraqi missiles were described as "crude," "wild," and "unpredictable." In weaponry as in approach, "*We* are systematic and reasonable; *they* are uncontrolled and mad."[11] Even the names we provided for the missiles reinforced these attitudes. The major missile we used was called "The Patriot," while we dubbed theirs

"The Scud." The Patriot versus The Scud—you know who's going to win that battle!

The word "neutralization" has a curious recent wartime history. It is traditionally a euphemism for assassination, but in Vietnam it meant bombing or burning entire villages. Then, in the Contra war against Nicaragua, the C.I.A. prepared a manual of terrorism for the Contras, including the recommendation that Nicaraguan leaders be "neutralized." The manual became an election issue in 1984. *New York Times* columnist Anthony Lewis summarized the controversy this way: "President Reagan . . . spoke sternly about the manual, saying . . . that those who put it out 'will be removed.'"[12] But after he was elected he changed his tune, saying the manual was not a call for murder. What was meant by "neutralize," Reagan now said, was "'You just say to the fellow . . . 'You're not in the office anymore.'"[13] It is not recorded if members of the press corps laughed derisively at Reagan's euphemizing claim; they should have.

B. Keller of the *New York Times* asserts the Pentagon has had some trouble in recent years in deciding what to call "little wars." They have mostly settled on "low intensity conflict," although the Navy insists upon using the more poetic phrase, "violent peace."[14] It also should be noted, says *New York Times* writer J. LeMoyne, that when the Pentagon converted a twin-propeller DC-3, especially designed for anti-rebel warfare, and provided it to El Salvador, they officially referred to it as an "airborne fire support platform."[15]

While some of these examples seem innocuous, maybe even cute, the language of warmakers is serious, deadly so. According to Professor L. R. Beres, nuclear war euphemisms such as "'crisis relocation,' 'limited nuclear war,' 'protracted nuclear war,' 'collateral damage,' 'countervalue' and 'counterforce' strategies and 'enhanced radiation warfare' (the neutron bomb) are insidious to the cause of peace."[16]

Again, I must quickly point out that any response to these wartime euphemisms is ideological. If you believe in the necessity of the wars in question, you doubtlessly applaud the euphemisms, for the language allows the participants to overcome moral repulsions to killing and get on with the job at hand. If you think the job has to be done, you applaud. If not, you jeer.

But most euphemisms are neither totally good nor totally bad. Professor Gibson explores a whole group that fall into this middle category—"developing nations," "senior citizens," "substandard housing," "disadvantaged," "underprivileged," "culturally deprived."[17]

I said these euphemisms were neither totally good nor totally bad. Why? Well, on the one hand, most of them are more humane than the words they replace and that is good. It is more humane to call someone culturally deprived rather than poor because "culturally deprived" spreads the blame. One can create one's own poverty, but creating your own cultural deprivation is a much more difficult matter. Again, the result of the euphemism is good. But, on the other hand, some people overreact to the label, blame all their failures on the culture, try to "get by," to "cash in" on their "cultural deprivation." And that is understandable, for the society at large has never found a convincing way to say, "Yes, the problem is partly created by the society. And we'll try to make that portion up to you. But in addition to what we do you have to go out there and bust your butt just like all of those non–culturally deprived people have to do."

One more comment about these middle-range euphemisms. Most of them take the blood out of the problem. "Senior citizen" takes the loneliness out of old age. "Culturally deprived" takes the hunger out of poverty. On the one hand, this may make the problem seem manageable. Like the fighter pilots, we may need euphemisms in order to act. But defining the suffering out of the situation may also make the problem seem tolerable, thus lessening our inclination to act. With these opposing possible reactions, who is to say whether the euphemisms are good or bad? I do not mean that no value judgments can be made, but that no one can make such a judgment for other people. We each have to make our own.

## ▶ Simplifications

We Americans like things to be simple. We want our lighters to light with a simple flick of the wrist. We want our lawnmowers to start first time every time. We want to be able to push a button on the top of a can and smell good all day.

And we want our public talk to be simple, not as "tinkling brass"—"full of sound and fury and signifying nothing." As anthropologist Edward Hall has pointed out, a "mumbling, halting speech pattern carries the implication of tormented honesty and deep hesitant truths. . . . With an American, the suspicion of the glib talker is almost an act of conscience."[18] We do not like long words—and the people who utter them are suspect.

Listen to Russell Baker of the *New York Times* complain of long words and attempt a psychological justification for his longing for simple speech: "We associate plain talk with the age of national confidence. . . . It is the campaign of 1948" when President Truman started a speech with these words: "I'm President of the United States and I'm trying to keep my job." Since then, suggests Baker, "campaign talk has become fatter and more pompous, as though we need sounds that seem weighty to conceal a thinness of the spirit from which they emanate."[19] So says Russell Baker, and I suspect most of us find his position psychologically satisfying. I know I find myself drawn to it, despite the fact that I consider his argument (to obey his injunction to be plain) a bunch of crap—historically inaccurate, analytically weak. But I am attracted by it. The desire for simplicity is so deeply ingrained in our culture that we rush to it even as we are intellectually repelled by it.

And politicians play upon our desire for simplicity. They take our philosophical preference for the simple and make it work for them. Political scientist F. Heer explains that when politicians give speeches, "they like to make things as easy as possible . . . . They would like to be genuises of simplification."[20] If simplicity is a philosophical value for most of us, Heer continues, it is an instrumental value for politicians. If politicians are speaking to audiences "who speak only the narrow, linear language of their job or professions,"[21] it clearly is to their advantage to use a simple vocabulary.

Gwen Brown, a rhetorical critic at Radford University, explains that Ronald Reagan, generally admitted to displaying a degree of incompetence as president, came to be perceived as competent through the use of simplification. She argues that Reagan's characteristic form of argumentation was the narrative, a form that "converts" the complications of reality "into compact, simple, easily digestible components." Because the complexities were filtered out, and because narratives are inherently difficult to refute, the resulting impression on the audience was "that the issue has been clarified as opposed to being simplified."[22] Thus Reagan was deemed competent even though his simplifications-through-narration often skirted or oversimplified the subtle details, overlooking the truth of the old adage that "The devil is in the details."

The point at which the consumers and producers of political rhetoric most clearly coalesce in their preference and propensity for simplicity is in the political slogan. Of all political rhetoric, the slogan is the simplest—and the emptiest. And the most popular. And (need I add?) the most insidious.

For slogans do strange things to us; or, perhaps I should say, we do strange things to ourselves through our slogans. We use them as shorthand for stating, defining, our beliefs. But what happens is that the slogans come to define us. Consider the process. A group of people are opposed to war. They want to live a peaceful existence. They don't want to hassle anybody. They want to be left alone. They want to be natural. They want to enjoy nature and nature's ways. So they select a flower, the simple daisy, as their nonverbal slogan, a slogan they think captures many complicated thoughts and encapsulates them in simple, direct terms. Having selected their slogan, they begin to think of themselves as flower children. The slogan started out to define their significant beliefs; it ended defining them as insignificant children, no more relevant to important questions than the flowers they carried.

Another, closely related, process of slogans is that they originate to express our beliefs; reiterated often enough, they come to be our beliefs. Take the right-wing slogan from the 1960s, "America—Love it or Leave it." This slogan originated in reaction to criticism of the country. It expressed a belief that America was a wonderful place—the highest living standard in the world, a benevolent climate, beautiful countryside, good people, a decent system of government, a place one just naturally loves, a place one would not want to leave. But as the slogan was reiterated it became a phrase with which to taunt the opposition. The beliefs about the country were forgotten. What was left was a shouted alternative: love it or leave it. And it was clear that the shouters preferred their opposition select the second alternative. The slogan quit expressing any beliefs about the country and came, itself, to be a belief.

It also should be mentioned that slogans, by simplifying reality, function to bring varying ideological positions under one roof. "Peace Now" was the slogan adopted by those who saw war itself as immoral as well as by those who merely believed the Vietnam war was immoral. "Pornography is the Theory—Rape is the Practice" is literally the banner under which anti-pornography feminists and antifeminist members of the New Christian Right find themselves marching side by side.

But slogans are only extreme cases of the simplifying tendencies in political rhetoric. I suspect nearly identical processes are at work in all political communication. More specifically, it seems to me that politicians respond to our desires for simplicity and their own; in turn, they come to believe their own simplifications. The alternatives would seem to be for them to spend inordinate amounts of time engaging in dissonance reduction to justify the ways they talk with us, or to callously dismiss the public as manipulable fools. And while there is some evidence that politicians occasionally assume we are fools whom they can manipulate, I do not see as much evidence of the assumption being as widespread among politicians as some pessimistic analyses would lead us to believe.

One obvious way we simplify the political world is by associating policies with the president. Murray Edelman, one of the foremost scholars in political communication, explains that this associational thinking saves us the trouble of trying to understand presidential policies. Because we react to a political event by praising or blaming those in power at the time of the event, even if they had nothing to do with it, we develop an "inability to analyze complicated issues and distaste for trying."[23] We simplify by associating policies with leaders. But the association soon becomes a confusion, and the reelection or rejection of the leader becomes all-important—the policy be damned. A major reason we cannot have issue-oriented elections in this country is that we voters refuse to keep our focus upon the issues. We refuse to try to understand them. We would much rather elect candidates we like; and if they do not solve the problems we will throw them out and elect other candidates we like, even if their stands on the issues are identical to those of the people we are throwing out. The manifestations of our simplicity can be so confusing!

Another mistake-through-simplification that we make in politics is simplifying complex human activities by comparing them to machines, forgetting that the most complicated machine—the computer—is simple by comparison with the human mind. Consider a prophetic analysis of this tendency written by satirist Russell Baker of the *New York Times* in 1969, in response to a comment by the president-elect's press spokesman, Ron L. Ziegler, that a Cabinet meeting was "part of the input process." Mr. Ziegler, suggests Baker, was thereby implying that Nixon's cabinet was "some higher manifestation of I.B.M. circuitry, undergoing input process and spewing forth coded readouts." The implication, Baker predicted, "will only intensify their embarrassment when their humanity is inevitably disclosed."[24] The decision-making processes of humans are not analogous to those of a computer. When we act as though they were we set ourselves up for a disappointment. Of course, we would be even more disappointed if they were. After all, Data is a brilliant android, but the best decisions rely heavily on the humanity of Captain Picard.

It should come as no surprise, by this point, if I say that a major problem with our attempts to solve public problems with politics is that we have oversimplified the issues we address. Take the whole area of "law and order," for example. When we identify a problem as a "law and order" issue, we are prompted by that label to look for the solution within the legal system. Unfortunately, however, those who are most exercised by "law and order" tend to stress the "order" portion of the "formula" (i.e., the police) and ignore "law" because they believe that one source of the problem is that same legal system. Thus, we find crime being blamed on "soft-headed judges" or "molly-coddlers" or "revolving door justice." While such persons might contribute in some way to the problem, it is doubtful that a single criminal ever selected a life of crime because his analysis of society showed him that certain judges and "do-gooders" would take pity on him when he got caught. Be that as it may, the point is that when we simplify an issue we may lead ourselves into incorrect diagnoses and unworkable solutions.

And simplified issues seem to have a way of hanging on, of being influential even when they are not, objectively, as pressing as before. For instance, in the 1994 elections many of those who took the "toughest" positions on crime got elected despite the fact that crime rates were declining. The major reason that crime can be a perennial campaign issue is that it is a simple issue, simply understood. There are clearly delineated good guys and bad guys. There are simple solutions from all sides—lock 'em up and throw away the key (conservative), three strikes and you're out (liberal), capital punishment (conservative), and gun control (liberal).

Despite the implications of what I have been saying in this section, let me state as *simply* as I can what I perceive the problem to be. We know that reality is ambiguous and complex. Yet we chop out a little chunk of it, a portion we perceive to be a problem, and give it a name—perhaps using a euphemism. We describe the problem with our logical language. We simplify it so that everybody, with a minimum of effort, can understand it. Then we become convinced that it is, indeed, a simple problem. So we institute a simple solution. Then we wonder why the solution does not work, maybe even kick out the person who proposed it.

Throughout, however, we cling to our demand for simplicity. And by doing so, comments *Saturday Review* writer T. H. Middleton, we preclude any realistic attempts to solve our problems, refusing to see the relationship between "pill popping" and "pistol packing," which, he says, is that "the well-stocked medicine chest and the well-stocked armory are both attempts to deal with problems simply and immediately but, in fact, unrealistically."[25] That is, because we oversimplify the problem we "buy into" the illusion that the cure will be easy; therefore, we institute a simple solution, which often actually makes the situation worse.

## ▶ Generalizations

The process of generalizing is understood as the method of looking at specific instances and arriving at a more widely applicable general rule. This process is basic to science, where it is known as "induction," the process of reasoning from the specific to the general. As handled by scientists, who understand the procedures for making sure all the specific examples are from the same class and taking into account negative examples, the process can generate accurate general statements. But most of us, most of the time, arrive at our generalizations in a sloppier way. We do not examine our examples carefully to make sure they are alike in all their essentials, we generalize on the basis of an insufficient number of examples (often on just *one* example), and we ignore negative examples rather than demonstrating how they differ in some essential way.

This section, then, is concerned with how most of us generalize rather than with the scientific process of induction. It also will consider how vague general statements are substituted for more specific examples and data. Such substitutions are especially troublesome if the vague generalization partakes of the mistakes that are noted above. But whether mistakes in the generalization process have been made is difficult to determine, for speakers often provide the generalization without even hinting at the process from which the general statement was derived.

To add to the analytic difficulty, both euphemisms and simplifications generalize, and lies are sometimes generalizations based on examples the speaker knows do not support the generality.

Given all these difficulties, we may wonder why politicians engage in generalizations. The answer, of course, is that general statements work for them. They use them for the same reason you and I do—because otherwise they would get bogged down in interminable detail. You and I might generalize, "I like chocolate ice cream," without thinking it necessary to say "except in freezing weather, or when I want something more refreshing, like strawberry, or when I feel like having a nuttier taste, when I have black walnut" or any of the hundred other "qualifiers" to the generalization. Yet when we hear a politician say, "I support Clinton's health care plan," we conclude that is the case under any and all conditions. We do not allow the politician to have the kind of qualifiers we demand for ourselves. Thus if, months later, the politician ends up voting for some other health plan, maybe one that was introduced after the statement of support was made, we conclude we were lied to.

So let us approach the phenomenon of generalizations this way. Rather than trying to determine whether all political generalizations are distortions, let's examine what seem to be the major functions of generalizations in political rhetoric: (1) they complement our all-encompassing two-party system; (2) they endanger the creation of meaningful distinctions; (3) they are dangerous to individualism; and (4) they allow leaders to manipulate us through an anxiety-reassurance cycle.

First, the two-party system requires generalizations. Unlike political parties in most countries, ours are not narrowly ideological or easy to identify as to their positions on issues. Although the leaders of each party tend to be ideological, they recognize that most people are not, so they have structured the parties to be broad and nonideological in order to try to appeal to practically everybody. They state their positions in broad generalizations rather than in narrow ideological terms. They hope thereby to win election as well as agreement with their policy positions, neither of which would be likely if they stated their positions too specifically. After all, we can all agree with the generalization that "the economy should be improved," but the specific ways in which any politician might seek to achieve the improvement are likely to meet with much opposition.

Unfortunately, the generalization process that is perceived as necessary to attain electoral victory and broad consent for measures is often self-defeating for the official once in office. The legislation or executive decision, once adopted, will be much more specific in application than the rhetoric implied. Take, as an example, Nixon's 1968 "Plan for Peace" in Vietnam. The "Plan" had no content. Those who wanted to bomb the North back to the stone age could assume that was Nixon's plan. Those who wanted an immediate withdrawal could hope Nixon planned to do exactly that. But once elected, Nixon had to select specific policies—and those specifics could not please as many people as had his rhetorical generalizations. Thus, those who had read their own preferred policies into his generalization felt Nixon had lied to them. The generalization that had helped Nixon gain the office made it difficult for him to govern once in office. It is always thus. The generalization is required by the necessity of appealing to a diverse audience. The disillusionment is inevitable because of the necessity of implementing a specific policy.

There is a sense, then, in which the country would be better off, as would the president, if the new president could take office without our having any expectations of what he would do. For instance, Reagan's 1984 and Bush's 1988 campaign promises of no tax increases made difficult the resolution of our economic problems. (Of course, I am not *seriously* suggesting we should elect presidents based on personality rather than policy; rather, I'm underlining how difficult it is for the elected to govern if they have hemmed themselves in too much with policy proposals during the campaigns.)

Second, generalizations endanger the possibility of making discriminations. The clearest example of this, suggests English professor A. Berger, is from the world of advertising. "As everything becomes inflated and tremendous, the word loses its currency. What is normal becomes *tremendous* . . . and we have reached the point of no return."[26]

Analogously, when "national security" is so broadened that it encompasses burglary, wiretapping, surveillance, wholesale invasions of privacy, and even murder, we have reached the point of no return. We can no longer discriminate between "national security" and "national interest." We are led to believe that "national security" is the totality of preserving our "national interest," forgetting that one of the most compelling facets of our national interest is freedom, and that wiretapping, surveillance, and invasion of privacy are inimical to freedom. "National security" is the "giant king size" of contemporary politics.

Third, generalizations are dangerous to individualism . . . and are encouraged by the technology of our mass society. To take all of the poor and lump them together into "the poor" or "the culturally disadvantaged" is to generalize away their individual differences. Some people are poor because they are culturally disadvantaged. Some have had home lives that denied the values of the culture. Some are lazy. Some are frozen out by the racism of the society. Some are stupid. Some have taken a vow of poverty for religious or political reasons. Some are the victims of unethical or illegal business practices. But we take one attribute of their lives, economic poverty, and use that generalization to define them.

And it strikes us as perfectly natural to do so. Our whole technology supports the tendency toward sameness. Oil paintings can be idiosyncratic;

computer graphics cannot. Handwritten letters can be personal; computerized form letters, even when "personalized" with insertion of the recipient's name and home town, cannot. As we wander rootlessly through our country we find security in the identical blandness of Howard Johnson motels, we feel at home under the golden arch of McDonald's, we take comfort in the fact that politicians all talk in similar ways about similar topics. We live our lives pretty much as others live theirs, enjoying our TV dinners while television news summarizes all the significant idiosyncratic activities of today's world in thirty minutes. (Well, twenty-one plus commercials, but why quibble?)

The current political reality is dependent on the media. In particular, television has transformed all our politicians into media creatures. Mass media operate with interpretative frameworks of their own that are embedded in specific linguistic characteristics ("story lines," "conventional structures," "dwindling drama," and so forth) within mass communication. The form of media affects the content.[27] There is a sameness in television news formats; audiences can predict content. Politicians have had to adapt their language and speaking style to the structure or grammar of the predominant medium. Speeches are being written in thirty- and sixty-second segments (paragraphs) to accommodate coverage. Needless to say, about all that can be put into a thirty- to sixty-second format is a generalization.

Fourth, generalizations allow our leaders to engage in a drama of suspense and solution that ensures our allegiance as it befuddles our minds. Murray Edelman explains that government "both encourages public anxiety and placates it through rhetoric and reassuring gestures." The anxiety is encouraged by discussion of domestic problems and foreign threats, and placated by reassurances of American power and the effectiveness of our leaders' actions. Thus, the anxiety-reassurance "cycle" "provides a supportive following."[28]

The threat is generalized beyond our individual power to ascertain. The reassurance is generalized, hidden behind walls of secrecy. Lacking the knowledge to challenge either the extent of the threats or the efficacy of the reassuring countermeasures, we are dangled on generalized rhetorical strings manipulated by our leaders. Betrayed by generalizations, we hang there helplessly—washing our cars, mowing our lawns, and supinely reelecting our leaders.

## ▶ The Art of Saying Nothing

I doubt much argumentation is necessary to prove to you that politicians often say nothing. The hot air quotient is so high that even casual observers of the political scene cannot help noticing it.

However, perhaps it is necessary to demonstrate that the facility of saying nothing is an art. That is less obvious; saying nothing seems as though it would be so easy. But apparently it is not. The mistake many newcomers to politics make is to say something. They enter the arena with ideological fervor, having bought the social studies textbook and the *New York Times* editorial calls for more debate on the issues. They stride to center stage, announce their positions clearly, and get swamped by their opponents.

They have not learned the first rule of the art of politics: don't offend anybody. Obviously, the best way to keep from offending people is to refrain from saying anything with which they disagree. And since the electorate holds lots of conflicting opinions, the only way to avoid offending at least a portion of them is to say nothing at all. But that does not mean politicians can stay home and become couch potatoes; they have to meet all those speaking engagements. They have to talk. To be successful, then, they have to learn the art of saying nothing.

How do they achieve this? What are the components of the art of saying nothing? We have been talking about some of them—euphemisms, simplifications, generalizations—and now I want to discuss, briefly, a few more: memorable phrases, earnestness, grand vision, jargon, and nice words.

## Memorable Phrases

Political economist J. K. Galbraith has written knowingly about memorable phrases, suggesting that some politicians (he specifically mentions Franklin D. Roosevelt and Adlai Stevenson, but there have been others) have been able, through the persuasiveness of their rhetoric, "to make their audience overlook the fact that the real questions were being avoided."[29] These phrases are part of our political heritage: Eisenhower's "military-industrial complex," Kennedy's "let's get America moving again" and his "New Frontier," Johnson's "let us continue" and his "Great Society." If you do not remember any for Nixon that is understandable. Memorable phrases were not his strong point, although "I'm not a crook" may go down in history. But certainly any dictionary of phrases would have to include Agnew's contributions, such as "nattering nabobs of negativity." Ford? None. Carter? None. Reagan? None, unless you count the borrowed ("Go ahead, make my day") or the banal ("A new beginning"). Bush? His "thousand points of light" might qualify, though it was actually provided by Peggy Noonan, a speechwriter he "inherited" from Reagan. Clinton? None, assuming we don't count "I didn't inhale."

Notice that the similarity among the memorable phrases is that they are vague. Everybody wants a New Deal, a Fair Deal, a part in settling the New Frontier, a chance to live in a Great Society or to overcome past mistakes via "A New Beginning." And anyone who has thought about our society knows what (s)he would do to achieve the promise of these catchphrases. The politicians who enunciate such contentless phrases do the voter the great service of not only allowing the dreams to continue, but of providing an opportunity to vote for them.

While some might argue that the dearth of memorable phrases among recent presidents says something negative about their ability to be original, my analysis suggests a different assessment. Namely, as long as the older phrases are still in use and still efficacious in garnering voters, as long as they still animate the political desires of the voters, there is no reason for politicians to entrust their political futures to new and untried phrases. If we want new phrases, we'll have to stop (re-)buying the old ones.

## Earnestness

A second tool of the art of saying nothing is earnestness. Politicians, says Galbraith, believe that "great earnestness is a surrogate for simple truth."[30] Knowing that the audience normally does not want to do the hard work of thinking through issues, they assume that if they can just *seem* sincere the audience will think they are telling the truth. Some saw such an attempt in Lyndon Johnson's unrelieved public seriousness, although leaks about his more mercurial character undermined his public facade. Others saw Nixon's often-repeated line, "let me make one thing perfectly clear," as his bid to be perceived as earnest and sincere. More recently, some have had fun with Bill Clinton's penchant for biting his lip as he "thinks how to answer," which makes the audience assume the subsequent answer came sincerely from the depths of the president's character.

This seeming earnestness, sincerity, was one of the weaknesses of the anti-war Left in the '60s and '70s. When the "peace movement" started in the 1960s it was composed of people of all ages. I remember that when I attended my first movement event, a candlelight vigil in 1968, I was one of the youngest participants. Yet a mere two years later, at another event, I noticed that I was one of the older people in attendance. What had happened was that the strategy (demonstrations), tactics (such as cursing, sewing an American flag on the seat of the pants, burning the American flag, and carrying Vietcong flags) and the life style (communal living, drugs), all of which the young protesters saw as necessary to demonstrate the sincerity of their opposition, had driven away the older adherents. As one of the movement leaders, Sam Brown, argued at that time, "behavior that is offensive to Middle America neither establishes nor identifies real political differences; it merely offends Middle America."[31]

But wait a minute: if the appearance of sincerity is a part of the art of saying nothing, a basic of politics, why were the members of the anti-war Left so despised for it? Simple. They broke the rule—they *were* sincere, and demanded that others demonstrate their sincerity. The *art* is the art of *appearing* sincere while leaving open the door to compromise. The Left *demanded* sincerity, slamming the door in the faces of those they considered ideologically impure, those who agreed with them substantively but who objected to their strategy, tactics, or life style. The politician accepts the dictum, "act sincere, whether you mean it or not," while the anti-war movement required adherents to *be* sincere, even if it meant destroying any chance of stopping the war.

Ronald Reagan was considerably more successful in his use of sincerity. Not only did his days as an actor prepare him with the ability to seem sincere when engaging in the art of saying nothing, but, according to S. R. Weisman of the *New York Times*, he often went the next step, making "his motivation a primary focus of the defense of his policies, transforming criticism of his actions into criticism of his sincerity."[32] Thus, when his civil-rights policies were attacked, he responded with a little story about how his family was so pro-Black that his father refused to allow him to see the classic film, "Birth of a Nation." When his economic policies were attacked as uncaring for the unemployed, he recalled the time his father was given a pink slip on Christmas

Eve. In short, he deflected attention from the policies themselves to his own motivation, his own sincerity.

President Clinton, on the other hand, has great trouble being perceived as sincere, at least partly because a significant number of citizens perceive him to have lied about whether he had extramarital affairs, about the events surrounding his attempts to stay out of military service, about whether he inhaled marijuana smoke, and about a myriad of other details of his life. When people do not trust you, it is difficult for them to perceive you as sincere; thus, your opportunity to employ sincerity as a strategy for saying nothing is destroyed. Perhaps we should call this the "boy who cried wolf" syndrome. At any rate, columnist Ruth Marcus, after examining some of the presumed lies of the Clinton White House, concluded that if trust is the coin of the realm, the Clinton Administration is "flat broke."[33]

## Grand Vision

A third component of the Art of Saying Nothing is Grand Vision, or what the British call "dawnism." John Kenneth Galbraith calls it the "adolescent tendency" to believe that some new approach—or leader—will usher in a new millenium, a generation of peace, or some other "dawn of a new day."[34] The election of every new president is accompanied with the hope that he will bring a resurgence of peace or prosperity or patriotism or whatever seems to be in short supply at that moment. Politicians play on that hope, pronounce grand schemes that advertise their ability to think great thoughts, then stumble over the most mundane and everyday things. There is an enormous difference between thinking great thoughts and performing grand deeds, which is perhaps the differential Jesse Jackson had in mind when he said, "he can talk the talk but can he walk the walk?" That is, isn't it possible that too many political grand visions replace any attempt at grand action?

Consider, for instance, the "Grand Vision" for the "flowering of the Atlantic civilization" enunciated by Barry Goldwater as he accepted the Republican Presidential Nomination in 1964. This Atlantic civilization was to be effected by the joining of all Atlantic Ocean countries with the United States as the central pillar, linking the Atlantic and Pacific civilizations. The entire complex was then to be used to achieve peace and guide emerging nations. It was, to say the least, a nationally egocentric vision that was undoubtedly psychologically satisfying to much of his audience. It was also just so much hot air, an excellent example of the value of Grand Vision in the Art of Saying Nothing—as is proven by the fact that Goldwater never mentioned the "flowering of the Atlantic civilization" again in the entire 1964 campaign.

Ernest Bormann has demonstrated that the way television covered the Reagan First Inaugural allowed Reagan to emerge as a symbol of a new day dawning. The juxtaposition of Reagan presenting his speech, the visual reminders of the founding fathers in the nation's capitol, and the glimpses of the planes returning the American hostages from Iran nicely supplemented

Reagan's thesis "that what was needed was . . . a change that would restore the basis of past national greatness—a great leap forward to be accomplished only after a firm step backward."[35]

## Jargon

Another tool of the Art of Saying Nothing is jargon. Many people confuse "jargon" with "cliche" or "bromide" but I mean more by "jargon" than the use of trite phrases. I use the dictionary definition: "a specialized language of a field." In most fields, the specialized language, the jargon, sets those in the field apart from nonmembers. Not so with politics, because politics is a *public* profession. There *is* a political jargon, but it is the language of the public. And the politician *must* speak this language. Regardless of ideology, politicians must be for hard work, God, and country and against the "military-industrial complex," "lawless crime," and "deceit in high places."

Murray Edelman points out that "Jargon is largely ritualistic and predictable. Its audience gets no surprises."[36] The politician who uses jargon, the language of the public, demonstrates identification with the public. Nothing has been said, but the right attitudes have been demonstrated. We can vote for him/her, that is, for one of us.

## Nice Words

Finally, nice words are a part of the arsenal that allows politicians to say nothing. Eric Goldman of *Holiday* magazine describes the effect of listening to a speech by the ultimate nice politician, Dwight David Eisenhower, and the language that kept that image shiny through eight years of his presidency: "There was the leader of my country, standing talking my native language, and . . . I could make little sense out of what he was saying." Goldman concluded that Eisenhower's muddled words demonstrated his political/rhetorical preference for "a sunny muddling through."[37]

But Goldman was wrong. Eisenhower was not just "muddling through"; he was engaging in the Art of Saying Nothing, an art he had mastered.

## How the Art of Saying Nothing Functions

Assuming for the moment that 1 have identified the major components of the art, it remains to be explained how it functions. Why don't we see through these windbags? Why do we vote for them and vote for them and vote for them, *ad nauseum*?

In order to understand that, we must first realize that most Americans are wedded to the *status quo*. They do not want change. The language of politics, the Art of Saying Nothing, "works" because it is not threatening. The code words reassure. The politician's language, says Edelman, is calculated to demonstrate that the speaker will do nothing to disturb "the established order or question its basic value premises."[38] In short, politicians who say nothing are not a threat; if they mouth language with which the audience is comfortable, they can be assumed to be safe, to favor the right things and oppose the wrong ones. They are properly middle of the road, recommended by their mediocrity.

When the people do contemplate change, which isn't often, they want that change to be on their own terms. Thus, the art functions to allow them to perceive the politician as recommending what they themselves prefer. "Ambiguities are useful . . . because they leave the auditors free to supply their own content for the ambiguities and thus persuade themselves."[39] Take this line from Nixon's Second Inaugural: "Let us resolve that this era will be what it can become: a time of great responsibilities, greatly borne, in which we renew the spirit and the promise of America as we enter our third century as a nation." The lack of ideological context in this line of the text, coupled with the high level of ambiguity, leaves the line empty of content. Thus, the audience members are "completely free to envision whatever future they desire."[40]

The Art of Saying Nothing, then, functions in two ways. First, it soothes the audience by talking its language. And second, it is structured so as to allow the audience to persuade itself. No wonder it is effective.

## ▶ The Language Mechanisms in Combination

To demonstrate the interactions between the various language mechanisms discussed in this chapter, I propose to look at a portion of the 1994 Republican "Contract with America." Regardless of what one thinks of the content of the "Contract," it is obvious that its authors, primarily Newt Gingrich, took great care in titling the various sections.

Section One of the Contract proposed a balanced budget amendment plus a line-item veto for the president. It was titled the "Fiscal Responsibility Act." The title was euphemistic, i.e., made things sound better than they were, in that it is not completely clear that a balanced budget requirement *is* fiscally responsible. (Many economists believe it is necessary for the government to engage in deficit spending during "hard times" in order to "prime the pump" of the national economic engine.)

The title was also a generalization—all titles are. That is a primary function of titles. It was also a simplification, partly because, as we have seen, a balanced budget is not simply a procedure of fiscal responsibility, especially if we take seriously the meaning of the word "responsibility" and the ramifications of that word in terms of the governmental responsibilities for the health of the national economy. The title is also a simplification in terms of the presidential line-item veto. While it is true that a president might veto some portion of a piece of legislation because of a perception that the portion is fiscally irresponsible, other possibilities exist: the portion might be vetoed for ideological reasons, for moral reasons, because it strengthens the president's political party to do so, or in retribution against the author of that portion of the bill. In short, to label the line-item veto "fiscal responsibility" unduly simplifies the uses and results of giving such power to the president.

The second provision of the "Contract" includes measures expanding prison construction, increasing sentences, and reducing the possibility of appeal for death sentence cases. It is titled the "Taking Back Our Streets Act." It can logically be argued that additional prisons in which to incarcerate criminals and longer sentences for them would in some ways allow us to "take back our streets." But it is not clear that such actions would have any more effect on street safety than, say, legalizing drugs so the addicted are not tempted to engage in violence to get their next fix. But at least prisons and longer sentences could be argued to have a relationship to safe streets; the third provision, reducing the possibility of appeal for death sentence cases, is in no way related to safe streets. The choices for those prisoners who want to appeal such sentences are between life imprisonment and the death penalty—getting back on the public streets is not in the equation at all.

I should point out that this second provision is the most popular provision in the contract. At the time the contract was being debated, 78 percent of the public said the government should be spending more money to halt "the rising crime rate." Of course, the crime rate was not rising, but most people did not know that. Ironically, says R. Morin of the *Washington Post*, support for spending to stem the crime rate was higher in 1994 and 1995, when the rate was declining slightly, than it had been when the crime rates were rising, in the 1970s and 1980s.[41]

The third plank in the Contract, called the "Personal Responsibility Act," concerned welfare reform. Here, two semantic phenomena are of interest. First, it is clear that if welfare is to be "reformed" in the sense of getting people off the welfare rolls and into jobs; that is, if the government is going to quit being responsible for people and they are going to become personally responsible for their own economic situation, they must somehow get jobs that pay a living wage . . . and to do so many of them will have to receive extensive training. The catch, wrote politician/journalist J. Fallows, is that it is more expensive to provide the job training and "find, provide and supervise jobs,"[42] than it is just to provide welfare. And since the Contract freezes the amount spent on welfare at the levels of the previous year, it cannot possibly fund these job-related activities that "most welfare analysts believe . . . could possibly bring about changes in a culture of welfare dependency."[43]

A second semantic anomaly about this plank is that its popularity primarily depends on use of the word "welfare" in its descriptive portions. "Welfare" is a word that has fallen upon hard times; Gingrich and Co. have, mistakenly I believe, concluded that the public wants to spend less on the poor and have structured the contract to do so. But public opinion polls do not support that analysis. A December 1994 poll by the University of Chicago's National Opinion Research Center, as reported in the *Washington Post* by R. Morin, found 59 percent of respondents saying the government spends too little on assistance to the poor: "the public wants to reform our public assistance programs. However, the public does not want to punish or neglect the poor, but to provide them with more assistance."[44]

The problems with plank three, therefore, are related directly to the language employed. Generalizing all public assistance for the poor as "welfare," the Republicans mistook the objections to "welfare" as objections to helping the poor. Thus, they froze the monies in this category, making impossible the solution they really preferred: moving people from welfare rolls to work rolls.

I could go on through the remaining seven provisions of the Contract, but that would be redundant. It should be clear by now that these language components interact, overlap, and reinforce each other, and that we critics need to understand not only the individual components but also how they mesh to provide an integrated whole.

## CONCLUSION

▶ While the language choices described in this chapter are not new phenomena, it does seem reasonable to hypothesize that they are newly dangerous.

▶ When the crises that face us are increasingly menacing, the results of miscalculation in a nuclear age increasingly serious, and the need for clarity thus increasingly demanding, continued reliance upon euphemisms may paralyze our ability and willingness to act.

▶ When the problems we face are increasing in complexity, the continued use of simplifications in both problem-description and solution-seeking becomes not just banal, but dishonest and stupid.

▶ When the population increasingly distrusts politicians, and that distrust has reached such proportions that the whole governmental system is distrusted, we know that generalizations are creating too many governing liabilities to be continued, despite their positive influence in persuading voter decisions at the polls.

▶ When the problems we face today turn out to be identical to the problems we were facing five, ten, fifteen, and twenty years ago, we know that politicians have become much too clever at the Art of Saying Nothing, and not clever at all at solving public problems. In a less complicated and dangerous age we could afford the political art of saying nothing, and even find an occasional senatorial windbag charming and quaint. But that day has passed. Though they are sophisticated and slick rather than quaint, the windbags are still with us . . . and will be as long as their rhetorical products can be sold to the consumers.

▶ Our only hope in reforming the societal dialogue, it seems, is to educate those consumers to want a better rhetorical product. It may be a long shot, but it also may be the only race in town. How that education should proceed I cannot say, but I suspect we could do worse than starting with the truths in this story told by an ancient wise man:

A Chinese sage of the distant past was once asked by his disciples what he would do first if he were given power to set right the affairs of his country. He answered: "I certainly should see to it that language is used correctly." The disciples looked perplexed. "Surely," they said, "this is a trivial matter. Why should you deem it so important?" And the Master replied: "If the language is not used correctly, then what is said is not what is meant; if what is said is not what is meant, then what ought to be done remains undone; if this remains undone, morals and art will be corrupted: if morals and art are corrupted, justice will go astray; if justice goes astray, the people will stand about in helpless confusion."

▶ I submit to you that, by and large, the American people today are standing about in helpless confusion . . . and will continue to do so unless they are somehow persuaded that they should be more sophisticated in consuming the language of politics, at least sophisticated enough to insist that politicians begin using language more responsibly. Unfortunately, most Americans, like the disciples of "the master," think the question of language use is "a trivial matter." I hope you no longer share that dismissive attitude.

## FOR FURTHER CONSIDERATION

1. Examine the remaining seven planks of the 1994 "Contract with America" to see whether the titles of those planks exhibit the characteristics of euphemism, generalization, and so forth, that are found in the first three planks.

2. If this chapter is correct in alleging that simplification is endemic in our politics, it should be true that all campaigns are fraught with simplifications. Are they? As you examine any one campaign, watch for simplification via "watered down" language, use of narratives, reliance upon slogans, identifying policies with people (such as "Clintonian," "Dole's proposal"), encapsulating a complicated series of positions under a single rubric ("family values," for instance), and so forth.

## NOTES

1. M. J. Stern, "What We Talk About When We Talk About Welfare," *Tikkun* 9 (November/December 1994): 29.

2. M. Tolchin, "First Principles of Artful Ambiguity," *New York Times,* 24 January 1984, p. A18.

3. M. G. Singer, "The Pragmatic Use of Language and the Will to Believe," *American Philosophical Quarterly* 8 (January 1971): 27.

4. W. Gibson, *Euphemism,* Harper Studies in Language and Literature pamphlet (New York: Harper and Row, 1974), p. 8.

5. *Ibid.,* 11.

6. G. Cheney, "'Talking War': Symbols, Strategies, and Images," *Studies on the Left* 14 (Winter 1990–91): 8.

7. R. L. Ivie, "Images of Savagery in American Justifications for War," *Communication Monographs* 47 (November 1980): 284.

8. Cheney, *op. cit.,* 10.

9. Gibson, *op. cit.*, 20.

10. W. Safire, "On Surgical Strike," *New York Times Magazine,* 16 June 1986, p. 12.

11. Cheney, *op. cit.*, 14.

12. A. Lewis, "The Buck Doesn't Stop," *New York Times,* 12 November 1984, p. A19.

13. *Ibid.*, A19.

14. B. Keller, "Essential, They Say, but Repugnant," *New York Times,* 20 January 1986, p. A24.

15. J. LeMoyne, "El Salvador Gets New U.S. Gunship," *New York Times,* 9 January 1985, p. A5.

16. L. R. Beres, "Embracing Omnicide: President Reagan and the Strategic Mythmakers," *Hudson Review* 36 (Spring 1983): 18.

17. Gibson, *op. cit.*, 17.

18. E. Hall, "The Freakish Passion; A Conversation with George Steiner," *Psychology Today,* February 1973, 66–67.

19. R. Baker, "American Fat," *New York Times,* 4 January 1973, p. 37.

20. F. Heer, "Man's Three Languages," *Center Magazine* 4 (December 1971): 66.

21. *Ibid.*, 67.

22. G. Brown, "The Conclusion of Ronald Reagan's Narrative: The Rest of the Story" (paper presented at the annual convention of the Southern States Communication Association, Louisville, KY, April 1989), 3–4.

23. M. Edelman, "On Policies That Fail," *Progressive,* May 1975, 23.

24. R. Baker, "The Process Epidemic," *New York Times,* 9 January 1969, p. 30.

25. T. H. Middleton, "Easy Solutions," *Saturday Review,* 12 July 1975, 61.

26. A. Berger, "Hot Language and Cool Lives," in *Language Awareness,* eds. P. A. Eschholz, A. F. Rosa, and V. P. Clark (New York: St. Martin's, 1974), 240.

27. R. P. Snow, *Creating Media Culture* (Beverly Hills: Sage, 1983), 25.

28. Edelman, *op. cit.*, 22.

29. J. K. Galbraith, "Who Needs the Democrats?" *Harper's,* July 1970, 56.

30. *Ibid.*, 56.

31. S. Brown, "The Politics of Peace," *Washington Monthly,* August 1970, 31.

32. S. R. Weisman, "The President and the Press; The Art of Controlled Access," *New York Times Magazine,* 14 October 1984, p. 80.

33. R. Marcus, "The White House Isn't Telling Us the Truth," *Washington Post National Weekly Edition,* 29 August–4 September 1994, p. 28.

34. Galbraith, *op. cit.*, 58.

35. E. G. Bormann, "A Fantasy Theme Analysis of the Television Coverage of the Hostage Release and the Reagan Inaugural," *Quarterly Journal of Speech* 68 (May 1982): 139.

36. M. Edelman, "Myths, Metaphors, and Political Conformity," *Psychiatry* 30 (August 1967): 222.

37. E. F. Goldman, "Party of One; On Presidential Prose," *Holiday,* April 1963, 18.

38. Edelman (1967), *op. cit.*, 221.

39. D. F. Hahn, "Nixon's Second (Hortatory) Inaugural," *Speaker and Gavel* 10 (May 1973): 113.

40. *Ibid.*, 113.

41. R. Morin, "What the Public Really Wants," *Washington Post National Weekly Edition,* 9–15 January 1995, p. 37.

42. J. Fallows, "The Republican Promise," *New York Review of Books,* 12 January 1995, 5.

43. *Ibid.*, 5.

44. Morin, *op. cit.*, 37.

# CHAPTER SEVEN

# Myths and Metaphors

> *. . . out of the mingled feelings that the multitude will prevail, and that the multitude, because it will prevail, must be right, there grows a self-distrust, a despondency, a disposition to fall in line . . . a loss of resisting power, a diminished sense of personal responsibility, and of the duty to battle for one's own opinions.*
> — JAMES BRYCE, 1870

D o not let the basic terms of this chapter throw you; they are not that complicated. By "myth" I do not mean green dragons and purple people-eaters, but a much more ordinary phenomenon: certain societal "truths" we tend to believe without any evidence. "Metaphor," too, is a relatively simple concept. A metaphor is merely a figure of speech in which a word for one idea or thing is used in place of another to suggest a likeness between them, as in "the ship *plows* the sea."

In this chapter I shall look first at metaphor, examining it not only as a basic language form but as a form often employed in politics. In doing so I lean heavily upon the approach of Kenneth Burke, a rhetorical theorist whose considerations of metaphoric language I find particularly insightful, and whom some people consider the most important rhetorical theorist of the twentieth century. I then examine three basic American political myths laid out by Professor Murray Edelman, a political scientist who has been heavily influenced by Kenneth Burke. Next, I consider a series of five myths identified by another political scientist, Michael Parenti, then provide a short examination of some types of metaphors that seem to reinforce the myths Parenti identifies. I end with a brief mention of some "lesser" myths of our society. Throughout the chapter you will find an interweaving of myths, metaphor, and political language. I hope you do not find that those three are too many skeins to keep track of at once, for understanding their relationships is basic to understanding how political language works.

## ▶ A Burkeian Approach to Language: Water Metaphors

Much of the rhetorical strength of basic metaphors (i.e., those based on common life experiences) is that they come from phenomena all audiences know about—air, fire, earth, water, human anatomy, the animal world, the seasons, "gardening" (planting, growing, decaying), and so forth. That prior

113

audience knowledge means the rhetor does not have to expend additional time and effort on meaning; "he's a bear of a man" is clear to most audiences.

At the same time, however, all metaphors (but especially the basic ones) carry with them a good deal of extra "baggage," so they are not as simple and direct as they seem at first blush. In that sense, then, via metaphors we express what we were not aware we were saying. For most audience members, "he's a bear of a man" means merely that the referent is a big person. To others, who have had nasty experiences with bears, it may mean the man is dangerous or dangerously powerful. Others may call to mind bear cubs, and conclude that the speaker is saying the man is playful, cuddly, and clumsy. Some may reflect on differences between humans and "lower" animals and conclude the speaker is classifying the man as something of a brute, less than human.

For the critic, the process of "teasing out" which of the possible meanings the speaker had in mind and which were "heard" by various audience members is a complicated one. To demonstrate something of the complications, I propose to look at water metaphors, relying heavily on the insights of Kenneth Burke.

My introduction to Burke as a political language theorist came when I attempted a Burkeian analysis of Goldwater's acceptance speech at the 1964 Republican convention. Following Burke, I looked at the imagery—and found the whole message could be summarized by collapsing Goldwater's images into one paragraph:

> Due to "foggy thinking," "the tide has been running against freedom" and we are sinking in a "swampland of collectivism." Therefore, despite the detractors who say "don't rock the boat," the "campaign that we launch here" will "set the tide running again in the cause of freedom." The "past will be submerged" and we will travel democracy's "ocean highway" where freedom will accompany the "rising tide of prosperity."

That was, I still think, the essence of the Goldwater message of 1964. But look again at the imagery. Note the number of liquid images—foggy, tide, submerged, ocean. Now think of Barry Goldwater, from the landlocked, partially desert, state of Arizona. Why is this man using water imagery? (Maybe he was in the Navy? No, the Air Force.) At the time, I could not give an answer—the only one that occurred to me, the fact that his name was Gold*water*, seemed inadequate. After all, the water images were mostly negative and I did not think he had a negative self-image.

Then I located an unpublished address given by Michael Osborn, a professor of speech communication at Memphis State University.[1] In it, Osborn argues that water imagery normally is used by those who perceive danger. It was a simple answer. And I applied it simply (simplemindedly?) to solve my conundrum. Goldwater saw the Ship of State in troubled water and wanted to save it by installing a new captain at the helm.

That insight allowed me to "close the book" on my Goldwater study, but it opened up a whole new vista. For the more I thought about it, the more I realized how central metaphor is to language and how ubiquitous it is in politics. To demonstrate the role of metaphor in political communication, let's stick with water imagery a few more minutes.

Water is one of the basic elements. Therefore, it is available for all kinds of uses, including to indicate danger. But water is also a cleansing agent. Thus, in politics we expect water metaphors of the danger variety to describe problems, those of the cleansing variety to describe solutions. That it is reasonable for water metaphors to be widely used in politics becomes more apparent, Professor Chris Johnstone of Penn State reminds us, when we realize that "govern" and "governor" originated from the Greek "gnomen," the name for the pilot who steered ships through narrow harbors.[2]

But water is also a romantic metaphor—the trite moon on a quiet lake, the archetypal midnight walk on the beach, the poetic suggestion of intercourse from the rhythmic sound of the waves pounding the sand, the 1960s poster urging us to "conserve water. Take a shower with a friend." And on and on.

It should also be remembered that many biologists think life started in the ocean (or the "ooze"). If we add the Burkeian idea of reversal (the fact that every concept has a polar opposite) we immediately perceive that if birth is introduced by oceanic metaphors, then death must be too. Both are related metaphorically to the ocean.

Birth and death—related via water metaphors and liquid realities; birth and death—basic processes; water—a basic element. It begins to make sense that our primary (even primal) concerns are encapsulated in the basic elements—earth, air, fire, water. And it also makes sense, of course, that those elements would be used as central images by our major institutions—politics and religion.

The ways in which religion and politics suggest and reflect each other should not be overlooked, for once the correspondence is suggested metaphorically, other interlocking perspectives are implied. Consider how a water metaphor that inherently carries both positive and negative implications—life and death—might animate the ways in which both politics and religion are suffused with negativism. For instance, in trying to "overcome" death by stressing an afterlife, religion is inevitably fear-producing. That is, the positive future being promised depends upon negating the present. Further, this wonderful future is attained through following a series of thou-shalt-nots. Negativism pervades. Now look at the Bill of Rights of the United States Constitution. Do you not find here a secular version of the Ten Commandments, a series of thou-shalt-nots that not only parallel several religions but suggest them, both in the magic number ten and in the negative approach? Even the words "Amendment" and "Commandment" sound alike, especially, one assumes, to the young religious citizen just learning of each in elementary school.

Before leaving the religion-politics parallel, but returning to our concern with water imagery, we might remember the importance of water in baptism, the political use of rivers, lakes, and oceans as national boundaries, the asserted ability of Christ to walk on water, and the military importance of ships and submarines. Life, death, religion, and politics all seem related to the water and to water imagery.

While it may seem to stretch the water metaphor nearly to the breaking point, I want, finally, to apply the general points here to a phenomenon from the 1960s. The 1968 Democratic nominating convention was held in Chicago.

Lyndon Johnson's handpicked successor, Hubert Humphrey, was to be nominated. Objecting to that impending nomination because they assumed Humphrey would continue Johnson's Vietnam policies, the youth of the "Peace Movement" descended upon the city to make their concerns known. Lacking money for hotel rooms (which were probably all booked anyway), most Movement participants stayed in public parks or slept "in the streets." Mayor Daley, Chicago's Democratic "boss" and a staunch supporter of Lyndon Johnson, did everything possible to make Chicago inhospitable to these young "visitors"—including having the police chase them from the parks, keeping them from "assembling," and locking public toilets.

As the clashes between the well-armed police and the unarmed demonstrators escalated in intensity, the young people hit upon a novel tactic. Having been denied access to toilets, they had "coped" by defecating in paper bags and urinating into balloons, which were then placed in the garbage containers. But as the police prodded and chased them, the protesters started using these waste matters as ammunition, throwing them at the police or dropping them on Daley's forces from tall buildings.

To at least this critic, the whole episode seems related to the concern we've been considering. The water is different, diuretic rather than oceanic, and the religious and political motives are subdued—but they are lurking there someplace.

Important to my analysis is the fact that toilet training is one of the earliest "civilizing" rules to which humans are subjected. Thus, breaking that first, most elemental inhibition is an incipient political act, for in breaking the first rule you learn, you threaten all other rules. The demonstrators, I suspect, had at least some dim recognition of this meaning as they hurled their bags of urine and excrement at the police. And the audience, I suspect, shared some of that dim understanding, for the American people overwhelmingly sided with the police— because, at base, "letting loose" is a revolutionary act, a revolt that revolts, a refutation of the infantile "no, no" of toilet training that implicitly denies *all* negations, especially the thou-shalt-nots of Church and State.

I have wandered pretty far afield from Goldwater's acceptance speech, I grant you. But that is what tends to happen when one tries to follow the various connections of political metaphors. Any phenomenon as central to politics as metaphors are is bound to lead in many directions simultaneously.

## ▶ Metaphor and "Terministic Compulsion"

So let's start off on another trek, this time to discover how metaphors provide arguments through the principle of terministic perfection and thereby reveal our individual thought patterns. We will begin with Penn State communication professor Tom Benson's article on "Poisoned Minds," an examination of the metaphor so often used in our society by those decrying the effects of some kind of literature—these days, usually pornography. These people, says Benson, talk as though the mind were a stomach with ears. And, since there is no way to give "an intellectual dose of mustard and warm water," those who use the metaphor naturally gravitate toward censorship as a solution: keep the poison out of the reach of the children because there is no antidote.[3]

Benson goes on to refute the assumptions of the metaphor, but that is not important for our purposes. What is important is an understanding of how one's chosen images lead directly to one's political solutions. Burke speaks of the principle of perfection that is implicit in any symbol system, providing "a kind of 'terministic compulsion' to carry out the implications of one's terminology."[4] In the present example, if one *de*scribes pornography as "poison," that term "compels" the rhetor to *pre*scribe a solution compatible with the description. In short, if you know the metaphors with which people describe a problem, you may be able to predict the nature of their solution even before they figure it out. Or to put it another way, you may know more about their thinking than they do. "Every writer has some . . . favorite images . . . that are analogous to a psychological tic."[5]

In his provocative essay, "The Second Persona," Edwin Black exemplified this point. Contending that the Far Right had taken over "exclusive property" of the communism-as-cancer metaphor, i.e., the idea that communism is analogous to a "cancer" on the "body politic," he examined that metaphor to find its "terministic compulsions." The result? He found that the metaphor and Rightist ideology are "not merely compatible; they are complementary at every curve and angle." That is, he found that the *de*scriptive metaphor "communism is a cancer" led those who used it to call for communists to be "cut out" of society. He also concluded that "there are strong and multifarious links between a style and an outlook,"[6] which is another way of saying that speakers create their own "terministic compulsions." In short, Black provided evidence that metaphor analysis can not only lead a critic to a rhetor's psychological tics; it can uncover ideologies.

But I keep wondering whether it did in this case. Granted that the cancer-of-communism metaphor was taken over by the Right, is that metaphor a *significant* variation of the genre of disease-remedy metaphors? Indeed, John Halverson's analysis of the writings of Robert Welch (founder of the John Birch Society) suggests that cancer was only one of the disease metaphors of this Rightist spokesman, who spoke often of viruses and festering boils. According to Halverson, use of disease-remedy metaphors allows destructive impulses to be "channeled into the 'respectable' figures of surgery and given a civilized guise."[7]

Of course, both Black and Halverson are anti-Rightist. One wonders how they would analyze a different disease-remedy metaphor—like this 1973 specimen, for example: "The body politic of America is on the operating table today. Watergate is the wound, an independent prosecutor must be the surgeon and Congress must supervise the operation on behalf of all the people of the country. If we do not heal the wound, if we do not investigate the case completely, if we allow a prosecutor to be appointed who is independent in name but not in fact, then we shall be sewing up the wound with the infection still inside."[8] Communism is not mentioned, nor is cancer. But the pattern is familiar; not, I think, because it is a Rightist style but because of the commonness of disease-remedy metaphors. (The example, incidentally, is from a speech by a leading liberal, Ted Kennedy.) And if the communism-as-cancer metaphor is only an extreme example of the common disease-remedy pattern, then perhaps in their language, as in so many other of their characteristics, the Far Right is just like the rest of us, only more so.

The realization that metaphor analysis might have led Black and Halverson to some false (or at least misleading) conclusions about Rightists and the possibility that analysis of the metaphors of an individual or a group might flounder on the shoals of broader societal metaphors suggest we should turn our attention to those broader societal beliefs and the metaphors with which they are communicated. To do so, let's examine the works of Murray Edelman, a political scientist whose groundbreaking work is indispensable to anyone studying political rhetoric.

## ▶ Edelman and American Mythology

We've seen that metaphors reveal individual thought patterns, but they also may reveal societal thought patterns, or myths. (Societal thought patterns are called "myths," not because they are wrong or fanciful, but because they tend to be accepted as true without proof, much as children accept the existence of ghosts or unicorns without proof.) Edelman contends that there are three basic American political myths: (1) all problems are caused by outgroups; (2) our leaders are benevolent heroes who will lead us out of danger; and (3) the function of the citizen is to sacrifice and work hard to do the bidding of the leaders.[9] Edelman did not examine the relation between these myths and societal metaphors, but the relationship is strongly implied by all the foregoing. That is, if there are *basic* political thought patterns (myths) that are accepted as true without proof, and if metaphors—as is often contended—are useful in helping to explain the unknown by analogy to the known, then it stands to reason that the basic myths would be "explained" or at least stated metaphorically. Let's see whether that is the case with the myths Edelman identified.

*All problems are caused by outgroups*, whether the ubiquitous "they" (as in "they did it") or some specified group. Outgroups are the archetypal forces of darkness, whether we are talking of the "black hand of tyranny" in international relations or identifying some "black-hearted villain" in domestic politics. In the water metaphor, too, we see this myth at work, as in the "tide of communism" threatening the "Ship of State."

Our problems are never caused by us. Some omnipresent "other" caused poverty, so we can mount a war against them. Our weapons are needed not because of anything *we* might want (Texas, Puerto Rico, Philippines, Grenada), but purely because of the existence of an "Evil Empire." Do we have racial problems? There must be outside agitators! Do we have inflation? There must be greedy union leaders! (Note that management never causes inflation when Republicans are in power and that unions are blameless when Democrats are in power.)

The thought that outsiders are at fault is a comfortable myth, because it means we do not have to engage in soul-searching or evaluate our own actions except in terms of whether they are sufficient to destroy the evil influences of those terrible others. The conspiracy theory of politics, embraced by both Far Right and Far Left, therefore, is merely the logical extension of the outgroup myth accepted by the Center. Theoretically, then, either end of the political spectrum is capable of capturing much of the vast middle at any given point.

The first myth blends in well with the second, that *our leaders are benevolent heroes who will lead us out of danger*. Metaphorically, they will provide the light to lead us out of darkness. They will calm the stormy sea and lead the ship of state into safe harbor. They will cut away the cancerous growth of communism and give us a healthy transfusion of capitalism.

They (and only they) know how to solve problems. This is how President Nixon established his preeminence as heroic, all-knowing leader in his address at Kansas State University in 1970: "I am, perhaps, more aware of the problems this nation has at home and abroad than most of you."[10] So who should solve our problems, the rest of us, who are unaware, or the president? But might not turning things over to a president risk despotism? Not with Nixon—his pronouns typed him as a *benevolent* leader. In his speeches, the pronoun "I" tended to be followed by action verbs, while "we" and "us" tended to be in the receiving position. The formula, then, was "I, President Nixon, have acted and we, the citizens, receive the benefits of the action."

If presidents "don" the mantle of office, much as one might "don" a mask, perhaps we can gain some insight into the process from examining cultures in which masks played a larger role than they do here today. When we do so we discover that although everybody in the primitive tribe recognizes that a member of the tribe is wearing the ceremonial mask, the recognition in no way undermines the ritual in which the masked tribesman is participating. According to mythologist J. Campbell, "He does not merely represent the God: he is the God."[11]

In like manner, our presidents do not just assume the office of the presidency, they *become* the office and thereafter have trouble distinguishing an attack on themselves from an attack upon the office. When Nixon's Watergate problems arose, his consistent position was that he was protecting the office, not himself. He could not release tapes because that would destroy the confidentiality of the office. And many believed him.

We do have an overpowering tendency to believe and make heroes of our leaders. As one of my political science professors once said, the American people had trouble revering Eisenhower as much as they wanted to because they already had a Father, Son, and Holy Ghost and couldn't work Ike into the sacred triumvirate. Our hero-worship gives incumbents several important advantages. First, they can take action against some "outgroup" and, since the results of any action are hard to measure, be presumed to have done the right thing. Taking action, thus, is more important than solving problems because they *seem* to be coping with the problems. If they actually solved the problems, of course, the result could be deleterious to them—as Churchill discovered when he was ousted from office after World War II. That is to say, if we elect somebody to solve problem X, and problem X is solved, we assume we no longer need that person . . . just as when we hire somebody to repair the water main, we no longer need those services once the main is fixed.

Another advantage of societal hero-worship is that the hero can *seem* to take action without actually doing so and thus gain "points" from every side. This is accomplished through what President Johnson used to call "jawboning." (And note the power that accrues to the user of such a phrase, thanks to the Biblical significance of a jawbone.) When Johnson castigated management, or Reagan jawboned unions, the consumers assumed the hero was protecting them, while managements and unions realized that they were still perfectly free to do whatever they wanted. The hero supposedly had acted, so the people were happy. Those involved knew he had not acted, so they were happy. Everybody won, especially the "jawboner."

If we are threatened by outside forces from which we can be saved by a leader, the third myth is obvious: *the function of the citizen is to sacrifice and work hard to do the bidding of the leader.* After all, a leader only can lead if there are followers to follow. There are common metaphors supporting this myth—"Too many cooks spoil the broth," "Too many chiefs, not enough Indians," and so forth.

The water, black-white, and disease-remedy metaphors we have been examining also apply to this myth, although not as strongly as to the other two. These metaphors are primarily applied to those who refuse to accept their role as followers. Those who strike off on their own may be referred to as "black sheep." If they get in trouble they are said to be "in deep water" or "in over their heads." And, of course, if they wander too far from the accepted path they may be considered "sick" and locked up in an asylum until they are well again.

Note also that the religious concept of discipleship reinforces the myth of the obedient follower. Like the citizen, the disciple is to follow quietly, except when propagandizing nonbelievers. Religions, too, are composed of silent majoritarians.

The citizen, says psychologist E. Fromm, "sees in the rulers the powerful ones, the strong, and the wise—persons to be revered. Citizens believe the rulers wish them well; they also know that resistance to those in power always is punished; so they are content when by docility they can win praise from these 'more superior' persons. These are the identical feelings which, as children, they had for their parents, and it is understandable that they are as disposed to believe uncritically what is presented to them by the rulers as just and true, as in childhood they used to believe without criticism every statement made by their parents. The figure of God forms a supplement to this situation; God is always the ally of the rulers. When the latter [who are always real personalities] are exposed to criticism, they can rely on God, who, by virtue of His unreality [in the temporal world] only scorns criticism and, by His authority, confirms the authority of the ruling class."[12]

Leaders reinforce the myth of the sacrificing followers with their rhetoric. Churchill offered Great Britain "blood, sweat, toil, and tears" and Kennedy reminded Americans to "ask not what your country can do for you, but what you can do for your country." Reagan undercut the myth slightly by arguing that all citizens can be heroes merely by doing their jobs. (The myth normally calls for citizen sacrifice, but Reagan implied no sacrifice was necessary.) But the real erosion of the myth came from Nixon's inability to inspire his followers. Analyzing Nixon's First Inaugural, rhetorical critic Robert Cathcart lamented Nixon's "reluctance to ask for sacrifice or new government programs" in the face of continuing crises, concluding that Nixon's "appeal is to those who want to occupy that comfortable moral middle ground between ease and sacrifice."[13]

Indeed, it is not surprising that Johnson and Nixon were unpopular or that we were critical of their Vietnam policies. They made life too easy; they minimized our sacrifices and maximized their responsibilities. In short, they overemphasized their roles as heroes and underemphasized our mythical role as sacrificing followers.

If the leader does not tell us how we can help, we feel unfulfilled, useless. We experience anomie (purposelessness, rootlessness). Our myth structure collapses and the leader becomes one of the "others," one of the outsiders. "Our" leader must then be defeated by a "man on a white horse," a new leader who will use our following to chase out the shadowy figure who arrogantly is posing as our leader and justifying his policies by constant reference to a largely nonexistent followership called "the silent majority." In short, Nixon's mythical following damaged the American myth about the role of followers and created a vague, uneasy feeling of helplessness. This feeling, in turn, weakened his ability to be perceived as a heroic leader and led us to wonder who the enemy really was.

So where are we? We have examined the nature of metaphors and found that through them we express what we were not aware we were saying. Metaphors provide arguments through the principle of terministic perfection. They reveal our individual thought patterns. Collectively, they reveal our societal thought patterns. And societal thought patterns are myths, some of which we have discussed.

But the myths we have examined, concerning where problems are thought to come from, whether the president is a benevolent leader, and the role of the citizen, are not the kind we meet every day in our political arguments. It is those "everyday" myths, I assume, that we should be most aware of, for they are the ones we are most likely to encounter in our daily lives . . . or even to use in our own argumentation. Therefore, I turn my attention to a series of axioms that political scientist Michael Parenti has identified as so common in our political rhetoric that they might well be considered myths by now.[14]

## ▶ A Parentian Approach

The myths that Parenti identified and that we will consider are: "you can't fight City Hall," "our leaders know best," "you cannot legislate morality," "the more things change the more they remain the same," and "it doesn't make any difference whom we elect, they're all the same." I chose these five from Parenti's list because they are functionally related—they all encourage passivity and conformity, a point to which I'll return after examining each phrase individually.

First, *"you can't fight City Hall."* I suspect we all have heard this locution at some point in our lives, perhaps even used it ourselves. It is a rationalization for quitting, normally delivered with a shrug that says, "I'd try, but what's the use?" The myth implies that we should not expect the government to respond to our demands; that we are too small and ineffectual to be considered, while the government is too big and powerful to be challenged. In effect, the phrase says the conservatives have been right all along: the government cannot solve our problems, or, in Reagan's formulation, government *is* the problem.

To the degree that we accept the "you can't fight City Hall" myth, we acquiesce in leaving government in the hands of the privileged and powerful . . . to legislate on behalf of themselves and their friends. That acceptance, in turn, means that there are far fewer people to object to governmental actions, making it easier for the government to treat those few to ridicule, attack and punishment because it is assumed that *any* proposal will attract a few nay-saying oddballs. So in the 1950s and '60s civil-rights leaders were called communists and investigated by the F.B.I. (which had over seven hundred pages on Martin Luther King, though most of it documented his sex life rather than any danger in his political activities). In the '60s and '70s anti-war protesters were called communist sympathizers (or, in Vice President Spiro Agnew's formulation, "com-symps") and investigated by the F.B.I. In the 1980s those opposed to government policies concerning El Salvador and Nicaragua were investigated by the F.B.I. (In more than two hundred cases, the F.B.I. illegally broke into organization offices to steal their records of membership and activity.)

However, and fortunately, not everybody has accepted the "you can't fight City Hall" dictum. As Parenti points out, "Many people still organize, agitate, protest, resist, and fight back—sometimes with an impressive measure of success. In recent decades we have witnessed a number of powerful democratic movements: the civil rights protests to enfranchise African Americans in the South and end lynch-mob rule and segregation, the civil liberties struggle against McCarthyism and government harassment of dissidents, the movement to end the Vietnam War, the anti-imperialist solidarity for El Salvador and Nicaragua, the attempts to build alternative educational and informational institutions, the movement for a nuclear freeze and an end to the arms race, and the struggles for women's rights, gay rights, ecology, and environmentalism."[15] So we *can* fight City Hall. And occasionally (though, obviously not always) we can win.

A second hardy myth is that *"our leaders know best."* And our leaders actively feed the myth. Lyndon Johnson was fond of saying, "I'm the only president you've got," and Richard Nixon, as I mentioned earlier, claimed, "I am, perhaps, more aware of the problems this nation has at home and abroad than most of you." Actually, Nixon started establishing his omniscient knowledge claim in his first Inaugural Address, in which he announced, "I know America's youth," "I know the leaders of the world," "I know the people of the world," and "I know America." Clearly, here was a president who knew best!

Most of the time, of course, we recognize that the president *doesn't* know best, but we tend to forget that truth in times of crisis. In a war, for instance, we are more likely to accept the idea that we should have faith in our leaders because they will "see us through" this difficulty. Yet, as Michael Parenti has commented, "what is overlooked is that they are likely the ones who *created* the crisis and should be held accountable for their actions. It is the essence of democracy that we *not* trust and 'have faith' in our leaders. Democracy is a system built on *dis*trust and accountability. At its heart is the idea that we must watch leaders closely, question them sharply, demand investigation, information, explanation, and open debate about policies."[16]

We have a lot of political talk in this country, an abundance of charges and countercharges, but we seldom have what Parenti said we need: open debate. The last *big* debate in the U.S. Congress, and in the country at large, immediately preceded our entry to the Gulf War. And it seemed like an open debate, with practically every member of both the House and the Senate taking part. But it was not an open debate—it was bogus from the "get-go," because President Bush had announced that he would not be influenced by the debate nor the resultant congressional vote, but would himself make the decision on whether to go to war. That presidential announcement reduced the debate to a sham exercise and simultaneously undermined the democratic premise of rule by the people and the constitutional provision that Congress should make the decision to declare war. Yet many in Congress, and most citizens, acquiesced in Bush's action because "our leader knows best."

Our third enduring political myth, often trotted out to explain and justify our unwillingness to tackle tough problems, is the idea that *"you cannot legislate morality."* This was a central argument used in the 1950s and 1960s against passing the civil-rights laws. Because the injustices were caused by prejudice, went the argument, and because prejudice cannot be solved by laws, legislation against those injustices would not solve the problems.

But this myth is wrong—in several ways. First, it incorrectly assumes that laws are directed primarily, or only, at the causes of behavior, and that the primary purpose of law is to eradicate those causes. But a little thought explodes that assumption—none of us presumes that the law against murder will eliminate all murderous thoughts. Rather, the law deters us from acting on those thoughts. When the law fails in its deterrence function, it still may be efficacious in its secondary function: punishment. Further, we hope the punishment meted out to one person will reinforce the deterrence function for others. In short, laws are *primarily* directed at actions, at behaviors, and only secondarily at thoughts—murderous thoughts, larcenous thoughts, prejudiced thoughts. The proposed civil-rights laws were to be laws against certain actions; whether those actions were caused by prejudice, ignorance, malice, greed, or patriotism was not a relevant question.

The second way in which the "you cannot legislate morality" myth is wrong is that it ignores the teaching function of law. There is a dialectical relationship between the teachings of the major institutions of the culture. If families, churches, schools, and government (via the law) teach that a behavior is wrong, their mutually reinforced teaching is powerful. But if even one of those institutions teaches otherwise, it can undermine all the others' teachings. Your family and church may teach that premarital sex is wrong; your sex education class may teach that it is stupid and immature; but as long as it is legal you are more likely to give in to the temptation. Your church, school, and government may all teach that taking drugs is wrong, but if "doing drugs" is a common occurrence in your family, the admonitions of those other three institutions are less likely to be effective.

So the relationship between morality and law is more ambiguous and complicated than the "you cannot legislate morality" axiom suggests. Indeed, Michael Parenti has gone so far as to suggest that not only can the law reinforce the morality teachings of other institutions, it also can encourage us to engage in *im*moral acts. He points out that the laws in Hitler's Germany turned normal people into SS torturers and killers. How did he know they were "normal people?" Because after the war, when the law no longer encouraged them to be murderers, most of them returned to leading "inconspicuously peaceful law-abiding lives."[17] So Parenti concluded that "the law not only can legislate morality, it can encourage immorality—which is the other side of the same coin."[18]

Rhetorically, then, the "you cannot legislate morality" myth functions to persuade people to give up on the law as an avenue for bringing the power of the state into consonance with the dominant morality of the citizens. In short, the myth is wrong where the morality in question is reinforced by the teachings of other major institutions from which we learn our morals. It is right only when the proposed "moral law" is undermined by countervailing rhetoric from a significant percentage of families, churches, and schools.

The fourth myth in Parenti's rhetorical formulations is *"the more things change, the more they remain the same."* This myth says history is "a dreary repetition of human folly and injustice."[19] It is a pessimistic formulation that somehow has managed to persist in this basically optimistic country, though I must admit that optimism has been waning in the latter part of the twentieth century. At the end of the nineteenth century a common belief was that "every day in every way the world is getting better and better," but as we approach the end of the twentieth we are likely to substitute "worse and worse" for "better and better."

Yet things demonstrably *have* gotten better. Consider, for instance, the three-hundred-year improvement in the lot of laborers. We have gone from conditions of near slavery to serfdom to underpaid sweatshop labor to organized well-paid labor. And the government, widely perceived these days as ineffectual, has been involved every step of the way, having initiated or endorsed by law "collective bargaining, arbitration, formal grievances, occupational safety, job benefits, unemployment insurance, seniority, and medical coverage."[20]

Or consider the improvements in conditions of and for women. Consider the movement from being considered property, to having limited property rights, to equity in the right to own and dispose of property. Consider the change from being barred from voting and holding office, to legal equity in the right to vote and be elected. Consider the improvement from absolutely no entry to the job market, to limited entry to low-paying jobs, to near-equity in the right to hold high-paying positions. Consider the movement from no access to birth control and safe abortions to fairly good access, at least for upper- and middle-class women.

Or consider the changes in the lives of African-Americans in the last two hundred years—from slavery to segregation to legal integration.

I do not mean to suggest there are no more battles for workers and women and African-Americans. The situations of all three groups still can and should be improved. But it is not true, for them, that "the more things change the more they remain the same." Important changes *have* taken place; things have *not* remained the same.

Again, the rhetorical function of the myth is to discourage us from attacking societal problems. To the degree we are convinced that the more things change the more they remain the same, to that degree we are persuaded to accept the status quo, not even to try for improvement. Ultimately, the myth has a hand in persuading us that the government can do *nothing* right. This myth and the rhetoric based on it have been important contributors to the contemporary success of the conservative movement, for the conservatives want the government to undertake less. If they can persuade us that government actions are always ineffective we may vote for them *even if* we *want* some changes made, i.e., even if we do not accept their ideology.

In this country, the idea that the more things change the more they remain the same leads to a corollary myth: *"it doesn't make any difference whom we elect, they're all the same."* Or, as practically everybody's charming maiden aunt is claimed to have phrased it, "Oh, my dear, don't vote—it only encourages them."

Yet the idea that there are no differences among politicians is obviously untrue. There are clear and important differences—moral, ethical, and ideological—between the Carters and Reagans, the Bushes and Clintons of this world. But I grant that it often *looks* as though it doesn't make any difference, so let me identify some reasons for that erroneous perception.

First, it doesn't look as though it makes any difference whom we vote for because the whole government is not changed. We reelect a large proportion of those in the House of Representatives—normally over 90 percent of them. Only one-third of Senate seats are even available in any election year. The Supreme Court changes little and slowly. The bureaucracy changes little and slowly.

Second, we citizens disagree on what we want, and on most issues divide along liberal-conservative lines in roughly equal proportions. Thus politicians, regardless of personal beliefs, are forced to hew fairly closely to the ideological midpoint. President Reagan was not, in office, as conservative as his campaign rhetoric had implied he would be, nor as conservative as his more right-wing supporters wanted. President Clinton is not, in office, as liberal as his campaign rhetoric had implied he would be, nor as liberal as his more left-wing supporters want.

Third, change is incremental. There were hundreds of steps between slave labor and well-paid union labor. But when we want action, when we want change, we want it *now,* not spread out over a two-hundred-year period.

So politicians are *not* alike. It *does* make a difference whom we vote for— it just doesn't, most of the time, make *as much* difference as we would like it to. And, it should be admitted, those of us who are involved in politics get a little tired of those who say it doesn't make any difference for whom we vote. Molly Ivins, the plain-speaking Texan political commentator, says it shouldn't take more than ten minutes "to figure which of two evils is the lesser, which of two dingbats vying for public office is just a shade brighter."[21]

I said earlier that these five myths were related. Let me now return to that point. I would argue that what the five have in common is that they all encourage passivity and conformity. Look at them again in that light:

▶ You can't fight City Hall, so you might as well not even try.

▶ Our leaders know best, so we should silence our objections and follow these wise ones.

▶ You cannot legislate morality, so don't even bring up the behaviors you object to. Work within the private sector; be one of Bush's "thousand points of light."

▶ The more things change the more they remain the same, so even if you got government to enact a law it wouldn't accomplish anything.

▶ It doesn't make any difference whom we elect, so don't bother to try to understand any differences among the candidates or their political parties or their platforms. Vote for the guy (so far, *guy*) you like . . . or think is smarter . . . or more handsome . . . or whatever. But VOTE—it's your duty. Your ONLY DUTY! Other, that is, than paying taxes (to support programs that wouldn't have existed if we'd voted for the other guy) and dying in a war (which we wouldn't have been involved in if we had voted for the other guy). But it doesn't make any difference whom we elect—as long as HE (so far) is a member of the ELECT.

So our cultural belief structure, captured in Parenti's myths, encourage passivity and conformity. But they do not do so in isolation; they are reinforced by discrete word choices dominant in our political rhetoric, especially by our political metaphors.

## ▶ Common Political Metaphors

Hundreds of metaphors used by politicians, and by us, encourage us to be passive and conforming, allowing the government free rein to do whatever it wants. In the interests of time, I'll mention only several metaphors.

First, some metaphors give human characteristics to government. We refer to the president as the *head* of state. Police are identified as the *long arm* of the law. We citizens, who live in the *heart*land, are the *body* politic. You will immediately note how these metaphors encourage passivity: the head controls the arms, the heart, the body. Therefore, we should do what the head says!

Second, we use a series of metaphors to characterize ideologically the people and programs we do not like. We've already seen how civil-rights leaders and anti-war sympathizers were characterized as communists and communist sympathizers. So let's consider how the same process has been used to attack a policy.

In 1994 the Clinton administration proposed a universal health care program. It immediately was attacked as "socialized medicine." The attack was effective but ignorant, obviously the product of people who did not know what socialism is. Socialism is "government ownership of the means of the production and distribution of goods." Medicine is not "goods." Medicine is a service provided by doctors and nurses. Doctors and nurses cannot be owned; therefore, medicine cannot be socialized.

But clearly the Clinton plan was calling for a change in the medical system. If it was not socialism, what was it? The answer is that the Clinton proposal would have converted medicine from the predominantly capitalistic *status quo* to a predominantly welfare-state system. Government control of a service (as opposed to ownership of goods) is called "welfare state."

Well, then, are welfare-state measures alien to the American system? Not really. The public-education system is part of the welfare state. Government builds the schools, pays and licenses the teachers, makes and enforces laws about school attendance. Lots of people have lots of complaints about public education, but I've never heard it attacked as socialistic. The road system is also part of the welfare-state structure of this country. Government builds the roads, licenses the drivers, makes and enforces the laws about who can drive and under what conditions. Again, there are lots of complaints about the highway system, but I've never heard it attacked as socialistic.

Now, as President Nixon used to say, let me make one thing perfectly clear: I am *not* arguing that the Clinton health plan should have been adopted. Maybe it should have been, maybe it shouldn't. What I *am* saying is that it should not have been defeated on the charge that it was socialized medicine. But the danger of such a defeat exists—it is easy to label a person or a program ideologically, easier than attacking them on their merits. And as long as those labels stick and people respond to the labels without examining the labeled, you can be sure politicians will use this shorthand method to influence our attitudes and votes.

## ▶ Myths and American Ideology

The myths that Edelman and Parenti identified are not our only political myths. From the beginning America has had a messianic myth. The Puritans wanted to establish a New Jerusalem. The Founding Fathers desired a New Athens. And the line goes on through "Manifest Destiny" . . . "making the world safe for Democracy" . . . Korea . . . Vietnam . . . Grenada. Even our dollar bill proclaims *Novus Ordo Seclorum*—a new order on earth. Even if we have to kill in order to establish it! And, as rhetorical critic Richard M. Weaver has pointed out, "as an indication of how innate the feeling for war is with us, we may recall that religions show no compunction about using metaphors of war. Consider the way in which the followers of the pacifist Christian religion sing 'Onward Christian Soldiers,' 'A Mighty Fortress is Our God,' and 'The Son of God Goes Forth to War.'"[22] The messianic myth, the idea that Americans are called on to save the world, may have been harmless enough in earlier centuries; but now, says Cogley, "it can be deadly dangerous. Establishing a *novus ordo seclorum* in isolation is one thing; extending it throughout the world in a nuclear age is another."[23]

We could also discuss other American political myths: for example, the myth of individualism and hard work as captured in the popular understanding of Robinson Crusoe, Davy Crockett, and Samuel Gompers. The myth of progress has been with us since at least the time of Zoroaster, who led the West to believe human societies can change and improve over time rather than being stuck in a repetitive cycle in which each new generation repeated the actions of the previous one (just as the seasons of the year return cyclically, bringing the same phenomena of budding, growing, decaying, and dying annually). Zoroastrian progress is more familiar to us, I suspect, in its "in every day in every way the world is getting better and better" strain, although, as earlier noted, today many people are likely to substitute "worse and worse" for better and better. It is not a difference that makes a difference, however, for, as Kenneth Burke has written, "any concept of 'development' or 'progress' gives rise to corresponding concepts of 'regression'"[24] and deterioration. That is so say, any idea implies its opposite. Movement implies stillness; the thought that society can improve implies that it also can deteriorate; the idea that the world can get better and better implies the opposite possibility that it can get worse and worse.

We also celebrate a myth of youth in this country. Our ideal is to get younger. We want to be twenty-five going on seventeen. Youth is all-pervasive. We live not only for but through our children. We rebel against age and, in doing so, identify with youth, the perfect mode for implying rebellion. Burke suggests that "once a social order (with its 'pyramidal' logic) has attained its scrupulous analogues in modes of 'self-control' . . . then imagery of youth can stand for general principles of resistance, however roundabout, symbolizing political or social motives not intrinsic to the biological condition as such."[25] That is, once we assume "self-control" accompanies "maturity" and that both are necessary for a society to be successful, we have established a system where lack of self-control is seen both as dangerous and as a natural characteristic of young people. Consequently, images of youth (who are assumed to be inherently out of control) can come to symbolize rebellion against self-control, thus against society itself.

But youth is not sustainable. The fountain of eternal youth does not exist. Thus, the youth revolution is doomed from the start. Knowing this, we lapse into fantasy and live young lives vicariously through our athletes, movie stars, and, mixing in the myths of Horatio Alger and Lady Luck, TV game shows.

Or we turn to the developing myth of love and openness as epitomized in encounter groups and twelve-step training programs. This emphasis upon the personal, the private, and the sexual is, says Professor P. Rieff, "an implicit criticism of the ugly and deforming thing that our sociability has become."[26] In this myth the world is irrelevant. Concerns for public policy, public action, and public life are replaced by concern for the self. The hero is the person who can screen out the chaos and ugliness of the outside and find peace within.

The rhetoric in support of this myth relies on the *anti-government attitudes* implicit in the myths Parenti identified. Conservatives and the authors of many self-help books claim society cannot be improved by government action but only by the improvement of each individual. Clearly, there is some truth in the claim, but it overlooks too much—the difficulty of individuals effectuating this "up by your bootstraps" philosophy, as well as the possibility that there may be incompatibilities between what individuals want to accomplish for themselves and what is necessary for those individuals to live with each other in a society. In short, the myth that self-love and self-improvement will inherently bring societal love and improvement reforms nothing, taking as its text the injunction of a 1960s comic, Brother Dave: "If the world's wrong, then right your own self." It is, at base, an antisocial masturbatory ideal at variance with the increasing complexity and interdependence of our world. And it, too, is doomed to failure because, as Rieff says, "an indifference to public ideas while teasing out the spirit of intimate relations, will not . . . bring either social peace or at last crown the power of love."[27] That is, while the major myths force citizens into passivity, this minor myth holds out the false hope that the passivity can somehow be employed to bring the hoped-for improvements.

## CONCLUSION

▶ We have covered a lot of diverse material in this chapter: positive myths about presidential power and citizen duties, as well as negative myths about the hopelessness of governmental action and the helplessness of citizens. We've examined the implications of liquid metaphors, the revolutionary implications of "letting loose," the "poison" of pornography, disease-remedy metaphors, light-dark and black-white metaphors, organic metaphors, and sexual metaphors.

▶ By and large, we have discovered that the myths and metaphors tend to empower the government and imply a quiescent role for citizens. Given all the language used to create citizen passivity and allow politicians to do what they want to do, it seems only natural that we have struck back with a phrase of our own—whereas we used to say we held elections to determine the lesser of two evils, these days we're more likely to claim we've elected the eviler of two lessers.

## FOR FURTHER CONSIDERATION

1. This chapter suggests that the congressional debate preceding the Gulf War was a "sham" because the debate could have no effect on the war-starting decision. But you might want to consider whether *all* congressional debates are more or less

bogus—that is, whether the "myth of rationality" (or "myth of deliberation") is just that: a myth.

In your analysis you might want to consider these points:

a) Can people who are dependent upon large campaign contributors be independent in examining societal problems?
b) Can a debate organized along *two* political party lines consider *all* the possibilities?
c) What is the function of debate in a body where everyone is a debater? (Remember that in the traditional idea of debate those who are debating are not those who are making the decision.)

2. A significant portion of this chapter was devoted to examining the political relevance of the water metaphor. Yet I also pointed out that any metaphor based on common life phenomena might yield an equally rich lode of politically relevant material. Examine one of these other phenomena—air, fire, human anatomy, the animal world, the seasons, gardening—to see whether it, too, provides insight into how political communication functions in our society.

## NOTES

1. M. Osborn, "The Rhetorical Metaphor in Criticism," Unpublished and undated manuscript, Memphis State University.
2. C. L. Johnstone, "Illuminating the Logos: Speech, Thought, and Being in the Philosophy of Heraclitus" (paper presented at the Eastern Communication Association convention, Ocean City, MD, May 1989).
3. T. W. Benson, "Poisoned Minds," *Southern Speech Journal* 34 (Fall 1968): 58.
4. K. Burke, *Language as Symbolic Action: Essays on Life, Literature, and Method* (Berkeley: University of California Press, 1966), 19.
5. *Ibid.*, 101.
6. E. Black, "The Second Persona," *Quarterly Journal of Speech* 56 (April 1970): 119.
7. J. Halverson, "The Psycho-pathology of Style: The Case of Right-Wing Rhetoric," *Antioch Review* 31 (Spring 1971): 103.
8. E. M. Kennedy, quoted in untitled editorial, *New York Times,* 13 May 1973, p. 49.
9. M. Edelman, "Myths, Metaphors, and Political Conformity," *Psychiatry* 30 (August 1967): 217–228.
10. R. M. Nixon, "Address at Kansas State University," *New York Times,* 17 September 1970, p. 28.
11. J. Campbell, "The Historical Development of Mythology," in *Myth and Mythmaking,* ed. H. A. Murray (Boston: Beacon Press, 1960), 33.
12. E. Fromm, *The Dogma of Christ and Other Essays on Religion, Psychology and Culture* (Greenwich, CT: Fawcett, 1955), 25–26.

13. R. Cathcart, "The Nixon Inaugural Address," in *Public Speaking as Dialogue: Readings and Essays*, ed. J. L. Ericson and R. F. Forston (Baton Rouge: Louisiana State University Press, 1970), 130.

14. M. Parenti, *Land of Idols: Political Mythology in America* (New York: St. Martin's, 1994).

15. *Ibid.*, 4.

16. *Ibid.*, 7.

17. *Ibid.*, 9.

18. *Ibid.*, 10.

19. *Ibid.*, 12.

20. *Ibid.*, 12.

21. M. Ivins, "Deep Voodoo," *Mother Jones,* January/February 1991, 12.

22. R. M. Weaver, *Visions of Order: The Cultural Crisis of Our Time* (Baton Rouge: Louisiana State University Press, 1964), 105.

23. J. Cogley, "A Mischievous Myth," *Center Magazine,* November/December 1972, 3.

24. Burke, *op. cit.*, 70.

25. *Ibid.*, 150.

26. P. Rieff, "A Modern Mythmaker," in *Myth and Mythmaking*, ed. H. A. Murray (Boston: Beacon Press, 1960), 268.

27. *Ibid.*, 256.

# Sexual Language and Politics

*Feminist politics is real only if women, together with their bodies, their works, and their voice, are present in a place where everyone can see them—let us say, in the marketplace.*
— MONIQUE CANTO[1]

To this point I have taken the noncontroversial position that language affects behavior. I have examined certain uses of language—such as definitions, form, generalizations, simplifications, and metaphors—in order to demonstrate that truth. I now turn to a slightly different and more controversial concern, examining not a type of language, but a subject of language: sexuality. The overarching purpose remains the same, however, which is to demonstrate that the language we use has behavioral effects.

What makes the material in this chapter more controversial than that in the preceding chapters is that the subject is sex, a topic that always stirs controversy in our society. Given our puritanical cultural background, given the centrality of religion in our culture and the centrality of sexual concerns to the major religions of our peoples, it probably should not surprise us that any mention of sex would become embedded in controversy. Nonetheless, the political language derived from our conceptions of sexuality is so important that we have no choice but to examine it if we want to understand political communication.

Not all interactions between sex and politics need come under our analytic gaze. We need not be concerned with the sexual activities of presidents and presidential candidates, with who, if anybody, has slept with Donna Rice or Gennifer Flowers or F.D.R.'s nurse or Dwight Eisenhower's jeep driver. We need not attempt to discover whether Thomas Jefferson had carnal knowledge of some of his female slaves or whether the Republican chant about Grover Cleveland ("Ma, ma, where's my pa?/Gone to the White House./Ha! Ha! Ha!") had any relationship to Cleveland's actual sexual history. That is to say, our interest is not in the sexuality of politicians but in sexual symbolism about politics, in sexual dialogue of and about presidents and other political participants. This interest is not a matter of idle curiosity or sexual titillation, but rather flows from the belief that gender-based discourse is basic in American political communication, and that manipulation of that discourse by political elites without corresponding understanding by the citizenry is dangerous.

We *are* interested, then, in (1) our language as a binary discourse system that is based upon the two genders; (2) sexual metaphors; (3) the effects of political language on women, keeping them out of the public realm of politics, focusing them on questions of beauty, and limiting their entrance into professional lives; and (4) the effects of the binary system on men, making them into warriors and focusing them on questions of machismo. Finally, (5) we want to speculate, at least, on possible causes for all of these language-based effects.

Because the relationships among language, sex, gender, and politics are so complicated (and, at times, convoluted), introducing this material takes some time. To try to bring some order to the chaos, I've divided the material into two chapters. This chapter is focused on sexual language in our culture generally, as well as more specifically in politics. The next chapter is devoted to tracing the influence of the marriage metaphor in politics, from courtship through divorce.

In this chapter, then, I explore the idea that our whole language can be said to be a binary discourse system because it is based upon the two genders. The system is always "in process," however. That is, the roles for each gender evolve as the language evolves, and vice versa.

At the present moment our binary language "stacks" the system in favor of the male: male-assumed "rationality" is favored over female-assumed "emotionality," male "activity" over female "passivity," male "hardness" over female "softness," and so forth. Further, our understandings of civilization, culture, capitalism, and "the battle of the sexes" reinforce the gender assumptions buried in the binary language structure.

Our sexual metaphors also reflect and reinforce the binary system. Metaphorically, males are depicted as warriors and sexual aggressors; women are framed as passive, acted upon rather than acting. Both genders accept as desirable a certain degree of violence and anger in sex, stemming from the male warrior mode. Thus, sex is seen as a male-dominated act in which men win and women lose, and often is described metaphorically in economic terms, as in suggestions of women "buying" financial security by marrying.

The attitudes about each gender are inculcated from childhood, but they are also affected by political and cultural changes. As more women join the work force, fewer are dependent upon men. As new birth control devices are invented, women are provided a degree of sexual freedom. As modern warfare becomes more technological, male physical strength is devalued.

Although contemporary changes would seem to be relieving women from dependency upon men, hence from the need to "play the sexual card" to achieve economic well-being, the culture still treats beauty as a female's most important asset. This idea structures how both males and females behave toward, think about, and perceive females. One clear effect is that the demand that females be beautiful interferes with the move of women into public realms, such as workplaces and politics.

In the nonverbal world, the different demands on men and women are reflected in their different modes of dress. Because men are evaluated only by what they do, their work clothes do not differ from their social attire: those of us who have to wear suits to work normally wear the same outfits in our social lives, while manual laborers are likely to wear the jeans and sport shirts that would be suitable on their jobs when they go out for the evening. For women, however, several wardrobes are required, with enormous economic (hence political) consequences—in mass media, in how stores are located, in the function of store windows, in the male/female relationship to shopping, in medicine (for example, face-lifts). Ultimately, dress is one component of how the system conspires to keep the female "in her place."

While the major effect of the binary discourse system on women is to keep them dependent, the major effect on men is to keep them cast in the warrior role. War is depicted as "sexy" and sexual metaphors are used to make violence attractive to men. For example, enemies are depicted as rapists who "penetrate" our defenses; the peaceful are depicted as "impotent."

## ▶ The Binary Discourse System

A major factor in how our minds work, says philosophy professor Mark Johnson, is that "We human beings have bodies. We are '*rational* animals,' but we are also 'rational *animals*,' which means that our rationality is embodied."[2] And the central fact about our bodies that affects our meanings, our comprehension, and our reason is that we are a gendered species. As English professor Margaret Higonnet and her colleagues have suggested, "A gender system consists not merely of a set of social roles but also of a discourse that gives meaning to different roles within a binary structure."[3]

In other words, the development of a binary discourse system is inevitable in a gender-controlled system. That is, we conceptualize the genders as polarized and then impose that polarity on our world views. Yet the orientation of our system is *not* inevitable, but rather is "filled in" for each age by what those living in the age choose to learn from the past, as filtered through their everyday experiences. In our own age, influenced as we were by Freud and his followers, says R. Scholes, "male and female have been defined as a fullness and a deficiency, a presence and an absence, a plus and a minus, an 'on' and an 'off.' The vagina and the penis, as an absence and a presence—the gap that needs filling and the magic wand that fills it—seem to divide the sexual world between them."[4]

### Our Binary Language Favors Males

While it may be possible to identify all the ways in which our binary language reflects genders, it clearly is not possible this side of a dictionary-like compendium. However, the major outlines may be clearly discerned: male versus female, rationality versus emotionality, activity versus passivity, hard versus soft, war versus peace, and so forth, with all the characteristics we associate with maleness on one side and those associated with femaleness on the other. The binary opposites are not clearly of the good-bad variety, yet they *are* stacked in favor of the male side, for "when push comes to shove" those on the "male side" are those for which we opt. That is, there is much to be said for softness, but in a showdown we'll choose hardness every time. Political ideas such as "negotiate" and "compromise" are somewhat neutral in terms of these binary opposites. Therefore, when "neutral" approaches seem preferable we tend to redefine those ideas as "hard" or "tough"; when they seem inadvisable we characterize them as soft, more like "caving in" or "giving up."

As I have implied, there is no escaping the existence of a binary language system because we are a gendered species and because we think with our bodies. There is no *inherent* reason why the binary system should be stacked to favor one gender, although ours clearly is—leading to a great deal of dissatisfaction, first among feminists, then throughout academia and beyond. The successes of the linguistic reformers—eliminating the use of "man" or "mankind" to stand for all humanity, for instance—have been small, but significant, in recognizing women as independent rather than subservient to men. But having largely succeeded at those first tentative steps at reform, the movement seems to have stalled. Perhaps the leaders have become daunted at the enormity of the task, for it is one thing to get a society to change a few nouns and pronouns, but de-gendering a whole discourse system is quite another thing. Yet that is precisely what is needed, for once a binary gender-based discourse system is established, the discourse system reinforces the gender system, which devises additional linguistic manifestations, and so forth, in an endless vicious cycle.

## Aggression and Passivity in the Binary Discourse System

Just how vicious that cycle can be is most easily demonstrated by examining the concurrence of our binary discourse system with the presumed differences between the genders in terms of aggression and passivity.

Whether it is true or not, it is assumed in American society that males are more aggressive than females, that aggression is "natural" in men. The acceptance of the "normality" of male aggression through a gendered discourse system that depicts men as active and women as passive has negative effects on societal activities such as marriage and law enforcement. Further, because females too often accept the notion that male aggression is natural, many women come to expect men to do the "dirty work" of aggression for them, thereby reinforcing the perception and reality of men as aggressive. Likewise, the belief and the language impinge negatively on female self-perceptions. Many women repress their own inclinations toward aggression, see themselves as unable to be "strong," and thereby perhaps set themselves up to expect and even "accept" physical and sexual abuse.

Whatever the originating cause, however, it is difficult, though not impossible, for the society to say aggression is natural and expected, then decry it when it is expressed against those who are "naturally" and "expectedly" depicted as weak and unaggressive. The system is so skewed in favor of male "natural" behavior that it may well be that patriarchy could not exist without the physical and sexual abuse of females to keep the dynamic intact.

Theoretically, of course, men could "tame" their "natural" aggressiveness and bend it to more productive pursuits. There is some attempt in our society for them to do so. One of the difficulties in accomplishing that objective, however, is found in the assumption that a "taming authority" is "school-marmish." And even when *some* diminution in male-based attributes is discovered, it tends to be denied. For instance, R. Wilkinson, in an excellent book on the tough-guy tradition, points out that although automobiles have been "styled and advertised as aggressive extensions of a driver's virility, cars have simultaneously become luxurious cocoons with push-buttons placed to economize on almost every body movement."[5] That is to say, even when men "give in" to "softness," the image that is projected ignores that "luxury" and stresses more "angular" qualities such as speed and power.

## Culture, Civilization, and Capitalism in Binary Discourse

A concomitant of the idea of "taming" aggression, thereby "taming" men, is the perception and definition of civilization itself as feminine. A part of the problem with culture, for men, beyond the fact that it involves such supposed "feminine" activities as art, music, dance, and literature, is that "culture" is enforced from above, leaving the individual no choice but to conform to the group or reject the entire package. To men imbued with the frontier approach to individualism, acceding to group standards is difficult to accept. And yet, in their own realms they do accept it. Competition in the business world, every bit as much as in the art world, requires the individual to strive and be judged by standards set by others.

Indeed, contradictions are rife between the gendered discourse system and the economic system that is presumed to represent "the manly virtues" of capitalism. Notice, for instance, how many "male" products are sold with images promising potency and activity, often with a violence motif, images quite different from those used to advertise "female" products. The contradiction is that in traditional views of capitalism men were seen as producers and women as consumers, but in order to sell goods it was also necessary to define men as consumers long before women were given the right to share in producing. The contradiction is necessary, it will be noted, because without it the system would have limited men to producers and women to consumers. And while the early days did see men as the predominant, if not exclusive, producers, it was always the case that they also had to be seen as consumers lest the system lose half the potential markets.

## The "Battle of the Sexes" in the Binary Discourse System

But undoubtedly the realm in which it is most obvious that reinforcing the gendered binary discourse system has negative results concerns the "battle of the sexes." Niccolo Machiavelli saw love as war, a struggle for domination. A leading scholar on Machiavelli, H. F. Pitkin, says that Machiavelli's writing relied upon "the metaphor of love as a military struggle between the sexes. A servant speaks of lovemaking in terms like 'attacking' and 'meeting strong resistance'; an old man preparing to make love to a young girl speaks of 'rousing up' his 'brigades' and adds, 'when one goes armed to war, one goes with double courage.'"[6]

I mention Machiavelli in this connection not because he is, these days, a negative source, or even because he seemed to be obsessed with the metaphor, but because he went to such pains to explain and justify the comparison. In his *Clizia* he made the metaphor quite literal: "Certainly the man who said that the lover and the soldier are alike told the truth. The general wants his soldiers to be young; women don't want their lovers to be old. It's a repulsive thing to see an old man a soldier; it's most repulsive to see him in love. Soldiers fear their commander's anger; lovers fear no less that of their ladies. Soldiers sleep on the ground out of doors; lovers on the wall-ledges under the windows of their beloved. Soldiers pursue their enemies to the death; lovers, their rivals. Soldiers on the darkest nights in the dead of winter go through the mud, exposed to rain and wind, to carry out some undertaking that will bring them to victory; lovers attempt in similar ways and with similar and greater sufferings to gain those they love. Equally in war and in love, secrecy is needed, and fidelity and courage. The dangers are alike, and most of the time the results are alike. The soldier dies in a ditch and the lover dies in despair."[7]

Though less disenchanted with romance than Machiavelli, Miguel Cervantes essentially agreed: "Love and war are the same thing, the stratagems and policy are as allowable in the one as in the other."[8] The binary gendered system of discourse, then, looks not only dangerous but dangerously off-course. For either gender to accept such a discourse system passively is to accept the continuation and reinforcement of inequalities, sexual violence, and perhaps war itself.

## ▶ Sexual Metaphors

At first glance, this poem by e.e. cummings seems to imply nothing more than a sexual encounter between a man and a woman.[9]

> (cccome?said he
> ummm said she)
> you're divine!said he
> (you are Mine said she)

On closer inspection, however, the poem reflects fundamental cultural truths about men's and women's attitudes toward sexual intimacy. The man can enjoy—indeed, delight in—sexual encounters and appreciate the woman's physical beauty ("you're divine"). But the prospect of "enjoying" a woman cannot be demanded: it is in the woman's power to grant or deny sexual favors. Thus, he must *ask* her to "cccome." The woman ought not—in fact, *must* not—enjoy sex for pleasure's sake. Thus, the woman in the poem offers a bargain: she will "ummm" with delight only if she also can proclaim, "you are mine."

The stereotype that women are looking for love while men are looking to score may have been somewhat mitigated in recent years. Yet in many ways the communication of such stereotypes causes, or at least reflects, deep-seated ambivalence about women's and men's willingness to engage sexually, intimately, and interdependently in the relationships they forge.

Male identity, according to philosopher Sam Keen, stems from "war, work, and sex, the triad of male initiation rites."[10] That men's identities are connected to the warrior psyche, that they are groomed to be able "to resort to violence," is "the major difference between men and women."[11] "The capacity and willingness for violence," he continues, "has been central to men's self-definition,"[12] and is communicated from man to man, father to son, in the metaphorical expressions that describe men's sexual attitudes toward women.

Metaphorically speaking, men are the primary aggressors in sexual relationships. Women may be stalked like animals ("he preys on young women," "he's a real animal," "he can't keep his paws off her") or hungered after like food ("she's a real dish," "she's a piece of meat"). Women can be "stroked," "cranked," or "turned on" like finely tuned machines, responding to the tinkering of the master mechanics. Women also may be won over or conquered, as in a game or a war. Men try to "score." They want to get past "first base," or, if at all possible, "make a home run." Certainly they don't want to "strike out." Men want to be known for their "conquests."

So pervasive are these male-dominant metaphors, such that "men's egos are nearly inseparable from their penises,"[13] that we can rarely hear words such as "potent," "penetration," and "thrust" without them conjuring images of man's anatomy. The metaphors associated with masculinity convey action, power, and control.

Not surprisingly, in a culture that reflects bipolar thinking, we find few examples of women being sexually active. Thus, women are *acted upon* by men. Metaphorically, they are the fruit to be savored. Baudelaire's passion for his mistress, Jeanne Duval, was captured in the metaphor of a bright red pomegranate bursting with red juice; Siddhartha's metaphor for his Kamala was a freshly cut, red, and fresh fig; in Octavio Paz's "Sun Stones," the woman's skin is "the color of peaches."[14] The image of the fruit, says Professor Thass-Thienemann, represents fertility: "the plant or fruit is alive as long as there is juice in it, when dry it is dead."[15] Thus, to preserve her "fruta sabrosa" ("delicious fruit") becomes the fervent hope of the young Tisbea, one of the more than two thousand women who are the "objects" of Don Juan's insatiable sexual appetite.[16]

The Don Juan character has become associated with the charmer, with the seducer, with unbridled sexuality. Interestingly, in Molina's play the hero actually takes his victims by force. But the violence Don Juan perpetrated became lost in the character's literary legacy.

Sex as a manifestation of violence and anger, however, is not lost in our linguistic repertoire. The anger men seem to harbor towards women in the sexual realm and the purported passivity of women that simultaneously fuels and receives this anger have concrete sources. The confusion, frustration, and miscommunication that surround sexual identities and inform the expectations for intimacy for both sexes are rooted in the socialization process. This process has a powerful influence on the sex- and gender-role identities of boys and girls, men and women. And the political effects of these culturally determined (and metaphorically reinforced) identities are also significant, with men in control of all realms that require power, strength, and force, and women relegated to realms more dainty, safe, and—ultimately—unimportant.

Given the confluence between the centrality of metaphoric expression in our linguistic repertoire and the importance of gender and sex in our cultural thought-patterns, it should come as no surprise to discover that the two factors become conflated with a third major societal influence, economics. Consider, for instance, these lines of poetry:[17]

> What is freely supplied me
> I shudder at,
> But if aught is denied me
> I long for that
> With constant mind.
> She who's effusive
> I flee:
> The girl who's elusive
> Suits me. . . .

The words in this nearly nine-hundred-year-old poem are woefully current. According to the poem, once a woman has sex with a man, she loses her power; she becomes less valuable and less cherished. Our language confirms that the idea persists even today: when a woman first has intercourse, she *loses* (her virginity); the man, through the same act, *wins* (her body).

Words used to describe sexual relations smack of economic brokering: "win," "lose," "power." Cultures, according to social anthropologist Kenneth Eckhardt,[18] establish power currencies to maintain equilibrium. Historically, sex has been an important commodity. Women used the potential for sex to solidify relationships. In return for sexual favors, men promised lifelong protection and security. Because virginity was traditionally the only way to assure a man that his children were truly his own, women learned to guard their prized treasure accordingly; they learned to withhold sex.

Sexuality as a power currency is rooted in the shift from an egalitarian agricultural society to the period when men became warriors (about 1700 B.C.). In the agricultural world, women were Mother Earth, the night, the moon, soft, flowing, and fertile. Men were Father Sky, the day, the sun, hard, penetrating, and shooting forth. Important to this dichotomy, Keen reminds us, was that neither domain was regarded as more powerful or more important: "That force that made the penis rise and the womb swell was thought to be the same as the power that pushed the bud through the fertile earth and ripened the grain."[19] Once a warrior mentality developed, the values of the agricultural society were no longer esteemed. Conquest replaced cooperation. More significantly, Keen continues, the dichotomous but equal relationship between Mother Earth and Father Sky disappeared, replaced by inequality: "In a warrior culture, once the sword had been proclaimed mightier than the plow, the soldier more potent than the farmer, a man's penis and his weapon became fused" and the idea of woman as a "land to be conquered, possessed, and, if necessary, humiliated" emerged.[20]

While women learn that love is a gift that can be given, men, according to Simone de Beauvoir, learn a different cultural imperative: they may actively expect, demand, and pursue sex and love.[21] As Nietzsche so powerfully articulates, women give the gift of love while men learn to expect and accept the gift.[22]

Keen links men's views on sex and their expectations for women to a shift in men's social roles. If men traditionally were valued for their role as provider and protector, and for their power to impregnate a woman, their valuation has shifted. With birth control and smaller families, impregnation abilities have slipped in value. Similarly, the existence of nuclear arms distances men from their role as combat warrior and protector of the home. Finally, the economic power previously wielded by men also has diminished, as is reflected by the rise of two-income families. As a result of these changes, says Keen, "for many men the erogenous zone seems to have replaced the battlefield as the arena for the testing of manhood."[23] More striking, perhaps, is Keen's assertion that it is *through* the penis, alone, that men have been allowed to feel, to unleash their emotions: "It is not that men are only interested in sex, but that we have been so conditioned to curtail our natural needs for intimacy that only in sex do we have cultural permission to feel close to another human being. . . . Emotionally speaking men are stutterers who often use sexual language to express their forbidden desires for communion."[24] Perhaps, he concludes, we can expect no more from a gender that has been trained to be warriors and workers, that has been schooled well in putting on a front of stoic silence.

The battle lines in the "battle of the sexes" are drawn by the contradictory expectations and roles for women and men. In nearly every facet of their lives, the rules for men and women clash. While both genders may be encouraged to seek love and intimacy, the terms themselves have different meanings for the two sexes. It is not surprising, therefore, that the rites of passage to manhood and womanhood have led to tremendous miscommunication, misunderstanding, and dissatisfaction in the relationships men and women seek: "We expect impossible things of one another, resent and blame each other for our lack of fulfillment. What is jokingly called the 'war between the sexes' is no joke, but the psychological reality that goes on constantly just beneath the masks of civility we have conspired to wear to satisfy our mutual needs."[25] But as you may have noticed, some of that "civility" is sometimes stripped away when women run for political office and have to face jokes about their presumed economic and military ignorance.

## ▶ Effects on Women: The Mask of Beauty

The admonition for young girls and boys to conform to prescribed physical norms begins at birth. Jesse Bernard[26] argues that from the moment a child is born, the first question asked, "Is it a boy or girl?" has a profound influence on the socialization process. And socialization, of course, is inherently political, for it determines who is allowed to be involved in politics, who is relegated to nonpolitical spheres.

When parents encourage female children to look pretty so they can "flirt" with others, and to dress in "pretty clothing," they are perpetuating a valuation of body image as intimately connected to esteem, self-worth, and future success. Too, being "daddy's little angel" connotes that the little girl always will be taken care of. The connection is obvious. If a good little girl conforms to the prescriptions to be pretty and cute—that is, "feminine"—she can depend on (or *be dependent on*) a man to take care of her in later life. Thus, appearance, dependency, and security become inexorably linked for the female child. The male child receives an entirely different message. He is expected to *do* something—to excel in sports, to *become* someone important through his accomplishments in the world.

These messages, initiated at birth, reflect both the explicit and tacit transmission of cultural norms. According to Susan Harter, a University of Denver child psychologist,[27] children are able to discern attractiveness characteristics in others as early as age four. While girls and boys *both* are concerned with appearance, young girls are judged *primarily* for appearance while the latitude for being judged attractive for little boys may include other traits such as being good at sports.

The danger in overvaluing attractiveness, Harter maintains, is that it becomes *the* major influence on self-esteem: "The tragedy is linking appearance to self-esteem, equating what a child looks like with the person inside. . . . If you're criticizing your child's looks, you're setting conditions for love."[28]

The impetus for young girls to accentuate their physical appearance and for boys to escape the need to be valuated for theirs begins in the home and is reinforced everywhere. Television alone, according to one study by William Leiss, has exposed the average 20-year-old American to 350,000 commercials.[29] These advertisements are strikingly obvious in orientation: females are treated as decoration and encouraged to buy products to improve their physical appeal: males are treated as "doers" and urged to buy products that will help them achieve (or appear to have achieved) expertise or success in some realm of action. The effects of these (and other cultural) emphases on the valuation of physical appearance are profound. The influences extend beyond the confines of the family unit and become insinuated into all realms of life—personal, professional, and political. If teaching women to prize beauty affected only how their own families responded to them, that would be *relatively* unimportant politically, but to the degree that physical attractiveness is fundamentally the only power currency at women's disposal to attract a man, secure a job, and enter the public realm, beauty is as much a political as a personal issue.

Within the past decade, several scholars, primarily in sociology and psychology, have begun to scrutinize the impact of beauty in today's society. Some of their titles reflect the ambivalent nature of beauty. Professor of psychology Rita Freedman,[30] for example, titles her work *Beauty Bound*. The term "bound" conjures the *pursuit* of beauty as a goal. It also connotes *restrictiveness,* for the pursuit of beauty literally *binds* women: in their clothing, in their diets, in their own bodies. Rhodes scholar Naomi Wolf's *The Beauty Myth*[31] similarly calls into question the mythic quality of beauty. While the term "myth" may suggest that beauty is a traditional value, thus resistant to scrutiny, the term also may suggest that our culture has bought into a dubious value that is merely a fiction of our own construction. And social psychologist Carol Tavris[32] uses the title *The Mismeasure of Woman*. The use of "mismeasure" connotes both the *figurative* and *literal* aspects of assessing women's emotional and physical attributes.

Many writers attribute our current obsession with beauty to the Industrial Revolution.[33] Once the family unit became separated, women retained responsibility for the domestic sphere while men moved into the work realm. Subsequently, says Wolf, "a new class of literate, ideal women developed, on whose submission to enforced domesticity the evolving system of industrial capitalism depended."[34] The cultivation of beauty became the one arena in which women could strive for and achieve success that would not compete with men. Talcott Parsons interpreted this pattern of beauty as "a compensation in female culture for exclusion from the male occupational world."[35]

Jesse Bernard argues that "the trade-off of female youth and beauty for male wealth and power has been a common theme in popular culture for many years."[36] This trade-off is played out in women's and men's relationships: how women evaluate their own looks, how men respond to women's attractiveness, how women's appearance influences their entry into public space—into work, politics, and so forth.

While beauty may be in the eye of the beholder, the definition of what is beautiful is culturally determined. Moreover, the ideal standard of beauty is mutable; it changes over time. Within the past fifty years alone, the ideal body for women has passed through three distinct phases: from voluptuous and curvaceous (for example, Marilyn Monroe and Jane Russell in the 1940s and 1950s), to unisex and slim (Twiggy in the 1960s and 1970s), to today's ideal of the full-busted but narrow-hipped woman (Cindy Crawford and Claudia Schiffer).

The changes may be related to a shift in cultural values. During pro-maternal eras, when motherhood and domesticity are regarded as women's primary roles, a fuller-figured woman is more positively valued. During periods when women enter the labor force, especially to pursue fields traditionally dominated by men, the thinner, more athletic figure becomes the norm.[37] Yet as long as the primary criterion for women is how they look, arenas that are more dependent on how one thinks—such as politics—may still largely be cut off from female involvement.

There are three basic problems with placing the burden of beauty on women and expecting them to conform to externally determined and ever-changing standards. First, if from birth women are told they must be beautiful in order to be successful, they begin to internalize an externally imposed standard and use it to measure their own self-worth. Beauty becomes the yardstick for evaluation. It takes a psychic toll on those who do not measure up. Culturally, the toll is that certain people are lost to the economic and political systems because their self-esteem is too low to allow them to become involved.

Second, if women accept beauty as a power currency in relationships, the emphasis on women's appearance becomes the major commodity they have to offer others. Studies consistently reveal that both women and men regard beauty as a woman's burden. In a 1977 study on twenty-eight thousand readers of *Psychology Today,* Tavris found that both genders valued physical attractiveness as an essential ingredient of the ideal woman, but not of the ideal man.[38] Similarly, a series of studies on college-age students by Elaine Hatfield and Susan Sprecher[39] determined that men consistently described their female partner's attractiveness to be of prime importance while women tended to value other traits in their male partners, such as personality, popularity, and intelligence—traits important for success in the world, including the world of politics.

And third, by perpetuating the expectation that women are the fair sex, expected to please and be pleasing to others, beauty becomes a goal in and of itself, a goal for which no price is too high to pay. Finding it impossible to measure up to the "ideal," women feel compelled to look outside themselves for help in becoming beautiful. They attempt to alter their weight through elaborate diet plans, as a $33-billion-a-year diet industry attests. They spend $20 billion annually on cosmetics to mask their faces and change their hair. And if all else fails, they pay $300 million on cosmetic surgery to literally recarve their bodies.[40] All this in the pursuit of the beauty society has told them they must have to be worthy human beings.

The efforts women expend on making themselves beautiful perpetuate an insidious gap between the genders. More than forty years ago, Simone de Beauvoir observed that femininity is a cultural rather than a biological imperative: "One is not born, but rather becomes, a woman . . . ; it is civilization as a whole that produces this creature intermediate between male and eunuch, which is described as feminine."[41] Because she is taught to derive pleasure from pleasing others, she becomes an object; "She is treated like a live doll and is refused liberty."[42]

The result of being other-focused interferes with developing autonomy. Carol Tavris says women who try to live up to male expectations develop the perception that "the woman's body is never right as it is and always needs to be fixed," a perception she predicts "will continue as long as women model themselves after the impossible male norm."[43] The continuous struggle to meet alternating standards of beauty exacts a toll on women. The struggle for women to appear simultaneously masculine and feminine has an enormous influence on how women, especially, will fare in the workplace. Stereotyped assumptions about women's appearance affect success.

### Beauty and the World of Work

Who works and who doesn't is a primary economic—hence political—question in any culture. Part of the problem women encounter in our culture when they attempt to enter careers (especially those traditionally dominated by men) stems from the nature of the male-determined corporate culture. Communication scholar Sue DeWine defines a corporate culture as a "set of expected behaviors . . . supported within the group. This set of expectations or norms usually consists of unwritten 'rules' that have an immense impact on behavior within the culture."[44] If we recall that the separation of the domestic sphere from the labor sphere impelled men to establish the work place, we can also expect that men set the standards for this environment, standards that women, socialized differently, might have trouble meeting.

In addition to establishing behavioral codes (such as objectivity, competition, aggressiveness, chain of command, risk-taking propensity, and teamwork strategies),[45] men also set the norm for acceptable workplace appearance. In his work on the relationships between fashion, culture, and identity, sociology professor Fred Davis connects the immutability of business attire to the Industrial Revolution and the Protestant work ethic: "[I]t fell to the adult middle-class male to serve as the visible embodiment of the ethos animating the great social transformation taking place. . . . Men's dress became more simple, coarse, unchangeable, and somber, sartorial tendencies that . . . survive to the present."[46]

Because men developed a "serious" work environment, exemplified in part by their attire, they essentially created and defined "professionalism" in their own image. How could women conform to this professional image while retaining those feminine attributes through which they learned to define themselves? Men, Davis argues, are essentially expected to convey one image. Women, in contrast, are bombarded with messages beckoning them to convey four distinct images: the maternal image of the doting and loving mother, the seductive siren who can attract and/or keep a man, the innocent ingenue who remains alluring through her perpetual youth, and the professional woman who must be reckoned with in the workplace. How can any one person—how can women—be expected to juggle these discrepant images simultaneously?

The irony is that to succeed in achieving one of the above cited images may doom women to fail in another arena. Consider the ads that entice women to maintain the baby-doll image. When women respond to this image, the essential self becomes buried beneath the child image. And the child image, of course, is inappropriate in public realms such as a serious work environment or politics.

Women, who are expected to maintain a cloak of femininity while simultaneously projecting a professional image (established by men), often encounter resistance in the job market. This is understandable if we consider that dress is one marker by which we judge others and by which we are ourselves judged. Women's clothing, Nancy Henley explains, is designed to reveal the body; it signals an invitation to be looked at. If men's work attire evolved to *minimize* physical differences, when women wear clothing that *accentuates* their physical appearance they risk being associated with a feminine stereotype that is incompatible with the stereotype of professional behavior. Thus, adherence to the gender-role expectation to "appear" feminine may serve as a barrier to getting hired or elected.[47]

How, then, can professional women reconcile the social expectation to be beautiful with the professional expectation that they sublimate their beauty? The competing urgencies have led to countless articles and books that serve up advice on dressing for success.

Dress as a symbol has undergone innumerable transformations. Yet, it is a powerful form of communication. While choice of public attire was actually legislated in eighteenth-century Europe according to an individual's station and line of work (anti-disguise legislation, if you will), the introduction of mass production in the nineteenth century brought with it greater freedom in choice of public dress.

This freedom of "expression," however, was qualified. Men were limited in their choice of clothing because *what* they wore "derived principally . . . from the overweening centrality accorded work, career, and occupational success for male identity. . . ."[48] This centrality, says Davis, consequently prevented men from displaying other facets of themselves in public: "for many decades to come, especially in the middle class, clothing was almost unavailable as a visual means for men to express other sides of their personalities."[49] Thus men's status (and clothing) derived from what they did; their dress disguised who they were outside the job. Consequently, they became less fully human, more fully bankers and teachers and ditchdiggers. Albeit at a lower level of intensity, this focus on occupation (and occupational dress) continues today.

Woman have been similarly limited in their choice of clothing because how they appeared served as both social and moral measuring rods. Women's social position, remarks Davis, was conveyed through their clothing as "the expressive vehicle for announcing the status claims of the family and of its male bread-winner in particular."[50] Women's moral fiber was similarly the subject of scrutiny: "Sexual status became personalized in public as strangers tried to determine whether someone, for all her seeming propriety, gave out little clues in her appearance which marked her as a 'loose' woman."[51] Thus women's wearing apparel was accorded prominence not only for what it said about her family, but also for what it revealed about the woman herself. If male clothing disguised personality, female apparel was designed to disguise, even deny, any public or occupational life. The distinctions persist today. Thus, the cultural imperative that traps men in public and professional lives precludes women from those lives. In short, culture limits the freedom of both genders.

While clothing presumably serves as a window to men's and women's status or disguises some aspect of their realities, the styles have been largely determined by the media. The mass production of clothing in the nineteenth century coincided with the rise of the department store. Store owners sought ways to attract potential customers. The window display became the lure: "Plate-glass windows were inserted on the ground floors of the stores and the arrangement of goods in them was made on the basis of what was most unusual in the store."[52] Anne Friedberg links the shop window to a sense of self: "By the middle of the nineteenth century . . . the shop window succeeded the mirror as a site of identity construction. . . ."[53] Yet the self these windows addressed was decidedly female, for shopping as a pleasurable activity became the purview of bourgeois women and provided them with an acceptable rationale to visit public space unescorted.[54] But this was the needed opening wedge, for once women could *visit* public space, it was a shorter step to becoming *employed* in those spaces . . . and eventually to start entering public life (and the life of politics) more fully.

Today all of the available media publicize current trends in fashion; however, no venue makes a more public display of these trends than the storefront window. While magazines pitching clothing are targeted to discrete audiences (such as *Golf World, Field and Stream, L. L. Bean, Vogue, Gentlemen's Quarterly,* or *Victoria's Secret*) the storefront window must "speak" to all who pass by.[55] Moreover, while individuals may *choose* to purchase a magazine or watch a television program that advertises wearing apparel, it is virtually impossible to go about our daily business without being assaulted by storefronts. Arguments about store-window assaults, of course, have been central in the political attack on pornography in the last half of the twentieth century.

The storefront window is the medium—and sometimes part of the message—to attract the prospective customer. Yet the desires of the proprietor may conflict with those of the urban (or mall) designer. The urban designer attempts to keep pedestrian traffic moving; the shopkeepers want to bring that traffic to a standstill. The design must say "you are *en route*," but the window displays call out "you have arrived" (in both senses). There are also class differences in the display of wares. Outlets catering to the lower classes have their clothes out on the street—accessible, affordable. But in upper-class stores the glass windows function as barriers, cutting the prospective customer off from the clothes, making the clothes inaccessible, suggesting they may not be affordable or that they may exist more as aspirations than consumable commodities.

At least *part* of the reason that malls have overtaken "downtown" shopping areas in much of the country is that malls cater exclusively to the buying and selling functions while downtown areas are more government-controlled. That is, in downtown areas local politicians are responsible for such things as keeping traffic moving, zoning regulations, and pedestrian safety, political functions that interfere with the unadulterated process of shopping and are irrelevant in malls.

The glass that separates the consumer from the store's interior becomes a metaphor through which individuals see not only their own reflections, but also a projection of how they would *like* to view themselves. In short, the socialization of citizens is carried out not only in the family and schools and churches, but also in commercial realms.

It is not surprising that women are the primary targets of advertisers when we realize that women account for about 80 percent of all consumer spending in the U.S.[56] Nor are we surprised, despite advertising executive Jane Newman's contention that the new trend in women's advertising is toward being realistic "versus having a mission or promise,"[57] that the "reality" advertisers reflect perpetuates an unattainable ideal. In order to sell their "disguises," advertisers first must make women dissatisfied with their realities. Little girls learn at home and school that they must be beautiful; from commercial advertisers they learn that they are not, that they must buy this or that product in order to fulfill the cultural imperative.

Despite the fact that women have entered the job market in ever-increasing numbers, despite the fact that nontraditional fields have opened their doors to women, the perception persists that women should not project a too-professional presentation. The window display reinforces this perception by providing the image and wares necessary for the totally sensual woman. The lingerie store is one example. The negligee originated in the eighteenth-century French parlor, and the term did not initially have a sexual connotation.[58] Rather, to dress *negligée* meant to don more comfortable, that is, less restrictive, clothing at home. It allowed a woman an alternative to what she was permitted to wear in public.

Lingerie stores, of course, still sell negligees for home wear, but, perhaps more important, they also sell g-strings, bustiers, teddies, and an entire array of provocative underwear. Therefore, professional women can cultivate the required dichotomous image (professional *and* feminine) by wearing erotic apparel beneath their business attire. Adherence to such artifice (even if the only person who sees the "disguise" is the woman herself) perpetuates the cultivation of sexuality and sensuality through the use of props. It suggests, moreover, that a sensual woman is identified by *what* she wears rather than by *who* she is.

It may seem to some that the question of women's underwear is a long way from political communication. But wait a minute. Politicians must exude self-confidence, which is gained in part from wearing clothing comfortable to them. Female politicians, then, are caught in a double bind. On the one hand they are required to wear nonrevealing clothing; on the other hand, they are (as women) required by the culture always to be feminine. So a situation has been set up in which the femininity of a female politician, important to building that required self-confidence, must be hidden from public view. What better place to hide it than beneath the visible clothing?

More than displaying the props that reinforce dichotomous images, the storefront window makes a public display of the ideal body. The mannequin serves as a constant reminder of how women, in particular, ought to look. By showing a woman what she *should* look like, the glass window erects a barrier. The mannequin in the window is nubile and svelte. The woman who peers in may be older and stouter. It is no wonder, then, that so many women, who are reminded daily of the distance between their own bodies and the idealized version in the store, are discontented. A recent study reports that "thirty-three thousand women told researchers that they would rather lose ten to fifteen pounds than achieve any other goal."[59]

Again, it may seem that we are a long way from politics and political communication. But consider this: medical insurance, operating under rules enacted by male legislators, does not cover cosmetic surgery. Why? Because males rarely feel the need to use that option: our culture allows greater deviation from normal standards of attractiveness for men without impeding their advancement in the public realm. Women, however, who are judged on a narrower range of acceptance, might have (or at least feel, as a confidence-building tactic) the need to have such surgery in order to enter the work force or the world of politics. If so, then they must pay in still another way to enter a life open to men without any alteration whatever. Anything that impedes only one sex from enjoying any cultural benefit or opportunity is inherently a political penalty for being born of that sex rather than the other. If any significant number of men had to have cosmetic surgery in order to "make it" in the world, you can bet coverage of such surgery would be legally required in health insurance programs. Making cosmetic surgery too expensive for the average woman has the effect, then, of keeping such women "in their place," that is, outside the public realm.

While the mannequins in store windows may be lifeless, the messages conveyed by them are unmistakable, for it is through the eyes of the forms in the window that we see ourselves reflected and our self-concepts reinforced. Mannequins, in a sense, partake of what Marshall Blonsky has called the "Vanna White myth": "The power of the Vanna White myth is her very emptiness. Everybody can identify with her, it is said, as a sister, Barbie doll, mother, friend, lover, wife, mistress."[60]

From storefronts we individual consumers learn something about keeping up our own fronts, our disguises. We learn what is stylish, what outdated. We learn to be open, if lower class, or cold and distant, cut off, if upper class. We learn how we should look, and that has an effect on how comfortable we are with ourselves . . . and who we shall become. We learn to reach for, maintain— or disdain—status, conformity, sexiness, and hundreds of other identity attributes. If clothes are masks or disguises, they reveal as much as they hide, for in taking on the appearance of another we tend also to *become* that other.

In Western society fashion has been a component of the societal machinery by which women are kept "in their place." In the latter part of the twentieth century that machinery has come to be seen as a problem, not only for women, but for our culture and our cultural politics. If women's "place" has been outside the public sphere, what can be done to remove the obstacles to women's entry to that sphere—the board rooms of business and the "smoke-filled" rooms of politics?

To those who still do not see any relation between beauty and politics, any effect of cultural stereotypes about beauty on political communication, perhaps a final example is in order. Consider why it is that Cindy Crawford is a model and Bella Abzug a politician . . . and how many changes in self-perception and cultural mores and societal dialogue would have to take place before the two could trade professions. At the very least, we would have to admit publicly that an attractive woman *can* be intelligent before Ms. Crawford would be allowed into politics.

## ▶ Effects on Men: Invitation to War

No action is unmotivated. Most actions most of us will take in our lifetimes we will perceive as being taken in response to the situations in which we find ourselves. However, what our responses are will be determined as much by how we define the situations as by the situations themselves. That is to say, naming a situation discloses our attitude toward it, and that disclosure, in turn, circumscribes our expectations, observations, and responses. As Kenneth Burke has written, a "symbolic act is the dancing of an attitude";[61] that is, what we call something summarizes our attitude toward it.

Perhaps because of powerful societal taboos concerning sex, gender-related terms are especially liable to carry subjective predispositions. Certain behaviors are legitimized and others proscribed by whether we define them as falling within "male" or "female" domains.

Thus, practically any male who wants to have a fistfight tonight can have one by the simple expedient of going into a bar and insulting somebody. Violence is a realm controlled by men. Any woman who wants to have a fistfight will have to work much harder at it. She may have to insult twenty people, or two hundred. If she is "lucky," she may find a fighting partner; more likely, however, she will go home with her desire unfulfilled.

On the other hand, practically any female who wants to have sex tonight can have it by the simple expedient of going into a bar and offering herself to somebody. Sex is a realm controlled by women. Any man who wants to have sex will have to work much harder at it. He may have to offer himself to twenty people, or two hundred. If he is "lucky," he may find a sexual partner; more likely, however, he will go home with his desire unfulfilled.

Each sex has its own traditional realm of power and is relatively powerless in the realm "properly" dominated by the other. This distinctly does not mean that men fight all the time and women have continual sex. Both genders are taught to hold a tight rein on their arenas of power. Those individuals who do not do so—bullies and "loose women," respectively—we view with a mixture of hatred and awe, contempt and longing, fear and fascination.

Further, each gender conventionally assumes that the realm of the other is dangerous to society: in a male-dominated society, sex is pornographic; in a female-controlled society, violence is pornographic. But no society, of course, is controlled totally by one sex. Thus, rape is the ultimate pornography, for it offends us all when the female prerogative (sex) is infringed upon by force, i.e., the male prerogative. By civilized rules, the male rapist has misapplied his domain of power, and the female has been deprived of hers against her will. Even here, in discussions of rape, women (as victims) focus on the violence while men (as rapists) focus on whether the woman "asked for it," that is to say, whether she maintained the accepted female power, the power to determine whether and when interpersonal encounters will become sexual encounters.

The tenuous relationship between the realms of sex and violence is illustrated in our relationship to the land. If the land is female ("Mother Earth," "the fertile soil"), then farmers should be male. They cultivate the land, which, left untilled, would grow wild; they plow the land ("plowing a furrow" being a metaphor for intercourse); they plant their seeds; they reap or harvest what they plant—all of which is appropriate within the bounds of consent. We become upset with the masculine treatment of the land only when it passes beyond the acknowledged limits of consent. Thus, when men "go too far" we complain of the "rape of the land." "Deforestation" is the ecological equivalent of "deflowering." The sexual overtones of "strip mining" are obvious.

Just as rape is the ultimate perversion of normal interpersonal relations, so war is the ultimate perversion of normal international relations. It is no accident that the word "intercourse" is used to describe normality in both interpersonal and international relations, nor that "rape" is the pejorative term used in each realm when force replaces friendly persuasion.

Because in our culture it is assumed to be the male prerogative and duty to protect females, language suggesting that an enemy or potential enemy is using sexual force commonly is used to justify our going to war. If the putative enemy is perceived as sexually dangerous, it is presumed necessary not only to blunt that danger but to reaffirm our own sexuality. As psychologist Lloyd deMause tells us, "All aspects of war have hidden sexual content, and much of war's excitement for both citizen and soldier is patently sexual."[62]

Thus, in the days leading into World War II, Americans were tantalized with what was called the "rape of Poland." In the Vietnam War, President Lyndon Johnson crowed, "I didn't just fuck Ho Chi Minh, I cut his pecker off."[63] President Ronald Reagan was more circumspect in his description of our invasion of Grenada; he merely called the airdrop of Marines onto the island a "vertical insertion" to stop the "Communist penetration." But the Marines were less circumspect; one sergeant announced, "I want to fuck communism out of this island and fuck it right back to Moscow."[64]

The words of Lyndon Johnson and the unnamed Marine reveal the ambiguity of the sexual motive for war, expressing simultaneous desires for (1) sexual aggression against the enemy and (2) neutralization of the enemy's male sexuality. Such ambiguity is removed, however, and the motivation for war purified when a masculine aggressor defiles a feminine victim. As Lyndon Johnson said of the communist threat in Vietnam: "If you let a bully into your front yard one day, the next day he'll be on your porch, and the day after he'll rape your wife in your own bed."[65]

Clearly, the male enemy is the sexual aggressor against the female America and her feminine neighbors. The masculine American mate must come to their aid. Thus, the sexual motive for war is most perfectly constituted by symbols of rape, symbols that feminize the threatened or victimized self while calling upon the masculine self to defend violently the female prerogative.

There is a certain weird logic to the use of the sexual metaphor for war, because sex and war are the two realms, other than sports, where people really do meet the requirement of the old cliche, "putting your body on the line." In both endeavors the commitment is absolute, the concentration total, the bodily involvement complete.

Especially in a country like the United States of America, where war has not actually impinged upon the totality of the population, no metaphor is more apt than the sexual for indicating the risk of war . . . or, for that matter, the fact that here is a decision that can affect fundamentally everything about one's life. Except for sex, there is almost nothing in American society, certainly nothing within the decision-making capability of the average citizen, that even approximates the totality of risk, the completeness of future causality, that is found in war.

There is consistent evidence of rape imagery throughout the American experience. Rhetorical scholars Kurt Ritter and James Andrews, for instance, report that the colonists talked of the British soldiers during the Revolutionary War as rapists, concluding, "Patriot orators' preoccupation with sexual assaults suggested an image of Britain as an incestuous parent raping his American daughter."[66]

Whereas the Federalists of 1798 were content to respond by means short of war to protect America from Napoleon's feminized challenge (characterized in Congress by a metaphor of seduction that featured French "syrens, wiles, sweet songs, veils, and opiates"), the Republicans of 1812 relied upon a metaphor of force (featuring terms such as "trampled, trodden, bullied, kicked, and pounded") to justify and declare war on "our inveterate, rapacious, and relentless enemy."[67] "As rapist," Sam Keen has observed, "the enemy is lust defiling innocence. . . . In American war posters he is the Jap carrying away the naked Occidental woman."[68]

In Woodrow Wilson's war message, the concern for sexuality was submerged in such language as "unmanly," "intercourse," "wanton," and "excited feelings," bubbling to the surface in Wilson's assertion that "we will not choose the path of submission and suffer the most sacred rights of our nation and our people to be ignored or violated" and that our goal would be "the early reestablishment of intimate relations" with the German people.[69]

Likewise, in Franklin Delano Roosevelt's World War II war message we find the warning that there "is no such thing as impregnable defense against powerful aggressors who sneak up in the dark," yet promising that we would not fight "for conquest."[70]

In 1950, the intentionally rhetorical document NSC-68 was written to convince Americans, through their decision-makers, that the United States must respond with increased military readiness to "frustrate" Soviet goals and preserve the principle of democratic consent.[71] Similarly, Secretary of Defense Weinberger's annual publication, *Soviet Military Power,* stressed the threat of Soviet "penetration" and "Western vulnerabilities."[72] Both these Cold War documents were written in the spirit of Winston Churchill's warning at Fulton, Missouri, that "Western democracies" must stand together so "no one is likely to molest them."[73]

The sexual characterizations of Jimmy Carter were created mostly by his relative inaction and ineffectuality in dealing with the Iranian hostage crisis. He was called "impotent" and was said to have "failed nakedly."[74] Because of that "impotence," he was blamed for having made Americans feel puny.[75] Carter's 1980 Republican opponents used quasi-sexual descriptions of the Carter approach. Candidate Reagan said Carter had "dillied and dallied," while Candidate Bush accused him of "pussy-footing around."[76]

Nor did Carter fare much better with what columnists Evans and Novak called the Soviet "rape of Afghanistan."[77] The attack was said to have caught Carter "with his military pants down,"[78] yet when Carter took a "hard" line some doubted we had the military "muscle" to back up the tough words. Senator Ted Stevens, Republican of Alaska, complained, "We're attempting to speak strongly while carrying a short stick."[79]

One of the more humorous manifestations of the concern for potency concerns a C.I.A. plot, acknowledged to Congress, to deprive Castro of "his copious beard through a chemical introduced in his cigars . . . The premise was that without his beard Fidel Castro would become politically impotent."[80]

It became a Cold War expectation that the feminine side of America's self—liberty, freedom, democracy, and peace—had to be defended by the masculine, militarized side from the constant threat of communist molestation. The most dangerous aspect of any American president, then, may come when he, like Ronald Reagan, perceives a potential enemy as "extremely active sexually."[81] But discovering such perceptions is not always easy. For instance, not many understood that when Reagan said "The Soviet Union underlies all the unrest that is going on. If they weren't engaged in this game of dominoes, there wouldn't be any hot spots in the world," he was giving away just such a perception. To understand that, says psychohistorian Lloyd deMause, you have to realize that in Reagan's "formative years in the Midwest . . . 'hot spots' were sexy places, such as nightclubs or brothels, where one went for some 'action.'"[82] Knowing that piece of generational/geographical linguistic construction, one could begin to understand that Reagan identified the Soviets with dangerous sexuality to the extent of associating international "hot spots" with the violation of respectable nations, i.e., with the corruption of free nations by turning them into international whores subject to the masculine will of totalitarian rulers.

In this perspective, even America could be raped. Indeed, the rape of America, in Reagan's mind, may not have been a farfetched fear, for he feminized her image as "Miss Liberty" in an extension of what rhetorical scholar Michael McGee identified as an Elizabethan "archetype of 'liberty' in Anglo-American political cultures."[83] In McGee's words, Elizabeth infused the concept of liberty with a spirit that taught the English-speaking world to like "the feel of 'feminized' power" and to "resent 'masculinized' versions of power."[84] In Reagan's words: "The poet called Miss Liberty's torch the 'lamp beside the golden door.' Well, that was the entrance to America, and it still is. . . . And through the golden door our children can walk into tomorrow with the knowledge that no one can be denied the promise that is America. . . . Her future is full; her door is still golden, her future bright. She has arms big enough to comfort and strong enough to support. For the strength in her arms is the strength of her people. She will carry on in the eighties unafraid, unashamed, and unsurpassed."[85] She will carry on, that is, giving birth to new generations of free men, if protected in her feminine vulnerability from the foreign intrusion of brutish masculine power.

That these views might have affected Reagan's policies is not just a matter of idle speculation. Reagan specifically focused his fear for Miss Liberty's safety in Central America, where what he called "freedom fighters" were struggling to prevent that region's "vulnerable" democracy from being "overwhelmed by brute force." The "threat of Communist penetration in our hemisphere" must be blunted, he argued.[86]

The sexual symbolism underlying Reagan's anticommunist rhetoric established a structural analogue between rape and otherwise nonsexual terms by systematically juxtaposing masculine terms of force and violence with feminine terms of nurturing and consent. Throughout his 1984 speech, the president contrasted America's efforts in Central America with those of the communist intruder by apposing "feminine" terms such as "promote," "help," "support," "aid," "train," "friendship," "gullibility," and "elect" with "masculine" terms such as "foment," "control," "wipe out," "slaughter," "herd," "abuse," "brutalize," "terror," "spread," "cynicism," and "overthrow." "El Salvador's yearning for democracy," Reagan argued, "has been thwarted by Cuban-trained and armed guerrillas, leading a campaign of violence against people and destruction of . . . their economy." Whereas the communists "want to shoot their way into power and establish totalitarian rule," the freedom fighters "have offered to lay down their weapons and take part in democratic elections." Thus, "It would be profoundly immoral to let peace-loving friends depending on our help be overwhelmed by brute force."

The underlying sexuality of this apposition of feminine and masculine terms, suggesting a male violation of that which is properly the female domain of power, emerged close to the surface of the text when Reagan spoke of the "new isolationists." They, like their counterparts in the 1930s, would prefer "a policy of wishful thinking, that if they only gave up one more country, allowed just one more international transgression . . . surely sooner or later the aggressor's appetite would be satisfied." Appeasement, then, only "emboldens" the aggressor.

Reagan's structural analogue invested his text with a sexual energy and moral fervor strong enough to blind him to other realities in Central America, realities that blurred the distinction between male rapists and female victims and caused the general public to ask, in effect, whether the struggle there was actually a fistfight between two nondemocratic forces rather than the rape of liberty by communist intruders. As historian Walter LaFeber wrote in 1984, the "reality" was that the "overwhelming number of Central Americans were in rebellion because their children starved, not because they knew or cared anything about Marxism."[87] In fact, U.S. power traditionally "has been the dominant outside . . . force shaping the societies against which Central Americans have rebelled."[88]

El Salvador's right-wing death squads and the atrocities that contras committed in Nicaragua were constant reminders of the "masculinity" of Reagan's "feminine" victims. Evidence of "Lady Liberty's" presence in Central America was hard to come by and difficult to establish against charges that "when the President speaks of 'freedom fighters' he means terrorist killers of unarmed civilians."[89] Thus, Reagan's ideological appeal to Cold War contain-ment sounded to many Americans more like antirevolutionary interventionism than a legitimate effort to keep the bully out of America's front yard.

The image of the counterrevolutionaries in Central America was never sufficiently feminized by Reagan's rhetoric to allow him to send in American troops. However, the possibility of some subsequent president doing so is increased by the American public's predisposition to respond favorably to a call to arms against Lady Liberty's sexual adversaries. Americans always have been prone to protect civilization from the forces of savagery, whatever their guise.[90] The enemy as rapist is one among many vehicles that a president may employ to decivilize the image of adversaries, but because of the power of sexuality the sexual metaphor may be the strongest weapon in the rhetorical arsenal.

In the Congressional debate preceding our entry into the Gulf War in 1991, a majority of pro-war spokespersons used sexual metaphors in their speeches. Additionally, a good deal of effort was expended to make the metaphor literal by focusing on actual rapes. Lots of testimony was introduced to demonstrate that the invading Iraqis were raping Kuwaiti women. But here is a statistic that did not come out in that testimony: between the time Iraq invaded Kuwait in August and the time we counterattacked the following January, the documented cases of Iraqis raping Kuwaiti women were surpassed by the documented cases of American servicemen raping American service-women. Thus it appears that the worried rhetoric about enemy sexuality *may* be countered with rhetoric *and* action supposedly "reaffirming" American sexuality and "manhood."

It should be noted, I suspect, that when we make war sound sexy, eighteen-year-old males will flock to it. And when they return to civilian life, to what we insist on calling "the battle of the sexes," we should not be surprised that a percentage of them batter their wives. After all, they are veterans . . . and in the Vietnam War "double veteran" was the honorific title bestowed upon a soldier who had sex with a Vietnamese woman and then killed her. When "battle" and "sex" become semantically intertwined, action and rhetoric in either realm may take on some of the coloration and partake of some of the substance of the other realm.

We are used to having our government "dance an attitude" by using subjective language to structure our perceptions, but when our leaders begin using language that implies that war is sexy and peace impotent, perhaps it is time to "sit this one out."

## ▶ Explanatory Hypotheses

We have touched upon a number of the relationships between sexual language and politics—how a binary discourse system is inherent in a culture that clearly differentiates between the roles of the genders, how sexual metaphors reinforce those roles, how stressing beauty affects the self-concepts of women and places barriers in their paths to professional (and political) success, how men are forced into the warrior role and the relations between that role and the tendencies of (male-run) governments to rely on war to solve international problems. And yet, I should indicate that all of this *barely* scratches the surface of the effects of sexual language on politics.

Nor have I devoted much time to exploring *why* sexual language should have these effects. So perhaps I should at least engage in some speculation about that question. In order to do so, let me return to several of the most important realms, the sexual language of war and the question of men and women as active/passive creatures.

We already have noted that war discourse is gendered, but we also should be mindful of the fact that war itself is largely "a gendering activity, one that ritually marks the gender of all members of a society, whether or not they are combatants. . . . During total war, the discourse of militarism, with its stress on 'masculine' qualities, permeates the whole fabric of society, touching both women and men."[91]

Because war traditionally has been fought by men, all those behind the front lines, men and women, come to experience their lack of participation as impotence. War is active, thus any passivity is perceived as feminine, or, more precisely, as effeminate. And while warfare has come to be perceived as an activity of the male gender, communication scholar Janice Rushing reminds us that it was not always so. In many societies the goddess of war and the goddess of love were the same—"chaste and promiscuous, nurturing and bloodthirsty."[92]

So how did this change come about? What cultural phenomena contributed to these romantic and sexual symbols becoming enmeshed with the idea of masculinity? The first answer, it seems to me, is found in the realm of biology.

Philosopher Mark Johnson, in his wonderful opus on metaphor, contends that if we want to understand how human minds work we must consider the fact that "We human beings have bodies. We are '*rational* animals,' but we are also 'rational *animals*,' which means that our rationality is embodied. The centrality of human embodiment directly influences what and how things can be meaningful for us, the ways in which these meanings can be developed and articulated, the ways we are able to comprehend and reason about our experience, and the actions we take."[93]

What Johnson suggests that impinges upon our topic was that one way, maybe the major way, in which we learn that "up" and "more" are positive and "down" and "less" are negative is by observation of the male penis. Maybe Johnson's right, maybe not, maybe you and I couldn't agree on that . . . but I think we can agree that, right or wrong, he was attempting to explain a fairly simple idea by correlation with a fairly simple biological phenomenon.

I'd like to try to stay at that same simple level of biological phenomena, but introduce what I think is a much more complicated idea or series of ideas and correlations. The phenomena in question are the simple facts that the penis is exterior and the vagina interior, and the question is, do those simple facts help us "get at" *anything* about human thought patterns explanatory of our gender relations? And immediately a correlation comes to mind: traditionally, in our culture, men are outside, in "public," whereas traditional women are inside, in the house. The biological exteriority of the penis and interiority of the vagina are perfectly matched in traditional placement of the "proper" arenas for male and female activity. And the match, one supposes, has been taken, down through the years, as proof of the moral, ethical, and practical perfection of the "assigned" sites for the gendered social practices appropriate to those sites, and therefore for the "naturalness" of the practices also.

But that "naturalness," as you know, has been denied in recent years by feminists, among others. And they have been successful enough that a countering "men's movement" has been spawned. And while I recognize that there is not a single ideology in the so-called "men's movement," any more than there is a single feminist ideology, at least one portion of the male movement, a portion called the "Men's Rights Movement," is afraid of women and devoted to returning them to their "natural" place, thus returning all of us to what they call "the sexual constitution."

Commentator George Gilder, for instance, supposedly speaking on behalf of many men, details his objections to what he calls the loss of "the sense of a defined male identity." He traces that loss to the fact that fatherhood these days requires a mate who agrees to motherhood, and such agreement is less likely now than in the past because there are fewer social and cultural pressures on modern women to fulfill some kind of "natural" law via motherhood. By comparison, Gilder says, in earlier times men felt sexually powerful because they could "have" many women and father many children, allowing them to be perceived with some degree of awe. But, bemoans Gilder, this "awe"-full power has slipped away from men in modern times, thanks to "women's liberation" and the "liberating" effects of modern birth control methods, so that by now "The male penis . . . has become an optional accessory . . . an instrument of sexual pleasure somewhat inferior to . . . a Coke bottle . . . an empty plaything . . . "[94] Gilder concludes that these attitudinal changes mark a "radical change in the sexual constitution."[95]

In rereading the position Gilder articulates, I am struck by the degree to which he is willing to *assume* that however the "sexual constitution" used to be was *right* and however it is now constitutes a *radical change*. For if we consider the values the loss of which he bemoans—the right and ability of men to impregnate women nearly at will, the right and ability of men to have "the decisive organ" to be foisted upon (or within) any woman, seemingly nearly at random, the right and ability of men to achieve sexual pleasure regardless of the pleasure or lack thereof for the woman, I hardly see how we can join Mr. Gilder in his nostalgic longing for the good old days before the "sexual constitution" was declared null and void. The biology that he considers "natural" I find anathema to practically everything I've learned since some time early in those tortured years known as the teens.

Yet I also know, as Higonnet has written, that "female dependency is almost always presented as 'natural,' as is the state of peace. War appears to be 'unnatural,' 'abnormal'—but warranted, in part, by men's need to protect and defend their women and families."[96] To those who see this gender division not only as natural and normal extensions of our biological makeups, but as exemplary, it is perhaps well to heed Princeton professor Joan Scott's reminder that "the Nazis also expressed anti-Semitism in explicit gender terms. The Aryan, masculinized nation was defined in contrast to representations of effeminate, homosexual Jews."[97]

Beyond the biological realm (with its presumed "natural" extensions), I think the other enormous cause for our perceptions of gender and for gendered language is religion. It is difficult to segue from biology to religion, so rather than try to make the leap on my own I rely on one of the most brilliant contemporary feminist writers, Luce Irigaray. Commenting on Freud's conclusion that woman is identified with orality, she says, "No doubt orality is an especially significant measure for her: morphologically, she has two mouths and two pairs of lips."[98] A few pages later Irigaray returns to this topic, commenting, "Two sets of lips that, moreover, cross over each other like the arms of the cross, the prototype of the crossroads between. The mouth lips and the genital lips do not point in the same direction. In some ways they point in the direction opposite from the one you would expect, with the 'lower' ones forming the vertical."[99]

Although I doubt that Irigaray so intended, her description of the two sets of lips as forming a cross metaphorically captures the attitude toward women found in the major religion that uses the cross as an icon, an attitude most perfectly captured by Margaret Miles in her retelling of the story of an encounter between a fourth-century monk and a beautiful woman:

> The monk immediately recognizes her beauty as a danger to him. The image of the woman has already entered his mind as a phantasm that will undoubtedly reappear later to disturb him as he tries to pray. The demons, he thinks, will bring her image to him as distraction and temptation. . . . The monk also notices that the woman is distressed about something. He is not fooled by this, however; he recognizes the woman's apparent distress as a trick of the demons to lure him to his downfall.
>
> If he were to attend to the woman's distress instead of to her beauty, he would need to treat her as a person, like himself, with an interior life, her own integrity, her own perspective, and her own universe. To respond to her in such a way, however, would seriously jeopardize his carefully cultivated tranquility and his spiritual progress.[100]

While this poor monk's conundrum and his solution to it may seem silly to us today, we should remember that many religions (including the one most practiced in this country, Christianity) indeed do preach that women are dangerous. In Ecclesiastes, for instance, we find these words: "From a woman sin had its beginning, and because of her we all die" (25:24). The gender roles that were built up in the Christian West, including this country, were related to these biblical teachings.

Gender differences were "thought to be biologically based, scripturally attested, God ordained, and unquestionable. Yet even though gender roles were considered 'natural,' men worried enough about the potential insubordination of the 'inferior' sex that they spent enormous amounts of time and energy on rearticulating and reaffirming what women are and should remain."[101] That is, culture was built up based on patriarchy's self-image. The representation of people found in culture is the representation of people as seen by the males who control the culture.

And in that representation "woman" is perceived and presented as "other," "inferior," "subordinate," a representation that is reinforced by the presumed "naturalness" of male understandings of biology, as reinforced by male understandings of religion. And part of the reason women have had trouble arguing against these formulations comes from the intersection of biology and religion, the imagistic coupling of the exteriority of the penis with the exteriority of God (God *the Father*, remember) and the interiority of the vagina with the lack of a Christian Goddess, the lack of a metaphysical entity representing the female principle. God and the male sexual appendage are "out there" for all to see: active, doing, being. There is no Goddess; the female sexual organs are hidden, passive, inert, visually absent.

From this intersection of biology and religion, then, we get the impression that women are passive while men are active . . . and chief among the activities of men is war. Man, says P. J. Bailey, "is a military animal, glories in gunpowder and loves parades."

## CONCLUSION

▶ In this chapter we have explored the binary discourse system and seen how that system is duplicated in the sexual metaphors common in the society. We have examined the effects of the binary system upon women, especially in terms of the societal focus on the beauty of women, as well as how the binary system propels men toward the warrior image. Finally, we have speculated on the contributions of our understandings of religion and biology to the meaning and continuance of the binary system.

▶ As I was finishing this chapter, a colleague asked me whether I had a piece of research I could present to a faculty research seminar he was organizing. I replied I'd be happy to come talk about "The Sexual Language of Politics." He looked a little startled, then asked, "Wouldn't that be a little esoteric for our group?" I'm sure that is the response at least some of my readers must have had when they first arrived at this material. If any are still of that opinion, the best I can tell you is what I responded to my colleague: "the sexual language of politics can be considered esoteric only if you consider the heart and soul of politics to be esoteric."

## FOR FURTHER CONSIDERATION

1. The differences in how women and men are treated, as traced in this chapter, are the result of socialization. Yet the danger in identifying such differences is that someone will read them as differences that are "natural" and due to the differing biological makeup of women and men (what feminists call "biological essentialism"). To make sure you have not so read the material, refer to Bonnie J. Dow's essay, "Feminism, Difference(s), and Rhetorical Studies."[102] While you are at it, you might also want to re-examine the chapter to make sure I have not "fallen over" into what Dow calls "gynocentric" criticism. Finally, consider this question: "How do we reclaim qualities and practices that are devalued by patriarchy as 'feminine' without reinscribing gender differences in a way that backfires politically?"[103]

2. Murray Edelman states that "Sexuality is always political because it establishes bonds, strains, hostilities, and constraints, and it generates symbols of the ideal and of the repugnant. The attribution of a unique measure of eroticism is blatantly political because it defines the group in terms that ignore individual characteristics and potentialities while highlighting a provocation to oppression."[104] Examine Edelman's allegation in terms of the myth of the "superior" sexuality of African-American women. Did this myth grow up in the postbellum South as a part of the

general repression and exploitation of African-Americans? Was it meant to, and did it, function to underline the powerlessness and subservience of both male and female African-Americans? Is the continuance of the myth in contemporary times a measure of the continuance of racism?

## NOTES

1. M. Canto, "The Politics of Women's Bodies: Reflections on Plato," in *The Female Body in Modern Culture: Contemporary Perspectives,* trans. A. Goldhammer, ed. S. R. Sulieman (Cambridge, MA: Harvard University Press, 1985), 339.

2. M. Johnson, *The Body in the Mind: The Bodily Basis of Meaning, Imagination, and Reason* (Chicago: University of Chicago Press, 1987), xix.

3. M. R. Higonnet, J. Jenson, S. Michel, and M. C. Weitz, eds., *Behind the Lines: Gender and the Two World Wars* (New Haven, CT: Yale University Press, 1987), 4.

4. R. Scholes, *Uncoding Mama: The Female Body as Text* (New Haven: Yale University Press, 1982), 128.

5. R. Wilkinson, *American Tough: The Tough-Guy Tradition and American Character* (New York: Harper and Row, Perennial Library, 1984), 60.

6. H. F. Pitkin, *Fortune is a Woman: Gender and Politics in the Thought of Niccolo Machiavelli* (Berkeley: University of California Press, 1984), 112–113.

7. A. Gilbert (trans.), *Machiavelli: The Chief Works and Others,* vol. 2 (Durham, NH: Duke University Press, 1989), p. 829.

8. M. de Cervantes, *The Ingenious Gentleman, Don Quixote de la Mancha,* in *The Portable Cervantes,* S. Putnam, ed. (New York: Viking, 1949).

9. e. e. cummings, *Complete Poems: 1913–1962* (New York: Harcourt Brace Jovanovich, 1972).

10. S. Keen, *Fire in the Belly: On Being a Man* (New York: Bantam, 1991), 70.

11. *Ibid.,* 37.

12. *Ibid.,* 37.

13. *Ibid.,* 70.

14. O. Paz, "Sun Stones," in *Selected Poems,* ed. E. Weinberger. (New York: New Directions, 1984), 31.

15. T. Thass-Thienemann, *The Interpretation of Language, Vol. II: Understanding the Unconscious Meaning of Language* (New York: Jason Aronson, 1968), 219.

16. T. de Molina, *El Burlador de Sevilla,* in *Diez Comedias del Siglo de Oro,* 2nd ed., ed. J. Martel and H. Alpern (New York: Harper & Row, 1968), 249.

17. Anonymous twelfth-century poem quoted in C. Cassell, *Swept Away: Why Women Confuse Love and Sex* (New York: Fireside Press, 1984).

18. K. W. Eckhardt, "Exchange in Sexual Permissiveness," *Behavioral Science Notes* 1 (1971): 1–86.

19. Keen, *op. cit.,* 92.

20. *Ibid.,* 95.

21. S. de Beauvoir, *The Second Sex,* trans. and ed. H. M. Parshley (New York: Vintage, 1952).

22. *Ibid.,* 712.

23. Keen, *op. cit.,* 76.

24. *Ibid.,* 78.

25. *Ibid.,* 79.

26. J. Bernard, *The Female World* (New York: Free Press, 1981).

27. S. Harter, cited in J. Salodorf, "Is Your Child Caught in the Beauty Trap?" *First,* 17 May 1992, 54.

28. *Ibid.*, 54.

29. M. Crawford, "The World in a Shopping Mall," in *Variations on a Theme Park: The New American City and the End of Public Space,* ed. M. C. Sorkin (New York: Hill and Wang, 1992), 12.

30. R. Freedman, *Beauty Bound* (Lexington, MA: D. C. Heath, 1986).

31. N. Wolf, *The Beauty Myth: How Images of Beauty Are Used against Women* (New York: Morrow, 1991).

32. C. Tavris, *The Mismeasure of Woman* (New York: Simon & Schuster, 1992).

33. Bernard, *op. cit.;* F. Davis, *Fashion, Culture, and Identity* (Chicago: University of Chicago Press, 1992); Freedman, *op. cit.;* L. B. Rubin, *Intimate Strangers: Men and Women Together* (New York: Harper & Row, 1983); Wolf, op. cit.

34. Wolf, *op. cit.,* 14.

35. Bernard, *op. cit.,* 477.

36. *Ibid.,* 477.

37. Tavris, *op. cit.,*

38. C. Tavris, "Men and Women Report Their Views on Masculinity," *Psychology Today* 10 (1977): 34–42.

39. E. Hatfield and S. Sprecher, *Mirror, Mirror: The Importance of Looks in Everyday Life* (Albany, NY: State University of New York Press, 1986).

40. Wolf, *op. cit.,* 17.

41. de Beauvoir, *op. cit.,* 301.

42. *Ibid.,* 316.

43. Tavris, 1992, *op. cit.,* 36.

44. S. DeWine, "Female Leadership in Male Dominated Organizations," *ACA Bulletin* 61 (August 1987): 19.

45. C. Berryman-Fink and V. Eman-Wheeless, "Male and Female Perceptions of Women as Managers," in *Communication, Gender, and Sex Roles in Diverse Interaction Contexts,* eds. L. P. Stewart and S. Ting-Toomey (Norwood, NJ: Ablex, 1987), 91.

46. Davis, *op. cit.,* 38–39.

47. N. M. Henley, *Body Politics: Power, Sex, and Nonverbal Communication* (Englewood Cliffs, NJ: Prentice-Hall, 1977).

48. Davis, *op. cit.,* 39.

49. *Ibid.,* 39.

50. *Ibid.,* 41.

51. R. Sennett, *The Fall of Public Man* (New York: Alfred A. Knopf, 1977), 164.

52. *Ibid.,* 45.

53. A. Friedberg, "*Les Flaneurs du Mal* (1): Cinema and the Postmodern Condition," *PMLA,* May 1991, 422.

54. R. Bowlby, *Just Looking: Consumer Culture in Dreiser, Gissing, and Zola* (New York: Methuen, 1985), 6.

55. Davis, *op. cit.,* 9.

56. B. Sharkey, "You've Come a Long Way Madison Avenue," *Lears,* March 1993, 93.

57. E. Pomice, "A Few Good Women . . . and How They're Changing the Way Advertising Addresses Us," *Lears,* March 1993, 104.

58. Sennett, *op. cit.*

59. Wolf, *op. cit.,* 10.

60. M. Blonsky, *American Mythologies* (New York: Oxford University Press, 1992), 221.

61. K. Burke, *The Philosophy of Literary Form: Studies in Symbolic Action* (Berkeley: University of California Press, 1973), 9.

62. L. de Mause, *Reagan's America* (New York: Creative Roots, Inc., 1984), 94.

63. *Ibid.,* 95.

64. *Ibid.,* 156.

65. *Ibid.,* 95.

66. K. W. Ritter and J. R. Andrews, *The American Ideology: Reflections on the Revolution in American Rhetoric* (Annandale, VA: Speech Communication Association, 1978), 9.

67. R. L. Ivie, "The Metaphor of Force in Prowar Discourse: The Case of 1812, " *Quarterly Journal of Speech* 68 (August 1982): 240–253.

68. S. Keen, "Faces of the Enemy," *Esquire,* February 1982, 72; S. Keen, *Faces of the Enemy: Reflections of the Hostile Imagination* (San Francisco: Harper and Row, 1986), 58–64.

69. W. Wilson, "War Message," in *Selected American Speeches on Basic Issues (1850–1950),* ed. C. G. Brandt and E. M. Shafter, Jr. (Boston: Houghton Mifflin, 1960), 301–310.

70. F. D. Roosevelt, "America's Answer to Japan's Challenge," in *Selected American Speeches on Basic Issues (1850–1950),* ed. C. G. Brandt and E. M. Shafter, Jr. (Boston: Houghton Mifflin, 1960), 412–420.

71. T. H. Etzold and J. L. Gaddis, eds., *Containment: Documents on American Policy and Strategy, 1945–1950* (New York: Columbia University Press, 1978).

72. C. W. Weinberger, *Soviet Military Power* (Washington: GOP, 1983).

73. T. G. Patterson, ed., *The Origins of the Cold War* (Lexington, MA: D. C. Heath, 1974), 16.

74. K. G. Hausman, "Now That Appeasement of Iran Has Failed," *New York Times,* 20 March 1980, p. A26.

75. R. Rosenblatt and L. I. Barrett, "Man of the Year: Out of the Past, Fresh Choices for the Future," *Time,* 5 January 1981, 11.

76. B. D. Ayres, Jr., "G.O.P. Again Assails U.S. Policy on Iran," *New York Times,* 28 March 1980, p. A10.

77. R. Evans and R. Novak, "Jimmy the Hawk Trims His Talons," *New York Post,* 12 March 1980, 29.

78. W. E. Brown, "As Carter Copes," *U.S. News and World Report,* 18 February 1980, 1.

79. M. J. Berlin, "The GOP Comes Out Fighting on Jim's 'Doctrine,'" *New York Post,* 24 January 1980, p. 14.

80. E. Desnoes, "Will You Ever Shave Your Beard?" in *On Signs,* ed. M. Blonsky (Baltimore: Johns Hopkins University Press, 1985), 12–15.

81. de Mause, *op. cit.,* 43.

82. *Ibid.,* 35.

83. M. C. McGee, "The Origins of 'Liberty': A Feminization of Power," *Communication Monographs* 47 (March 1980): 26.

84. *Ibid.,*35.

85. R. W. Reagan, "Remarks of the President at the Eureka Commencement Ceremony," Washington, DC: Office of the Press Secretary, 9 May 1982, 2.

86. R. W. Reagan, "Address to the Nation, May 9, 1984," *Weekly Compilation of Presidential Documents* 20 (1984), 676–682.

87. W. LaFeber, *Inevitable Revolutions: The United States in Central America* (New York: Norton, 1984), 274.

88. *Ibid.,* 12.

89. A. Lewis, "Freedom Fighters," *New York Times,* 10 April 1986, p. A31.

90. R. L. Ivie, "Images of Savagery in American Justifications of War," *Communication Monographs* 47 (November 1980): 279–294.

91. Higonnet, et. al., *op. cit.,* 4.

92. J. H. Rushing, "Evolution of 'The New Frontier' in Alien and Aliens: Patriarchal Co-optation of the Feminine Archetype," *Quarterly Journal of Speech* 75 (February 1989): 3.

93. Johnson, *op. cit.*, xix.

94. G. F. Gilder, "Politics' Hidden Dimension: Sex and the Social Order," *New Leader*, 3 September 1973, 7.

95. *Ibid.*, 7.

96. Higonnet, et. al., *op. cit.*, 5.

97. J. W. Scott, "Rewriting History," in Higonnet, et. al., *op. cit.*, 27.

98. L. Irigaray, *An Ethics of Sexual Difference* (Ithaca, NY: Cornell University Press, 1993).

99. *Ibid.*, 18.

100. M. R. Miles, *Carnal Knowing: Female Nakedness and Religious Meaning in the Christian West* (New York: Vintage, 1989), 182.

101. *Ibid.*, xiv.

102. B. J. Dow, "Feminism, Difference(s), and Rhetorical Studies," *Communication Studies* 46 (Spring 1995): 106–117.

103. E. Schiappa, "Interdisciplinarity and Social Practice: Reflections on Dow, Condit, and Swartz," *Communication Studies* 46 (Spring–Summer 1995): 140–147.

104. M. Edelman, *Constructing the Political Spectacle* (Chicago: University of Chicago Press, 1988), 84.

# The Marriage Metaphor in Politics

*Political and economic ideologies are framed in metaphorical terms. Like all other metaphors, political and economic metaphors can hide aspects of reality. But in the area of politics and economics, metaphors matter more, because they constrain our lives. A metaphor in a political or economic system, by virtue of what it hides, can lead to human degradation.*
— GEORGE LAKOFF AND MARK JOHNSON[1]

In Chapter 8 we saw that sexual language has enormously important effects on both women and men, determining their outlooks on life, the kinds of lives possible for them, and the roles they are allowed to play in public life. In a sense, this chapter is a continuation of the previous one, for its central concern, an analysis of the marriage paradigm to electoral politics, is an extended application of the influence of gendered language on the political system.

Every marriage is different . . . and every elected official has a somewhat different relationship to his/her electorate. Nonetheless, nearly every marriage comes about and goes through similar stages—courtship, the marriage ceremony, and a honeymoon—and ends with either death or divorce. Electoral politics parallels these stages, especially at the presidential level. Hence, candidates "woo" the voters, who say "yes" or "no." If the answer is yes and the person is elected, there is a public ceremony that "cements" the bonds, called the "Inaugural," in which the person elected vows fealty to the Constitution (a kind of "'til death do us part" pledge). This is followed by a honeymoon, after which the "marriage" proceeds until the president dies in office or is replaced at the polls by a new suitor or is impeached.

First we will examine the presidential courtship of the public. Like all courtships, it not only precedes but continues after the marriage ceremony. Yet, unlike the courtship before and in most marriages, presidential "courting" is false from beginning to end.

## ▶ False Intimacy in the White House

Since the inception of the modern presidency, the American president has assumed a central role within the American polity.[2] Presidents not only symbolize the nation, they are the center of the nation's emotional life.[3] The role puts a burden on them to satisfy national emotional needs through their public

165

communication.[4] The primacy of the emotional component in presidential communication makes it useful to analyze presidential discourse through the metaphors of courtship and intimacy that surround it.

Metaphors reveal a great deal about the audiences that are constituted by their use.[5] That is, when we listen to a speech, if it doesn't appeal to us we "turn off." Thus, what the speaker says determines who the audience is and whether there are any successful "conversions." Discourses call for certain kinds of behavior from audiences and create certain kinds of communities through the metaphors that they employ.[6] Therefore, it says something about the American public that the discourse of presidential politics depends heavily upon the metaphors of courtship.[7] Perhaps we Americans are hungry for intimacy, desirous of being courted; at any rate, campaigners "woo" voters and "court" political elites. In the electoral "beauty pageant," the victor is the one who most effectively establishes an intimate relationship with the electorate.

This intimate relationship, however, is not one of authentic closeness, which would involve reciprocity and genuine sharing.[8] It is a rhetorical invention, involving the creation of the appearance of intimacy and emotional attachment. It attends to the formalities of courtship, but it is not the authentic act.[9]

This false intimacy or pseudo-relationship has been described by Anne W. Schaef in her provocative book, *Escape From Intimacy*.[10] Schaef provides a lengthy list of behaviors that assist in the construction of false intimacy.[11] For our purposes, this list can be condensed to three broad categories: first, the establishment of "instant intimacy" through sharing secrets and displaying empathy; second, the fostering of mutual dependency through enacting the role of savior; and third, the privileging of the intimate relationship through denying needs and other facets of life for the relationship's sake.

In establishing their "pseudo-relationship" via "instant intimacy," politicians seek to establish close emotional bonds with their constituents.[12] Rhetorically, professional politicians emphasize these bonds and thus enunciate the importance of the connections. Presidents in modern times have emphasized an ever-increasing intimacy with their audiences: In 1945, Harry Truman said, "the President of the United States is your president."[13] By 1960, Dwight Eisenhower extended the bond, saying that personal ties were "not merely geographic; rather they are shared principles and connections. Together we believe in God, in the dignity and rights of man, in peace with justice, and in the right of every people to determine its own destiny."[14] The friendship based on the enunciation of those bonds became even more seemingly intimate by 1974, so that upon taking the oath of office, Gerald Ford delivered "not an inaugural address, not a fireside chat, not a campaign speech—just a little straight talk among friends."[15]

Sometimes the intimacy exceeded friendship, as when Nixon declared in his first Inaugural Address, "I speak from my own heart, and the heart of my country . . . "[16] But perhaps the acme of instant intimacy was achieved by Jimmy (never the more distant "James") Carter, who defined his presidential responsibility as "to stay close to you, to be worthy of you and to exemplify what you are"[17] and who noted that "Your strength can compensate for my weakness, and your wisdom can help to minimize my mistakes."[18]

These claims of intimacy do not stand alone and unsupported. They are buttressed by other rhetorical devices that suggest the discourse is among intimates. The most important of these is the sharing of secrets. From the famous picture of Johnson lifting his shirt to show us his scar from his gallbladder operation, to Nixon's mawkish paean to his mother, to Carter's revelations of his born-again experience, to Clinton's admissions of "past troubles" in the marriage, we have been treated to intimacies with our presidents as personal as any with our closest friends.

What makes each of these acts an act of intimacy, of course, is that we get from it some information that otherwise would have been secret. In like manner, the whole secrecy apparatus of the government makes uncovering a secret an act of intimacy, as when Lyndon Johnson, in responding to a press conference question about negotiations to end the war in Vietnam, told of a private contact with the leaders of the North through an unnamed nongovernmental source, then said, "It is a confidential message but I will unclassify a paragraph or two of it for you."[19] The "paragraph or two" was inconsequential in its own right; thus, no information that was thereby declassified was as significant as the act of declassifying, for by that act the President *seemed* genuinely to be sharing. The act was intimate, even if the worthlessness of the information made it a false intimacy.

In addition to sharing their secrets, presidents must also convey the impression that they are listening to the secrets of their audience—their intimates. Ironically, "listening" is a prominent aspect of presidential speech. Franklin Roosevelt, for instance, said, "I have come, not primarily to speak but rather, to hear; not to teach, but to learn. I want to learn of your problems, to understand them and to consider them as they bear on the larger scene of national interest."[20] John F. Kennedy asked for the nation's "suggestions and ideas."[21] Even Richard Nixon promised that, "for its part, government will listen."[22] It is not surprising that Jimmy Carter, a (rhetorical) populist, went even further, often praising himself for his attentiveness to the public: "I've had a chance, the last two years, to travel around our nation, perhaps more than any person in history, in a two-year period, to talk some, but to listen a lot."[23]

These presidents did not just listen for the sake of listening, however. By listening, or appearing to listen, they opened for themselves the opportunity to claim that they had heard; that they uniquely understood the polity, had entered the electorate's world, and could thus speak and act of and for that world. As Dwight Eisenhower said, "One of the continuing problems of government, of course, is how to keep in touch with the grass roots, how to get the understanding of the last citizen, in the remotest hamlet, of the things he should know about his government, so that he can make intelligent decisions, and how, conversely, government is to know what these people are thinking."[24]

It is not just the electorate's thoughts that are important. Presidents also rhetorically strive to take on, and feel, the electorate's emotions. Roosevelt excelled at this. His depression-era and war rhetoric was full of empathetic emotional appeals: "These are troubled times we of this generation are living through. Some of us, I know, are tempted to give way to doubt and fear, even to despair. But when we are beleaguered by thoughts like these, let us remember how the nation has come through its dark hours of the past, and take courage."[25]

Roosevelt was not alone in offering empathy. Eisenhower, for instance, noted that "Not everyone is filled with happiness and hope in this season of rejoicing. There is weariness—there is suffering for multitudes. There is hunger as well as happiness, slavery as well as freedom in the world tonight."[26] Kennedy, too, felt the need to discuss his emotional bond with the American people: "In short, the Federal Government is not a remote bureaucracy. It must seek to meet those needs of the individual, the family, and the community which can best be met by the nationwide cooperation of all, and which cannot be met by state and local governments."[27]

In contradistinction, Ronald Reagan thought he heard citizens saying that no government could meet our needs. Those were the citizens with whom he empathized. He said he could hear better plans out in the hustings than in Congress, and suggested it was time for government to seek solutions by listening "to the genius of industry, the imagination of management, the energy of labor—not to some sprawling Cabinet office in Washington which never should have been created in the first place."[28]

Sometimes presidents even have admitted to listening lapses—theirs *and* ours—as when President Clinton tried to explain the continuing causes of racism in 1995 by saying that some causes "are rooted in the fact that we still haven't learned to talk frankly, to listen carefully, and to work together across racial lines."[29]

Perhaps nowhere in presidential rhetoric does the rhetorical act of empathizing with the audience reach the raw emotions as it does in the funeral oration. Yet from the end of the dominance of Ancient Greece to the beginning of the Reagan Revolution the funeral oration as a political document languished somewhere lower than at the presidential level. Political scientist H. Graff writes, "While previous Presidents wrote occasional letters of condolence to families and celebrated the bravery of particular servicemen, Mr. Reagan's direct participation in religious services has only minor precedent."[30] During the Reagan presidency the presidential eulogy nearly became "the defining public ceremony."[31] President Reagan presented numerous eulogies: for the 241 Marines killed in Beirut and the 18 lost in the Grenada invasion in 1983, for soldiers and advisers in El Salvador in 1984, as well as for noncombatants such as Princess Grace of Monaco, former President Harry Truman, Senator Henry Jackson, former Vice President Hubert Humphrey, and Terence Cardinal Cooke; for soldiers who died in an air crash in Newfoundland in 1985, for the crew of the *Challenger* in 1986, for Berlin disco-goers and bombardiers over Libya and sailors from the frigate *Stark* in 1987.[32] Professor Fred Greenstein has determined that "in five of his first six years in office, funeral orations and speeches made directly to religious audiences made up nearly 10 percent of his prepared remarks."[33]

Sharing secrets with us, listening to our dreams and our problems, empathizing with our heartaches and sufferings, our presidents pretend to be our intimates. But, of course, they can not really be intimate with us. We are too numerous and their power is of another dimension entirely from our lives. The pretended intimacy is false, just one more weapon in the presidential rhetorical arsenal.

Turning now to the second set of behaviors politicians use to establish intimacy with the public, fostering dependency via the "savior" role, I note that we are all dependent upon our intimates; the very fact of intimacy makes us dependent. In encouraging the appearance of intimacy and ensuring the perpetuation of their position at the emotional center of American life, presidents also foster dependency. It is important to the rhetorical achievement of intimacy that this dependency appear reciprocal, and important to this analysis that it is not in fact reciprocal. Rhetorically, presidents claim to depend on the public for ideas, input, and emotional support. In actuality, they do no such thing, and everybody knows it. But for the sake of the relationship, the pretense continues.

Lyndon Johnson spoke in the manner of all modern presidents when he said, "I am here today to say I need your help; I cannot bear this burden alone. I need the help of all Americans and all America."[34] But what kind of help can the average citizen give a president? When a president says, "Ask not what your country can do for you, but . . . " what is it he is asking us to do? Pay taxes? Avoid crime? Vote for him? Support him quiescently? Clearly, it is of a different order of assistance from when friends call and say they need our help . . . and just as clearly, the intimacy too is of a different order.

Presidents not only foster dependence through their need of the public, they also rhetorically strive to ensure that the public needs them. The world has become such a dangerous and threatening place that the very survival of the nation sometimes seems to depend on presidential wisdom, courage, and action. Presidential discourse is full of allusions to threat and reassurance.[35] Dwight Eisenhower spoke for all modern presidents when he reminded us that "we live in an age of peril."[36] Richard Nixon drew the relationship between that peril and the presidency when he said, "When Americans are risking their lives in war, it is the responsibility of their leaders to take some risks for peace."[37]

Lest the knowledge of peril threaten to overwhelm the public, the presidential rhetor is there to provide reassurance. After making the potential threat apparent, presidents enact the role of savior and protect the polity from the threat. Such was the case when Roosevelt was bringing "order out of chaos,"[38] when Eisenhower promised to "go to Korea,"[39] when Ford ended "our long national nightmare,"[40] and when Reagan offered us "a rebirth" that would "put America back."[41]

Murray Edelman's examination of presidential myths includes the myth that if only the right person is placed in the White House all will be well.[42] Unsurprisingly, then, whoever is in the White House tends to employ rhetoric that says "I am the right person." Richard Nixon, for instance, preferred locutions such as "That is why I shall do *all that a man in my office can do* to preserve the economic freedom that built this nation."[43] The "right man" demonstrates he is the "right man" (and that we are right to depend on him) by using the powers of the office. If the powers of the office are used correctly, the man holding the office must be the right one.[44] And since most Americans have no basis for determining whether the powers *are* being used correctly, any president need only act to appear to be the one on whom we should rely. The action proves he *is* the president, the right man; all will be well.

The false intimacy in all this is that presidents really are not dependent on us, no matter what they say; nor are we dependent on them, despite their attempt to prove that we are by pointing to all the threats and perils in the world, then trying to reassure us with reminders that they are on the job. As we have painfully learned, when presidents tell us there are threats to the national security the threat is more often to their tenure than to our security. Likewise, the pretended intimacy is more useful to their continuance in office than to our needs. The intimacy is false, for in true intimacy the dependence is truly reciprocal.

The third set of behaviors politicians use to establish intimacy with the voters is summarized under the heading "privileging the relationship." To "privilege" one thing over another is to establish a hierarchy of importance; in this case, it is to act as though the president-voter relationship takes precedence over all other facets of life. For presidents to maintain their position as the emotional center of American political life, they must rhetorically ensure the primacy of their relationship with the American polity by laying aside their own needs, ignoring other facets of existence for the relationship's sake, and expecting the audience to do the same.

Presidents make it clear that they, in their role as savior, are making sacrifices for the polity, for the sake of their relationship with that polity. Truman stressed the "burdens and . . . responsibilities" of the office[45] and was often "overwhelmed by responsibilities."[46] Johnson stated Kennedy's martyrdom in terms of himself, saying he would have given "all I have . . . not to be standing here today."[47] Nixon excelled at martyrdom, making his historic trip to China even as he complained that "it will be a difficult trip from the physical standpoint."[48]

Their selflessness, in turn, justifies their actions. "A leader is respected who puts aside personal gain and acts for the good of the Nation—a selfless leader for a selfless nation."[49] Actions that are taken without ulterior motives, by individuals or by nations, are assumed to be moral; indeed, the lack of self-interest *proves* their morality. That is why war-bound presidents always proclaim our lack of interest in gaining land or subjects (or, more recently, oil): if the action is not driven by ulterior motives, if it can be perceived as a sacrifice, it must be moral . . . and right . . . and necessary.

The burdens do not all belong to the presidents, however. To keep the savior ever-present in their lives, the American people are called upon to make sacrifices as well. Kennedy exhorted Americans to "Ask not . . . . "[50] Johnson reminded them that "the oath I have taken before you is not mine alone, but ours together. We are one nation and one people. Our fate as a nation and as a people rests not upon one citizen but upon all citizens. That is the majesty and the meaning of the moment."[51]

In addition to providing the standard call for national unity, such appeals have the effect of bonding the audience to the speaker. Theoretically, then, a president's failure—or the failure of the presidential relationship—is as much the fault of the people as of the president. But as Carter learned from the American response to his "malaise speech," it is not good form to blame the people. Assessing blame suggests the courtship is over, the bonds of intimacy are broken, and the divorce is near.

Despite media use of the metaphors of courtship and relationship, despite presidents' attempts to prove they are intimate with the public, there are indications that the public does not want presidents as their intimates. Heroism and distance are much more highly regarded than intimacy. Lacking royalty, we feel the need of ceremony. And it is difficult to be awed by someone with whom we have been intimate (no matter whether the intimacy concerned personal finances or the shape of abdominal scars). The destruction of awe explains why the Nixon campaign hated the discussions in 1968 revolving around the question of whether Nixon really shaved the hair on his nose, and it is why, as communication scholar Josh Meyrowitz has reminded us, "in pursuing our desire to be 'close' to great people or to confirm their greatness through increased exposure, we often destroy their ability to function as great people."[52]

Nixon's nose hairs aside, presidents who seek to consolidate their power by extending the appearance of friendship can end by limiting their persuasive options and undercutting their claims to expertise by allowing the electorate to feel they know the president all too well. Familiarity may not necessarily breed contempt, but, as presidents have increasingly discovered, it doesn't do much to encourage respect, either.

As with many marriages, the beginning of disrespect may take place as early as the marriage ceremony itself, to which we now turn our attention.

## ▶ The Presidential Inaugural as a Marriage Ceremony

A successful romantic courtship often culminates in a marriage ceremony; a successful presidential candidate's courtship of the public culminates in an inaugural ceremony. In both cases the ceremony is a public affirmation of previously agreed-to commitments and a promise or affirmation of a future relationship based upon qualities such as honor, love, and respect.

What is achieved in both ceremonies is a unification. In marriage two people are brought into a union. In an inauguration, the whole nation is unified. Each ceremony is more than an outward manifestation of an inner resolve, for a ritual does more than express; it performs. Roger Grainger, speaking of the power of any ritual, says "It affects all who take part in it at a fundamental level, a level much deeper and more profound than the satisfaction which comes from expressing shared emotions or proclaiming a common philosophy or ideology. The act itself expresses and asserts social solidarity and belonging . . . "[53]

What is "performed" in the marriage and inaugural ceremonies are transitions. And the major transitions of lives—birth, graduation, marriage, death—normally are celebrated with rituals. (Lesser transitions—first job, divorce, retirement, and so forth—may also involve rituals, though of a more informal and unofficial nature.) Transitions seem to "call out" for ritual; and rituals, says Ronald Grimes, provide means for "greeting, deepening, condensing, and negotiating"[54] the transitions. Dirk Johnson, writing of the 1993 Clinton inauguration in the *New York Times*, commented, "For Americans everywhere . . . Inauguration Day marks the start of an uncharted journey, not only for their leaders but also for themselves."[55] To demonstrate that point, Johnson quoted one citizen as saying "we're all excited because we feel we're on the brink of something," and another who identified the nature of that brink: "It feels like history is being made."[56]

One unfortunate parallel between a marriage and an inaugural is that both often are perceived as rescues. Both the president and the groom sometimes are depicted and perceived as men "on white horses" who will rescue the nation or the damsel from some unsavory fate.

Just as, in the nineteenth century, marriage was depicted in novels as a goal rather than a reality . . . and came to be presented as desirable only when true friendship was added to the traditional sexual passion as a benefit of marital life,[57] so it may be that we only will become happy with and accept our presidents when we quit hoping for a "man on a white horse" and begin more carefully evaluating whether the president is doing all a person in that difficult role could possibly do; i.e., when we begin evaluating our presidents as humans rather than as contemporary supermen.

Then, perhaps, we could respect and even like our presidents. We certainly could have better relationships with our presidents if we relied on the prescriptions for marriage written by Nigel Nicolson in his description of the marriage of the novelist Virginia Woolf: "When two people of independent minds marry, they must be able to rely upon each other's tolerance, affection and support. Each must encourage, without jealousy, the full development of each other's gifts, each allow the other privacy, different interests, different friends. But they must share an intellectual and moral base. One of them cannot be philistine if the other is constantly breasting new ideas. They cannot disagree wildly on what is right and wrong. Above all, their love must grow as passion fades . . . "[58]

Another parallel between marriage and inaugurals is that each partakes of both religious and governmental aspects. It was not always so. In Roman times, Paul Veyne of the College de France reminds us, "marriage was a private act, which did not require the sanction of any public authority. Bride and groom did not have to appear before the equivalent of a priest or justice of the peace. No written document was necessary; there was no marriage contract . . . . "[59] Likewise with political leadership. Absent elections or predetermined succession, there was no transitional ceremony equivalent to an inauguration by which the new leader was "invested" in the office.

But by now both ceremonies are public as well as private, religious as well as civil. While marriages are private they are also public, especially in contractual aspects such as when they start, when they end, the "duties" of the contracting parties, and the matter of inheritance. Despite the supposed proscription of religion in politics, religion does play a major role in presidential inaugurals. As journalist Peter Steinfels has written, an inaugural "has, at its core, the solemn administration of an oath on the bible, preceded and followed by prayers and accompanied by hymns as well as patriotic music."[60]

Inaugural oaths and marriage oaths both may include problematic language. In George Bernard Shaw's 1908 play, *Getting Married,* "the bride-to-be reads the marriage service, is shocked, and almost refuses to go through with the ceremony."[61] Later in the century, of course, many couples insisted on alterations in the ceremony, especially in removing the "and obey" phraseology.

There never has been any parallel movement in presidential politics, although perhaps there should have been. What, exactly, does it mean that a president must pledge to "take care" that the laws be "faithfully executed?" Is he pledging to force all of us to obey the law? Merely saying he will not undermine the decisions of judges? What?

Both institutions—marriage and the presidency—are perceived as existing, at least in part, for the care of children. That marriage might be so perceived is obvious. The possibility of seeing the president as a metaphoric father is more farfetched, but seems to have its roots in medieval times and to be related to religion. According to Georges Duby, due to "the christianization of kingship, the king," the male secular agent of "God the Father," began "to be perceived as a father himself."[62] Once that perception was in place, "people began to conceive of the state as a kind of family."[63] Given that background, and also considering the twentieth-century U.S. laws giving government power to protect and care for children—protecting them from abusive parents, feeding them in Head Start programs, schooling them, and so forth, as well as the broadening tendency to treat adults as children and to see the whole nation as one extended family, perhaps it is not surprising to find Bill Clinton announcing in his inaugural address that "We must provide for our nation the way a family provides for its children."[64]

Both marriages and inaugurations are perceived as potentially transformative. Just as a recent study of women's romance novels found that the man is "healed and redeemed"[65] by marriage to a good woman, so in politics do we talk about presidents "growing into" the job. Maureen Dowd of the *New York Times* reminds us that in 1969 Richard Nixon was thought to have been transformed by the presidency from "the impulsive, wrathful man of the 1950s, so eager for combat and lustful for vengeance, to the man in the White House, cautious and thoughtful, intent on conciliation."[66] Although we later learned that no such transformation had taken place, the revelation did not dampen our belief in the transformative nature of the office. Thus, William Safire, comparing Clinton's inaugural address with his prepresidential tendency to talk his audiences to death, commented, "Famous for his prolixity, Clinton proved here he could edit himself, a happy augury of discipline elsewhere."[67] The "growing into" had already begun; the presidency was saving Clinton from himself.

One minor way in which marriages and inaugurations can be seen to partake of the same characteristics is reflected in the fact that in both, the clothing worn is apparently important to some people. In writing about the Clinton inaugural, Dowd and Rich "applauded" Virginia Kelley (Clinton's mother) for lending "a bit of Vegas glamour to the inauguration."[68] While the description may be read as either a literal compliment or a backhanded criticism, the columnists left no doubt about their assessment of Mrs. Clinton's outfit, saying they were alarmed by "the blue unidentified flying object that landed on Hillary Clinton's head or the tan tourniquet applied to her neck."[69] Whatever your politics, I doubt you will invite Dowd and Rich to cover *your* wedding!

One final similarity between weddings and inaugurations is that they both involve love. The fact that Clinton's inauguration was attended by many leading lights of Hollywood led *New York Times* correspondent Bernard Weinraub to remark that "the links between the Clinton Administration and largely Democratic Hollywood are, for the moment, like a love affair."[70] Richard Cohen of the *Washington Post* said Hollywood was not alone: "Washington is head-over-heels in love with Clinton."[71] "Love," of course, is probably too strong a word for how most people feel for their president, but it is clear that people care more for a president they feel cares for them, and at the time of Clinton's inauguration 75 percent of the public felt that Clinton "cared 'about the needs and problems' of people like themselves."[72]

Obviously, if there is love (or a high degree of caring) there is also the possibility of heartbreak. Broken campaign promises may be seen as analogous to marital infidelity.

Although some in attendance at a wedding may think one or the other of the participants is marrying the wrong person, there is never any doubt about who are actually marrying. But one problem with applying the marriage metaphor to presidential inaugurals is that the persona of the bride is unclear. Because the people were courted, it should be the people who, collectively, compose the bride. But there are other possibilities, as when Adam Clymer of the *New York Times* spoke of Clinton's inauguration as a "marriage of political convenience" with Congress, especially with congressional Democrats.[73]

Alternatively, the fact that the new president swears fealty to the Constitution suggests the marriage is between the president and the whole system of government. R. W. Apple captured this possibility in his account of the Clinton inaugural, when he said, "The solemn magic of the moment . . . lies in what it symbolizes: the unquestioned acceptance by victor, vanquished and public alike of the continuity and legitimacy of governance."[74] Whereas the investiture of a king once led the populace to shout "long live the King," there is a sense in which the inauguration of a president calls for the unverbalized cry, "long live the system," or, more poetically, "long live America."

Regardless of who gets married at the presidential inaugural, it is followed, as marriages are followed, by the honeymoon. To explore that phenomenon we will look at one particular presidential honeymoon.

## ▶ The Passionless Honeymoon of President George Bush

Even before George Bush took the oath of office, pundits predicted that his would be "the briefest honeymoon in history, a gridlock of indecision."[75] The reasoning behind their prediction included the difficulty of following the Ronald Reagan "act," public and congressional delayed reactions to the negativity of Bush's 1988 campaign, and Bush's lack of an agenda—or even a vision from which one could be fashioned.

Despite that prediction, after nearly three months in the Oval Office President Bush maintained an unusually high approval rating, with polls indicating that 71 percent of the public approved of the way he was handling the job. That rating compares quite favorably with the 62 percent approval that Ronald Reagan had at the same point in his presidency.[76] At the same time, however, the *Washington Post* reported that "almost half of those interviewed said they only somewhat approve of Bush's performance, suggesting that support for Bush remains tentative."[77] Thus, the Bush honeymoon can best be described as "passionless."

That every president has a "honeymoon" with the media is about as surprising as "the room decor at a Holiday Inn."[78] Yet there seems to be a misunderstanding about the reasons for the honeymoon. In common parlance it is assumed that the honeymoon is a time when the media suspend their own self-interest and allow some time for the new president to become acclimated to the job before resuming "their traditional roles as adversaries."[79]

This common assumption overlooks the fact that the honeymoon is created by the convergence of presidential and media interests during the early months of a new presidency. As Grossman and Kumar have said, "during this period the White House and the news media share the same definition of the news."[80]

How long does this convergence of interests last? How long is a honeymoon? Those who write of the phenomenon are wary of identifying a time period. Grossman and Kumar say the honeymoon ends when "controversies and conflicts"[81] replace the feel-good rhetoric of the early days. Political scientist E. E. Cornwall refers to the honeymoon as a "temporary period" that ends "at some point during his first term . . . "[82]

In their textbook on the presidency, Edwards and Wayne suggest the honeymoon lasts until the new president begins "making hard choices that inevitably alienate segments of the population."[83] Political scientists Press and VerBurg attempt to "nail down" the time element in these words: "This euphoria lasts from the evening of election day to several months after inauguration. President Kennedy suggested that the end comes by August in the first year, or sooner. Jarol Manheim, examining the presidencies of Kennedy, Johnson, Nixon, and Ford, argues that 'a turning point occurs in late March, about two months after inauguration day.'"[84]

Despite all this wavering, the unofficial time period for a honeymoon seems to be one hundred days. At least, after the first hundred days, the media present their assessments of how good the honeymoon has been.[85] There also seems to be agreement that, one hundred days or no, the honeymoon ends when the president and media disagree over some major item in the news. Press and VerBurg note that "Carter's honeymoon ended as he defended his budget director, Bert Lance, from charges of improper banking activities. Ford's ended when he pardoned Nixon. Reagan ended his when he started budget and tax proposals through Congress."[86] And George Bush? The answer is not as clear. Maybe he never had a honeymoon. We'll return to this point later.

In our interpersonal lives we tend to equate courtship with rhetoric (wooing) and honeymoons with more active lovemaking. But a presidential election, despite the language about "wooing the voters," does not culminate in a marriage. The honeymoon phase of the presidency is not a period of love-making but a continuation of the courtship, still a time of rhetoric; presidential actions end it.

Grossman and Kumar explain why ingrained habits of reporters make them unlikely to attack early presidential rhetoric: First, reporters present criticism in the form of a comparison between the president's rhetoric and his record. Since the president has no record at this time, his rhetoric is presented as the news story. Second, reporters seldom present critical stories on their own authority—they prefer to pluck critical words from the mouths of public figures. At this early stage of an administration, however, most public figures are unwilling to criticize the president in strong and thus newsworthy terms because it is not yet clear in which direction the president is moving. He may be on their side and they do not want to antagonize him prematurely.[87]

After the honeymoon, Press and VerBurg note, when the president has taken a series of actions against which his rhetoric can be measured and when opponents are more willing to speak out, "No longer is the president's rhetoric the only story. Now conflict and controversy claim the reporter's attention."[88]

One of the first problems facing a new president is differentiating himself from his predecessor. With a president elected on the "throw-the-rascals-out" model, such differentiation is easy. But George Bush had no such platform. He owed his election largely to his predecessor and dared not alienate the Reaganauts in his own administration, in Congress or in the electorate. The public had loved Ronald Reagan, so Bush seemed not so much a new husband as an interloper; the "true love" had been forced out of the house and a new husband foisted upon the hapless homemaker nearly against her consent.

Differentiation *was* needed—not only because Bush had to establish himself as rightfully installed in the husbandry role, but also because Reagan's "hands-off" "management style," his lack of attention to details (sometimes lack of attention at all), slothful work habits, slick media packaging, and lack of knowledge and/or intelligence all had come under attack. The trick was to differentiate without hinting at repudiation.

Bush began the process immediately, in his inaugural address. After thanking Reagan for "the wonderful things you have done for America," Bush immediately and repeatedly noted that "a new breeze is blowing."[89] That image may not be as stark as that of a torch being passed to a new generation of Americans, but it did indicate that Bush intended not to be a Reagan clone. Indeed, much of the inaugural *could* (but need not) be read as a partial repudiation of the Reagan years—of public and private greed, of contentiousness between the presidency and Congress, of indifference to the ailing and destitute.

Several days later, conservative columnist William Safire toted up what he called Bush's "semiotics of dissimilarity":

▶ more press conferences

▶ "being prepared"

▶ noncontroversial Cabinet choices ("Not one thumb in the eye; no Haig, Casey, Watt, or Meese . . . ")

▶ family focus

▶ cultural change ("Farewell Adolfo, hello L. L. Bean.")

▶ respect for Blacks

▶ high ethical standards[90]

Other columnists noticed the changes. Bernard Weinraub of the *New York Times* commented that Bush's "energetic schedule" was "strikingly different from Ronald Reagan's."[91]

These were not just confirmatory observations of anti-Reagan columnists and reporters. President Bush *intended* that the differences be noted. Said one of his close friends, "It's important to . . . establish the fact that this is a new President with a distinct style very different from the old President."[92] Several weeks later, conservative columnist Kevin Phillips noted that Bush's aides were pushing stories "about how nice it is to have a President who can read a memo, stay awake at meetings, repudiate racism and eschew vulgarity."[93] That President Bush was able to accomplish the differentiation is not surprising; that he did so without puncturing the honeymoon with the Reaganites is more of a feat—not miraculous perhaps, but certainly a deft piece of politics.

Theodore Sorenson, no stranger to presidential beginnings, notes that the key to the success of the honeymoon is the president's rhetoric, not his actions.[94] That is to say, political honeymoons are evaluated by evaluating the rhetoric of the new president. Yet throughout the Bush honeymoon the most consistent criticisms of Bush touched on his inability to frame "the vision thing." Various commentators found him indecisive and hesitant, vague, and uninformed—agendaless and visionless. Although these various assessments all culminate in the question of vision, is it instructive to look at them separately. *Time* explained that Bush's predilection for indecision resulted from his unwillingness to disappoint his friends and was "exacerbated by his inherent cautious nature and his lack of ideological commitments."[95]

Bush's indecisiveness and hesitancy concerning the U.S.S.R. got him into trouble during the honeymoon period when he said and did nothing in response to a slashing of the Russian arms budget, a new Soviet election, and the beginning steps of Poland and Hungary toward parliamentary democracy. When publicly asked about his inaction, Bush remarked petulantly, "We'll be ready to react when we feel like reacting."[96] A former White House official suggested Bush had not yet made the transition from vice president to president: "The President weighs in at an appropriate moment when he can have a significant impact. A vice president does whatever he wants to."[97]

But not all journalistic voices were critical of Bush's "wait and see" approach. A somewhat surprising voice favoring Bush's moderation (or caution, hesitancy, or indecision) was the former J.F.K. speech-writer

Theodore Sorenson, who said it was preferable to have "Mr. Bush plodding . . . in the Oval Office than John Kennedy launching the Bay of Pigs invasion, Gerald Ford pardoning his predecessor or Ronald Reagan organizing the Nicaraguan contras . . . "[98]

Obviously, Bush's first hundred days were marked by caution. Whether that cautiousness should be seen as just that or as indecisiveness and hesitancy is somewhat unclear, but it is doubtful that Bush could have been helped by a pictorial sequence that appeared on CBS in early April, about seventy days into his presidency: First, "Oil, miles of it, spread across Prince William Sound. Then ducks drenched in oil. Then President Bush playing horseshoes."[99]

The issue of Bush's hesitancy in responding to developments in the old Soviet empire also was used in the charge of vagueness. R. W. Apple suggested that the vagueness, perhaps intentionally, mollified both sides. Promising a policy review prior to action implied enough "to give hope to those who favor new departures and enough suggestion of foot-dragging to persuade those who like the status quo that he will not go too far."[100]

Another arena where the question of Bush's vagueness surfaced was in the budget battle. There, once again, according to the *New York Times,* the vagueness may have been intentional, "because he wanted to use it as an instrument for negotiations with Congress."[101] Representative Leon E. Panetta, Democrat of California and chair of the House Budget Committee, was less than enthusiastic about the vagueness: "If you're serious about negotiations, you've got to put something on the table."[102]

While Hendrik Hertzberg undoubtedly went too far when he complained that Bush was "contentedly wallowing in a mire of puppy-tickling, Polaroid-shooting, horse-shoe-chucking, amiable vagueness,"[103] it does seem obvious that Bush's vagueness was a manifestation of (or contributor to) the lack of vision and that it sometimes led him across that fine line separating pragmatism from opportunism.

Perhaps because Bush was obviously so much better informed than Reagan, the charge that he was uninformed was relatively light and poorly documented. Yet there were a few nagging indications that his reputation for being well informed may have resulted more from Reagan intellectual liabilities than from Bush assets.

Ann Devroy suggests that the Bush parallels to Martin Van Buren were more serious than Bush's own jokes about how alike he and the last president to win the Oval Office directly from the vice presidency would suggest. She notes that the following Bush responses all came from the same press conference: "We're in the process of discussing that." "No decision on that yet." "Not sure now." "We take whatever the next step is." "I'd have to talk to him about it because I don't know."[104] Yet, except for the final response, most of these responses seem more like delaying tactics than indications of lack of information.

Likewise, when Molly Ivins had some fun when Bush professed ignorance of one of the trial balloons that Secretary of the Treasury Nicholas Brady floated about the Savings and Loan bailout, claiming it proved he was, although president, "out of the loop,"[105] she surely knew that Bush was saving face, not admitting ignorance.

If Bush was uninformed, the evidence to prove it is paltry. Most examples that were set forward can be understood better as delaying tactics or face-saving maneuvers. But the one good example, his failure to get beyond old Cold War thinking,[106] *did* suggest that a lack of information may have contributed to his lack of "the vision thing."

As we have seen, we may disagree on whether Bush was indecisive and hesitant, vague or uninformed, but there seems little doubt that he lacked ideological vision. Molly Ivins suggested that the totality of his ideology was "a basic decency, patriotism and desire for people to be accommodating."[107]

Many columnists and reporters who wrote about Bush's lack of vision during the honeymoon tended to give him the benefit of the doubt. For instance, Tom Wicker wrote that the world was waiting for an indication of "*his* ideas, *his* convictions, *his* goals. It's weak leadership . . . that the President of the United States has let himself appear so far to have none."[108] That *seems* like a strong indictment, but look at the escape clause: "let himself appear so far." Wicker seemed to imply that there *was* a personal fund of ideas, but that Bush had mistakenly "so far" not unveiled them.

Likewise, the *Wall Street Journal* wrote that Bush "invites trouble by not telling Americans what his presidential priorities are," as though Bush's failure in this respect was merely a strategic oversight. The newspaper did go on to admit that "many Republicans worry that the real reason Mr. Bush isn't articulating a clear message is that he doesn't *have* a clear strategy."[109] Again, however, the admission points to a lack of *strategy*, not vision.

The Bush Administration defense was to say that the search for vision had to do with perception rather than reality because it was based on a Roosevelt-Reagan activist model not applicable to a presidency following a caretaker model.[110] And the public did not seem to notice a vision deficiency: two-thirds of those polled said they thought Bush had a "clear idea" of his presidential goals.[111]

Perhaps the term "vision" is too grandiose. No one ever has explained why a president has to have a "New Deal" or "Great Society" in mind when he takes over the office. On the other hand, the lack of an agenda, of clearly articulated goals, of any solid convictions other than "a basic decency, patriotism and desire for people to be accommodating" seem to be deficits that would be bound to mar any honeymoon.

Even without any overarching vision, however, it is possible to establish a strong presence with rhetoric. As already indicated, the fairest evaluation of any presidential honeymoon is a rhetorical assessment. And on that count, if no other, the Bush honeymoon was a failure. Just as a real marriage may founder when it is discovered on the honeymoon that neither member has a clear idea of where the marriage will "go" after the holiday, thus ruining both the honeymoon and the marriage, so did Bush's lack of vision hamper both his honeymoon period and his subsequent presidency.

Despite a few flourishes in the Inaugural, the Bush speeches of the honeymoon period were largely forgettable. As Bernard Weinraub noted at the time, the honeymoon speeches "faded like premature crocuses."[112]

More important, perhaps, than the quality of the speeches were the speech occasions missed altogether—such as the "oil spill in Alaska, human rights violations in China, starvation in the Sudan, ethical misconduct in Washington, gun control in America,"[113] and so forth. A president who understood the importance of rhetoric in a honeymoon would not have missed these occasions; a president with a vision, if not of how the world should be, at least of how the presidency can be used as a "bully pulpit," would not have missed these occasions. John Kennedy would not have missed these occasions. Ronald Reagan would not have missed them. That George Bush did tells us much about his leadership or lack thereof.

So, was it a good honeymoon? That depends, is seems, on who is doing the assessing. George Bush himself claimed, "I don't even think in terms of 100 days because we aren't radically shifting things,"[114] yet "cranked up his staff . . . to give upbeat assessments of his first 100 days, in a public relations blitzkrieg."[115] Bush provided this assessment: "In three short months we've made a good start coming to grips with issues demanding urgent attention and decisive action."[116]

The public, as we have seen, seemed to think it was an acceptable honeymoon. That may be explained, says Richard Morin, director of polling for the *Washington Post,* by a simple fact: "He hasn't done much, so he hasn't made people mad."[117]

The media, on the other hand, gave quite mixed reviews. These may reflect nothing more than the semantic inappropriateness of talking of "the" honeymoon. With one groom and many brides there are many honeymoons of varying durations and passions. Some journalists saw the honeymoon as wasted: "He's inarticulate and occasionally silly. His administration is a crashing bore."[118] Others were able to change their criteria and still like the President: "He may not be strong on the vision thing. But so far, he's no slouch at dealing with what's right in front of America's eyes."[119]

Some, like R. W. Apple, announced that the honeymoon was over in February;[120] others, like Seib and McQueen, argued in April that the honeymoon was continuing.[121] And, of course, for those like Molly Ivins there was never a honeymoon; she saw Bush as having an "incurable tendency toward moments of transcendent dorkiness" and concluded that "Deep down, he's shallow."[122] The rhetorical importance of these disagreements about when the honeymoon ended is that as journalists announced the honeymoon was over, they were really announcing that it was time to take off the gloves and start fighting, that the period of "making nice" was over.

All of us can agree with Hendrik Hertzberg that judging a president on the basis of a hundred days is an "idiocy,"[123] but, like Hertzberg, we continue to do so. Misled by the metaphor we have adopted, we all continue to talk about "the honeymoon" as though there were just one rather than hundreds. We all continue to disagree on presidential performance, just as we continue to disagree on how to cast our ballots. And we all continue to make mistakes, just as we continue to make mistakes behind the voting-booth curtain.

The final application of the marriage metaphor to presidential politics concerns the ending of a presidency. Again, we will look to a specific presidency to illustrate the metaphor.

## ▶ Richard Nixon and the Presidential Divorce

In the introduction I indicated that a presidential marriage could end any of three ways—death in office, replacement by a new suitor, or impeachment (the action most clearly equivalent to divorce). To examine this phenomenon more closely, let's look at the only time a president was removed from office via the impeachment route (although, technically, Nixon was not "removed" from office by impeachment but rather scared into resigning before the impeachment process was completed).

Given the propensity of Americans for divorce in their personal lives and the falseness of the political intimacy between presidents and citizens, the amount of public disillusionment with government in general and presidents in particular is not surprising. And the fact that only one president has been removed by impeachment is downright astounding.

Perhaps the paucity of impeachments can be explained in part by the changing nature of bride and groom in the political realm. That is, unlike marriages between two people, the marital metaphor as we've applied it to politics involves a succession of brides. Presidents and presidential candidates woo the public, marry either the public or Congress or "the system," honeymoon with the media, and are divorced via impeachment from Congress.

Indeed, I want to suggest that once the election and honeymoon are over, the president and the public never again are perceived as groom and bride. In both press treatments and in presidential actions, the marriage and family metaphor undergoes a transformation, producing this configuration: the president is the father of the people and the husband of Congress; together they act as parents to the children, the role played by the American people. Thus, the president plays the role of the adoring husband and wise father, whose function is to be the family figurehead, representing the integrity and values of his family. The Congress is the mother, who molds her children, supports her husband, and builds the foundation for a healthy and stable environment. The American people represent the children. They often confront problems in their daily lives that they cannot solve on their own, whereupon they contact their parents, asking for guidance and support. But, like most children, they have little or no control over the parents' actions and they must obey the rules the parents set forth in the form of national laws.

Before we turn our attention to Nixon's resignation, a short recounting of the major outlines of Richard Nixon's career is in order.

In the 1950s, of course, Nixon was Dwight Eisenhower's vice president, a president-in-waiting, so to speak (and is it an accident of language that we say that a vice president is being "groomed" for the presidency?).

In 1960 Nixon tried to move into the presidential bedroom, but John Kennedy was perceived as the more handsome suitor, so Richard Nixon's advances were spurned. It was, as it turned out, eight years before Nixon could claim the presidential prize, and by then the prize seemed somewhat tarnished, as he took his presidential vows under turbulent conditions.

The consummation of the marriage took place on January 20, 1969, when Nixon was sworn in as president of the United States. As with any new relationship, there were rough times. The newlyweds (Congress and Nixon) were having their fair share of conflict. Additionally, some of the children, unhappy with the war in Vietnam, were rebelling via student protests and antiwar marches. By the fall of 1969 the honeymoon was clearly over. To placate the kids, Nixon presented his plan for "Vietnamization" of the war (which supposedly would lead to an eventual withdrawal) and started to confront other issues causing turmoil in the family.

To some extent, at least, Nixon was successful. He built some confidence in the home environment, had some success in dealing with the other governmental families of the world, and secured renomination for another four years as husband and father. During the reelection campaign there was a bumbled burglary attempt by those close to the president, but the subject did not become a major issue during the campaign. Fairly soon after the election, however, the congressional wife became suspicious about the burglary and doubtful of the husband's explanations of where he had been that night. Ultimately, these shenanigans at the Watergate, a nearby apartment building, became the grounds for "divorce," although to the end President Nixon claimed the affair was of little consequence. Congress, on the other hand, like a suspicious and vindictive wife, continued to investigate the issue, ultimately causing havoc in the family.

As time passed, Nixon found it impossible to work for the interest of the nation while constantly having to defend himself against the bill of particulars in the congressional divorce suit. Because of the mounting tension, and seeing less and less chance for reconciliation, Nixon resigned from the presidency on August 9, 1974, essentially agreeing to the divorce.

Having accepted the terms of the divorce, it was time for him to confront the children. They were the audience for his resignation address. For months they had heard how he had betrayed both Congress, to whom he was supposed to remain faithful for better or for worse, and them, to whom he was supposed to be a model. But Nixon, brokenhearted at losing his coveted position at the head of the table, made his final appeal to his children in hopes of retaining their love and support. He asked for their patience and help while simultaneously saying goodbye and trying to prepare them for the road ahead without him.

In explaining why he had to leave he simply stated, "America needs a full-time President and a full-time Congress,"[124] i.e., a full-time father and mother. In this statement, we can see how Nixon began to sacrifice himself in an effort to do what was in the best interest of his children.

Never admitting any wrongdoing, Nixon maintained that the choices he had made as president were in the best interests of the family. He portrayed himself as a victim, without quite identifying the victimizer. Driving a wedge between the children and their mother is not acceptable behavior, so he could not point a finger at Congress, though he came close to doing so when he implied that the resignation/divorce was necessary because he had lost the support of Congress.

It is certain that the children did not learn in this speech why Congress was pulling the plug on the marriage. Speaking in the first person, President Nixon appealed to the emotions of his children, saying, "I have shared in the turbulent history of this era. I have fought for what I believe in. I have tried, to the best of my ability, to discharge those duties and meet those responsibilities that were entrusted to me."[125] Clearly, nothing in the speech even hinted that a divorce was called for.

The problem, however, is that *somebody* must have been guilty of *something*. In trying to exonerate himself, Nixon came perilously close to lashing out in resentment and pain against his ungrateful spouse and children. Talking of his own accomplishments—the efforts he had made that were not appreciated, the work done in China and the Middle East that was not recognized as significant, the ending of America's longest war without being thanked, the crucial breakthroughs in limiting nuclear weapons that were now forgotten—he was clearly agitated that he received so little acknowledgment for those achievements and not a little resentful that those for whom he had undertaken those actions were kicking him out of the house. Although he occasionally dropped the "I" and employed "we" in an attempt to unite himself with his children, the essence of his message was "I did all these things for you and this is the thanks I get."

He told his family that he would have preferred to carry out his job to the finish, but, because of Congress, this would not be possible. Having thereby given the back of his hand to the spouse, Nixon turned noble, commenting: "I would say only that if some of my judgments were wrong—and some were wrong—they were made in what I believed at the time to be in the best interest of the nation."[126] In other words, whatever he had done he had done for them, as any father would have. His only admission was that he occasionally used poor judgment, but since when is that a reason to end a marriage?

But it *was* ending, so Nixon, who had dedicated more than a quarter of a century to his family, to the nation, continued to play concerned father by attempting to prepare the American people for the road ahead. He explained that a new man would be stepping in to fill his shoes. This man, Gerald Ford, could be looked upon by the nation as a stepfather taking his place. For this new man Nixon asked for "the understanding, the patience, and the cooperation"[127] of all the people. Nixon, still holding on to the role of father, offered further advice. He asked that the bitterness and divisions of the recent past be put to rest. He encouraged the children to rediscover those shared ideals that lay at the heart of their strength and unity as a great and as a free people.

I have no doubt that Richard Milhous Nixon loved his family, his nation; his twenty-five years of service on the national scene testify to that. Nor do I doubt his sincerity in this speech when he said, "In all the decisions I have made in my public life, I have always tried to do what is best for the nation."[128] He seems truly to have believed that he had done nothing wrong, so it is a triumph of his love—a father's love, if you will—that in his final sentence he was able to overcome his bitterness about being "wrongly" accused and his resentment at being underappreciated, and say, simply, "May God's grace be with you all the days ahead."[129]

So it was that on August 9, 1974, the divorce papers were signed, sealed, and delivered. Nixon's words that day, alternating between resentment and love, forced all of us to grow up a little, to recognize that the perfect family does not exist; that any member of the family can get in trouble; that the family can not be depended upon always for support; that honesty, purity and security are always temporary, constantly in danger of metamorphosis into their opposites.

And finally, in 1994, we learned that no judgment is ever final and that all actions have unintended consequences. For in that year, we buried Richard Nixon, his reputation largely reestablished through his prolific and prescient postpresidential writings. And since 1994 we have seen the congressional wife grow ever more powerful and overbearing, to the point where the power she now possesses is at least equal to the president's. She has become the chief lawmaker, reducing the president's power. And the children? As ever, they remain the victims of the constant power struggle between the parents . . . and will as long as they continue to allow the family to be constituted in this fashion; that is, as long as they content themselves with political language that condemns them forever to the role of children, in abject ignorance of their true constitutional role as rulers.

## CONCLUSION

▶ In this chapter we have traced the marriage metaphor in presidential politics from the courtship of the public through the marriage to the public or Congress or the system, the honeymoon with the press, and the divorce from Congress. As is obvious from, if nothing else, the lack of consistency in the persona of the bride, the metaphor is flawed. But it is also flawed in that the courtship is not authentic . . . hence the marriage is false from the start.

▶ I would like to conclude by recommending that we purge our language of such a misleading metaphor, yet I know that is not likely to happen. At the least, then, I want to encourage you to realize, every time you hear the metaphor or see it in print, that it is an inaccurate metaphor, that it implies an integration of public and presidential motives that may neither exist nor, in the final analysis, be possible or desirable.

## FOR FURTHER CONSIDERATION

1. While this chapter has traced the "marriage metaphor" in electoral politics, that is not the only political realm in which it is employed. For instance, welfare has been described as an arrangement of "loveless marriages between impoverished women and their government."[130] Try extending this metaphor into an analysis of welfare policies. Among other things, you might want to consider whether the metaphor provides insight into why childbearing is so central to our male-authored

welfare laws; why so many welfare laws written by our predominantly white legislators have attempted to exclude African-American women, immigrants and women with "lax" standards of sexual morality; and why the laws came under attack as they came to be perceived as primarily benefitting African-American women and "promiscuous" teenagers.

**2.** If political elections are described metaphorically as "courtships," and if cultural courtship continues to be a matter of male-initiated pursuance of females, it is reasonable to conclude that cultural understandings will make it difficult for women to be candidates for office. It would be useful, therefore, to examine female campaigns to see how the successful ones have coped with the "courtship question." Did they adopt male (electoral) courting behavior? Did media coverage of their campaigns drop the courtship metaphor? Were other metaphors adopted that legitimated the campaigns? How, exactly, were the campaigns run (and covered by the media) so as to allow their election despite the prejudice against women actively "courting?"

## NOTES

1. G. Lakoff and M. Johnson, *Metaphors We Live By* (Chicago: University of Chicago, 1980), 236.

2. S. Kernell, *Going Public: New Strategies of Presidential Leadership* (Washington, DC: Congressional Quarterly Press, 1986); T. Lowi, *The Personal President: Power Invested, Promise Unfulfilled* (Ithaca: Cornell University Press, 1985).

3. B. Rockman, *The Leadership Question: The Presidency and the American System* (New York: Praeger, 1984).

4. M. Stuckey, *The President as Interpreter-in-Chief* (Chatham, NJ: Chatham House, 1991).

5. E. Black, "The Second Persona," *Quarterly Journal of Speech* 56 (April 1970): 109–119.

6. J. Bineham, "Some Ethical Implications of Team Sports Metaphors in Politics," *Communication Reports* 4 (Winter 1991): 35–43; C. Blair and M. Cooper, "The Humanist Turn in Foucault's Rhetoric of Inquiry," *Quarterly Journal of Speech* 73 (May 1987): 151–171; M. Charland, "Constitutive Rhetoric: The Case of Peuple Québécois," *Quarterly Journal of Speech* 73 (May 1987): 133–150; K. H. Chen, "Beyond Truth and Method: On Misreading Gadamer's Praxical Hermeneutics," *Quarterly Journal of Speech* 73 (May 1987) 183–199; Lakoff and Johnson, *op. cit.*

7. H. Stelzner, "Humphrey and Kennedy Court West Virginia, May 3, 1960," *Southern Speech Communication Journal* 37 (Fall 1971): 21–33.

8. R. Denton and M. Stuckey, "Presidential Speech as Mediated Conversation" (paper presented at the annual meeting of the Speech Communication Association, New York, November 1980).

9. Stelzner, *op. cit.*

10. A. Schaef, *Escape From Intimacy: The Pseudo-Relationship Addictions* (New York: Harper and Row, 1991).

11. *Ibid.*, 103–105.

12. R. Fenno, *Home Style: House Members in Their Districts* (Boston: Little, Brown, 1978).

13. H. S. Truman, "Remarks at Pemiscot County Fair, Caruthersville, MO," *Public Papers of the Presidents of the United States,* 7 October 1945.

14. D. D. Eisenhower, "Radio and Television Address to the American People on the Eve of His South American Trip," *Public Papers of the Presidents of the United States,* 21 February 1960.

15. G. Ford, "Remarks on Taking the Oath of Office," *Public Papers of the Presidents of the United States,* 9 August 1974.

16. R. M. Nixon, "Inaugural Address," *Public Papers of the Presidents of the United States,* 20 January 1969.

17. J. Carter, "In Changing Times, Eternal Principles," *New York Times,* 21 January 1977.

18. *Ibid.*

19. L. Johnson, "The President's News Conference of June 17, 1965," *Public Papers of the Presidents of the United States,* 17 June 1965.

20. F. D. Roosevelt, "Campaign Address on Public Utilities and the Development of Hydro-Electric Power, Portland, OR," *Public Papers of the Presidents of the United States,* 21 September 1932.

21. J. Kennedy, "Remarks to Delegates to the Youth Fitness Conference," *Public Papers of the Presidents of the United States,* 21 February 1961.

22. Nixon, *op. cit.*

23. J. Carter, "Remarks and a Question-and-Answer Session with HEW Employees,"*Public Papers of the Presidents of the United States,* 16 February 1977.

24. D. D. Eisenhower, "Remarks at the Eleventh Annual Washington Conference of the Advertising Council," *Public Papers of the Presidents of the United States,* 22 March 1955.

25. F. D. Roosevelt, "Radio Address to Farm Dinners Held Throughout the Country," *Public Papers of the Presidents of the United States,* 8 March 1940.

26. D. D. Eisenhower, "Remarks at the Pageant of Peace Ceremonies," *Public Papers of the Presidents of the United States,* 20 December 1956.

27. Kennedy, *op. cit.*

28. R. W. Reagan, "Text of Reagan's Speech Accepting the Republicans' Nomination," *New York Times,* 18 July 1980.

29. W. Clinton, "Remarks by the President in Address to the Liz Sutherland Carpenter Distinguished Lectureship in the Humanities and Sciences," White House Press Release, 16 October 1995, 2.

30. H. Graff, "Presidents Are Not Pastors," *New York Times,* 27 May 1987, p. A23.

31. V. Navasky, "Engulfed," *Nation,* 6 June 1987, 749–750.

32. Graff, *op. cit.;* F. I. Greenstein, *Leadership in the Modern Presidency* (Cambridge, MA: Harvard University Press, 1988); Navasky, *op. cit.*

33. Greenstein, *op. cit.*

34. L. Johnson, "Address Before a Joint Session of Congress," *Public Papers of the Presidents of the United States,* 27 November 1963.

35. M. Edelman, "Myths, Metaphors, and Political Conformity," *Psychiatry* 30 (August 1967): 217–228.

36. D. D. Eisenhower, "Radio Address to the American People on the National Security and Its Costs," *Public Papers of the Presidents of the United States,* 19 May 1953.

37. R. M. Nixon, "Terms of Peace," *Public Papers of the Presidents of the United States,* 14 May 1969.

38. F. D. Roosevelt, "Second 'Fireside Chat' of 1934," *Public Papers of the Presidents of the United States,* 30 September 1934.

39. J. R. Greene, *The Crusade: The Presidential Election of 1952* (Lanham, MD: University Press of America, 1985), 2.

40. Ford, *op. cit.*

41. Reagan, *op. cit.*

42. Edelman, *op. cit.*

43. R. M. Nixon, "Excerpts from Nixon Talk on Confidence," *New York Times,* 10 March 1971. Italics added.

44. R. Gonchar and D. Hahn, "The Rhetorical Predictability of Richard M. Nixon," *Today's Speech* 19 (Fall 1971): 3–13.

45. H. S. Truman, "Radio Address to the American People after Signing Terms of Unconditional Surrender with Japan," *Public Papers of the Presidents of the United States,* 1 September 1945.

46. H. S. Truman, "Remarks in Missouri, Indiana, and Ohio, En Route to Washington," *Public Papers of the Presidents of the United States,* 4 November 1948.

47. Johnson, 1963, *op. cit.*

48. R. M. Nixon, "Remarks at a Luncheon of the 'National Citizens for Fairness to the Presidency,'" *Public Papers of the Presidents of the United States,* 9 June 1974.

49. Gonchar and Hahn, *op. cit.,* 7.

50. J. Kennedy, "Inaugural Address," *Public Papers of the Presidents of the United States,* 20 January 1961.

51. L. Johnson, "Inaugural Address," *Public Papers of the Presidents of the United States,* 20 January 1965.

52. J. Meyrowitz, *No Sense of Place: The Impact of Electronic Media on Social Behavior* (New York: Oxford University Press, 1985).

53. R. Grainger, *The Language of the Rite* (London: Darton, Longman and Todd, 1974), 2–3.

54. R. L. Grimes, *Marrying and Burying: Rites of Passage in a Man's Life* (Boulder, CO: Westview Press, 1995), 1.

55. D. Johnson, "From Afar, New Hope for Change," *New York Times,* 21 January 1993, p. 9A.

56. *Ibid.,* 9A.

57. C. G. Heilbrun, "Marriage Perceived: English Literature 1873–1941," in *What Manner of Women: Essays on English and American Life and Literature,* ed. M. Springer (New York: New York University Press, 1977), 160–183.

58. N. Nicolson and J. Trautman, eds., *The Letters of Virginia Woolf: Volume II, 1912–1922* (New York: Harcourt Brace Jovanovich, 1976), xiii.

59. P. Veyne, "The Roman Empire," in *A History of Private Life, 1: From Pagan Rome to Byzantium,* ed. Paul Veyne (Cambridge: Belknap Press of Harvard University Press, 1987), 33.

60. P. Steinfels, "Beliefs," *New York Times,* 23 January 1993, p. 7.

61. Heilbrun, *op. cit.,* 170.

62. G. Duby, "Private Power, Public Power," in *A History of Private Life, II. Revelations of the Medieval World,* ed. Georges Duby (Cambridge, MA: Belknap Press of Harvard University Press, 1988), 14.

63. *Ibid.,* 17.

64. "A Dawn of Promise," *New York Times,* 21 January 1993, p. A18.

65. G. G. Pathey-Chavez, L. Clare, and M. Youmans, "Watery Passion: The Struggle Between Hegemony and Sexual Liberation in Erotic Fiction for Women," *Discourse and Society* 7 (January 1996): 100.

66. M. Dowd, "Clinton as National Idol: Can the Honeymoon Last?" *New York Times,* 3 January 1993, p. 12.

67. W. Safire, "Clinton's 'Forced Spring,'" *New York Times,* 21 January 1993, p. A19.

68. M. Dowd and F. Rich, "Picking Up the Perks of Presidential Power," *New York Times,* 21 January 1993, p. A7.

69. *Ibid.,* A7.

70. B. Weinraub, "Hollywood Crowd Gives Capital Two Thumbs Up," *New York Times,* 20 January 1993, p. A11.

71. R. Cohen, "An Uncompromising Start," *Washington Post National Weekly Edition,* 18–24 January 1993, p. 28.

72. A. Clymer, "Americans Have High Hopes for Clinton, Poll Finds," *New York Times,* 19 January 1993, p. A7.

73. A. Clymer, "Congress and Clinton: A Handshake if Not a Kiss," *New York Times,* 10 January 1993, p. E5.

74. R. W. Apple, Jr., "A Day of Dreams, a Time of Commitment," *New York Times,* 21 January 1993, p. A1.

75. D. Beckwith, "What to Expect," *Time,* 21 November 1988, 26.

76. A. Devroy and R. Morin, "Surprisingly High Marks for Bush," *Washington Post National Weekly Edition,* 10–16 April 1989, p. 37.

77. *Ibid.,* 37.

78. M. J. Robinson and M. Sheehan, "Brief Encounters with the Fourth Kind: Reagan's Press Honeymoon," *Public Opinion* (December–January 1981): 57.

79. M. B. Grossman and M. J. Kumar, "The White House and the News Media: The Phases of Their Relationship," *Political Science Quarterly* 93 (Spring 1979): 40–41.

80. *Ibid.,* 41.

81. *Ibid.,* 43.

82. E. E. Cornwall, Jr., "The President and the Press: Phases in the Relationship," *Annals of the American Academy of Political and Social Sciences* 427 (September 1976): 57.

83. G. C. Edwards, III, and S. J. Wayne, *Presidential Leadership: Politics and Policy Making* (New York: St. Martin's, 1985), 109.

84. C. Press and K. VerBurg, *American Politicians and Journalists* (Glenview, IL: Scott, Foresman, 1988), 174.

85. D. Bonafede, "White House Report: Ford's First 100 Days Finds Skepticism Replacing Euphoria," *National Journal,* 16 November 1974, 1711–1714; D. Bonafede, "From a 'Revolution' to a 'Stumble'—the Press Assesses the First 100 Days," *National Journal,* 16 May 1981, 879–882; A. Devroy, "George Bush's First 100 Days," *Washington Post National Weekly Edition,* 1–7 May 1989, p. 14; J. Chamberlain, "Ford's Hundred Days," *National Review,* 28 March 1975, 329–332; T. C. Sorenson, "Bush's Timid 100 Days," *New York Times,* 27 April 1989, p. A31.

86. Press and VerBurg, *op. cit.,* 176.

87. Grossman and Kumar, *op. cit.,* 42.

88. Press and VerBurg, *op. cit.,* 176.

89. G. Bush, "Transcript of Bush's Inaugural Address: 'Nation Stands Ready to Push On,'" *New York Times,* 21 January 1989, p. 10.

90. W. Safire, "I'm Not Reagan," *New York Times,* 23 January 1989, p. A25.

91. B. Weinraub, "Bush's Bold Message: Reagan Doesn't Work Here Anymore," *New York Times,* 24 January 1989, p. B7.

92. *Ibid.,* B7.

93. K. Phillips, "Did We Elect Another Carter?" *New York Times,* 9 February 1989, p. A27.

94. Sorenson, *op. cit.,* A31.

95. Beckwith, *op. cit.,* 26.

96. H. Hertzberg, "Has It Really Been Only a Hundred Days? Feels More Like a Thousand," *New York Post,* 25 April 1989, 27.

97. M. Santini, "Bush's First 100 Days," *New York Daily News,* 30 April 1989, p. 33.

98. Sorenson, *op. cit.,* A31.

99. M. Oreskes, "The Many TV Faces of a Presidency," *New York Times,* 4 April 1989, p. B10.

100. R. W. Apple, Jr., "For Bush, Free Shave," *New York Times*, 27 January 1989, p. A12.

101. R. Pear, "Lawmakers Assail Bush Over Budget, Terming It Vague," *New York Times*, 11 February 1989, p. 1.

102. *Ibid.*, 9.

103. Hertzberg, *op. cit.*, 27.

104. Devroy, *op. cit.*, 14.

105. M. Ivins, "Back in the Tall Cotton," *Progressive*, March 1989, 40.

106. Beckwith, *op. cit.*, 29.

107. *Ibid.*, 29.

108. T. Wicker, "Pushing From the Top," *New York Times*, 11 April 1989, p. A31.

109. G. F. Seib and M. McQueen, "His Own Mind," *Wall Street Journal*, 12 April 1989, pp. A1, A6.

110. Weinraub, 24 January 1989, *op. cit.*, p. B7.

111. B. Weinraub, "How the President Lost His Tongue," *New York Times*, 7 April 1989, p. A14.

112. *Ibid.*, A14.

113. *Ibid.*, A14.

114. R. W. Apple, Jr., "Trying Hard to Make It All Look Effortless," *New York Times*, 26 April 1989, p. A24.

115. *Ibid.*, A24.

116. B. Weinraub, "Bush on 100 Days: Off to 'Good Start,'" *New York Times*, 25 April 1989, p. A26.

117. R. Morin, "No Views Are Good Views for Bush's Approval Rating," *Washington Post National Weekly Edition*, 8–14 May 1989, p. 15.

118. Hertzberg, *op. cit.*, 27.

119. "President Bush's Hundred Days," *New York Times*, 23 April 1989, p. E22.

120. R. W. Apple, Jr., "Realities for Bush," *New York Times*, 9 February 1989, p. B14.

121. Seib and McQueen, *op. cit.*, A6.

122. Ivins, *op. cit.*, 40.

123. Hertzberg, *op. cit.*, 27.

124. R. M. Nixon, "Resignation," in *Presidential Rhetoric: 1961 to the Present*, 5th ed., ed. T. Windt (Dubuque, IA: Kendall/Hunt, 1994), 229–232.

125. *Ibid.*

126. *Ibid.*

127. *Ibid.*

128. *Ibid.*

129. *Ibid.*

130. F. A. Kornbluh, "The New Literature on Gender and the Welfare State: The U.S. Case," *Feminist Studies* 22 (Spring 1996): 171–197.

# Secrecy, Surveillance, and Lies:
## Government Impediments to the Societal Dialogue

*If a government is responsible to an electorate it has to communicate with the electorate, whether by deceiving it, debauching it, pandering to it, or striving to make political sense with it.*

— I. ROBINSON[1]

**S**ecrecy, surveillance, and lies might seem to be strange topics in a book devoted to communication, yet I maintain that they are some of the more communicative activities of our government.

Governmental secrets, like personal secrets, say something about how the secret-holders perceive others, about what kinds of information they think are too damning to trust to others, about what arenas of their activities they think are too important and too dangerous to be shared.

In our personal lives, when we find that friends are keeping secrets from us, we may be hurt because we conclude the friends do not trust us. And we may also be suspicious, because we conclude that our friends have something to hide, probably something that would lead us to make negative judgments about their personalities or activities.

Government secrets probably should, but seldom do, conjure up identical thoughts. That is, we probably should conclude that the government does not trust us. And we probably should be suspicious of the motivations that led to the secrecy; we should want to know what has been going on that the government doesn't want us to know about.

In our personal lives, when we are stung by friends' secrecy, we often conclude that, although it hurts to admit it, our friends have a right to keep whatever secrets they want and determine for themselves how close they want their relationships with us to be. But with government secrets such conclusions are inappropriate. The government does not have a right to keep whatever secrets it wants because the government is engaged in public business; hence, the public, whose business it is, has the right to know what is being done. Further, the relationship between government and citizen is not for the government to decide; only the citizens legitimately can make that decision.

Surveillance is the consort of secrecy. By secrecy the government keeps information it does not want others to have; by surveillance the government gathers information others do not want it to have. Ultimately, of course, government information—gathered surreptitiously and kept secret—leads to policies. And these policies themselves are often secret, so that citizens have no entry at all to what the government is doing, supposedly in their name and for their benefit, no opportunity to voice their opinions or to enter the ongoing conversation.

And the societal conversation itself is damaged by government lies, just as our private conversations are damaged by lies. Of course, most people *expect* government lies, hence are not particularly upset when they encounter them. That acceptance, I suspect, at least partly stems from the fact that we engage in lies in our own lives. We may not tell important "whoppers"; we may console ourselves with the thought that we tell only "little white lies," but we *do* know that we lie. As communication researchers Robert Hopper and Robert A. Bell have pointed out, we even lie nonverbally: "We smile at people we do not like. We act busy to deter others from asking for favors. We hide our anger to avoid conflicts and pretend to be angry to force concessions."[2]

But I hope nobody thinks that government lies bear any but the most superficial resemblance to the "lie" in the "good to see you" smile. The latter does not determine who will be president, whether a war will take place, or whether our democracy will continue. Getting caught in a conversation with somebody we dislike because we lied by smiling can be uncomfortable; lies in government are not just uncomfortable, they are dangerous.

There is, then, a clear relationship between secrecy, surveillance, lies, and communication—the first three are, in some ways, the antitheses of communication. To be communicative is to be open (although there are varying degrees of communicative openness); to be secretive is to be closed (again, with varying degrees). Further, "open" and "closed" are more than merely strategic communicative choices—they are ways of life that affect all aspects of our being, including our psychological makeup and our ideological value structure.

For these reasons, Professor Edwin Black of the University of Wisconsin has argued that "those who value freedom preeminently also value disclosure, while those who value order preeminently are disposed to abide mystery."[3] As we already have seen, both liberals and conservatives prize freedom, and both prize order. Nevertheless, on this issue, it is generally true that liberals opt for open government and conservatives for governmental secretiveness, surveillance, and, under extreme circumstances, lies.

Like most generalizations, however, this one is not absolute, so we find many conservatives, especially those with a libertarian bent, who will bow to no one in their opposition to governmental secrecy, surveillance, and duplicity. Again, Professor Black is persuasive in explaining why many who otherwise hew the conservative line oppose secretive government. He suggests that total openness, in both our personal lives and in government, can at least be imagined, but none of us can even imagine lives or governments that exist in total secrecy. In an individual life, total secrecy would lead to hermitlike existence, while in government it not only would undermine the societal dialogue, but eliminate it. Thus, he concludes, "We can . . . find an unqualified approval of openness but only a qualified approval of secrecy."[4]

Additionally, of course, all of us, liberal and conservative and all shadings in between, believe in democracy. Our belief predisposes us to openness rather than secrecy, to thinking responsibility is attached to authority, and to the thought that one responsibility of government is to be honest with its bosses, the people. We even have cemented this boss-worker relationship semantically by conjuring up a single name for all government employees, from the simplest janitor to the president of the United States; we say they are all "public servants." This mind-set obviously does not take kindly to secrecy amongst the servants, to having the servants spy on the bosses and lie to them.

This chapter, then, is devoted to an examination of ways in which secrecy, surveillance, and lies damage the societal dialogue. First, however, we will want to examine the scope of such activities and the justifications for them as set forth by the government, giving special attention to the major "justification" that these three communicative activities are necessary to protect national security. Having accomplished the preliminary steps, we then turn to the question of the relationship of these activities to political communication. We will examine how their antidemocratic nature endangers the free marketplace of ideas, how they are dangerous in that they allow the government to determine the relationships between the government and the citizens, how they cast a "chilling" effect on our willingness to engage in the activities of citizenship, and how, eventually, they destroy our trust in the government. First, however, the preliminary steps.

## ▶ Scope

Each week the Pentagon alone classifies a stack of documents higher than the Empire State building. Each week! And the Pentagon is only one of twelve government agencies authorized to use the "top secret" stamp, one of twenty-five agencies allowed to use the "secret" stamp. There is almost no way of knowing the total amount of material secreted away from citizens in any given year by the thirty-four thousand individual government employees who are authorized to determine which secrecy stamp to use on documents, although it has been estimated that the yearly secrets increased by 40 percent during the Reagan years[5] and another 5 percent in the first year of the Clinton presidency.[6] The U.S. House of Representative's Subcommittee on Government Information, in the years between 1955 and 1960, "held 173 public hearings and investigations and issued 17 volumes of hearings transcripts and 14 volumes of reports, all of which documented secrecy in the federal government."[7] According to the U.S. Information Security Oversight Office, the number of documents classified as secret in 1989 was 6,796,501—or thirteen per minute.[8]

A 1994 audit by the Office of Management and Budget discovered that the *process* of secrecy—determining what should be kept secret, sorting the secrets into some kind of schema that theoretically would allow retrieval of the secrets, and guarding the secrets behind locked doors—costs approximately $16 billion a year.[9]

Surveillance is a relatively new activity of the United States government. Prior to the end of World War II about the only Americans who knew anything about, or were concerned with, surveillance (outside an occasional paranoid) were scholars on Nazi Germany and Communist Russia and a few writers of political fiction such as Aldous Huxley and George Orwell. But by the 1990s, we all have to be concerned, for the surveillance is not just of other governments—U.S. citizens are being watched, too.

We are used to defining the contemporary social situation as an "information society," but that phrase, says communication professor Oscar Gandy, "is a misnomer that hides the extent to which industrial societies have in fact become surveillance societies."[10] As the former Chairman of the Board of I.B.M. has testified, "In the past you had to be famous or infamous to have a dossier. Today there can be a dossier on anyone."[11] In 1974 Senator Sam Ervin "discovered 858 Federal banks containing more than one billion records on American citizens."[12] Only 10 per cent of these federal data banks are specifically authorized by statute; 60 percent of them regularly share information on individuals with other government agencies; 50 percent do not allow the subjects of the files to review or correct their records; and 40 percent of the subjects are unaware of the existence of records on them.[13]

Almost the extreme opposite is the case with lies—we all know the government tells them. The mendacity rate of our contemporary government is so high that only the hopelessly naïve and romantically patriotic fail to notice it. The habit of telling lies is clearly endemic to politics, from the start of the campaign, where, as correspondent Timothy Smith points out, the candidate denies candidacy, claiming to be "only testing the waters, and so forth"[14] to the end-of-career autobiography, in which the retired politician puts a nice gloss on everything done when in office. Because of the ubiquity of political lies, we assume all politicians lie; as a correlate, we also assume that it is naïve to believe otherwise, or even to complain about it. As Russell Baker of the *New York Times* comments, "Anyone who accepts campaign talk at face value, goes the tolerated view of politics, deserves the gulling he will inevitably get."[15]

## ▶ Are They Ever Legitimate?

I am not making a blanket denouncement of all secrecy, surveillance, and lies. Sometimes secrets are legitimate. Sometimes intelligence sources must be protected. Official plans such as combat operations and even economic plans that, if divulged, would lead to land or commodity speculation; matters of individual privacy; and information that might compromise friendly foreign governments or leaders might legitimately be kept secret. Privacy is necessary in a number of arenas: military, economic, and legal.

While there are many possible purposes for surveillance, those that come nearest to legitimacy are those avowed by the agencies that engage in the process. For instance, the United States Army justifies its domestic surveillance as necessary to carry out its responsibility for warning against the outbreak of civil disturbances.[16] That is, Army officials cannot warn against such an outbreak unless they gather information that might indicate that a civil disturbance is on the way. And, while they are at it, they also collect information that might be useful to Army troops if they are sent into the area where the outbreak is taking place.

The Justice Department requests warrants to wiretap if "there is probable cause for belief that an individual is committing, has committed, or is about to commit a crime." The warrantless wiretaps, one supposes, are used when Justice officials *think* something like that is going on but do not have enough evidence to convince a judge that there is "probable cause." The Justice Department also is allowed to wiretap foreign governments and individuals without a warrant. Prior to 1972 it also could wiretap suspected domestic groups without a warrant, but had so abused that "right" in the 1960s that its doing so was outlawed in 1972—which explains why Reagan decided to allow the C.I.A. to take over that "responsibility."

Local police departments engage in surveillance when they think an event has "a potential for violence" or will create problems for them (such as traffic, crowd control, noise, or group conflict problems).[17]

It is more difficult to find legitimate arenas of governmental lies, although the individual white lies of politicians probably should not be considered worrisome.

Yet, I would insist that much too much governmental communication is poisoned with secrecy, surveillance, and lies. There are, it seems to me, too many secrets and too many lies; the legitimations for secrecy and surveillance are drawn much too broadly. An enormous leap into openness may be necessary if American citizens ever expect to retake control of the societal dialogue (and the government).

But I am not denigrating the importance of national security. I want to protect both national security and civil liberties.

Ultimately, many think secrecy is necessary to protect the national security. Yet it could be said that even if secrecy does advance national security (a somewhat shaky proposition), that fact alone does not establish it as desirable in a democratic state. Unfortunately, I find that the national security "cover" used to justify secrecy, surveillance, and lies is often illegitimate. It has not been many years since the director of the National Security Agency appeared before a congressional committee and refused to answer any questions because "he did not consider that the National Security Agency was subject to the Constitution . . . "[18] Imagine, a government official who believed he could keep all his activities secret because he thought the Constitution did not apply to him! On this issue I agree with Stansfield Turner, a former Director of the C.I.A., who said the risk of governmental secrecy is that "our government will operate without the consent of the governed . . . will do things in secret that the governed would not consent to if they knew about them."[19]

Further, I would argue that "national security" is not the totality of "national interest" any more than "personal security" is the totality of "personal interest." Most of us remember a time early in our "dating years" when we wanted to go somewhere our parents were worried about. They argued that it was "dangerous" (i.e., they were concerned for our personal security), but we thought the advantages more than compensated for the danger (i.e., that our other interests outweighed the security interest). No doubt we would have been safer if we had stayed home, but we can't stay at home all our lives just because it is safer. In a similar way, it is undoubtedly true that the government could improve public safety with a giant infusion of secrecy, surveillance, and lies; the question is, are there other interests as important to us as safety? For instance, is it possible we are willing to accept some degree of insecurity in order to gain access to information we need to exercise influence over public policy? Is it possible we would rather be free to travel about the world as we wish than have our every step traced by the government in order to ensure our safety?

About ten years ago a friend of mine whose family originally migrated here from Russia decided to return to the "homeland" to visit a cousin he had never met. When he arrived at the cousin's home town, he stopped at a filling station to ask directions to the address he had for the cousin. Before he even got out of his car, a police car pulled into the station behind him. The police approached his car and said, "Mr. _____ (using his correct name), your cousin is waiting to meet you at his home—go two blocks east, turn south, third house on the right."

For ten years I thought this to be a perfect example of the kind of unfreedom that results when a society is totally under surveillance . . . and felt sorry for the Russians. Then this past summer I returned to the town of my childhood in the Midwest. When I got to town I stopped at a store to buy a house gift for my cousin, with whom I was to be staying a few days. When I arrived at his house fifteen minutes later he called out, "Hi, I heard you were in town." He had heard it on the police band on his radio—the local police had run a check of my car license through the national system. My short stop for a present had given them sufficient time to complete their "investigation." The local police were merely protecting the security of their little town, but that security was purchased with my freedom.

I immediately thought of my friend's experience in Russia, and wondered if our system had become too much like theirs. Clearly, there are many ways to lose freedom, and the most pernicious may not be the most obvious. People may be able to go about their daily lives in seemingly total freedom, but, as Frank Donner noted over twenty years ago, "if their steps are tracked by spies and informers, their words noted down for crimination, their associates watched as conspirators—who shall say that they are free?"[20]

As with secrecy and surveillance, we often hear that the government has a right to lie to us because of national security, national interest. The government *depends* on you to assume that national security equals national interest, thus making it easier to prove that lying to protect that national security is in the best national interest. But we can dismantle this hoax by asking how we would be safer, with a democracy or a dictatorship? No political scientist would deny that our streets would be safer and our shores more secure if we were a dictatorship. Because of their secrecy, their decision-making speed, and their ruthlessness, dictatorships are more able to protect national security and to make the society safe from external and internal enemies.

The next question is, is it in our national interest to abandon our democratic orientation and become a dictatorship? I hope you agree that it is not, that the price we would have to pay for that increased security is too high. And I hope, concomitantly, that you now agree that national security is not the be-all and end-all of national interest, that, indeed, they can be incompatible.

At the very least, we should be able to agree that most of the major lies of the modern era, rationalized as having been necessary for the national security, did not improve our security at all.

▶ How was our security improved when Dwight Eisenhower's government lied to us about the U-2 plane shot down over Russia?[21]

▶ How was our security improved when John Kennedy lied to us about the Bay of Pigs invasion?[22]

▶ How was our security improved when Lyndon Johnson lied to us about the level of our troop involvement in Vietnam in the mid-'60s?[23]

▶ How was our security improved when Richard Nixon told us we had respected the neutrality of Cambodia when the truth was that we had bombed Cambodia with 3,630 B-52 raids?[24]

▶ How was our security improved when Gerald Ford lied to us about the Cambodian "piracy" of the *Mayaguez,* an American ship?[25]

▶ How was our security improved when Jimmy Carter misled us about the nature of the 1970s energy crisis?[26]

▶ How was our security improved when Reagan's White House spokesman, Larry Speakes, said it was "preposterous" to think U.S. forces might invade Grenada and that no invasion would take place?[27]

▶ How was our security improved when George Bush lied about being willing to wait a year for the sanctions against Iraq to work, then attacking Iraq militarily only five months later?

▶ How was our security improved when Bill Clinton lied about keeping guns out of Bosnia?

The point has been made: many lies for reasons of national security do not increase our security. Even if they did, that, in itself, would not justify them because national security is not the totality of national interest.

It should be obvious that what makes all these "national security" lies possible is secrecy. The so-called "security classification system," says David Wise, allows the government "to keep from public view policies, decisions and actions that are exactly the opposite of what the public is told."[28] The danger is not only that we are being lied to, but what the government *does* that it has to deny—such as attempting to replace governments through military coups in Laos in 1959 and Cuba in 1961; getting the public to support actions taken for other reasons, as was the case with the lies about the Gulf of Tonkin activities in 1966, which garnered public support for widening the Vietnam War; planning or actually attempting to assassinate leaders such as Fidel Castro and Muammar Qaddafi; and trading arms for hostages with a sworn enemy, Iran.

Ultimately, of course, the combination of secrecy, surveillance, and lies in the international arena becomes a way of life. As Norman Cousins has argued, it is but a short step from withholding information and lying about foreign politics to using "deceit and underhanded tactics in the general affairs of government."[29] The Declaration of Independence refers to a "decent respect for the opinions of mankind," but contemporary American administrations have not even shown a decent respect for the opinions of Americans. Keeping the truth from us, lying to us, spying on us, the government in recent years has forgotten that "our society was dedicated to the proposition that it is a human enterprise before it is a national enterprise."[30]

## ▶ Relationship to Political Communication

Secrecy, surveillance and lies are anti-democratic. All three endanger the free marketplace of ideas, either by distorting the available information or by altering the relationships of the people involved. The use of the word "marketplace" here cues us to the capitalistic analogy being used. But the metaphor is not just a *figurative* metaphor; in our system it is *literally* the case that the citizens are supposed to be the bosses and the government is designed to work for us.

If you look at our system through the capitalism lens you immediately perceive how illegitimate secrecy, surveillance, and lies are and how debilitating to political decision-making. Workers never have the right to keep secrets about the business from the boss; they never have the right to spy on the boss; they never have the right to lie to the boss.

So if we citizens are the bosses, then government officials have no right to keep secrets from us, to spy on us, or to lie to us. Such government actions immediately should raise the question, "who's in charge here, anyway?"

All three governmental actions impair democratic decision-making. If the government keeps secrets from us and lies to us, then we do not have the information we need to evaluate public policies. Nor do we have the information necessary to judge how well the office-holders are doing their jobs. Likewise, if the government spies on us when we get together to protest a government action, we are intimidated into silence and inactivity, i.e., into abandoning our right to decide policy, to be the bosses, to communicate with each other openly and freely about what we think we as a country ought to be doing.

People do, of course, judge government policies, whether they have sufficient information or not. If the government withholds the needed information, that judging will be done in ignorance. A public opinion not founded on facts, however, is worth little.

In addition to judging policies, we also judge public officials—presidents, congresspeople, judges, bureaucrats, and so forth. Indeed, we often judge officials by their policies. But without the ability to judge policy rationally, there is no rational basis for judging the officials.

Unfortunately, government officials often rely on citizen ignorance. Knowing that their secret policies and actions cannot be judged, they have less reason to be honest and responsible. Running through the congressional testimony about "Irangate" were stories of how officials achieved "plausible deniability" by a combination of secrecy and lies. Reading the "Irangate" hearings, we can clearly see that the Reagan Administration learned well the lesson of Watergate, namely, as I. F. Stone notes, that "the key to successful conspiracy is that the higher-ups do not ask what's going on, and the lower-downs do not tell them."[31]

The "move" from secrecy to conspiracy is neither fanciful nor unusual. In fact, conspiracy is a near-certain, natural result of a policy of secrecy. Senator Edmund Muskie traced the relationship in his commentary on Watergate: "Secrecy encouraged isolation. Isolation inspired contempt for uninformed opposition. Contempt bred conspiracy. . . . national security became the excuse . . . . So they began not to tell the truth. They began to lie."[32]

Senator Muskie talked of a "National Security elite" unable to trust others. Our national experience is that any insular and insulated bureaucracy soon begins to perceive outsiders as troublemakers and their own actions as beyond the law. William C. Sullivan, once third in command at the F.B.I., has testified at a Senate hearing that not once in his thirty years with the Bureau "did I hear anybody, including myself, raising the question: 'Is this course of action which we have agreed upon lawful, is it legal, is it moral?'"[33]

Clearly, then, removing the citizen as a participant in decision-making is a serious violation of democratic principles. If the government can make decisions and lie to the citizens, either about the nature of the decisions or the motivations for them, it leaves no role for the citizens to play. As constitutional scholar Mark Yudof has written, "When government keeps its policy initiatives secret or characterizes events in the absence of other sources of information, it undermines full discussion of public policy matters and, ultimately, the electoral process. The obvious danger is that government persuaders will come to disrespect citizens and their role of ultimate decider, and manipulate them by communicating only what makes them accede to government's plans, policies, and goals."[34]

Obtaining access to information about alternatives that were debated and discarded before a decision was made can be as important as the actual government decisions that are announced. It is important to be able to evaluate the decision-making process while it is still a process. Citizens have the right to know whether an administration really is committed to the policies it claims to support. Citizens have the right to know how far an administration really is prepared to go in trying to help allies and what the consequences of these actions are likely to be. They have the right to participate in or otherwise influence these decisions.

The removal of citizens from participation in decision-making endangers individual rights and participatory democracy; threatens the purpose of the First Amendment protections of speech, press, assembly, and petition; and diminishes the free marketplace of ideas and the information essential to intelligent self-government in a democratic system. It is amazing (and amazingly accepted without complaint) that while we have laws making it illegal for the executive branch to lie to the legislative branch, there are no laws forbidding any branch of government from lying to the public.

Not every citizen, of course, *wants* to be involved in decision-making, but democratic theory suggests that *at a minimum* each citizen should have the right to cast an informed vote. That is, democratic doctrine requires that policy be based on the rational consent of the community. And rational consent, indeed rationality itself, cannot be achieved without adequate understanding of all the pertinent facts. Hence, any substantial withholding or distortion of information by the government conflicts with the basic assumption of the democratic system.[35] As Joseph Lyford has commented, "The framers of the Constitution can hardly have envisioned the state as an enemy of the people,"[36] yet how else can we perceive a government that refuses us the information we need rationally to evaluate the actions of our elected officials? Constitutional scholar Thomas Emerson has noted that allowing the government to control access to the facts "ultimately confines the whole decision-making process to those who possess the crucial information."[37]

Democracy, to work, requires trust in both the intelligence and the honor of the citizenry. When that trust is missing, the government comes to fear citizen involvement. Apparently the Nixon Administration succumbed to some such fear, leading to that whole complex of events that has become encapsulated in the term "Watergate." As the *New York Times* editorialized at the time, "Where fear is chronic, such terms as right and wrong, moral and immoral, legal and illegal lose their meaning."[38] Thus, the White House defended its break-in and burglary of a psychiatrist's office as an act of national defense. In that climate, one of Nixon's lieutenants, asked whether the president's power might extend beyond burglary and even to murder to protect the national interest, refused to draw any firm line outlawing such an act.

I suspect the people would have drawn a firm line, not only against murder but also against burglary. But the people were not involved in the decision-making, and can never be involved without information.

Not only does governmental withholding and distorting of information contradict general democratic theory, interfering with the accuracy of information between the branches of government contradicts the system of checks and balances set up in our democratic Constitution. Separate but coequal powers can only work if both branches have the information. It should not even be necessary for the legislative branch to subpoena the information from the executive branch—that information should automatically be shared.

## ▶ Relationship between Government and Citizens

In some sense, the secrecy program may function as much to communicate a differentiation between the government and the citizens as to protect government information. Carl J. Friedrich, professor emeritus of political science at Harvard University, has commented that psychologically the "lure of secrecy" is that it "gives the possessor of a secret a certain sense of exclusivity whereby he is set apart from ordinary mortals; every one of us has at some point smiled at eager young diplomats clutching their brief cases, carefully locked and containing—the morning newspaper."[39]

Governmental contempt for citizens is an attitude we tend to associate with the Russian communist experience, yet it is not clear that the attitude—or the existence of secrecy—was ever any more prevalent in Moscow than in Washington, D.C., today. And the fact that we are drawn to make this comparison is itself ironic, for these two most secret governments have had moments when they opted for openness. In 1917 Lenin proclaimed that the Soviet Government "abolishes secret diplomacy and, for its part, expresses its firm determination to conduct all negotiations quite openly before the whole world." At about the same time President Woodrow Wilson, in one of his Fourteen Points, declared there would be "open covenants of peace, openly arrived at, after which there shall be no private international understandings of any kind but diplomacy shall proceed always frankly and in the public view." How far both countries have strayed from those announced intentions!

From a general contempt for citizens it is a short step to contempt for their constitutional rights. Recently obtained files indicate that from 1981 to 1985 the F.B.I. "ran a surveillance operation aimed at hundreds of people and organizations opposed to the Reagan Administration's policies in Central America . . . "[40] While the F.B.I. may not have violated any law in this endeavor, it certainly demonstrated a degree of callousness toward the rights of citizens opposed to government policy. Indeed, it could be said that a major result of domestic surveillance has been a diminution of freedom. Consider how many constitutional rights are violated by surveillance: freedom of speech, freedom of assembly, freedom of association, the right to petition the government, and the Fourth Amendment ("the right of the people to be secure in their persons, houses, papers, and effects against unreasonable searches and seizures").

Another outgrowth of governmental contempt of citizens is to keep them ignorant. Of especial interest to the field of communication is the fact that secrecy "insulates" bureaucrats and thereby affects their subsequent persuasiveness. Obviously, those who have information have advantages over those who do not have it. Less obvious, but equally important, is the effect of information in allowing government authorities to talk as "experts" to an audience of "uninformed citizens." As communication scholar Eugene Garver points out, "the persuasion of experts claims not to be persuasion but something else, demonstration or instruction," which creates in the audience a feeling "that they have no choice . . . that they are bowing to necessity."[41] Secrecy, therefore, lifts its holders (government officials) to the category of "experts," while simultaneously lowering the audience (citizens) to the level of "learners." The resulting relationship is hardly to be desired in a society supposedly designed so the citizens can be the masters.

Further, those who hold secret information can affect the societal dialogue by selectively leaking their secrets. A bureaucrat who wants to strengthen the secrecy apparatus, for example, could leak the "secret" that some potential enemy country had discovered the identity of our agents in their country. That leak might scare the Senate and the House into "shoring up" secrecy requirements. How common are such occurrences? Forty-two percent of government officials admit they have leaked information to affect decision-making.[42] Perhaps their motives were honorable, but one wonders what kind of a public debate can result when those who have a stake in the outcome of the debate can control what information is made available, what is kept secret. Anthony Lewis of the *New York Times* concludes that "Knowledge in government is power. . . . Secrecy is the modern battleground of the eternal struggle for power in the American system of divided government."[43]

And that modern battleground, suggests communicologist Oscar Gandy, is not being fought between individual citizens outside of government, or even between individuals within government. Rather, he says, the battle is located in "the widening chasm of power between individuals and bureaucratic organizations,"[44] that is, between citizens and the government.

And that informational chasm, in turn, makes us susceptible to lies. H. L. Mencken once said that "nobody ever went broke underestimating the intelligence of the American voter." But the present point is not that citizens are unintelligent but that government secrecy and lies make them under- and mis-informed. And that lack of information leads to feelings of helplessness. Because we do not understand public problems, we assume we should not be called upon to decide how to solve them. And since we feel we have no role to play in solving problems, we do not get upset when the problem-solvers, those in government, lie to us.

## ▶ The "Chilling" Effect on Active Citizenship

Every time you write a letter to the editor protesting some government policy, or engage in a rally or demonstration favoring something the government opposes or opposing something the government favors, you run the risk that somebody in the government will start a dossier on you, a file that might eventually be used to keep you from getting the job, the loan, the visa, or passport you want. If the fear of "getting in trouble" with the government keeps you from engaging in those activities, it has succeeded in one of its purposes. That is, if the Constitution guarantees freedom of speech, so that the government officials cannot directly prohibit you from speaking out, they can accomplish the same thing by intimidating you.

Does the government actually do such things? Yes. In the F.B.I.'s "National Crime Information Center" there is a list of people who the Secret Service has told the F.B.I. are "anti-authority or anti–law enforcement." It is not clear how one gets on such a list—or even why such a list exists, inasmuch as holding beliefs inimical to authority or law enforcement is not illegal in this country.

Many Vietnam-era veterans who subsequently joined the anti-war movement believe their official Pentagon files have been "contaminated" by information about their anti-war activities and that the information has been used to cause harm in their lives, but they are powerless to prove their suspicions because of Supreme Court stands. Christopher Pyle, a communication analyst, explains that the Court refused to allow the innocent subjects of the army's computerized political data banks to challenge the constitutionality of that surveillance. The chilling effect on political activists caused by the existence of the files was not enough, Justice Burger ruled, to give the plaintiffs standing to sue. They had to prove that the surveillance had caused them more tangible injuries, such as the loss of jobs, mortgages, or reputation. Of course, they could not prove such injuries unless they could learn what the army had done with the files, but the Court would not "allow the plaintiffs to examine the records. Burger's ruling was a classic Catch-22 decision . . . and it effectively immunized the internal security data banks from constitutional challenge in court."[45]

It appears, then, that fear of government retribution may be a sane response, equated neither with lack of intelligence nor lack of bravery. Max Lerner, in his brilliant opus on American civilization, demonstrated just how logical that fear of retribution might be by tracing post–World War II assaults on civil liberties: "the Smith Act prosecution of Communist leaders, the security purges of government officials, the Congressional investigations of 'Reds' and 'subversives' in government agencies and in colleges and universities, the sharp restrictions on foreign travel, the security surveillance of scientists, the scrutiny of the associates and even the families of men in the armed services, the wide-spread use of wiretapping in the effort to get evidence on political suspects, the heaping up of dossiers which were often filled with trivial and hearsay material, the setting up (under the McCarran Act of 1950) of emergency detention camps for political suspects, the grant of unprecedented power to put together an 'Attorney General's list' of subversive organizations which in effect served as a measuring stick for loyalty, the deportation of aliens as political undesirables, the blacklisting of movie, radio, and TV performers, the use of anonymous evidence against 'security' suspects who had no chance to confront their accusers, the dismissal of political unreliables from presumably sensitive posts in private industry, and group pressures within small communities against suspected books and individuals in a movement that came to be called 'cultural vigilantism.'"[46]

And the foregoing list, please realize, was written before the activism of the 1960s and '70s, when a good deal of the dissent (and "chilling effect") took place, when the government was actively "taking names" and creating dossiers. At the end of those turbulent anti-war years, one of the nation's experts on civil liberties, Frank Donner, reviewed the "chilling effect" and pointed out that political surveillance "produces the greatest return of repression for the least investment of power."[47]

## ▶ Destroying Our Trust in the Government

In our individual lives we do not trust people who keep secrets from us, spy on us, and lie to us. Nor do we trust a government that does so.

One way that our trust is shattered is by the illegal or immoral acts the government engages in because it thinks it can keep them secret, acts it would eschew if openness were required. Numerous examples of government burglary and even government murder that were hidden behind walls of secrecy have been common knowledge for years. Perhaps some of the most egregious government actions are just now coming to light, such as the experiments conducted in the 1940s, 1950s, and 1960s in the development of military applications of atomic energy. In 1994 Hazel O'Leary, Clinton's head of the Department of Energy, made public some long-held secrets about how the government used American citizens as guinea pigs for radiation experiments. Some Americans "were given experimental doses of radioactive substances by government scientists seeking to determine their organic impact and retention in the body."[48] Others, of course, were exposed to radiation in the course of their work in uranium mines, at nuclear weapons plants, and at A-bomb test sites. As well, many unsuspecting "civilians" downwind of the tests were exposed to radioactive "fallout." The potential dangers to all these people were kept secret.

That the secrecy about deleterious effects of bomb tests and the experimentation on American citizens was intentional government policy can be demonstrated from a secret Atomic Energy Commission directive to doctors at the Oak Ridge National Laboratory dated April 17, 1947 (declassified February 22, 1994): "It is desired that no document be released which refers to experiments with humans and might have adverse effect on public opinion or result in legal suits."

So the experiments were secret. Were they illegal? The Nuremberg Code, written in Germany by American lawyers in 1947 after the discovery of Nazi experimentation on World War II prisoners of war, declares that in medical experimentation "the voluntary consent of the human subject is absolutely essential" and that subjects must be protected from "even the remote possibility of injury, disability or death."

In the 1990s, it was revealed that the government had engaged in "nuclear experimentation" on some people and recklessly disregarded the health of others. Anthony Lewis of the *New York Times* editorialized that those acts, and the secrecy surrounding them, had contributed to the destruction of faith in the responsibility of the government, for to be responsible to the electorate the government must be held accountable for its actions: "The premise of the American Constitution was that the governors must be accountable to the governed. . . . In departing from their wisdom we have learned how right they were."[49]

Another realm in which secrecy, surveillance, and lies lead us to distrust the government is through information "leaks." That is, by selectively releasing information when it will do the most good to your side, the most harm to the other, you can use information that has been kept secret for political advantage. Political communication scholars David Paletz and Robert Entman have toted up the various reasons why politicians might "leak" classified information: "to intimidate or warn an adversary, protect one reputation, harm another, advance policy proposals, stimulate support, woo the voter."[50] The chairman of the House Armed Services Committee in 1986, Les Aspin, put it this way: "Every administration wants to have it both ways—to keep its secrets, and to reveal them whenever doing so is useful for their politics and policies."[51]

Unfortunately, because most leaks contain negative information about politicians or their policies, the net effect of leaks (and a side effect of secrecy) is to undermine citizen confidence in the government generally, and especially in the president. Tom Wicker of the *New York Times* adds that because secrecy "will almost always force a President to lie—to the American public [and] the world—its exposure also erodes the public's trust in his integrity."[52] That is to say, the possibility of secrecy leads leaders to do things they shouldn't do; the people can keep leaders honest and honorable only through information. True, we sometimes do stupid things with the information once we get it, but, subject to error though we may be, the one thing you can guarantee about "the people" that nobody can guarantee about any set of leaders is that they are incorruptible.

Secrecy, therefore, ultimately leads to disaffection from government. Emerson explains: "concealment of information tends to engender anxiety, fear, panic and extremism," which lead "to suppression, and . . . more secrecy."[53] One of the inevitable accoutrements of secrecy, leaks, tends to escalate the acceleration: "this method of informing the public . . . is often biased, partially true, or such a small part of the whole picture as to create a false impression."[54] Leaks hardly can be argued to be a good way of producing an informed public.

The distrust created by secrecy, surveillance, and lies, in turn, makes the lives of public officials more difficult, fulfilling their public duties less possible. How can the president lead if we don't trust him? How can the legislature debate policies calmly if we're standing on the sideline shouting "liar" at them? In my lifetime I've seen two presidents—Johnson and Nixon—forced from office precisely because things had gotten so bad during their administrations that we didn't trust a thing they said to us.

In the case of Johnson the primary factor activating our distrust was his lies. In the case of Nixon, surveillance was an important contributing factor. (The original break-in at the Watergate was for the purpose of gathering information against Nixon's 1972 opponents—in other words, it was a surveillance operation—and the final crushing blow to the Nixon defense came because he even had "bugged" himself and had to turn over the tapes of the Oval Office bugging to the Courts.)

And it can be argued that the same distrust that destroyed the Johnson and Nixon presidencies, in somewhat lessened proportions, has damaged every recent presidency: Ford's secretly decided pardon of Nixon; Carter's violation of a central campaign promise ("I'll never lie to you"); Reagan's secret policy of trading arms for hostages with Iran; Bush's "no new taxes" lie; Clinton's series of "small" lies that cumulatively convinced us we could not trust him all had their effect. None of these presidents, as clever as they may have been in other realms, seems to have learned that they cannot reestablish trust until they abolish secrecy, surveillance, and lies and adopt open, honest, unobtrusive governmental communication.

## CONCLUSION

▶ Secrecy, surveillance, and lies are the weapons of those who want to exercise arbitrary and unbridled power—the kind of power those who wrote our Constitution were attempting to eliminate. Consequently, it is no surprise that there are no constitutional justifications for any of the three. Their negative effects on our societal dialogue—endangering the free marketplace of ideas, impairing democratic decision-making, interfering with the right to cast an informed vote, letting the government determine the relationship between itself and citizens, holding citizens and their rights in contempt, keeping citizens ignorant, "chilling" our willingness to engage in the activities of citizenship, and destroying our trust in the government—should suggest that their dangers may outweigh their advantages. I'm not sure what you will conclude, of course, but I have come to agree with the former attorney general of the United States, Ramsey Clark, who said "if we really want to have democratic institutions . . . we had better start working awfully hard toward the abolition of secrecy in government."[55] As a first step, we could follow Justice Hugo Black's admonition to "not be afraid to be free."

## FOR FURTHER CONSIDERATION

**1.** In light of the material presented in this chapter—and your own thinking as prompted by the material—evaluate this argument: "Democracy requires thinking. Totalitarianism, for all the inconvenience it provides by eliminating individual freedoms, is comfortable in that it does not require any thinking on the part of the inhabitants. Totalitarian systems do not create—or need—citizens; they rely on 'masses.' Eventually, however, all totalitarian systems crumble from a lack of citizens, for only citizens—not masses—can have dignity. And dignity flows from thinking, and sharing that thinking with others in an attitude of mutual respect, i.e., from open and honest communication."

**2.** When Clinton first became president in January 1993 he ordered a wholesale review of the entire secrecy apparatus. The White House began to draft a new executive order on classification; the Department of Defense and the Central Intelligence Agency (C.I.A.) began a review of their security practices; the Justice Department attempted to "open up" the process through a new set of guidelines governing the Freedom of Information (F.O.I.) Act; and the State Department began a re-examination of its embargo policies as they affect the free trade in ideas. What happened to these reforms? Did they just get lost in the shuffle? Did the Clinton Administration bow to special interests within and outside the government, or find that the proposed changes were too dangerous to make? Note: be prepared to be frustrated in your attempt to research this topic. Delving into the arcane topic of governmental secrecy of necessity involves butting your head against an occasional brick wall.

## NOTES

1. I. Robinson, *The Survival of English: Essays in Criticism of Language* (Cambridge, MA: Harvard University Press, 1973), 66.
2. R. Hopper and R. A. Bell, "Broadening the Deception Construct," *Quarterly Journal of Speech* 70 (August 1984): 289.

3. E. Black, "Secrecy and Disclosure as Rhetorical Forms," *Quarterly Journal of Speech* 74 (May 1988): 137.

4. *Ibid.,* 148.

5. C. M. Cannon, "Reagan Faulted for Growing Secrecy," *People for the American Way Press Clips,* October-November-December-January 1987–88, 1.

6. B. A. Franklin, "In Washington They've Got a Secret—Or Maybe Three Billion of Them, No One Can Say," *Washington Spectator* 20 (1 July 1994): 3.

7. H. N. Kruger, "The Access to Federal Records Law," *Freedom of Information Center Report No. 186,* September 1967, 1.

8. "Shrinking Secrets," *New York Times,* 18 April 1990, p. A24.

9. Franklin, *op. cit.,* 2.

10. O. H. Gandy, "Surveillance Society: Information Technology and Bureaucratic Social Control," *Journal of Communication* 39 (Summer 1989): 61.

11. F. T. Cary, "On Safeguarding the Right of Privacy," *New York Times,* 15 June 1974, p. 31.

12. H. Shields and M. Churchill, "Kids in the Computer," *Progressive,* October 1974, 37.

13. *Ibid.,* 37.

14. T. G. Smith, "The Lying Campaigners," *New York Times,* 8 July 1973, p. 33.

15. R. Baker, "Hardened to Lies, Perhaps," *New York Times,* 1 March 1971, p. 39.

16. C. H. Pyle, "Spies Without Masters: The Army Still Watches Civilian Politics," *Civil Liberties Review* 1 (Summer 1974): 39.

17. D. Burnham, "Lawyers Assail Police on Files," *New York Times,* 10 February 1973, p. 64.

18. M. Halperin, "We Need New Intelligence Charters," *Center Magazine* 18 (May/June 1985): 52.

19. S. Turner, "Intelligence and Secrecy in an Open Society," *Center Magazine* 19 (March/April 1986): 2.

20. F. Donner, "Rx for Surveillance," *Civil Liberties Review* 1 (Summer 1974): 17.

21. S. Pett, "Are Many Government Statements Lies?" *Arizona Daily Star,* 6 March 1966, p. D9

22. *Ibid.,* D9.

23. *Ibid.,* D9.

24. L. Charlton, "An Inquiring Capital Debate: What Is Falsification?" *New York Times,* 12 August 1973, p. E3.

25. D. F. Hahn, "Corrupt Rhetoric: President Ford and the Mayaguez Affair," *Communication Quarterly* 28 (Spring 1980): 38–43.

26. D. F. Hahn, "Flailing the Profligate: Carter's Energy Sermon of 1979," *Presidential Studies Quarterly* 10 (Fall 1980) 583–587.

27. A. Marro, "When the Government Tells Lies," *Columbia Journalism Review* 23 (March/April 1985): 37.

28. D. Wise, "The Institution of Lying," *New York Times,* 18 November 1971, p. 47.

29. N. Cousins, "America's Need to Know," *Saturday Review/World,* 23 October 1973, 4.

30. *Ibid.,* 4.

31. I. F. Stone, "It Pays to Be Ignorant," *New York Review of Books,* 9 August 1973, 6.

32. E. S. Muskie, "Secrecy Corrupts," *Progressive,* September 1973, 46.

33. Marro, *op. cit.,* 37.

34. M. G. Yudof, *When Government Speaks: Politics, Law, and Government Expression in America* (Berkeley: University of California Press), 1983.

35. R. J. Steamer, "A Self-Evident Assumption," *Freedom of Information Center Publication No. 32,* July 1960, 3.

36. J. P. Lyford, "Journalism in Government," *Center Magazine* 7 (July/August 1974): 7.

37. T. I. Emerson, "The Danger of State Secrecy," *Nation,* 30 March 1974, 395.

38. "Spirit of Watergate," *New York Times,* 5 August 1973, p. E14.

39. C. J. Friedrich, *The Pathology of Politics: Violence, Betrayal, Corruption, Secrecy, and Propaganda* (New York: Harper and Row, 1972), 188.

40. P. Shenon, "F.B.I. Again Called Lax on Liberties," *New York Times,* 31 January 1988, p. E5.

41. E. Garver, "Ancient Rhetoric and Modern Problems," in *Rhetoric 78: Proceedings of Theory of Rhetoric, An Interdisciplinary Conference,* eds. R. L. Brown, Jr. and M. Steinmann, Jr. (Minneapolis: University of Minnesota Center for Advanced Studies in Language, Style, and Literary Theory, 1979), 80.

42. "42% of Ex–U.S. Aides Admit Disclosing News," *New York Times,* 27 October 1986, p. A19.

43. A. Lewis, "Secrecy and Folly," *New York Times,* 24 December 1987, p. A19.

44. Gandy, *op. cit.,* 62

45. C. H. Pyle, "The Invasion of Privacy," in *The Communication Revolution in Politics: Proceedings of the Academy of Political Science* 34 (Number 4, 1982), ed. Gerald Benjamin, 140.

46. M. Lerner, *America as a Civilization: Life and Thought in the United States Today* (New York: Simon and Schuster, 1957), 455–456.

47. Donner, *op. cit.,* 9.

48. Franklin, *op. cit.,* 2.

49. A. Lewis, "Secrecy and Cynicism," *First Principles* 18 (December 1993): 23–24.

50. D. L. Paletz and R. M. Entman, *Media, Power, Politics* (New York: Free Press, 1981), 59.

51. L. H. Gelb, "Use of Disclosures," *New York Times,* 2 June 1986, p. A15.

52. T. Wicker, "Covert Doesn't Pay," *New York Times,* 4 April 1987, p. 27.

53. Emerson, *op. cit.,* 395.

54. Steamer, *op. cit.,* 1.

55. R. Clark, "The Case Against All Forms of Government Secrecy," *Center Magazine* 11 (January/February 1978): 72.

# Media and Political Campaigns

*New forms of communication create different kinds of public discussion, and even different publics.*
— MICHAEL SCHUDSON[1]

It is no criticism of academia to say that academics have not yet arrived at a settled opinion of the relationship of media and politics. Not even a generalization about the effects of each on the other can be made that all researchers would agree upon. And I must admit to a degree of vacillation in my own thinking: some days I am of the opinion that the media have destroyed politics; other days I think the influence has gone the other way, that politics have destroyed the media.

In this chapter I explore one aspect of the relationship between these two great institutions in American life, identifying major ways in which the media have, over the years, changed the nature and functions of political campaigns. The next chapter (Chapter 12) is devoted to the effects of mediated campaigns on voters, examining how citizens can be misled by media coverage of campaigns and how the media structure our perceptions of candidates and their stands on the issues. Chapter 13 explores a less often noted phenomenon, the effects of media on politicians themselves. It argues that the media, in bringing politicians "down" to our level, eliminate the possibility of old-style "great" leaders while simultaneously encouraging us to evaluate these "lowered" figures by the old standards of "greatness."

## ▶ Effects of Media on Campaigns

In the eighteenth and nineteenth centuries, candidates for president did not campaign. They did not "run" for the office. To do so was perceived to be "unseemly," to appear to want the office "too much." Consequently, as political scientist Marvin Weisbord has written, prior to the twentieth century "the United States picked its presidents largely sight unseen, without hearing from their lips what they would or would not do if elected."[2] The first candidate to break this pattern was the 1860 Democratic candidate, Stephen A. Douglas. And the first candidate who campaigned and won was Woodrow Wilson in 1912.

But, of course, campaigns *did* exist. People who ran for "lesser" offices campaigned for themselves. And there were presidential campaigns, but those who spoke on behalf of the candidates, the surrogates for those personages, were the friends of the candidate and the leading lights of the candidate's party. National campaigns were, in a sense, local in nature, as the major speakers on behalf of a candidate were the "local" politicians, senators, governors, and members of the House of Representatives, speaking in their own states and districts. It was thought that these people, who often knew a large percentage of "their" voters, could "come off" better than an unknown "foreigner" from another state. Yet as the country got more and more populated, the advantage subsided. Consider, for example, the fact that the totality of the first Congress represented only forty thousand voters whereas by now the average congressional district contains six hundred thousand people.[3] Even "local" politicians no longer speak to "a family of friends." Thus, the value of surrogates has lessened considerably; there no longer is reason to think they would be more persuasive with the "home folk."

Two developments of the twentieth century, in addition to the population increase, changed the nature of campaigning—improved transportation and electronic media. As trains became faster and more reliable, cars became common, the road system was expanded and improved, and air travel became an everyday phenomenon, it became *possible* for candidates to get out to meet and greet a significant number of people. Over time, what was possible became what was desirable and, ultimately, necessary.

The improved transportation made it possible for candidates to travel to various parts of the country to campaign. Equally important, it made it possible for voters to travel to the venues where the candidates were speaking. Obviously, candidates' ease of travel, thanks to their money, preceded citizen access to some degree, but I remember my own father telling how, at age eleven, he and his family made a two-day, sixty-mile trip by horse-drawn buckboard to hear presidential candidate William Jennings Bryan speak during the 1908 campaign.

By now, of course, we do not travel at all to hear candidates. Since the invention of the remote control we don't even have to travel across the room to change the channel. From the comfort of our chairs and couches we can access any candidate we want to hear—and blip out those we find disagreeable. And whether the ability to tune in is a more significant development than the ability to tune out is a toss-up in most people's minds.

Interestingly, however, research in communication suggests that campaigns conducted by candidates themselves rather than by surrogates may give voters a better chance of uncovering deceptive candidates. A study of interpersonal communication by Buller, Strzyzewski, and Hunsaker found that the more we look for deception the less likely we are to recognize it, but also found that this result is more true for conversational participants than for observers.[4] If we extrapolate this finding to the political arena, it would be postulated that politicians who work closely with each other are least likely to detect lying (thus a surrogate speaker for a candidate, often a friend, might not be able to recognize the candidate's lies). Likewise, reporters who are close friends with politicians are not likely to detect a lie. But reporters who keep their distance from the politicians stand a good chance of detecting deception, as do citizens. It may be, then, that knowing candidates only through their media presentations (i.e., from a distance) may not be the worst way to evaluate them.

To "get at" modern media effects on the structure of campaigns in a somewhat more rigorous and organized manner, I turn now to issues that have been raised in the literature since television started being perceived as an important "player" on the political stage in the early 1950s.

## ▶ Eliminating Potential Candidates

It has been argued that television has eliminated many potential candidates because of their unseemly appearance, lack of wealth, poor speaking ability, or lack of a national office. These allegations will be examined in this section.

In the midst of the 1960 race between John Kennedy and Richard Nixon, newspaper columnist Arthur Krock speculated that some candidates might be hurt or eliminated "by the state of not being photogenic,"[5] suggesting that if television had existed in 1884 the good-looking Blaine might well have defeated the more stodgy-appearing Cleveland.

It is probably no accident that the suggested effect surfaced during the 1960 campaign. J.F.K. *was* better looking than Richard Nixon, though many Nixon supporters countered that their man looked more "presidential" than Kennedy. Nor is it surprising that the effect disappeared in 1964, when a gangly, big-eared Lyndon Johnson crushed the more dapper and manly-proportioned Barry Goldwater in an electoral landslide. Aesthetic judgments are just too idiosyncratic for candidate looks to be a very important factor.

A second alleged effect is that television has pushed wealth to the forefront. Do the new electronic media eliminate the poor from the race? The evidence on this point is, at best, inconclusive. Perot's millions did not win him the 1992 election; Steve Forbes's millions did not garner him the 1996 Republican nomination. Yet, it is doubtful that either would even have been in those races without their immense wealth.

A lot of nonrich politicians have gained the White House even since television, an admittedly costly medium, has become the major campaigning tool. Yet it remains true that candidates without wealth, even when backed by their parties and receiving matching funds from the government, must spend an inordinate amount of time seeking financial backing—time (and energy) that perhaps could be used better in attempts to appeal to the voters.

Some have suggested that the influence of money could be lessened considerably if we could figure out a way to get free TV time for each candidate.[6] In the 1996 campaign some small amounts of free time *were* provided by the various networks. As welcome as the 1996 free time was (and as a completely reformed system might be), it should be recognized that television did not introduce wealth as a new element to politics, though it may have exacerbated the political problems associated with it. Nor is there much reason to believe that if television were completely free, and open access were guaranteed to all declared candidates, the poor candidate would have a much better chance than is the case today. Which of us would choose to be led by those who haven't even figured out how to take care of themselves?

A third supposed effect of contemporary media is to make public speaking ability more important. The argument here is that both radio and television allow "slickness" of delivery to substitute for excellence of content. From my perspective, this contention is simply not true. Dwight David Eisenhower was exceedingly dull on the speaker's platform; Jimmy Carter was no whiz at persuasion; Hubert Humphrey's tendency to talk too much did not deprive him of the 1968 Democrat nomination; and George Bush's mangled syntax did not preclude him from defeating Dukakis in 1988.

If anything, the influence of television has been in the other direction. Before TV, candidates fought out their campaigns in public speaking appearances and on radio. Television provided alternative tactics for poor public speakers—such as advertising spots (in many of which the candidates do not even appear), informal interviews, and films.

In the early days of television a fourth effect was alleged: that television was so nationalizing the culture that it exempted all but national figures. Historian Emmet John Hughes, writing in 1960, argued that "In the future of television, it would seem doubtful if the most distinguished governor, whatever his record or personality, could come close to national candidacy."[7]

But Hughes was writing before Governors Carter, Reagan, and Clinton were elected president. More important, he was writing before the impeachment proceedings against Richard Nixon brought politicians to a state of ill repute, opening the way for non-Washington candidates to run against Washington and giving "outsiders" improved chances against the "insiders" who were receiving more national television exposure.

I conclude, then, that the new electronic media of the twentieth century did not automatically eliminate any potential candidates from the race. Looks, wealth, speaking ability, and nonnational exposure do not seem to be factors that have been raised prohibitively above their pre-TV importance,[8] although some minimal effects may be noted in each realm.

## ▶ Effects on Primary Elections

The most obvious effect of television on primary elections has been to make them more important. Primaries first appeared on the American scene at the beginning of the twentieth century, yet did not attain prominence until the 1950s and did not prove conclusive until 1960. The 1956 Democratic primaries were given wide coverage on television, but the inconclusive results of the various primaries confused rather than clarified the race for the nomination. In 1960, after an indefinite result in Wisconsin, the West Virginia primary eliminated Humphrey and nearly assured that Kennedy would be the nominee. In 1964, the California primary ensured the Goldwater nomination. In 1968, the assassination of Robert Kennedy obviated voters' intentions and obscured the results. Since 1968, the only nominating campaign where the results of the primaries were at all ambiguous has been in 1976, when Ronald Reagan came fairly close to unseating the incumbent (but unelected) president of his own party, Gerald Ford. But presidential politics is not horseshoes—close doesn't count.

Television increased the importance of primaries by making state primaries nationwide events. Concomitantly, television coverage shifted the focus of primaries from the immediate purpose of selecting delegates to the national convention to the wider purposes of popularizing the winners and proving their vote-getting ability.

Television coverage also affected what candidates could say in a primary, making it necessary for them to appeal simultaneously both to the immediate state audience and the larger national audience.

Television, in its daily coverage of primaries, has increased the difficulties for the party without an apparent nominee. It has made the primaries more important, forcing all serious candidates to take part in them, yet it has spread the angry words exchanged in these familial battles to every corner of the country. Television has forced the party without a nominee to commit political hara-kiri. No matter which candidate emerges the victor, the real winner is the party whose candidate did not have to go through the primaries.

In 1964 the Johnson campaign relied on what other Republicans had said about Goldwater in the primaries. One of the most effective Johnson ads focused on the fallen placards of the various other Republican candidates for the nomination, supposedly lying in the dust after the San Francisco Republican convention, and quoted what these Republicans had said about Goldwater when they were running against him for the nomination.

In 1996 President Clinton had no opposition in the primaries. Meanwhile, although the Republican primaries decided the nomination relatively early, the eventual Republican nominee had been badly battered by nine primary opponents. He began the election campaign bruised and tired, facing a fresh opponent who was armed with all those nasty quotations about him culled from the speeches and negative ads of the other Republican primary candidates. Under those circumstances, Dole had much more to overcome than did Clinton, who had not been challenged for the Democrat nomination.

How has television affected primaries? It has made them more important, increasing the necessity of carefully phrased appeals on the part of the candidates and harming the party that has to engage in bitter primary battles to select a candidate.

## ▶ Effects on Nominating Conventions

The traditional pretelevision nominating convention was a strange amalgam of seriousness and play, a deliberative body encased inside a giant party. On the serious side were debates about the content of the platform and the selection of the candidate, including a good amount of "wheeling and dealing." Less serious were the parties, marching bands, balloon drops, waving placards, meeting and greeting of friends from other states, demonstrations on behalf of the various candidates, and imaginative and entertaining speeches attacking the other political party.

Television, partially because it is so predominantly a visual medium, was unable to catch the true nature of a convention. As Theodore White has chronicled: "TV displays events, action, motion, arrival, departure; it cannot show thought, silence, mood or decision. And so the TV camera caught the carnival outer husk of the convention in all its pageantry and motion."[9] What television could not picture was the important clash of ideas taking place in the platform committee and in the minds of the delegates, so the political parties had no choice but to change the nature of conventions.

The most important and obvious change was a change of focus. Where prior to television a convention was a rough-and-tumble fight for the nomination, the purposes of the convention are now not so much to nominate a candidate as to sell the obvious candidate to the public and weld together the warring factions of the party after the vicious primaries. The change from nominating a candidate to ratifying the candidate chosen in the primaries means that a convention no longer merely signifies the end of the nominating process; rather, it is the beginning of the campaign proper.

An effect of television on conventions that has been widely applauded is the seeming demise of the bosses. There are two possible explanations about what happened to the bosses. On the one hand, they may have become more open, changing from dealing to leading. On the other, they may have been driven even further behind the scenes. If the latter interpretation seems more likely, that possibility first was predicted immediately following the 1952 conventions, when sociologist Emory S. Bogardus commented on how Americans had reacted to seeing the bosses work on the floor of the convention: "doubtless the 'bosses' in the future will be more forehanded and subtle."[10] With the single exception of the machinations of Mayor Daley, boss of Chicago at the 1968 Democrat convention, the prediction has been accurate.

Another effect of television on nominating conventions has been to make them earlier. The party with a nominee does not need an early convention, but the party that has been divided by primary battles needs to get into the convention early in order to make the reconciliation that will allow it to fight the campaign as a unified party. That is why the party out of power nearly always schedules its convention in July (although in 1996 the Republicans put off their convention until August so as not to compete with the Atlanta Olympics). The party inhabiting the White House waits until August for its convention.

Television also has lessened the artificiality of demonstrations in support of candidates put forward for the nomination. In 1952 the Republican convention allowed each nominee 150 paid demonstrators. Reacting to the ensuing adverse criticism, the Democrats ruled out the use of paid paraders, who have disappeared forever. This action helped curb, but did not eliminate, the silliness of such demonstrations. Often delegates seem to take part in demonstrations more to get the exercise than to show support, as is indicated by the fact that some delegates take part in several demonstrations. This aspect of national conventions should still be refined, although I doubt there is really a dignified way to parade, blow horns, shout, and let off the steam of emotional enthusiasm.

Television coverage also has brought about changes in the nature of convention speeches. Three such changes are easily observable. First, the speeches are shorter now, although they are still too long and too numerous for all but the most diehard political supporter. The speeches are also less emotional, because what seems to a supporter to be an honest outpouring of emotion seems like acting to the unconvinced. Third, the speeches now denounce the opposing party less, although the 1992 Republican convention speeches were criticized for returning to the old norm of bitterly denouncing the opposing party.

Almost all the changes that television has forced upon the political convention have been designed to attract and hold the home audience. How helpful any of the changes have been to the American system of nominating is debatable. The conventions have been streamlined for the convenience of the voters in television land. To the degree that the streamlining is only a surface show and the "wheeling and dealing" have been driven underground, however, the surface reforms may be more harmful than helpful.

## ▶ New Campaign Devices

The most obvious device that television introduced is the spot advertisement. Although spot ads are expensive and eat up much of every candidate's budget, they are relatively cheap per voter reached. Further, they have the power to reach those who are otherwise unreachable. Only interested citizens will watch a half-hour political program, but spots can reach the apathetic, ill-informed, and presumably persuasible portions of the electorate.

Another function of ads, often overlooked in critiques, is that they provide arguments for the already persuaded to use in their discussions with family, friends, and coworkers. That is to say, spot ads function as all "big ticket" advertising does. None of us goes out to buy an expensive item, such as a car, just because of an ad we saw on television. Yet the airwaves are jammed with automobile company ads. Why? Because they are providing arguments to recent buyers of that brand to use when somebody asks, "how do you like your new car?" Voting is, for most people, a "big ticket" item, and the ads for the candidates supply answers to partisans for the question, "why are you going to vote for that person?"

None of this, of course, suggests that political advertisements are in any way a boon to democracy. They are, of necessity, designed as nonintellectual appeals: it is impossible to provide a reasoned argument in thirty or sixty seconds. They are filled with suggestion and innuendo, and they are often negative because it is easier to attack others or their programs in a few seconds than to explain your own strong points or explain why your proposals are more sound.

It would be difficult to overstate the illogicality of most television spots. For one thing, candidates often misrepresent their opponents' positions, essentially attributing to them what might be called "straw men" positions that are easy to destroy . . . and their ease in destroying them, according to communication researcher Robert Bierstedt, "is used to demonstrate one's own critical skill."[11] For another thing, proof is rarely proffered in these ads. Max Frankel, correspondent for the *New York Times,* concluded in his examination of the 1994 congressional elections, "Charges of drug dealing, tax cheating and criminal coddling crowd the screen, with not even a pretense of proof."[12]

While many researchers have studied spot ads, sometimes finding they were helpful, sometimes not, what has not been studied (and may not lend itself to objective research) is what may be their most important deleterious effect: getting the populace used to evaluating politicians and politics by nonlogical, overly simplistic methods and criteria.

A device closely related to spot advertising is "hitchhiking." A hitchhike, so called because it gives the politician a "free" ride on the end of a popular show, is a five-minute commercial at the end of a shortened hour or half-hour regularly scheduled program. The sponsors of these popular shows are forced to give up the five minutes by the threat that the campaign will buy the entire time slot if they refuse, something they do not want to happen because campaigns take place during the fall, when all shows are competing for audience (thus advertising revenue) for the new TV season. The five minutes are valuable because the audience is captive—most would rather tolerate the political ad than switch to another station for the last five minutes of another show. Besides, most people do not look at their watches; they do not know they are watching the beginning of a five-minute ad. They assume, since the program is over, that they are merely seeing the normal glut of ads between the end of one show and the start of another.

Perhaps the most insidious hitchhike is when a candidate buys the first five minutes of whatever show immediately follows a newscast, then designs a five-minute ad to look like a news show. Most viewers do not realize that the hitchhike is not a part of the news, thus their critical antennae may be switched off.

But the hitchhike is not a foolproof technique. Many people are unhappy about having their favorite program shortened. When Adlai Stevenson preempted five minutes from the end of the popular "I Love Lucy" show in 1956, he received this telegram from an irate viewer: "I like Ike and I Love Lucy. Drop dead."[13]

Another device introduced by television is the "telethon." The idea of a telethon is to have people call questions in to the candidate at the studio, to answer on the spot. The questions are usually screened so that the candidate need not handle any crackpot. By the 1968 presidential election the "screening" had gotten so out of hand that candidate Nixon was not actually answering called-in questions, but rather responding to questions made up by his own campaign, questions he had practiced answering before the telethon began. Because of the Nixon maneuver, telethons have fallen into disuse, but they still are available and could be valuable for any candidate who used them in an honest way.

Television also has introduced documentary films, usually candidate biographies, into the campaign process. They seem most useful during primaries, when they introduce candidates to the voters. Because the people who vote in such elections are more knowledgeable about and interested in politics than those who don't, they are more likely to be willing to watch a half-hour documentary on one candidate. Documentaries are rarely used during general elections, because only a small percentage of the potential voters will watch them. Therefore, to the degree films are used in general elections, they are presented at the nominating conventions as a part of the process of introducing the party nominee. The 1996 biography of Clinton at the Democratic convention seemed more aimed at proving he had a good marriage (a response, perhaps, to the widespread whispers about his alleged extramarital affairs) than at any directly political aspect of his life.

The new device that has been most widely hailed, condemned, and studied is the television debate. This is not to say that candidate debates are new; nearly everybody has heard of the Lincoln-Douglas debates. But many people do not know those debates were not during a presidential campaign or between presidential candidates; they were in 1858, during the race in Illinois for the U.S. Senate. The first *presidential* candidate debates were in 1960, between Kennedy and Nixon, and were initiated precisely because they could be televised to the whole nation.

For the next three elections, 1964, 1968, and 1972, there were no debates, because in each election one or both candidates refused to participate. But there have been debates in every presidential election from 1976 to the present, and they seem so firmly ensconced by now that any candidate who tried to wriggle out of participation probably would be badly damaged in the polls.

So what have been the effects of political debates? That question is impossible to answer. Some candidates have been thought to have benefited from debates, some hurt; but for every suggested "lift" or "drop" there have been alternative explanations.[14] The debates seem to change very few votes; Robert Friedenberg, a professor of communication at Miami (Ohio) University, has succinctly (and I think correctly) concluded that "the principal effect of debates upon voting behavior seems to be to reinforce the existing attitudes of voters."[15]

But that does not mean debates are worthless. One extremely useful function of such exercises is that they force citizens to listen to the opposing candidate. Perhaps they are not persuaded to vote for that other candidate, but the listening still is valuable. As Katz and Feldman observed after the 1960 debate, "It seems that the debates might make for a greater acceptance of the winning candidate . . . one knew more about him, one felt he was more human and more accessible."[16]

Still, it must be admitted that the great hope for presidential debates, that they would contribute substantially to the education of the public,[17] has not happened, partially because the format seems to militate against education and partially because the candidates "ignore, twist, or broadly interpret questions to facilitate providing the answers they want to provide . . . avoid specifics . . . and fall back on the stock responses they have utilized throughout the campaign."[18] Yet to me, the best response to the "uneducational" charge has been provided by communication scholar Robert Friedenberg: "While such criticism has merit, it frequently seems to be offered without consideration of the rhetorical situation that governs political debates. From the standpoint of the two participants, the motivating exigency is not the desire to educate the public. It is the desire to win the election. From the standpoint of panel journalists, the motivating exigency is not the desire to educate the public. It is the desire to create a news-worthy event. Hence, none of the participants in national political debates are highly motivated to provide an educational experience for the viewer."[19] Additionally, it is questionable whether the audience tunes in as much to be educated as to be entertained by a good confrontation and cheer for their already-chosen favorite.

So, has the new device of televised campaign debates been a help or a hindrance? I don't know, nor do I think a definitive answer can be given for some time in the future, if ever. The debate is a new technique, unmeasurable in importance, with which politicians may play. Debates may have caught the fancy of a few, or many, people. Whether those few or many voted more intelligently or more stupidly than they would have otherwise is a contested point. What is uncontested is that the debates add a new dimension that we will not easily be rid of, nor, perhaps, endure.

The final new device television introduced is not so much new as a device that television has brought into its own, "the direct appeal." Nixon used the direct appeal in his famous 1952 "Checkers" speech to respond to charges of financial impropriety. Bill and Hillary Clinton relied upon it to address the "infidelity" issue in 1992. Interestingly, no other direct appeals took place in the forty years between Nixon and the Clintons, although if pressed I might admit the 1960 Kennedy appeal for religious tolerance to the list. But there *were* other points at which the device perhaps should have been used. Barry Goldwater well could have employed a direct appeal in 1964 to respond to the "warmonger" charge, and Tom Eagleton, briefly the vice-presidential candidate on the Democrat ticket in 1972, might have refuted charges of emotional instability in a direct appeal. Considering what eventually happened to both Goldwater and Eagleton, I can't imagine how a direct appeal could have worsened anything.

## ▶ The Continuation of Barnstorming

In the nineteenth century, when few towns had commodious town halls and few high schools had large theatres (or gymnasiums, since basketball hadn't been invented yet), when candidates went about the countryside speaking they frequently did so in the biggest farm barn in the area. So the process of traveling from place to place to present the campaign speech came to be called "barnstorming."

When television first was introduced to politics people commonly believed that it would eliminate barnstorming. Television was to allow politicians to address the voting millions from their own offices, appealing to more from that one spot than ever had been possible in the longest, hardest barnstorming campaign. Yet that is not what happened. Instead, campaigns have become harder and longer, with more miles traveled and more speeches presented than in the pretelevision years. What happened to the predicted change? Why didn't it occur?

One reason television has not replaced barnstorming is that when a candidate is traveling from place to place the same speech can be given at each stop. Complete reliance upon television, however, would require a new speech each day, for television, as Robert Bendiner has said, is "a voracious consumer of material."[20] While there may be candidates who have enough to say to fill two months of campaigning via television, they could not do so without getting into such intricacies that the audience soon would be lost, along with the election.

A second reason barnstorming has not been eliminated is that candidates must still appeal to regional and group interests. They must visit every part of the country, preferably every state, and must speak to certain groups. Every presidential candidate tries to find a farm group and a veterans group to address. No Democrat candidate can pass up a speech to some union organization on Labor Day; no Republican candidate can afford to bypass the National Association of Manufacturers.

Additionally, barnstorming is still with us, in part, because it is required by local politics. The "head" of the ticket, the presidential candidate, needs to go into states in order to give a hand to the campaigns of the party candidates for governor, Senate, House, and so forth. Not only are state and local candidates in need of such a boost from the top, the whole party apparatus depends upon it. If a potential party worker knows the candidate will not come to town, there is less incentive to volunteer to work for the party. But if there is a chance the presidential nominee will grace the area with a visit, volunteers are easier to recruit, partially because they hope that when the nominee comes they at least will be able to meet him, perhaps even meet *with* him.

Even if barnstorming were not necessary to get the glory-seeking to work for the party, it still would be necessary in order to fire up the enthusiasm of the party workers. This is, after all, a major purpose of barnstorming. The purpose is not to gain votes from the uncommitted; those who come to the airport during the jet-stop are not the undecided, they are the committed. And they come away from the airport more committed than ever. Before, they were working for the nominee of the party of their choice; now they are working for George or "the Duke" or Bill or Bob. Because the campaign is now more personal they put more of their person into campaigning. Those who predicted that television would bring the demise of barnstorming just did not understand this aspect of campaigns.

The final and perhaps most important reason barnstorming has not disappeared is that no one really knows how effective television is. No candidate wants to throw away barnstorming, a proven method, for a technique on which no one ever has depended exclusively. As long as it is not necessary to choose between the two, barnstorming will continue. Politicians use television, but they do not altogether trust it; they yearn to get out into the hinterlands, to "feel the pulse" and "press the flesh" of the electorate themselves. Perhaps someday a candidate will eschew the old barnstorming method and campaign entirely via the air waves. If and when this happens—and if that candidate wins—it will revolutionize campaigning. But don't look for it in the near future.

## ▶ Issues and Images

I will return to the general question of issues and images in the next chapter, when I discuss the effects of mediated campaigns upon voters. Because it commonly is asserted that television has *caused* such a change in the nature of campaigns, however, we should address the specific question of whether such a change has occurred here.

In order to answer this question, we must first ask whether the campaign focus in pretelevision days was on issues. And the answer is clear: it was not. While the first televised campaign relied heavily on sloganeering ("I Like Ike"), so did the pretelevision 1840 election, in which the Whig slogan was "Tippecanoe and Tyler Too." Nor was the televised 1964 Johnson attack upon the Goldwater image as a "warmonger" all that different from the 1932 pretelevision Roosevelt campaign against "Hoovervilles."

I contend that the focus always has been upon image, or on image as a manifestation of the issues. When pretelevision voters cast their ballots for "The Great Commoner" (William Jennings Bryan) they were voting for image-plus, i.e., for a whole series of issues that somehow were tied in with the image, issues about what the common people wanted versus what was good for New York bankers, issues presumably comfortable to someone raised on a farm in Nebraska. Likewise, a vote for Bill (not the more formal William) Clinton in 1992 was a vote for image-plus, a vote that assumed that a person who knew so many statistics could perhaps do something about them, a vote that assumed that somebody who had had marital problems would understand something about the average person living in a society where one out of every two marriages ends in divorce, a vote that prayed that somebody from a town named Hope would approach problems hopefully rather than cynically.

Despite all the campaign speeches about various policies, leadership (as encapsulated in candidate images) has been the issue in every televised election, as it was in pre-TV days. And in our complex world there is little doubt that leadership will continue to be the issue in presidential campaigns. Perhaps there are better ways for voters to "get at" leadership questions than by relying upon candidate images. Perhaps some changes in media coverage of campaigns would be useful in helping us focus more realistically on leadership questions. But to those who deplore the emphasis on image and blame that emphasis on television, I only can reply that while we might wish for a world in which the electorate would weigh issues carefully, this is not the case today; it never has been the case; and it is unrealistic to condemn television for the condition. In many ways, the "new" televised campaigns are just like the old pre-TV ones: equally noninformative; equally frightening in what they tell us about our intelligence, our willingness to be misled, our eagerness to have the campaign "done with" so we can get back to our own private lives; and equally focused on images rather than issues, as has been the case from George Washington's election through our most recent one.

## ▶ Distrust of Government and Politicians

While it often is argued that media have created the present high level of distrust among citizens about government and, especially, politicians, such mistrust always has existed. The "founding fathers" mistrusted government; that's why the Constitution was designed with a series of checks and balances to keep any one group of politicians from gaining too much power. And we *always* have distrusted politicians. Political scientist E. T. Jack reminds us that Alexis de Tocqueville observed as long ago as the 1830s that "Americans as a group think of politics as a dirty business and politicians as confirmed scalawags, not to be trusted for a minute."[21]

Further, distrust is the *logical* outcome of any form of government. That is because every government engages in actions to address contemporary problems, and the actions taken must, of necessity, hurt some citizens. Naturally, those hurt come to distrust the government.

But the tracing of historic distrust and identifying the logic of distrust should not be read as denials that distrust has increased in contemporary times. Clearly, there is less faith in government (and politicians) now than at any other time in our history. But it may not be fair to blame this change solely on the media. After all, it was L.B.J.'s dissembling that led to the "credibility gap" in the 1960s. It was Nixon's lies and the impeachment proceedings against him, Ford's pardon of Nixon, and Carter's campaign "against Washington" that fueled the distrust in the 1970s. It was Reagan's constant anti-Washington position, his argument that "government cannot solve problems, government *is* the problem" that reinforced the distrust in the 1980s. And it was Bush's reneging on his "read my lips, no new taxes" campaign promise, Clinton's anti-Washington campaign and presumed misleading statements about his sexual and economic affairs that broadened the mistrust in the 1990s. If we do not trust politicians, much of the blame for our attitude must be laid at the feet of politicians themselves.

But there is plenty of blame left over, so we should not allow the media to get off scot-free. I see two major media developments that have contributed to the increasing distrust: changes in how media cover politics and the rise of "hate radio."

First, there have been changes in the nature of media coverage. Following the assassination of John Kennedy, stories started to surface about his sexual peccadilloes, specifically about the possibility that he had had an affair with Marilyn Monroe and might, in some way, have been implicated in her death. The media were taken to task for not keeping us appraised of Kennedy's personal life; consequently, the media started focusing on the personal lives of politicians, especially sexual escapades. One result, since none of us are free of personal problems, has been to discover something "bad" about everybody in politics. Equally important, focusing on personal lives has increased the focus on personality, with a concomitant lessening of focus on political positions and issues.

Then, in the aftermath of Nixon's "Watergate" problems and the success of investigative reporters in "bringing down" Nixon, the popularity of investigative reporting increased. Obviously, such investigations sometimes turn up illegalities and shady dealings, raising questions about the honesty of politicians, especially in the economic realm.

These two changes in the nature of reporting, increased focus on personal matters and increased investigative reporting on economic matters, have had the effect of increasing citizen distrust of politicians. That effect can be seen most clearly in media exposés of Bill Clinton. The amount of media time and attention given his alleged extramarital romances and his (and Hillary's) prepresidential economic arrangements probably exceeds the time and attention given the sexual and economic contrivances of all 1950s and 1960s politicians combined. The increased coverage is the logical result of the changes in media coverage.

The second recent development in the media that has contributed to the increased distrust of government and politicians has been the rise of "hate radio." While it may be argued that so-called "hate radio" was merely the result of the opening of the airwaves to ordinary people, and that, therefore, it is not really a *media* effect, that explanation overlooks too much. Specifically, it overlooks the takeover of "national talk" in the media by political partisans. And this alteration *may* be fairly blamed on the media, especially television. In trying to "jazz up" political talk shows, the media increasingly hired political partisans rather than journalists, but pretended they were journalists. Thus, John McLaughlin, a former Nixon speech-writer, was redefined as a journalist and given *three* TV shows to host. Pat Buchanan, another former Nixon speech-writer, was redefined as a journalist and given a permanent spot on *Crossfire,* to be replaced by former Reagan-Bush Chief of Staff John Sununu.

Note that much of this change took place in the 1970s, when Democrat Carter was in the White House, so it made sense for the media to hire conservative partisan talkers. But the "sense" disappeared in the 1980s, with Reagan's and then Bush's elections. Yet, the media continued to use conservative partisans, who now became cheerleaders rather than critics. In the 1990s, with the Clinton's election, the partisans went back to being critics. And now radio began to get into the act, especially with the hiring of conservative partisan Rush Limbaugh and a large cast of other conservative (often *more* conservative) Rush wannabes.

So "hate radio," although it features the voices of angry citizens (Robin Toner calls it "an echo chamber for their discontent"),[22] really is fueled by extremely conservative political partisans, who are pretending to be journalists and "egging on" the angry (conservative) citizens. Audience statistics gathered by the Times Mirror Center for the People and the Press and reported by Richard Morin suggest something of the disparity between those who listen and those who do not: "listeners are more likely to be Republican and conservative . . . and conservatives are twice as likely to be talk radio regulars as liberals are."[23] While 9 percent of Americans are white evangelicals, Thomas B. Edsall reports that "35 percent of Limbaugh listeners said they were white evangelicals."[24]

But the problem with "hate radio" is not just that it is overwhelmingly conservative, nor that it replaces journalists with political partisans, nor even that the callers are unrepresentative of the nation as a whole—though all these things are true and are problematic in some ways. No, the basic problem is deeper and more basic than any of these. In brief, it is that opinions are put forward as truth, often before the truth is known. We all have opinions, of course, and psychologists say our opinions are important to the development of our individuality, personality, and identity. Yet, as Albert 0. Hirschman has written, democracy requires "that opinions *not* be fully formed *in advance* of the debate." When that happens, he says, "there will be an *overproduction* of opinionated opinion," and a "wholesale embrace of an 'ideology,'" in "knee-jerk" fashion."[25] *That*, I would argue, is what contemporary hate radio is doing. In substituting (primarily conservative) opinion for the give-and-take of deliberation, it is providing us with a constant "kneejerk" antigovernment and antipolitical position. The sheer volume of such opinions on the airwaves of both radio and television drowns out all other voices, leaving us at the mercy of "opinionated opinion."

So perhaps the media *do* bear some blame for the current level of distrust, for the fact that by now "politician" and "bureaucrat" are epithets, that "politics" and "government" are mostly negative words.

Politicians have been largely ineffectual in struggling against all the negativism, although they have tried to prove themselves trustworthy. For instance, they constantly use campaign posters showing them with their families and run ads showing themselves doing familiar things such as wearing jeans (Carter in 1976), playing horseshoes (Bush in 1988), and wearing plaid shirts (Lamar Alexander in 1996 Republican primaries). They also take care to align with the values of the audience (on the assumption that we trust people who believe as we believe). That is one reason they do so much polling—so they will know which values to embrace as they campaign.

But, of course, the major way in which politicians try to prove they are trustworthy enough to elect is by running negative ads showing their opponents as *un*trustworthy. That tactic has the ultimate effect of undermining all politics, for what the public tends to conclude is not just that the opponent is not to be trusted but that *all* candidates are untrustworthy. The damage that negative advertising does to our perception of politics would be difficult to overstate.

## CONCLUSION

▶ So what can we conclude about the effects of media on the nature and function of campaigns? I have argued that the media have had very little effect in terms of "automatically" eliminating anyone from the race, eliminating "barnstorming," or changing the focus from issues to images. I found somewhat more media responsibility for the increasing distrust of government and politicians. But the major effects of the media seem to have been to make primaries more important and increase the difficulties for the party without an apparent nominee; to convert nominating conventions from nominating battles to a process for ratifying the nominee chosen in the primaries; and to introduce new campaign devices, such as spot ads, telethons, and televised debates.

▶ But tracing the effects of media on the nature and function of campaigns does not give us the complete story, for those campaigns are now mediated. That fact has effects, too, to which I turn in the next chapter.

## FOR FURTHER CONSIDERATION

**1.** This chapter argues that media coverage of campaigns has forced campaigns to change to "fit into" that coverage. Examine the 1996 presidential campaign to see whether the "forcing" continued in that campaign. Then examine ways in which the Clinton and Dole campaigns attempted to "skirt" the coverage, hence avoiding being forced to "fit into" coverage, by "going directly to the people" through talk shows, computer contacts, direct mail, and televised advertisements.

**2.** Since political conventions no longer serve any purpose except to advertise the party nominees, perhaps they should be eliminated. Tote up as many arguments as you can find for and against this proposal. If you had the power to make the decision, which position would you favor?

## NOTES

1. M. Schudson, "The Limits of Teledemocracy," *American Prospect,* Fall 1992, 42.

2. M. R. Weisbord, *Campaigning for President: A New Look at the Road to the White House* (Washington, DC: Public Affairs Press, 1964), 4.

3. S. Smith, "Saving Our Cities From the Experts," *Utne Reader,* September/October 1994, 67.

4. D. B. Buller, K. D. Strzyzewski, and F. C. Hunsaker, "Interpersonal Deception: II. The Inferiority of Conversational Participants as Deception Detectors," *Communication Monographs* 58 (March 1991): 35.

5. A. Krock, "'The Man Who'—Not 'The Issue Which,'" *New York Times Magazine,* 6 October 1960, p. 110.

6. M. Frankel, "Election Day Fantasy," *New York Times Magazine,* 6 November 1994, p. 26.

7. E. J. Hughes, "52,000,000 TV Sets—How Many Votes?" *New York Times Magazine,* 25 September 1960, p. 78.

8. D. F. Hahn, "The Effect of Television on Presidential Campaigns," *Today's Speech* 18 (Spring 1970): 4–17.

9. T. H. White, *The Making of the President 1964* (New York: Atheneum, 1965), 182.

10. E. S. Bogardus, "Television and Political Conventions," *Sociology and Social Research* 37 (November–December 1953): 116.

11. R. Bierstedt, "The Ethics of Cognitive Communication," *Journal of Communication* 13 (September 1963): 200.

12. Frankel, *op. cit.*, 26.

13. Hughes, *op. cit.*, 19.

14. G. F. Bishop, R. G. Meadow, M. Jackson-Beeck, eds., *The Presidential Debates: Media, Electoral and Policy Perspectives* (New York: Praeger, 1978); R. V. Friedenberg, R.V., ed., *Rhetorical Studies of National Political Debates, 1960–1992* (New York: Praeger, 1993); K. H. Jamieson and D. S. Birdsell, *Presidential Debates: The Challenge of Creating an Informed Electorate* (New York: Oxford University Press, 1988); S. Kraus, ed., *The Great Debates: Background, Perspective, Effects* (Bloomington: Indiana University Press, 1962); S. Kraus, ed., *The Great Debates: Carter vs. Ford, 1976* (Bloomington: Indiana University Press, 1979); S. Kraus, *Televised Political Debates and Public Policy* (Hillsdale, NJ: Lawrence Erlbaum, 1988); M. Martel, *Political Campaign Debates: Images, Strategies and Tactics* (New York: Longman, 1983); L. D. Mitchell, *With the Nation Watching* (Lexington, MA: Lexington Books, 1979); A. Ranney, ed., *The Past and Future of Presidential Debates* (Washington, DC: American Enterprise Institute for Public Policy Research, 1979); K. Ritter, ed., *The 1980 Presidential Debates* (Special issue of *Speaker and Gavel*, V. 18, No. 2) (Lawrence, KS: Allen Press, 1981); J. L. Swerdlow, *Beyond Debate: A Paper on Televised Presidential Debates* (New York: Twentieth Century Fund, 1984); J. L. Swerdlow, ed., *Presidential Debates: 1988 and Beyond* (Washington, DC: Congressional Quarterly Press, 1988).

15. Friedenberg, *op. cit.*, 207.

16. E. Katz and J. J. Feldman, "The Debates in the Light of Research: A Survey of Surveys," in Kraus, *The Great Debates, op. cit.*, 218–219.

17. Jamieson and Birdsell, *op. cit.*

18. Friedenberg, *op. cit.*, 201–202.

19. *Ibid.*, 207.

20. R. Bendiner, "How Presidents Are Made," *Reporter,* 9 February 1956, 17.

21. E. T. Jack, "A Community's Public Talk," *PS: Political Science and Politics*, December 1993, 722.

22. R. Toner, "In Limbaughland, Election Jitters," *New York Times,* 3 November 1994, p. A11.

23. R. Morin, "Look Who's Talking," *Washington Post National Weekly Edition,* 19–25 July 1993, 37.

24. T. B. Edsall, "America's Sweetheart," *New York Review of Books,* 6 October 1994, p. 9.

25. A. O. Hirschman, "Opinionated Opinions and Democracy," *Dissent,* Summer 1989, 395.

# CHAPTER TWELVE

# Effects of Mediated Campaigns on Voters

*The effective political discourse
reaching the mass public is mostly
the shrinking soundbite, a medium
that reduces political debate
to messages worthy of bumper
stickers or fortune cookies.*
— J.S. FISHKIN[1]

Televised political spot ads and televised campaign debates have been around for so long they are probably what most people think of when they hear the phrase "mediated campaigns." And, indeed, I include these facets among the phenomena of mediated campaigns. But I also include those interminable Sunday-morning talk shows, campaign coverage in the news, news specials, documentaries about one or both candidates and/or their positions on the issues, media reports of the latest polls rating the candidates, editorials and op-ed pieces in newspapers, interviews and opinion (or opinionated) pieces in magazines, call-in shows on TV and radio, and the contributions of the newest medium, the computer. Except for those few people who actually see and hear candidates live, and the even fewer who talk with the candidates in person, all of us get all of our information about campaigns through the media, from the candidate, the candidate's campaign apparatus, or those hired by the media— journalists and political ideologues posing as journalists. The totality of all this media "coverage" is what I mean by a "mediated campaign."

Consider, for instance, the 1992 campaign in terms of "talk" shows alone. Writing just before the election, Howard Kurtz toted up *some* of that portion of the campaign that was fought out on the talk shows. Perot, of course, *announced* his candidacy on the Larry King ("Kingmaker"?) Show, but also appeared there an additional five times; President George Bush, says Kurtz, "popped up on almost any programs that would have him," including eight talk shows and "nine televised town meetings"; meanwhile, Bill Clinton, "also closed with a talk-show blitz," appearing on five talk shows "and a town meeting at WWOR in New Jersey."[2] Please note that Kurtz focuses only on *talk* shows during the last week of the campaign; most of the "mediated campaigns" of the three candidates, even in that final week before the election, aren't included in his summary.

There are two major sets of players in mediated campaigns—the candidates (including their whole campaign apparatus) and the media. Although the average citizen usually does not distinguish between the contributions of the two sets, we should. Therefore, I first will examine the mediated campaign as "produced" by the candidate, then turn to the media coverage of the campaign.

In neither case will I attempt a complete analysis of the techniques used, for that would require a separate book, but rather focus on a few of the more important and newer tactics in order to give a flavor of what is happening.

## ▶ The Mediated Campaign

First, then, I want to look at how citizens can be misled by the mediated campaigns of the candidates, as the candidates focus on issues only to prop up their images, take us in with their televised ads, numb us, bypass the national media, stage the news, avoid argumentation, and avoid taking clear stands on issues.

Probably the most obvious misleading comes from the fact that candidates talk about issues. There is nothing wrong with that, of course; they should talk about issues. But the effect of such talk is that we come to think that the election must be about issues, when nothing could be farther from the truth. Issues, as Professor Ruth Gonchar and I demonstrated in 1972, are largely irrelevant.[3] That is to say, the purpose of all that "issues talk" is not to clarify ideological positions but rather to provide us voters with an image that will distinguish the candidate from the opponent in our minds.

The issues themselves are largely irrelevant, partially because the stands taken on the issues may reflect the candidates' polls more than their own thoughts, partially because the stands are stated vaguely in order to persuade us that candidates agree with us even if they do not, partially because candidates may alter their positions once elected. But perhaps the most important reason that issues are irrelevant relates to the fact that our elections are determined by the calendar rather than by the emergence of important issues. That is, we have a presidential election every four years, whether we need one yet or not. Therefore, campaigns concern whatever "issues" might be "lying around" when the calendar says it is time for an election, even if those "issues" are relatively unimportant. That is why the 1960 election focused so much attention on what to do about Quemoy and Matsu.

About who?

Quemoy and Matsu were two small islands off the coast of the island of Formosa, the island to which Chinese "nationalists" fled when the Communists took over China. The U.S. government had pledged to come to the defense of Formosa if it were attacked by China, but never had made a corresponding pledge regarding Quemoy and Matsu. So, somehow, whether such a pledge should be made became a major issue during the 1960 campaign.

Why was the question about Quemoy and Matsu a campaign issue? Because elections demand issues! And if there is not a major issue that the candidates want to focus on, they will find (or invent) an issue that can be escalated from minor to major standing.

Issues may also be irrelevant because they confuse the voter. As communication scholar Donald Zacharias has stated, "America's hidden political crises have too long a history, too many tentacles wrapped around social institutions and corporations to be topics for meaningful debate in an election year."[4] Consider, for instance, how many of us, during the 1996 campaign, in which we were asked to "ratify" or "repudiate" the so-called Republican revolution of 1994–1996, could even identify the major outlines of the ten bills of the Republican "Contract With America," much less give reasoned evaluations of the Republican and Democratic positions on the separate bills, or address the more arcane question of the differences between the versions of the bills as passed by the Republican House of Representatives and the Republican Senate!

The difficulty in citizen understanding of the issues is the reason campaigns are designed so that images contain the issues. The campaign, then, is organized this way: (1) the candidate first selects a theme that is dictated by the personality and world view of the candidate; (2) issues are chosen that are consonant with the theme; then (3) those issues are framed in language that reinforces the theme.

Thus issues and stands on issues are chosen to demonstrate the theme in operation and thereby reinforce the image. The 1984 Reagan reelection campaign is a perfect example of the process. Reagan's theme was "America is back and standing tall," a theme that perfectly reflected his generally cheerful persona and his patriotic focus on "what's right with America." The two issues that were consonant with the theme and emphasized throughout the campaign were the improvements in American economic health (improved, that is, over the 1982 recession, which had been brought on by Reagan policies, not over the pre-Reagan 1970s) and the increases in military power during his reign. As an example of how the language chosen framed the issues in a way that reinforced the theme, consider how Reagan compared Democrats and Republicans on economic issues: "To the Republicans, every day is the Fourth of July; to the Democrats every day is April 15." That is to say, Republicans, like Reagan, are cheerful and positive; Democrats, like Mondale, are crabby big spenders (hence big taxers). Notice how the issues got "rolled into" the theme, which, in turn, reinforced the Reagan image.

In addition to misleading us by talking about (often) irrelevant issues in (frequently) irrelevant ways, mediated campaigns can mislead us with ads. Of course, none of us thinks we are "taken in" by the ads. We have been "consuming" ads since our toddler years and pride ourselves on our ability to "take them in stride." Political ads *look* and *sound* like product commercials, so we figure we can handle them. Yet, as Robert Spero points out in *The Duping of the American Voter,* there is one important difference between a political commercial and a product commercial: "Political commercials are in no way regulated for truth in advertising, nor can they presently be regulated."[5] That single fact, Spero continues, explains why political ads are "the most deceptive, misleading, unfair, and untruthful of all advertising . . . Today the sky is the limit in political advertising with regard to what can be said, what can be promised, what accusations can be made, what lies can be told."[6]

In short, our years of experience in front of the tube watching product commercials have not prepared us to watch political commercials. For while we are used to illogicality, truth-stretching, and ambiguities, we are not prepared for downright lies. We are used to discounting ads a certain extent, so when we hear a political advertisement in which a candidate says the opposing candidate has voted for twenty-seven tax increases we automatically cut the number back to, say, twenty, then think: but even twenty is too many. However, since there is no "truth in advertising" requirement for political ads, the truth may be that the opponent never voted for *any* tax increases. Even with our automatic discounting, we have been misled. All the sophistication we think we have gained in watching hundreds of thousands of product ads down through the years itself misleads us by making us think we know how to consume such ads. We are duped—partly by the ads, partly by our own arrogance about our advertisement decoding abilities.

Not quite convinced yet? Okay, try this: take a minute and jot down the differences you would expect between incumbent and challenger ads. If you said the logical thing, that incumbents say they've been doing a good job and challengers say the incumbents have been doing a bad job, you would be partially right. Incumbents *do* talk about their own competence and their accomplishments in office, but that is not their main focus. As communication researchers Anne J. Wadsworth and Lynda Lee Kaid have discovered, incumbents' advertising "focused on their 'presidential qualities' and reinforced voters' images of them as tied to the office of the president."[7] In 1972 the Nixon campaign "tag line" at the end of commercials said "Re-elect the President," as though if we did not reelect Nixon we wouldn't have a president any more! And while challengers do attack the shortcomings of the incumbent's administration, the major thing that sets their ads apart from the incumbents' is that they much more often appear in and have speaking roles in their ads.[8] The major characteristics, then, are that incumbents stress personality while not appearing in person, leading us to think not of Mr. Bush or Mr. Clinton but of Mr. President. Challengers talk about issues, but present the ads themselves, leading us to think of them as competent *thinking* persons. The election, then, is not between the ideas of the incumbent versus the ideas of the challenger, but the image of "The President" versus the image of "The Thinker."

Another way in which we are misled by office-seekers' mediated campaigns is by how well they "fit into" the whole media world. Often this process of "fitting in" is called "the manipulation of the media." But that phrase makes me uncomfortable. If I know that you will like me better if I do X, so I do it, have I manipulated you by doing X . . . or have you manipulated me into doing X? Something like that is going on in what usually is called the "manipulation" of the media. Candidates act in certain ways because they know they'll get better coverage if they do. I call that "fitting in" because I can't figure out who is manipulating whom!

But, whatever you call it, it happens in every campaign. When a natural disaster hits—a flood, tornado, hurricane, whatever—the candidates do not do the *useful* thing, i.e., go to Congress to get disaster relief funds. No, they fly into the stricken area (for about fifteen minutes) to get their pictures taken stacking sandbags to stop the flood, helping to rebuild a damaged house, and so forth.

Knowing that only one story can be the lead story on the evening news, they strive mightily to give the media just one story a day . . . and to make sure that everybody in their entourage sticks to a single "line" on that story. They try to take credit for everything good that happens and to blame everything bad on the other candidate.

The damnable thing about television, and about candidates fitting into television, is that the whole phenomenon is simultaneously distracting and dull. Television distracts us from our own lives, from thinking about our families and our friends and from our work. Politicians on television, then, become a part of that distraction, rather than what they'd like to be—a part of our lives.

After a while, of course, televised distraction becomes dull. As Anna Quindlen puts it, "familiarity can numb."[9] We become numb with distraction— and react numbly to the latest report of disaster in Africa, rumblings of war in the Middle East, genocide in Bosnia, and whatever the politicians are crowing or complaining about today. We become neither angry nor sad about the latest starving child or ranting madman. We become, rather, uncaring and un-involved. Nothing seems real; image and images are all. And into our homes, with us in distracted and numbed states, come the politicians . . . trying to "fit in." Unfortunately, they fit only too well, as *Esquire* writer Doug Marlette points out: "if Reagan was his own spin doctor . . . Bill Clinton is his own spin shrink . . . the talk-show host, the anchorman, the televangelist, the actor, the carnival sideshow snake-oil salesman, Slick Willie."[10]

Maybe at that point, when we become too distracted and too numb, when the politicians begin fitting into our television regime *too* well, we would be well-advised to click off the tube and play with the kids or watch a sunset or read a book or even have a real conversation with a real person. Naturalist Bill McKibben suggests that we "take the long view and remind ourselves that no one ever lay on his deathbed wishing he'd watched more *Matlock*."[11]

The more politicians try to "fit in" to avoid critical coverage, the more journalists the Washington press corps assign to cover campaigns. In days gone by candidates could escape most of that national coverage by traveling outside Washington, where they would face only the local media, which tends to be less critical. But by now such a large entourage of national reporters accompanies candidates that candidates invented a new way to avoid them. Candidates now give interviews to local media from the "privacy" of their campaign headquarters in Washington via satellite.

National reporter Ken Auletta provides this report on the new campaign approach during the 1992 campaign: "Starting with President Bush in January, the candidates used satellites to conduct live interviews with local stations around the country. During the 1992 primary season, the Freedom Forum Media Studies Center at Columbia University found that twice as many local stations used satellite interviews as they did in 1988; and partly to save money, one in ten local stations now accepted video news releases produced by candidates—a threefold increase over 1988—with half failing 'to reveal the source of this material to viewers.'"[12] The satellite coverage and videos not only bypass the critical national media, they also "demonstrate" that the candidate "cares enough" about the local area in question to talk directly with local reporters who are known and trusted in that area. And the video news releases, with the campaign source unrevealed, give the candidates the opportunity to structure voter perceptions directly rather than through critical journalists, who might ask tough questions.

Another way candidates get their position covered by the media is by "staging" events, or what Daniel Boorstin called "pseudo-events."[13] The idea is that candidates know there is going to be some coverage on the evening news, so they might as well make sure the coverage relates to what they want to have covered rather than leaving the choice up to the journalists. *Time* correspondent Thomas Griffith traced this phenomenon as President Reagan used it: when Reagan was concerned about the farm vote he traveled to a midwestern state fair, where he could "speak against a backdrop of hay," and the media "went along for the ride. The networks . . . are all too willing to play along with staged news, and thus share a complicity."[14]

If a president, vice president, or leading candidate goes someplace to make a speech, it is assumed that the media would be derelict in their duty if they did not cover it. That assumption gives campaigns wide latitude in deciding what to say, where to say it, and what props to use to drive home the campaign theme. The media are forced, then, to "pass on" pictures and accounts of the event to the voters.

Because campaigns are focused on pseudo-events rather than on persuading voters with position arguments, there has been a diminution of argumentation in campaigns. Philosopher and law professor George Anastaplo has written knowingly about the disappearance of argument in contemporary politics. He says that contemporary public speeches "are filled with short, one-paragraph sentences, little snatches of things"[15] rather than detailed arguments.

You can prove the Anastaplo assertion to yourself very easily. Take almost any speech by President Lincoln and almost any speech by any modern president. You don't even have to read them—just hold them up at arm's length and note that in the Lincoln speech the paragraphs normally went for half a page to one and a half pages, whereas the contemporary speech has six to eight paragraphs on a page. This is not a change in the idea of how to do paragraphs. If you now bring the speeches closer and examine them you will discover that Lincoln was constructing arguments, with premises, assertions, evidence in support of the assertions, and conclusions, whereas the contemporary politician has only unsupported assertions, statements designed to appeal to our already-held beliefs and stated as pithily as possible for media ease in pulling out a "news bite" of ten to fifteen seconds.

That campaigns adapt to media was demonstrated in 1996 by James Fallows, a former political speech-writer turned journalist. He wrote: "the pressure to keep things lively means that squabbling replaces dialogue. The discussion shows that are supposed to enhance public understanding may actually reduce it, by hammering home the message that issues don't matter except as items for politicians to fight over."[16] If the media treat issue arguments as mere "squabbling," politicians have very little choice but to avoid argumentation so as to avoid being depicted as "squabblers."

So political campaigns have come to avoid issues as much as possible. In addition to not wanting to be treated as "squabblers," politicians have learned that every position offends some portion of the electorate, perhaps a portion they need in order to get elected. They have also discovered that when they do address issues, they're accused of manipulation. Therefore, when Senator Dole in 1995 attacked the values in Hollywood movies, the attack was treated as an attempt to pick up some Christian Conservative support. When Clinton addressed the same subject in 1996, the media addressed the question of whether Clinton was trying to preempt a Republican position. Nobody in the media seems to have considered seriously the possibility that both Dole and Clinton were concerned about what films and television fare may be doing to the culture; the assumption was that issue discussion is always a campaign ploy.

A somewhat more legitimate—or at least logical—reason why candidates may not want to address issues is that once they are elected they need to govern. If a problem looks different after two years in the White House, with altered circumstances and new information, they are "roped in" by the position they took in the campaign. That is a major reason George Bush did not win a second term in office. He had promised in 1988 that there would be no new taxes; once in office, though, he discovered that new taxes were needed, so he approved them. In 1992 he was punished for that changed outlook. Bush would have done better if he had not taken a position on taxes in 1988. (Of course, it might also have been better if in 1992 he had argued that the new taxes had been necessary, rather than saying he had made a mistake in "caving in" to the Democrats on taxes. But, as we've seen, argumentation no longer takes place in campaigns, so the voters were left to choose between a Democrat who *might* raise taxes and a Republican who *might* cave in again. They voted against the one they suspected did not have the courage of his convictions.)

One major way in which candidates avoid issues, or at least tone them down, is through language choices. Their pollsters with their focus groups are useful in these choices. For instance, after Newt Gingrich suggested that the children of teenaged mothers who cannot care for them should be taken away and put into orphanages, and after the outcry that the suggestion occasioned, Frank Luntz, a top Republican pollster, came to the rescue. He found that although there was some support for the proposal, the support increased significantly when "foster homes" replaced "orphanages" in the proposal. Thereafter, the modification became part of the Republican proposal.[17]

Another Frank Luntz success concerned the order of provisions in the 1994 Republican "Contract with America." On the basis of his polling, "the balanced-budget amendment, the contract's most popular provision, was put at the top, and term limits, the second-most-popular provision, at the bottom."[18] The least popular planks were placed in the middle, in the hope that the casual reader would either not notice them or at least not think about them very much.

Mediated campaigns, then, as structured by the campaigning politicians, focus on issues only to prop up images, take us in with their televised ads, numb us, bypass the national media, stage the news, avoid argumentation when possible (thus damaging the "ongoing conversation"), and avoid taking too clear a stand on issues. But politicians cannot be blamed for all that is wrong with mediated campaigns; the "contributions" of the media are also responsible. But before we look specifically at media coverage of candidates and issues, we need to examine more generally how media structure our perceptions.

## ▶ Media Coverage of Campaigns

The changes brought about by developments in communication always are faced with a mixture of hope and fear. Extravagant claims are made, frightening predictions set forth. But by now we are far enough into the "television age" that we can begin to sort out some of the effects and separate fact from fiction.

Communication researchers Susan Drucker and Gary Gumpert have been especially prescient on how the electronic media have "altered and transformed" political rhetoric.[19] They point out that "political communication" is a phrase that "evokes images of platform oratory before masses gathered in public places,"[20] but that in contemporary society the electronic media have led to a "shifting from the domain of public spontaneity to controlled and privatized relationships."[21] That is, while we used to gather together to hear candidates in person, we now huddle solitarily in front of our TV sets and computer screens. In that sense, a contemporary televised political speech is not so much a *public* event as a private one.

Concomitantly, the "public" is not so much a community as a series of atomistic individuals, each reacting without any concern for others. As professor of law Ronald Collins points out, television short-circuits democracy "by undermining the significance of assembly . . . in our own privatized TV world, we are civic in name only. . . . Television . . . is inherently alienating; it caters to the solitary life."[22]

W. Lance Bennett, a political scientist who focuses on communication issues, points out that this atomization "marginalizes audiences from power."[23] He says "people live now in imagined electronic communities. In these communities of the mind, citizens are drawn together primarily through political spectacles, as they are simultaneously disconnected from traditional forms of society and politics like parties, trade unions, and even the family."[24] The result of this process "is that people find short term personal meanings in these episodic, dramatic framings of political events, but carry little information or social understanding away from the television set with them."[25] Thus, they are not positioned to act in any kind of politically efficacious way. Consequently, he concludes, "when frequently excluded citizens cannot imagine themselves as part of any larger political community, then political order, democratic or otherwise, becomes a questionable proposition."[26]

The "political order" requires at least a modicum of feeling that "we're all in this together," some bare-bones minimum of tolerance of and respect for the opinions and beliefs of others, some willingness to accept a degree of compromise in order to keep "the system" going. Those characteristics of "polity" have been undermined by television—not intentionally, but as a natural outcome of television's approach to covering the world, which might be called the melo-dramatic imperative. In all of television, from the "pure entertainment" shows to news "stories" to coverage of campaigns, the focus is on conflict, the delineation of the good and the bad. In international arenas we are given the "American gladiator" against some aggressive heathen, and domestic political campaigns are covered in much the same way. Nuances are lost; moral absolutism is stressed. As a result, as journalist Robert Hughes has bemoaned, "the traditional American genius for compromise, which is the heart of a pluralist democracy, is breaking down."[27] The fault is not completely television's, of course, but television is a major contributor, encouraging us to mistake their stereotypes for reality. Thus, the 1950s television classic, *Ozzie and Harriet,* "gets recycled as another fantasy about statecraft and morality."[28]

One result of contemporary television, then, is that it is increasingly difficult for citizens to separate the serious from the silly. Ken Auletta, writing in *Esquire* magazine, points out that it is "not without reason" that "the public tends to confuse the trash news programs with the ostensibly serious ones. Programs like *Hard Copy* or *Geraldo* are, after all, broadcast on network-owned stations."[29] When Sally Jessy Raphael has a program entitled "Mom, I'm a Teen Prostitute," Jenny Jones focuses on "Deadly Erotic Teen Games," and Montel Williams features "Teen Girls Who Have One-Night Affairs," both the national audience and the national journalists are primed to look not only at teen sex but also at the sex lives of politicians rather than the issues of the campaign. Both are conditioned to approach those lives in terms of moral absolutes, forgetting that very few of us can measure up to some kind of "purity" standard in our personal lives.

More important, perhaps, all of us who consume television on a daily basis learn to sneer at everybody, on and off the set. Todd Gitlin, a professor of communication at New York University, says that the "jokey come-back" and the "put-down" are the "common currency" of television. Thus, "a free-floating hostility mirrors, and also inspires, the conversational style" of the television audience. Ultimately, he says, "rather than learn one subject well, [TV audience members] acquire a sophisticated repartee and light banter."[30] Glibness replaces thoughtfulness, and, especially in politics, becomes a standard by which to judge, so that if a candidate is seen to pause, even for a moment, to gather the thoughts needed to respond to a tough or trick question, the audience sees that lapse in glibness as something else, perhaps a lapse in morality, with the assumption being that the candidate is pausing to consider the best way to befuddle us rather than to determine which of several possible responses is the most honest under the circumstances. Thus it is that absolutists, who never have to pause to consider nuances or recognize that changed circumstances might call for changed responses, come off on television as more honest than other candidates.

That was one of the Buchanan's appeals in the 1996 Republican primaries. Many voters swung to him because he "says what he means and means what he says"; but that description did not represent the real difference between Buchanan and the other candidates. Rather, the difference was that Buchanan was an absolutist whose ideology did not admit that a different judgment might be called for when comparing a robbery engaged in for kicks with the same act perpetrated by a parent trying to get food for a starving child. The unvarying nature of his responses, then, meant that he not only "said what he meant," but that he always meant the same thing, thus always had a glib answer—without hesitation, because without thought.

Having now examined some general ways in which the media structure our perceptions, it is time to turn more specifically to political campaigns and to how the media structure our perceptions of candidates.

The most important effect of the move from print coverage of campaigns to television coverage is that it has exacerbated the media, hence public, tendency to focus on personality. The point is not that personality was not a question before television. As political communication professor Doris Graber reminds us, "when candidates shook hands firmly, kissed babies, and handed out cigars the thrust was not on issues." The politicians were trying to "convince the voters that the candidates were strong, compassionate, and generous."[31] The point, rather, is one of balance and perspective: prior to television the candidate's personality was one, perhaps relatively minor, criterion. With television it has been promoted to the primary, and at times the only, evaluative category. As long ago as 1978, David Broder, one of the more insightful journalists in the second half of the twentieth century, wrote that, compared to the print media, television "is personality dominated."[32] Consequently, television coverage creates "giant waves of personal publicity that drown out almost any other consideration of qualifications for the office."[33]

Believing they are searching for clues to "character," television journalists bombard candidates with personal questions. For instance, during the 1992 Democrat primaries Sam Donaldson of ABC asked Senator Bob Kerrey of Nebraska, who was seeking the presidential nomination, whether he had ever used drugs, specifically marijuana or cocaine. What that has to do with anything is, at least to me, unclear. If he had smoked a joint at some point would that mean he was ineligible for the presidency? Or maybe that, because he had done what most of us had done, he was *more* qualified to be our leader? Because he would have broken a law, maybe he shouldn't be the chief "lawmaker?" What about somebody who had driven through a stop sign? What, exactly, would we know about somebody's "character" if we knew the person had—or had not—once in a lifetime tried a recreational herb?

Fortunately, not all, maybe not even most, voters are as obsessed with such an approach to "character." On April 1 during that same primary season, Bill Clinton made an appearance on the *Donahue* show. Ken Auletta reports the outcome: "Donahue prowled the stage with a microphone, asking Clinton: 'Have you ever had an affair?' 'Have you and Hillary ever separated?' Then the sheepish host had his microphone gently taken by a female member of the audience who exclaimed, 'Given the pathetic state of the United States at this point—medicare, education, everything else—I can't believe you spent half an hour of airtime attacking this man's character. I'm not even a Bill Clinton supporter, but I think this is ridiculous!'"[34]

But the electronic media did not change. The 1996 campaign coverage on television was as devoted to "character" as the '92 campaign had been.

Interestingly, one reason television has the power to focus our attention on what *it* wants to focus on, to the exclusion of what the people want, is precisely because we assume it does not have *that* much power. We think television portrays campaigns as conflict-filled because they are, never stopping to think that the conflict is *created* in campaigns because of the need to get on television. We think television covers the "flashy events" in campaigns because that is how campaigns are, never dreaming that the candidates' staffs stage events in a "flashy" way in order to get television coverage.

Many people, for example, assume recent campaigns have focused on angry white male voters because there is something in politics that has angered white males. Yet *Washington Post* writer Henry Allen suggests that it is not politics *per se* that has angered them, but how they have been depicted in the media—another indication of the interaction between media and politics. To check out this position, he suggests we ask, "Does white male anger have anything to do with 25 years of being described . . . as rabid racists; as self-loathing gynephobic rape addicts; as phallocentric redneck gun nuts;"[35] and so forth.

Has Mr. Allen just gone off on a diatribe against how men are treated in the media; is he just being bitter about how his gender is represented in the media (forgetting that women are depicted negatively, too)? Or might he be "on to" something here? As you ponder this, consider the average husband and father as depicted on television entertainment. Is he capable or a bumbler? Compassionate with his kids, or concerned only about his own image? Understanding of his wife, or more likely to beat her at the slightest provocation? A practitioner of sexual fidelity, or juggling several affairs? Given those depictions, who would want to become a husband or father? What image do we have of men in general? Given those depictions, what husband or father would not be angry?

The collective image we have of men *is* affected by the images we receive from television. Indeed, journalism professors Michael Gurevitch and Anandam Kavoori have pointed out that our "collective memory" of all of history since the introduction of television is carried in images: "Rodney King keeps writhing on the ground; 'Bull' Connor keeps deploying fire hoses . . . and John F. Kennedy remains forever young, bronzed, and embodying hope."[36] The images we carry around in our heads, both of historically important events and personages and of average people, are reality to us. So although we think television is not *that* influential and discount its power, we are fooling ourselves. Television helps determine what we think, how we think, indeed, *whether* we think.

What we think about specific political activities, for instance, is determined by how television presents them to us. For example, in 1993 the United States sent "peace-keepers" and food to Somalia, largely because of the pity evoked by televised pictures of the suffering, starving people. Then at some point an American soldier was killed and we were shown his body being dragged through the streets by the triumphant band of killers. Shortly thereafter another of our soldiers was captured by another (or maybe the same) band, and we were shown his face on television, maimed and tortured. But we didn't know what to do with all those images. As Walter Goodman wrote at the time, the viewer didn't know whether to focus on the hostage, the corpse, or the earlier picture of the suffering Somalis. Goodman asks, "what sort of policy making is it to have Washington's actions decided, even in part, on the latest affecting pictures on the evening news?"[37] Are dramatic pictures, the central contribution of television, of any use to us in policy-making?

In like manner, we can ask, what sort of vote determination is it to make our decisions on fetching pictures of candidates with their families, on images of "character" created by journalists poking around in the bedrooms of the candidates, or on the presumed "common man" image created by Lamar Alexander's plaid shirts? The media can't determine our vote? Yes they can, by what they choose to show us, by what they choose to focus on, by the images they create or help create of the various candidates. We say "I vote my conscience," in complete ignorance that our consciences have themselves been affected by television.

But not only our views of candidates and candidate images are structured by television. Our understandings of candidates' stands on the issues are also affected. Roger Ailes, an advisor to George Bush, offers an insight into media coverage of issues that he calls his "orchestra-pit" political theory: "If you have two guys on a stage and one guy says, 'I have a solution to the Middle East problem,' and the other guy falls in the orchestra pit, who do you think is going to be on the evening news?"[38]

I would go even farther and suggest that even if the other candidate did not fall into the orchestra pit the electronic media would not report the substantive solution to the Middle East morass. Instead, they would report who won the debate. Both the Middle East solution and the nose dive into the orchestra would be presented as tactics to manipulate the voters. In short, the focus of the media would be on what has been called the "horse-race" aspects of the campaign.

Professor of communication Vincent Fitzgerald has made an in-depth study of these aspects of the media. He reports that "the media appear more interested in reporting pre-election polls as a sporting event focusing on winners and losers rather than reporting serious presidential candidates debating national and international issues."[39]

Many journalists admit to this tendency. Howard Kurtz, of the *Washington Post,* suggests one reason is that some stories are "too hot" for them to handle. They dare not examine too carefully why so few prisoners are white, or whether welfare assistance is sufficient as a safety net, or why it is that crack was not newsworthy until it passed out of the slums and into the suburbs. Says Kurtz, "to delve into these subjects is to risk charges of racism or sexism . . . ."[40]

Journalist Ken Auletta agrees that concern for their own image keeps journalists from focusing on issues. "Reporters pursue surface questions for many reasons, not the least being that it is easier to maintain objectivity by reporting who wins or loses than by reporting who's right or wrong. By judging the quality of a candidate's ideas, we risk being seen as partisans, a view that would drain the press of what credibility it retains."[41]

On the other hand, James Fallows suggests that journalists cover the horse race rather than the issues because of their desire to talk about what they know best, the strategic and tactical side of politics. He traces the emphasis in the coverage of that horrible explosion at the federal building in Oklahoma City in 1995. The discussion in the media, he suggests, "changed quickly from the event itself to politicians' 'handling' of the event. On the Sunday after the blast President Clinton announced a series of new anti-terrorism measures. The next morning, on National Public Radio's *Morning Edition,* Cokie Roberts was asked about the prospects of the proposals taking effect. 'In some ways it's not even the point,' she replied. What mattered was that Clinton 'looked good' taking the tough side of the issue. No one expects Cokie Roberts or other political correspondents to be experts on controlling terrorism, negotiating with the Syrians, or the other specific measures on which Presidents make stands. But all issues are shoehorned into the area of expertise the most prominent correspondents do have: the struggle for one-upmanship among a handful of political leaders."[42]

For that reason, suggests Fallows, "the natural instinct of newspapers and TV is to present every public issue as if its 'real' meaning were political in the meanest and narrowest sense of that term—the attempt by parties and candidates to gain an advantage over their rivals."[43]

Whether to protect their own credibility or just to steer the discussion into realms where they feel more comfortable, journalists covering campaigns clearly focus on "who staged the best events, who looked smooth, who sounded good, who was winning, who gave the best performance."[44] But those are not aspects that the citizens care about. Fallows points out that in town-hall forums and on radio and TV talk shows, "the citizens asked overwhelmingly about the *what* of politics: What are you going to do about the health-care system? What can you do to reduce the cost of welfare? The reporters asked almost exclusively about the *how:* How are you going to try to take away Perot's constituency? How do you answer charges that you have flip-flopped?"[45]

The disparity between citizens' and journalists' questions is a main reason that candidates in 1992 and 1996 emphasized media that allowed them to talk directly with the voters rather than relying on journalistic coverage. As Bill Clinton told one reporter, "Real voters don't ask me—as you journalists always do—about the political process and polls. They ask how their lives are going to be changed."[46]

What the candidates in '92 and '96 were trying to do, in addition to getting elected, was to engage the public in dialogue, to focus on the problems facing the country. That focus, they feared, was being lost by the way journalists were covering their campaigns. Fallows, who often writes more as a political participant than as a journalist, agreed: "a relentless emphasis on the cynical game of politics threatens public life itself, by implying day after day that the political sphere is nothing more than an arena in which ambitious politicians struggle for dominance, rather than a structure in which citizens can deal with worrisome collective problems."[47]

In addition to the media's general tendency to focus on "horse-race" aspects, several other tendencies make media coverage troublesome. One is that the coverage is so shallow, so lacking in depth. This, of course, is not just true of campaign coverage, but of media coverage at all times. For instance, communication professor Gail Hankins argues that the media did an inadequate job of analyzing the possible causes of the urban riots of the '60s, neglecting "to explore alternatives such as economics, poverty, and degradation as possible causes of the urban chaos."[48] The result was that uninformed viewers used their own, often prejudicial, attitudes to conclude that Blacks were "looters." Then in 1968, when the Kerner Commission reported that "unemployment, under-employment, police practices, and inadequate housing" were root causes, those facts were "never addressed effectively by the media."[49]

Another example: since the "end of the Cold War," the media have returned time and again to a "peace dividend," asking what happened to it, when it is going to come, and so forth. But it is clear that they always refer only to a financial dividend. Yet isn't it possible that the Cold War cost much more than money . . . and that the *real* peace dividend may be in other—ultimately more important—areas, a dividend that will never be located by journalists who seek it only in the military budget?

To see the shallowness of media campaign coverage one can examine the 1988 Bush-Dukakis race. At a time when the Soviet Union was collapsing and the various Republics were "spinning off" into independent countries (or trying to do so), media coverage of the campaign focused on "flag burning, dirty records and government funding of offensive art."[50] It is true, of course, that some of that coverage was created because Bush was giving patriotic speeches in flag factories and Dukakis was riding in a tank for a "photo-op," but much of the coverage (and the campaign activity) was driven by the media's inability or unwillingness to attend to more important international phenomena.

Even more troubling is that fact that we citizens view the coverage of flags and pornography and think we are informed about the campaigns. Philosopher George Anastaplo thinks this is even more important than the shallowness of the coverage itself because "it deceives you into believing that you *are* informed."[51]

Much of the shallowness of television, of course, is related to the fact that it is predominantly a visual medium. Television commentator Marvin Kalb comments, "television news was seduced by the photo-op, its news judgment drained by the values of entertainment. Producers allowed . . . the image to supplant the substance."[52]

With television, if there is no picture there is no story. Jay Rosen, professor of journalism at New York University, points out that "the savings and loan scandal and other complex maneuvers of finance . . . occur in a political field that is fundamentally nonvisual and thus of negligible interest"[53] to those responsible for deciding what we'll see on the evening news—responsible, that is, for deciding what is news.

The final point to be made here about media coverage of campaign issues, though hardly the final point that would be covered in a *complete* account of media coverage, concerns "sound bites," five- to twenty-second statements that candidates make that are later excerpted by television for news shows. According to U.C.L.A. sociologist Steven Clayman, the media select sound bites according to three criteria: narrative relevance, conspicuousness, and extractability.[54] Sound bites have been around for a long time, but probably came into their own during the 1984 Democrat primary when Walter Mondale, in criticizing opponent Gary Hart's supposed lack of substance, appropriated a slogan from a popular TV fast food commercial: "Where's the beef?" Probably a larger percentage of the American public could have identified that popular quotation than could have answered any substantive question about differences among the candidates.

By 1988, according to communication professors Joseph Opfer and Peter A. Anderson, "campaign speeches actually were written with sound bites embedded in them," and television newscasters not only repeatedly showed the "bites" but used them "as a kind of points system to keep track of which candidate performed better."[55]

Not all commentators, it must be admitted, find the reliance on sound bites a purely negative phenomenon. Andrew Savitz and Mark Katz, for example, deny that sound bites replace substance: "Read Einstein's lips— $E=mc^2$ —and a scientific revolution is born; the Ten Commandments—the Ten Sound Bites—and monotheism makes its debut."[56] Of course, Savitz and Katz are political communication consultants, i.e., the kind of people responsible for the development of sound bites. And it should also be noted that Einstein's formula is embedded in a corpus of words explaining it and the Ten Commandments are part of the Bible, a rather long text that puts the commandments in perspective. Likewise with the memorable phrases that are a part of our political heritage. Franklin D. Roosevelt did say "the only thing we have to fear is fear itself," a "sound-bite" if you will, but he did so in a speech that spelled out why we should not be fearful and why fear is a debilitating reaction to events. Consequently, his admonition was a pithy way of summing up his central message. Such "summing up" is a very different phenomenon from the contemporary one in which such phrases are inserted into speeches, not to summarize important substantive points but to substitute for them, not to make an argument but to make the six o'clock news.

## CONCLUSION

▶ So the electronic media *have* made a difference. They have covered campaigns in a way that privileges absolutism over compromise; confuses the serious and the silly, substitutes the "put down" for the rebuttal; replaces thoughtfulness for glibness; and focuses on personality rather than issues, on images rather than content, on the "horse race" rather than the national problems the candidates address. The coverage is shallow, as the media fail to investigate alternative explanations for events, prefer to focus on the most visual rather than the most important and rely on the campaign sound bites rather than whatever substance might be there. And because we do not normally think the media have the power to do all this harm, it is even easier for them to do it.

▶ Not only are the voters affected by media coverage, so are the politicians. Indeed, we have seen that much of what politicians do is in response to knowledge of how the media cover events and people. But their adaptation does not exhaust the effects of the media on politicians, the topic of the next chapter.

## FOR FURTHER CONSIDERATION

**1.** None of us likes to think we are influenced by mediated campaigns. Yet most of us are. Without doing any research, try to remember any ads from the last presidential campaign. Why do you remember those particular ads? Is there any chance your evaluation of the candidate was affected (either positively or negatively) by that ad? Do you think others might have been influenced by it? Why them and not you?

Now do the same thing for media coverage. Do you remember any particular news report (print or electronic) on the campaigns? Was anything "blown out of proportion" by the media? Did the media ignore any aspect of either campaign that you thought should have received better coverage?

If you had been a news reporter in that election, what would you have done differently?

**2.** One seeming change in political campaigns in recent years has been the emergence of candidate humor. In 1996, for example, Vice President Gore, generally considered stiff and conventional, "played" with his image with several self-deprecating pieces of humor: (1) "How can you tell Al Gore from a roomful of Secret Service agents? He's the stiff one." (2) "Al Gore is so boring, his Secret Service code name is Al Gore." Why this change? Was it only the "humanizing" of Al Gore, or is something more important happening? Did all the 1996 candidates employ humor? Was this really a change from earlier campaigns? Does it symbolize something about contemporary campaigns, changes in the campaign audience, or changes in media coverage?

## NOTES

1. J. S. Fishkin, "Talk of the Tube: How To Get Teledemocracy Right," *American Prospect*, Fall 1992, 48.

2. H. Kurtz, "When Stories Seem too Hot to Handle, We All Get Burned," *Washington Post National Weekly Edition*, 28 January–3 February 1991, p. 27.

3. R. Gonchar and D. Hahn, "Political Myth: The Image and the Issue," *Today's Speech* 20 (Summer 1972): 57–65.

4. D. W. Zacharius, "Communication and Social Change," *Quarterly Journal of Speech* 58 (April 1972): 217.

5. R. Spero, *The Duping of the American Voter: Dishonesty and Deception in Presidential Television Advertising* (New York: Lippincott and Crowell, 1980), 2.

6. *Ibid.,* 3.

7. A. J. Wadsworth and L. L. Kaid, "Incumbent and Challenger Styles in Presidential Advertising" (paper presented at the annual convention of the International Communication Association, Montreal, June 1987), 29.

8. *Ibid.,* 29.

9. A. Quindlen, "Threshold of Pain," *New York Times,* 3 March 1993, p. A15.

10. D. Marlette, "Never Trust a Weeping Man," *Esquire,* October 1993, 71.

11. B. McKibben, "Sometimes You Just Have to Turn It Off," *Esquire,* October 1993, 67.

12. K. Auletta, "Loath the Media," *Esquire,* November 1992, 112.

13. D. J. Boorstin, *The Image: A Guide to Pseudo-Events in America* (New York: Harper and Row, 1961).

14. T. Griffith, "Making News and Non-News," *Time,* 1 September 1986, 70.

15. G. Anastaplo, "Education, Television, and Political Discourse in America," *Center Magazine* 19 (July/August 1986): 26.

16. J. Fallows, "Why Americans Hate the Media," *Atlantic Monthly,* February 1996, 48.

17. R. Toner, "G.O.P. Is Tutored on Strategy for Budget Debate," *New York Times,* 2 February 1995, A10.

18. E. Kolbert, "The Vocabulary of Voters," *New York Times Magazine,* 26 March 1995, p. 48.

19. S. J. Drucker and G. Gumpert, "The Mediation of Political Talk" (paper presented at the annual convention of the International Communication Association, Miami, May 1992), 1.

20. *Ibid.,* 2.

21. *Ibid.,* 3.

22. R. Collins, "TV Subverts the First Amendment," *New York Times,* 19 September 1987, p. 31.

23. W. L. Bennett, "White Noise: The Perils of Mass Mediated Democracy," *Communication Monographs* 59 (December 1992): 403.

24. *Ibid.,* 404.

25. *Ibid.,* 404.

26. *Ibid.,* 405.

27. R. Hughes, "Why Watch It, Anyway?" *New York Review of Books,* 16 February 1995, 38.

28. *Ibid.,* 38.

29. Auletta, *op. cit.,* 177.

30. T. Gitlin, "Glib, Glib, Glib," *Utne Reader,* March/April 1994, 116.

31. D. A. Graber, "Television Coverage of the 1984 Campaign" (paper presented at the annual convention of the International Communication Association, Montreal, June 1987), 1.

32. D. S. Broder, "Of Presidents and Parties," *Wilson Quarterly* 2 (Winter 1978): 109.

33. *Ibid.,* 114.

34. Auletta, *op. cit.,* 179.

35. H. Allen, "The Year of the White Male," *Washington Post National Weekly Edition,* 2–8 January 1995, 12.

36. M. Gurevitch and A. P. Kavoori, "Television Spectacles as Politics," *Communication Monographs* 59 (December 1992): 418.

37. W. Goodman, "The Effect of Images on Governmental Policy," *New York Times,* 7 October 1993, p. B3.

38. Auletta, *op. cit.,* 177.

39. V. M. Fitzgerald, "Public Opinion Polls and Network News Coverage of Presidential Campaigns" (paper presented at the annual convention of the Speech Communication Association, San Antonio, November 1995), 3–4.

40. Kurtz, *op. cit.,* 27.

41. Auletta, *op. cit.,* 51.

42. Fallows, *op. cit.,* 51.

43. *Ibid.,* 51.

44. Auletta, *op. cit.,* 112.

45. Fallows, *op. cit.,* 48.

46. Auletta, *op. cit.,* 179.

47. Fallows, *op. cit.,* 55.

48. G. A. Hankins, "Western Media Coverage of Conflicts in Their Own Backyard: An Analysis of News Media Coverage of the African-American Community" (paper presented at the annual convention of the Speech Communication Association, Chicago, November 1990), 4.

49. *Ibid.,* 4.

50. D. S. Broder, "Trivial Pursuits," *Washington Post National Weekly Edition,* 25 June–1 July 1990, p. 4.

51. Anastaplo, *op. cit.,* 26.

52. M. Kalb, "TV, Election Spoiler," *New York Times,* 28 November 1988, p. A25.

53. J. Rosen, "The Whole World Is Watching CNN," *Nation,* 18 May 1991, 623.

54. S. E. Clayman, "Defining Moments, Presidential Debates, and the Dynamics of Quotability," *Journal of Communication* 45 (Summer 1995): 118.

55. J. Opfer and P. A. Andersen, "Explaining the Sound Bite: A Test of a Theory of Metaphor and Assonance" (paper presented at the annual convention of the Western Speech Communication Association, Boise, February 1992), 1.

56. A. Savitz and M. Katz, "Sound Bites Have Teeth," *New York Times,* 26 March 1990, p. A17.

# Effects of the Media on Politicians

*The art of the campaign is the art of attracting positive media attention for a candidate. The task of governing is obviously very different and much more complex.*
— GARY WOODWARD[1]

Some ways in which media affect politicians have already been identified in the last two chapters: (1) The cost of television forces candidates to spend much of their time and energy raising money and thereby makes them vulnerable to major contributors. (2) In beaming the "intrafamily" squabbles of primaries to all voters, the media make it more difficult for politicians to shore up their intraparty base before engaging with the opposing nominee. (3) The increased focus on candidates' personal lives, which started in the 1960s, chases some people out of politics, scares others into not getting involved, and puts enormous stress on politicians' personal and family lives. (4) Politicians are forced to campaign in certain ways in order to get coverage in the media, for instance, to structure their speeches as a series of "sound bites" to get on the evening news. (5) The demand for glibness robs politicians of the ability to pause for a moment's thought before responding, ultimately privileging absolutism and forcing nonabsolutists to talk like absolutists even if they are moderate themselves.

## ▶ The "Lowering" of Politicians

But that list does not exhaust the ways in which media affect politicians. Perhaps the most important and debilitating effects were traced by communication scholar Josh Meyrowitz,[2] who argued that television brought politicians "down" to our level, thus eliminating the possibility of their presenting themselves as old-style "great" leaders. Television accomplished this, he said, by invading the "back region" of politicians. That is, before television a politician could come on stage; give a speech; then "retreat" to a "back-stage" area; talk with friends, family, and campaign aides about the speech; plan how to do better next time; and so forth. But television ended that, for it follows the candidate off stage. There is no place to which the candidate can escape. "On stage" continuously, then, the candidate loses all ability to "rehearse" the "on-stage" presentations.

Think about this in terms of the most important "presentations" most of us make in our personal lives: our romantic courtships. What if the object of our affections could watch us on television as we "get ready" for the date, listen in as we discuss the upcoming date with our friends, listen to commentators reflect on our "possible moves" during the date and imply that those "moves" are "manipulative," then follow us home after the date, listen in as we respond to questions about "how the date had gone" and discuss with friends what we plan to do differently on the next date? That would be analogous to the ways that television invades the "back regions" of candidates, making it difficult for them ever to be "off stage," ever to have a comfortable arena for evaluating the last presentation or preparing for the next.

Yet politics, like courtship, requires a degree of "mystification." We all want to present ourselves as we want to be seen, maybe as we want to become, rather than as we are. The audience—to our courtship "moves" and to the tactics and strategies of politicians—*wants* to be mystified. Robert Brustein suggests that the public insists on thinking that "certain specially endowed individuals can heal our disorders, realize our dreams, and solve our problems."[3] Yet, television precludes that mystery for politicians, as the unblinking camera lens intrudes into all aspects of their lives. Television thus, says Columbia history professor Henry F. Graff, "robs statesmen of the distance between themselves and the people that heads of government have historically required and savored and for which they have not yet found a substitute."[4] As Meyrowitz concludes, "In the new communication environment the political actor faces a disquieting paradox: to audition for the role of traditional hero is to end up playing the fool."[5] Indeed, who but fools would attempt to put themselves forward as logical candidates in a media environment in which, as the president of the CBS Broadcast Group, Howard Stringer, has put it, "we seem to want our leaders to be asexual, atypical and without intellectual or personal histories."[6]

In short, the ubiquity of television coverage means politicians will always be what Michael Lerner, the editor of *Tikkun,* calls "wounded healers," "people who do not yet fully embody the ideals to which they aspire."[7] But the public has not yet tumbled to that imperative; somehow we have convinced ourselves that our leaders are, or ought to be, some special kind of beings, so that when their mortality is revealed to us "we feel shocked, feel that they have been unmasked and disappointed us,"[8] so we resolve never to trust them again.

It could be argued, then, that much of Ronald Reagan's success in politics came from the fact that his Hollywood notoriety before entering politics had accustomed him to having little back-region freedom. He was used to media invasions of his privacy and had learned to live in the public eye before entering politics. Thus he always seemed at ease, while his opponents, just becoming "media creatures," seemed stiff and unsure of themselves.

## ▶ Effect on Issues

A second way in which the media affect politicians is by impinging on the content of the political positions of candidates. As we have seen, issues are not always central to campaigns, yet they *can* make a difference, as the *New York Times* claims they did in 1932: "Hoover's position was that you aren't as hungry as you think. Roosevelt's position was that you are."[9] And we know who won *that* election!

In determining the effect of the media on issues, consider what political stances are possible on the issue of crime in a culture inundated with "shoot-em-ups" (both cowboy and urban). As television critic Walter Goodman has pointed out, the melodramatic focus of TV crime shows and westerns leads the audience to support either capital punishment or gun control, despite the position of the law-enforcement community "that whatever the merits of those ideas, neither is likely to affect street crime very much."[10] In the last few campaigns, as Francis Clines comments, candidates of every ideological position have "once again judged the nation 'soft on crime,' even though crime rates were declining and government already was underwriting the greatest non-totalitarian prison construction binge in history."[11] Given the "climate" of the country, a climate largely created by Hollywood's propensity for "shoot-em-ups," no politician could afford to "ease off" on the crime issue.

Politicians, of course, are not dumb people. They realize that the stands they take on issues, both during campaigns and while in office, will have consequences. That is why it is common, according to former Senate majority leader George J. Mitchell of Maine, for politicians to worry about "what kind of campaign commercial could be made from a particular vote as they stand in the well of the Senate and prepare to cast their yeas or nays."[12] And they are not thinking so much of the positive ads they could make but of the negative ads their opponents could devise. Obviously, that fear may have an impact on their votes.

## ▶ Effect on Rhetoric

Not only do the media force politicians to be careful about their positions and votes, but also to exercise caution in what they say. Politicians must simultaneously denounce anybody who engages in "class warfare" and boast about how much they have done (or will do) for the middle class.

Politicians must talk "nicely," but not too nicely. They must reveal a steel edge behind their nice talk, for what we want, as playwright Arthur Miller reminds us, is a president tough enough, ruthless enough, "to do our dirty work . . . to fight dirty in a dirty world."[13]

To be credible, politicians must be perceived as sincere, a factor that may be as related to how they say things as to what they say. Credibility is, at base, as much an "acting" criterion as a political one—which is why Robert Brustein, Dean of the Yale School of Drama, is a good person to give insight into the phenomenon. He claims credibility is basically an acting criterion, not a political one, for it concerns "simulating the role of sincerity" rather than "verifying facts or discovering truth."[14] The concern for credibility, for sincerity, takes us right back to the previously mentioned media focus on personality. As Brustein comments, television convinces us that Shakespeare was right, that "all the world's a stage." Our attention, therefore, is distracted from the political action and focused on the political actor. Thus do issues get lost from view as our attention is switched to personalities, to praise and blame.[15]

The imperative to talk in a certain way may be one reason presidents seem to present all issues as crises. Television allows the people to get familiar with the president; and although the president cannot reciprocate (as demonstrated in Chapter 9), he can separate us from our focus on the one-sidedness of the relationship merely by making every instance in which he speaks to us a matter of crisis. The crisis brings us together as a people, making us far more manageable than if we were a bunch of individuals feeling dejected by a president who cannot respond to our needs. Fundamentally, however, the resulting sense of familiarity may work to the disadvantage of some unsuspecting president. As anyone who ever has been involved in a manipulation while in the context of an intimate relationship can attest, there is indeed no vengeance like that of a partner scorned.

Other, more minor, media effects on politicians include how nattily politicians dress (the "uniform" seems to be a dark blue suit, light blue shirt, and well-matched tie) and whether they use visual aids in their presentations. (In 1995 Newt Gingrich went to a press conference carrying two congressional bills and a golf club, to make the point that Congress was hard at work while President Clinton was off on a golfing trip.)

## CONCLUSION

▶ In this chapter we have seen how, in bringing politicians "down to our level" by invading their "back stage" areas, the media have eliminated the possibility of old-style "great leaders" while simultaneously encouraging us to evaluate these "lowered" figures by those old standards of "greatness."

▶ Just as religion controlled the medieval world, television controls the contemporary world. In both worlds, the central icon provided the individual with a sense of belonging to a larger whole, although the older culture focused on sacraments concerning suffering, death, and redemption and today the only sacrament is to market conformity. Medieval politicians had to pay obeisance to the church, which built them up into nearly sacred creatures; today politicians must bow at the altar of television, which brings them down to nearly subhuman levels. Meanwhile, for those of us in the audience the wafer and the wine have been replaced by the Big Mac and Coca-Cola.

## FOR FURTHER CONSIDERATION

1. As you think back on the last presidential campaign, can you identify any points at which the campaigners seemed to suffer from having to adapt to the media? Were there points where either candidate seemed uncomfortable with media

questions or with situations into which they the media forced them? How did you evaluate that uncomfortableness—did it affect your evaluation of the candidate or did you get angry at the media?

**2.** In the middle of the 1996 campaign, commentator Maureen Dowd wrote that President Clinton, rather than leading, "settles for being a mirror. The role suits him. He perfectly reflects the confessional, narcissistic, cynical, opportunistic, personality-driven times."[16]

The question is, can any of the change in Clinton's behavior be laid at the feet of the media? Did they force him to change from leadership to mirror image? And did they affect the "times" to which he adapted? That is, are the 1990s confessional, cynical, and personality driven because of the media, or are the media, too, just adapting to the people?

## NOTES

1. G. C. Woodward, *Perspectives on American Political Media* (Boston: Allyn and Bacon, 1997), 133.

2. J. Meyrowitz, "The Rise of 'Middle Region' Politics," *Et Cetera* 34 (June 1977): 133–140.

3. R. Brustein, "News Theater," *New York Times Magazine,* 16 June 1974, p. 36.

4. H. F. Graff, "The 'Ordinary Man' as President," *New Leader,* 2 September 1974, 8.

5. Meyrowitz, *op. cit.,* 140.

6. H. Stringer, "The Oxidizing Effects of Heroism," *New York Times,* 31 August 1991, p. 15.

7. M. Lerner, "Clinton's Hypocrisy Factor," *Tikkun* 9 (May/June 1994): 8.

8. *Ibid.,* 8.

9. A. Miller, "Politics as Theater," *New York Times,* 4 November 1972, p. 33.

10. W. Goodman, "What's Bad for Politics Is Great for Television," *New York Times,* 27 November 1994, p. H33.

11. F. X. Clines, "'Old Sparky': Not Just a Punch Line," *New York Times,* 27 November 1994, p. 18.

12. R. Toner, "'Wars' Wound Candidates and the Process," *New York Times,* 19 March 1990, p. B6.

13. Miller, *op. cit.,* 33.

14. Brustein, *op. cit.,* 7.

15. *Ibid.,* 36.

16. M. Dowd, "The Man in the Mirror," *New York Times,* 12 September 1996, p. A23.

# CHAPTER FOURTEEN

# Avoiding Media Influence

*The Jeffersonian dream of citizens sharing a common body of facts or ideas . . . will be more difficult . . . because so many other sources of information will compete for the public's attention.*
— R. SCHMUHL[1]

There once was a Chinese emperor who put out a decree that only he was allowed to use the personal pronoun "I." He thereby reserved to himself exclusively not only the power to decide but also the power to persuade and, ultimately, the power to think. Today, says commentator David Watson, the media have metaphorically adopted the emperor's role as arbiter of thought: "The contemporary erosion of people's capacity to think for themselves and the monopolization of meaning by media seem to be succeeding at what the legendary emperor could only have imagined."[2]

Fortunately, however, we have no laws decreeing that we citizens have to rely on the media. If we do rely on them it is because we have decided to follow that route. Yet, as the last few chapters indicate, such a decision on our part is wrought with peril. Is there an alternative? Is there any other way to make decisions about where to stand on the issues of the day, which candidates to support for office, what meanings to assign to events? Obviously, I think there are alternatives.

Each of us is capable of interpreting data and evaluating people and events. We do it all the time in our daily lives. The only difference is that we have firsthand knowledge of the data to be considered when we make decisions about our own lives. The trick in political decision-making, then, is to figure out how best to approximate the informational level we demand when making decisions in our own lives.

When we are trying to decide between two health insurance companies our employer offers, we read the prospectus of each company, seek out people who are in each plan to see what their experience with it has been, and try to get a "reading" on the comparable abilities of the doctors and hospitals available under each. The same options are available to us when presidential candidates

---

Most of the evaluative criteria in this chapter are derived from Ruth M. Gonchar Brennan and Dan F. Hahn, *Listening for a President: A Citizen's Campaign Methodology.* LISTENING FOR A PRESIDENT, Ruth M. Gonchar Brennan and Dan F. Hahn. Copyright © 1990 by Ruth M. Gonchar Brennan and Dan F. Hahn. Reproduced with permission of GREENWOOD PUBLISHING GROUP, INC. Westport, CT.

are putting forward alternative proposals in any realm. We can read the opposing proposals, listen as each candidate explains (or fudges on) the details, seek out others who have information relevant to the question at hand, and try to get a "reading" on the comparable effects of the two proposals on both ourselves and the society.

When we are trying to make a decision about a person, we do not rely exclusively on what others say about that person, but try to gather firsthand information. If possible, we talk with the person; if that is not possible, we try to find out what the person said and did under as many circumstances as possible. Likewise in politics. If possible, we try to meet the candidates. Where that is not possible, we move to the second alternative: we try to get access to the person's speeches (available from the campaign offices of each candidate), interviews with the candidates conducted by both print and electronic media, and debates among the candidates. We pay *some* attention to what others say (both in the media and in our circle of friends), but we try to rely mostly on our own impressions of information drawn from primary sources.

One other thing: when we are evaluating a person in our daily lives we have evaluative criteria, determined by the role the person is to play. If we're trying to decide whether we want to work for the person, we have different criteria from those we use if we're trying to decide whether we want to date the person, and those criteria are different still from those we use when trying to decide whether we want to move next door. Unfortunately, the choice of criteria is probably the point on which most of us are weakest when it comes to politics. We're not sure what we want in a president, or congressional representative, or mayor. And that lack of criteria makes us susceptible to the others' evaluations—in and out of the media—who may not be using criteria we would endorse if we took time to think about it.

In 1990 Professor Ruth Gonchar Brennan and I published a book titled *Listening for a President: A Citizen's Campaign Methodology,* in which we suggested five sets of criteria that citizens could use in evaluating candidates: personality orientation, leadership ideal, ideology, epistemology, and axiology.[3] What follows is an application of that material, presented here as a set of recommendations for what to look for in primary sources (and how to use it) when we evaluate candidates—always keeping in mind that evaluations are subjective and interpretive and must be made by each individual.

## ▶ Personality Orientation

One school of thought says we should vote issue rather than personality. Yet as Walt Anderson, former contributing editor to the magazine *Human Behavior,* once said, "The trouble with this line of thinking, attractive as it may be, is that we don't elect issues. We elect people . . . "[4] And, as political scientist James D. Barber has argued, once we elect a president that person "copes, adapts, leads and responds not as some shapeless organism in a flood of novelties, but as a man with a memory in a system with a history."[5]

At the same time, however, we should recognize that not every facet of a person's personality should be held up for consideration. In classical rhetorical studies, the Greeks held that "civic virtue" was the most important aspect of ethos, which was itself the most important of the three proofs: ethos, pathos, and logos. Yet, as rhetorical theorist G. Hauser has written, civic virtue "was unlike the Christian virtues of faith, hope, and charity . . . which are best practiced beyond the glare of publicity. They had in mind practical virtues that would help in forming prudent public decisions."[6]

The first problem, then, is to determine the facets of civic virtue, that is, which facets should be brought into the public sphere and which are best kept private. Should we be more concerned about Kennedy's, Hart's, and Clinton's "affairs of the heart" (and Carter's imagined ones), or should we concern ourselves with their heartfelt public speeches and their sometimes heartless governmental acts?

From my perspective, it is a matter of sadness that we are now more likely to see politics through a private-morality than a civic-virtue lens; that we are more likely to focus on Clinton's prepresidential finances and possible marital indiscretions than his public persona and acts, indeed, to perceive those public activities through a private and dark Puritan filter; that we are more likely to insist that our own private moral standards—on abortion, reading materials, premarital sex, and family values—become public policy, and to evaluate politicians on their stances on those private morality beliefs, than to examine the justice or prudence of their public decisions or the temperance and magnanimity of their public utterances. But I realize this is only *my* perspective; yours might be different.

At the least, however, we should recognize that private character and public character are not the same thing. We all know bankers who cheat on their wives but would never dream of stealing a penny; alternatively, we know contractors who substitute shoddy materials for the more expensive ones their clients paid for, yet would never dream of having an illicit affair. Likewise with politicians. Political expert Hugh Sidey has reminded us that as president, John Kennedy embodied many admirable traits, but he did not escape the later assessment of those critics who linked some of the activities of his private life to a "gravely flawed character."[7] Similarly, although Lyndon Johnson was often chided for his boorish behavior and philandering, Sidey acknowledges that, in his public life as a politician, Johnson was fundamentally devoted to achieving what was best for the country.[8] On the other hand, Sidey reminds us that despite the abiding consensus that Jimmy Carter embodied the personal qualities valued by U.S. culture, he was not regarded "as effective." Sidey concludes that character is not the sole arbiter of success for a president.[9]

So we can't just lump all aspects of character together and assume we have criteria for holding office. Rather, we have to try to factor out which aspects are relevant, which irrelevant. Partly that means we must decide which aspects are relevant to each of us, but more importantly it means we must decide which are relevant to the office in question. For instance, that Lyndon Johnson was a "boor" might not have been relevant to his presidential capability; that he was a "congenital liar" certainly was. The first aspect tells us more about his personal than his civic life, but the second is absolutely central to his handling of public life.

In trying to "tease out" these personality characteristics, I have found that the most useful materials included in primary sources concern self image, ego ideal, and handling of stress.

One aspect of candidates' self-images is evident in the values inherent in statements they make about themselves. Clinton's reminiscences about his childhood and Dole's recollections of his wartime activities were especially rich in the 1996 election. Never mind that Clinton told his stories to demonstrate that he would stand up for what he believed in and Dole told his to remind us that Clinton did not serve in the armed forces; we needn't be "sucked in" by their motivations.

More important is what the stories tell us about how the two men would conduct themselves in office—and here is where our own values become important to the interpretation. For instance, if we believe that parents are to be obeyed at all times, we will not be impressed with Clinton's challenge to his stepfather; on the other hand, if we believe that spouse abuse is a heinous act, we applaud his attempts to shield his mother from his father. Further, we assume he will support attempts to strengthen the spouse-abuse laws.

If we think that it is a citizen's duty to serve in the military, we will respond positively to Dole's stories and sneer at Clinton's lack of service. But if we think that citizens are duty-bound to support the country only when they think the government is in the right, we are more sympathetic to Clinton's doubts about the morality of the Vietnam War and his anti-war activities. There are, after all, two equally long-standing, respected positions on citizen duty. One says "my country, right or wrong." The other avers "my country, when right to be kept right, when wrong to be put right." Which of those positions you adhere to will determine which wartime experience resounds most positively with you.

Another aspect of self-image is reflected in how candidates labels themselves. In 1988 and 1992, for instance, there was a great deal of controversy surrounding George Bush's labeling of himself as a Texan, since he had grown up in Connecticut, had spent most of his adult life in Washington, D.C., and didn't even have a home in Texas. At the same time, however, he *had* lived in Texas; he started his political career there; and it was the last place he had lived before moving to the nation's capital for a series of jobs in various Republican administrations.

So was he a Texan? I don't know, and don't care. It isn't important. But it *is* important that he thought of himself as a Texan. To see that it was important, all you need do is consult your own knowledge of what it would mean to identify yourself as coming from Texas versus Connecticut. If there are differences between these two sets of self-identifications, given the fact that self-perceptions are important in determining actions, it clearly is significant that George Bush identified himself as a Texan, regardless of what he "really" was!

A third important aspect of self-image can be plumbed by considering contrasts within the public image or between the public and private images. To get at such contrasts you can compare what is said with what is done. For instance, Ronald Reagan always *talked* the extreme conservative position on social issues (abortion, family values, and so forth), yet he never pushed to get that position enacted into law. Or you can compare what is done now with what was done earlier. For instance, at campaign time George Bush made a point of being photographed playing horseshoes, but when there was no campaign there were no horseshoes—there were, instead, golf clubs and powerboats.

A fourth aspect to which you should be sensitive is the candidate's negative self-image, that is, the characteristics the candidate warns against. When Richard Nixon said he believed that when the action is hot the rhetoric should be kept cool, was he giving away his own tendency to respond in the heat of the moment rather than taking time to cool down? Perhaps so.

Beyond self-image, candidates' ego-ideals are important; that is, what they think of revered others. These are important because what we revere in others is usually a characteristic we ourselves have not yet mastered. Think, for instance, of somebody you respect highly, then try to think what it is you respect about that person. Chances are you will find that what you respect is some quality you do not feel you yourself have.

Politicians, as we too often forget, are just people like us. Thus, when they identify characteristics they respect in others, they are probably characteristics they feel they lack. So when Richard Nixon said that what most impressed him about President Eisenhower was that he always was the coolest man in the room, that is additional evidence that Nixon believed he himself had not yet mastered coolness. Combine that with his warning to keep the rhetoric cool, and a pattern begins to emerge, a pattern that can (but perhaps needn't) be read as a self-criticism.

Another aspect of personality that seems especially significant in evaluating candidates, especially presidential candidates, is their handling of stress in times of crisis, attack, or failure. At such times, does their rhetoric become filled with discomfort and anxiety words? Do they become bitter? Do they claim to be misunderstood or misquoted? Do they strike out at others? Do they try to deflect our attention to another realm? Or do they take responsibility? As government professor Ronald A. Heifetz has said, it isn't easy to know which candidate to trust, "but the odds may favor candidates that do not pretend to have all the answers, who acknowledge mistakes and take pride from being able to learn, even from opponents."[10]

Before I leave the topic of personality, a warning is in order. As we delve more and more deeply into any single personality, we tend to get involved with the "person" rather than the "persona," or role. When we do, we run the risk of ourselves being transformed—from critic to supporter, from feeling we have a "secondary" relationship with this person as a potential president to feeling a "primary" relationship, more like friendship. At that point we are most vulnerable, for we lose our ability to be objective.

## ▶ Leadership Ideal

When you and I interview for a job, we put our ideal selves forward. When we're asked how we would handle such and such a situation, we answer with how we *hope* we would handle it, even if we know that we have sometimes responded differently to similar situations in the past.

In trying to understand political campaigns, it is helpful to see them as analogous to interviews. The candidates are interviewing for the job. So we shouldn't be surprised that they try to put forward their ideal selves—the selves they *want* to be (or become). And we shouldn't be too upset that the self they put forward is somewhat different from what we know their past selves to have been. After all, most historians tell us that presidents really do "grow into" the position once they're there. That is the natural evolution most of us go through. We may major in engineering, but we don't really become engineers until we've been on the job for a while. It would be as unfair to compare us as new graduates with engineers who have twenty years experience as it would be to judge the aesthetic beauty of a butterfly by the ugliness of the caterpillar.

That candidates put forward idealized versions of the job they would do if we elect them should not bother us. As Ruth Gonchar Brennan and I have pointed out, "we should want to know what the candidates aspire to even as we realize they probably will not be able to live up to all their goals. Better to vote for one who will fall short of lofty goals than to vote for one who will achieve only the mediocre ones expressed in his or her campaign."[11]

Two especially significant aspects of candidates' leadership ideals are found in the orientation the candidates divulge toward power and the comments they make about the office and past office-holders.

The two time-honored positions about presidential power are (1) that presidents can do only what the Constitution specifically delegates to them and (2) presidents can do anything that is not prohibited to the presidential office by the Constitution. A third position, that presidents can do anything they can get away with, though some presidents seem to have it, is not a position you will ever find any candidate espousing.

But the positions candidates take on this question *are* important. While it is true that a good deal of presidential power is institutional and systemic, passed on from earlier presidents, it is also true that much of the president's authority is not systemic but personal. As presidential scholar Robert Hirschfield has noted, "Because the Presidency is a personal office, the incumbent's own view of his power plays an important role in shaping the actual dimensions of that power. . . . however a President reaches his concept of presidential power, and whatever form that concept assumes, his own attitude and behavior are major determinants of the power he in fact possesses."[12]

And presidential perceptions of their own power are, in turn, crucial in determining the destiny of the nation. As John Kennedy noted during the 1960 campaign, "the history of this nation—its brightest and its bleakest pages—has been written largely in terms of the different views our Presidents have had of the Presidency itself."[13]

But which pages are bright and which are bleak? On that there is little agreement. In 1991 the vast majority of Americans reveled in nationalistic pride at our military success in the Persian Gulf. Others, a clear minority, were concerned that President Bush, like so many of his predecessors, had emasculated the spirit of the Constitution, if not the letter, in leading us into that war. Even before the war started, as Lewis Lapham of *Harper's* wrote, some critics were concerned that during the past four decades "the American government [would] wage a war at the will and discretion of the foreign-policy apparat in Washington . . . [ignoring] the wishes or opinions of the broad mass of the American people."[14]

From George Washington to the present there has been a long, slow accumulation of power in the office of the president. As the Roman apothegm had it, *historia non facit saltum*—history makes no leaps. Yet the major battle over the power of the presidency was fought out in the early years of the twentieth century. On one side was William Howard Taft, who believed that "the President can exercise no power which cannot be fairly and reasonably traced to some specific grant of power or justly implied within such express grant as proper and necessary to its exercise. Such specific grant must be either in the federal Constitution or in an act of Congress passed in pursuance thereof. There is no undefined residuum of power which he can exercise because it seems to him to be in the public interest."[15] On the other side of the question was Theodore Roosevelt, whose belief was "that it was not only his right but his duty to do anything that the needs of the nation demanded, unless such action was forbidden by the Constitution or by the laws."[16]

Clearly, Teddy Roosevelt won that argument. Today most Americans, presidents included, seem to think that the fact that the president is commander-in-chief means he has the right to lead us into war, despite the fact that the Constitution assigns the war-declaring power to the Congress. As a result, since World War II we have followed our presidents into wars in Korea, Guatemala, Vietnam, Nicaragua, El Salvador, Cambodia, Grenada, Libya, Lebanon, Panama, Iraq, and a number of other places, all without a congressional declaration of war, and forgetting the constitutional presumption that Congress should be responsible for determining whether we go to war.

While the president's power to determine the issue of war or peace is important, it is not the only issue in which we should examine the candidates' orientations toward presidential power. Attitudes toward all sharing of power should be considered, whether it is with Congress or the courts or state governments. For instance, consider whether you would trust the author of the following "story" to share power as president: "Imagine a football team and I'm the coach, and I'm also the quarterback. I have to call the signals, and I have to center the ball, run the ball, pass the ball. I'm the blocker. I'm the tackler. I'm the passer. I have to catch the pass."[17] Would you trust that man to share power once he became president? If not, and you had been voting in 1964, you would not have voted for its author, Lyndon Johnson.

More generally, in addition to finding any insights you can into the candidates' positions on presidential power, you should examine any and all comments the candidates make about the office and the people who have held it. For instance, you no doubt would have been heartened during the 1976 campaign to find Jimmy Carter recognizing how unrealistic the demands on the president are: "Our people ask that a president be both tough and gentle, both statesman and politician, both dreamer and fighter. You expect him to have the drive and stamina to reach the White House, and the wisdom and patience to govern wisely there."[18] But your gladness would have been cut short if you had recognized that Carter's patterned behavior in the face of contradictions was inaction, a fact you could have discovered from his actions as governor of Georgia.

Much also can be learned by examining what activities of other presidents the candidates attack and which they defend, applaud, or forgive. Probably few people who remembered that Bush supported Nixon to the bitter end of that troubled presidency, for instance, subsequently voted for Bush.

Obviously, however, one needs to be aware of the possible image-making in a good percentage of the comments candidates make about past presidents. Lauding Washington and Lincoln is a little too easy, as easy as attacking Richard Nixon. But we should attend to the candidate who finds something in a Washington or a Lincoln to attack or something to applaud in the Nixon White House or in the presidential career of a recent incumbent of the other party, for some principle is being enunciated that is even more important to the candidate than adhering to the usual stereotyped images of presidential heroes and devils.

In all the examination of candidate leadership ideals, we must remember that the goal is to determine what the candidate thinks the presidency *should* be, but that the determination is useless to you as a voter unless you know what *you* think the presidency should be . . . and can be.

## ▶ Ideology

The study of a candidate's ideology is important for the insight it provides into the assumptions, motivations, ideals, worldviews, opinions, and expectations of that person. At the most general level you need to know whether the candidate leans toward conservatism or liberalism, but more than that you want to know whether the candidate is *your* kind of conservative, *your* kind of liberal.

The ideological materials that are most important in evaluating candidates stem from conceptions of human nature, society and social causality, and the moral conflicts of the day.

How do the candidates view human nature? Are humans basically good (the liberal position) or basically evil (a more conservative approach). One way to "get at" candidates' views of humans is, interestingly, through their views of God. If they perceive God as angry and punishing they probably view humans negatively (i.e., as motivated by fear and deserving of punishment). Candidates who believe in a more loving God, however, are more likely to see people as basically good, motivated more by rewards than punishment. Thus if God is depicted as wrathful and fear-provoking you can conclude the candidate sees humans as untrustworthy and evil, but talk of "love" and "brotherhood" suggests the candidate has a more positive view of humanity.

Candidates' views of humanity also are implied in the way they speak to us. Do they treat us as equals or inferiors? Of course, no candidate will *say* they see us as inferior, but such judgments are implied in their words. For instance, if a candidate talks about the populace as "children," that should be taken as a perception of citizen inferiority. When Jimmy Carter, in 1979, said "We have demanded that the American people sacrifice and they've done very well,"[19] was he not, in effect, patting us on our collective heads as if we were children?

We also should be concerned with the information a candidate does *not* provide, i.e., does not trust us with. The 1992 campaign was something of a classic on this score. George Bush did not trust us with information on his involvement in "Irangate" or his and his family's involvement in the savings and loans crises; Bill Clinton did not trust us with information on his attempts to evade the draft or on his relationship with Gennifer Flowers; and Ross Perot did not trust us with information on what he planned to do about anything.

The issues chosen for consideration may also be revealing. Literary critics have known this for a long time; for instance, Seymour Chatman notes that "the subjects that an author elects to write about themselves characterize . . . the author's persona, or role."[20] So, when people are dying of starvation we have a right to be suspicious of the character of a candidate who concerns himself with a few flag-burnings; when racial problems are plaguing the country, we have a right to look askance at any candidate who manipulates our resentments of each other rather than addressing the problem; when children are dying in drive-by shootings, we have a right to be concerned that a candidate is paying back the National Rifle Association for its financial support rather than discussing what can be done to ensure some degree of safety. I once read that the worth of a culture is determined less by the quality of its answers to questions than by the quality of the questions addressed. That may be true of candidates, too. Mussolini, after all, fulfilled his promise to the Italian voters to make sure the trains ran on time; he just didn't bother to tell them that he would join Adolf Hitler in an attempt to take over the world.

Conceptions of human nature also may be apparent from the feelings to which the candidates appeal. The 1992 campaign, while not as personally nasty as the '88 campaign, nonetheless may have hit rock bottom in terms of the feelings the various candidates intentionally activated. As I saw it, Bush appealed to our fears, especially our fear that Clinton would be a "tax and tax, spend and spend" liberal; Clinton appealed to our anger, especially our anger that Bush had reneged on his "watch my lips, no new taxes" pledge and thus, by implication, our anger at the possibility that Bush might again prove untrustworthy in his campaign pledges. Meanwhile, Ross Perot appealed to our disgust: disgust with a campaign again filled with undeliverable promises; disgust with a retinue of candidates we did not trust; disgust, in short, with "politics as usual." Fear, anger, disgust—hardly the "better angels of our nature!" A far cry from the 1950s, when Dwight Eisenhower, according to Hugh Sidey, was able to bring people together despite their divergent views: "His patience, his common sense, his concern for the national good . . . [resulted in] an unusual persuasiveness, almost irresistible at times."[21]

Finally, candidate views of human nature may be deduced from whom the candidate identifies with. Consider these lines from George Bush's acceptance speech at the 1988 Republican convention: "Some people who are enjoying our prosperity have forgotten what it's for. But they diminish our triumph when they act as if wealth is an end in itself. . . . The fact is prosperity has a purpose. It is to allow us to pursue 'the better angels,' to give us time to think and grow. Prosperity with a purpose means taking your idealism and making it concrete by certain acts of goodness." At first blush, of course, those words seem filled with lofty sentiments. But think about the American audience to whom those words were addressed. Think about the majority of us who are unprosperous. What role would a bricklayer or a teacher or a McDonald's employee have in a Bush presidency? Maybe we could be the recipients of the "acts of goodness" of the prosperous? What about the unemployed? What about the two-thirds of American mothers who are single, divorced, or poor? Where would they fit in a Bush presidency?

The candidates' views of humans will be related to their views of the society those humans have created. Candidates who are optimistic about society think people are capable of rational decision-making. Liberals tend to believe this way. The more negative belief, that people are open to manipulation and therefore in need of direction, tends to be a conservative view.

These views, in turn, determine the kind of government actions a candidate will back. A candidate who believes people can make their own decisions supports government policies that use sanctions. Such policies try to lead citizens into making right decisions. Our traffic laws are based on this strategy. Fines for violating traffic laws are calibrated on the assumption that people are able to determine and act on the possible results from various driving alternatives. One individual might not be willing to risk a ticket under any conditions while the next might be willing to risk a $10 ticket for going 5 miles over the limit but will not risk a $50 ticket by going 20 miles over the limit.

A candidate with a more pessimistic evaluation of citizens' ability to make rational decisions would structure the laws differently, perhaps forcing automobile companies to design cars incapable of exceeding the speed limit. Most of our laws concerning poor people are based on this strategy, which is called the strategy of correction. For instance, the poor are provided food stamps rather than cash on the assumption that they are incapable of deciding for themselves how to spend their money.

As with so many other realms of ideology, however, liberals and conservatives are inconsistent on their views of human and social strategies, as can be seen when we examine how the two sides approach the issues of free will and determinism. Here the question is whether deviations from the laws of the society are completely controlled by individual decision (the free will position) or whether the actions of the individual in question were to some degree determined (or predetermined) by the nature of society (the determinism position).

Conservatives tend toward the free-will end of the spectrum, believing, for instance, that anybody who breaks the law *willfully* decided to break it and should bear the total brunt of the responsibility. Liberals, tending toward determinism, are more likely to say that something about the nature of the society "pushed" the individual toward breaking the law, so leniency should be shown.

Notice how the points contradict each other. Conservatives believe people cannot make up their own minds, so the laws should be based on correction strategy . . . but they can make up their own minds (have free will) so if they break a law they should be punished severely. Liberals believe people can make up their own minds, so the laws should be based on sanction strategy . . . but their actions are determined by societal structures, so lawbreakers should be treated leniently.

What causes both sides to hold these contradictory positions? I suggest that the contradictions dissolve if we move back to the broader level of pessimism versus optimism about human nature. That is, it makes sense that those optimistic about the goodness of humans (liberals) will use the sanction approach and also hold that those who break the laws just "made a mistake" and shouldn't be punished too heavily. Likewise, it makes sense that those more pessimistic about people will both think they can't make rational decisions (believe in the strategy of correction) and also that law-breaking is an indication of their basically evil nature. Seen from this perspective, the contradiction between how laws are written (based on strategies of correction or sanction) and how they are enforced (on the basis of free will or determinism) largely disappear.

Looking through the simplest possible lens, we know a great deal about candidates when we know whether they are conservative or liberal. We know conservatives will be "tougher" on individuals—if passing laws they will make it tough for the individual to qualify for any kind of government support; if enforcing laws they will push for maximum levels—high fines, capital punishment, and so forth. Liberals, on the other hand, we know will be "gentler"— they will try to make it easier for the individual to qualify for some kind of government support or "break," and will opt for less draconian penalties, lesser fines, and life imprisonment rather than the death penalty. All of which goes a long way toward explaining why conservatives refer to liberals as "bleeding hearts" and liberals accuse conservatives of having "Nazi mentalities."

These same characteristics, then, explain a good deal about the differences between liberals and conservatives in terms of the third aspect of ideology to be considered here, conceptions about the moral conflicts of the age. Liberals tend to think morality is relative; that is, that an act may be moral in one set of circumstances but immoral in another. Conservatives, on the other hand, tend to believe that any act they perceive as immoral is always immoral, regardless of the circumstances. Consequently, conservatives call liberals "wishy-washy" and liberals label conservatives "absolutists."

Attitudes toward divorce provide a good example of the difference. At the liberal extreme, divorce is held to be the moral alternative under certain circumstances; for instance, if one of the partners is a spouse-abuser. At the conservative extreme, all divorces are perceived as immoral. Toward the middle of the spectrum is the attitude that divorce, while always sad, is sometimes necessary. Those leaning in the conservative direction will argue for rather severe penalties on the party responsible for the breakup, while those of a more liberal stripe will argue for "no-fault" divorce.

Because more people tend to be rather traditionalist in their thinking about society, in a morality-based campaign the more conservative candidate is more likely to win. That is why conservative candidates try to structure campaigns around morality . . . and why liberal candidates try to make economics (their stronger point) the central issue.

## ▶ Epistemology

"Epistemology" is one of those words most of us encountered in some philosophy class or another, but because we didn't see how it was important to us, we mostly just skimmed over it. At the most basic level, though, "epistemology" has to do with "how you know what you know." Thus it *is* relevant to campaigns, for when a candidate says we should adopt policy X because that will produce result Y, one question we want to ask is "how do you know it will have that result?"

Any logician will tell you that if you want to know how a person knows anything, the place to begin is with the person's assumptions. Epistemological analysis, then, tries to determine what the candidate assumes. Assumptions, in turn, tend to be hidden in premises. In formal logic, premises and conclusions are organized in structures called "syllogisms."

Most of us remember syllogisms from junior high school . . . and chances are astronomically high that we were taught about them with the identical example:

> All men are mortal.
>
> Socrates was a man.
>
> Therefore, Socrates was mortal.

We may not have understood exactly what the syllogism meant, but we memorized it, reproduced it on a test, and promptly forgot all about it.

But the syllogism is the basic form of argumentation. If we do not understand syllogisms we do not understand how to make an argument, or how to evaluate an argument made by another. The easiest way to evaluate a syllogism, I think, is through drawing related circles that include the categories found in the syllogism. Thus, in the above example, we know the largest category is the circle of mortality; within that circle is a smaller circle for "men"; and within that circle is an even smaller identification, "Socrates." So the circles would look like this:

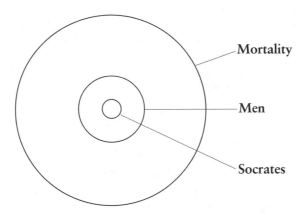

The series of circles demonstrates that the argument is logical: every element of the syllogism is accounted for and the relationships between them are as the syllogism suggests. But suppose the syllogism had been somewhat different, like this:

> All entities except gods are mortal.
>
> Socrates was an entity.
>
> Therefore, Socrates was mortal.

Let us check this one out with our series of circles. Again, the largest category is mortality, so that is the largest circle. The second circle (encompassing entities), however, we're not sure where to place. Apparently part of the circle goes within the circle of mortality, part outside. And now, where should we place Socrates within the "entity" circle? We don't know. Lacking any independent knowledge of whether Socrates was a god or a nongod entity, we do not know whether he goes in the part of the entities circle inside or the part outside the mortality circle. Thus, we are precluded from accepting the conclusion that Socrates was mortal; he may have been mortal, or he may have been a god, hence immortal.

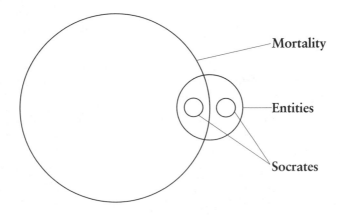

If, at this point, it dawns on you that this is all very well, but you don't think it's relevant because you've never heard a candidate talk in syllogisms, you would be partly right. Candidates do not talk in syllogisms, nor do we in our everyday lives. We talk in something called "enthymemes," which are partial syllogisms. Hence, to evaluate the way they (and we) talk, we have to transpose what is said (enthymematically) into syllogisms.

How do we do that? Well, the truth is that we do it almost subconsciously. Let's examine a hypothetical example from everyday life. Suppose you and I were driving through a strange town, and I turned onto a one-way street going the wrong direction. I am blabbing away about the changes I want to make in the next edition of this book, completely oblivious to my driving. You, however, are not oblivious at all. So as we approach the next intersection you interrupt me with "You'd better slow down, Dr. Hahn, there won't be a stop sign at the corner." You have uttered an enthymeme. If I do not translate it into a syllogism, if I look at you and say "Huh?" and barrel into the intersection, we may both be killed. But if I translate your enthymeme into a syllogism, we may be saved. The syllogism would be something like:

> There are no stop signs facing the wrong direction on a one-way street.
>
> We are traveling the wrong direction on a one-way street.
>
> Therefore, there will be no stop signs facing us.

So if I, probably somewhat unconsciously, convert your enthymeme into a syllogism, I will understand your message. If I do not, I will not.

Likewise with politics. If the politician's audience translates the candidate's utterances, the various enthymemes employed, into syllogisms, the message will be understood . . . and then can be evaluated. Absent such a "translation," what the candidate says is just so much hot air, as meaningless as "there won't be a stop sign at the corner" is to someone who does not know (s)he is driving the wrong way on a one-way street.

But now, unfortunately, we need to add an additional complexity. It is not enough to evaluate the syllogism to see whether it is formally logical; we also must determine whether the assumptions are correct. Consider, for instance, the "trickle down" economics of the Reagan-Bush years. One argument supporting that theory was that trickle-down economics produces more jobs. Syllogistically, here was the argument:

> The more money you have, the more you can invest.
>
> The more you invest, the more jobs are created.
>
> Therefore, jobs will be created if taxes are cut so you have more money.

You can draw the series of circles and see that the argument is logically valid. Therefore, you understand why a Reagan advisor referred to the adoption of trickle-down economics as "the most incredible job-creating machine the world has ever seen."[22] Such a conclusion makes sense, is logically valid according to the syllogism. Unfortunately, it turns out to be wrong. Here are the

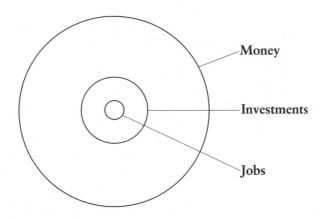

statistics on how much job growth took place in various administrations since 1960: Kennedy, 2.3 percent; Johnson, 3.8 percent; Nixon, 2.3 percent; Carter, 3.1 percent; Reagan, 2.1 percent; Bush, 0.6 percent; Clinton, 2.4 percent.[23] In short, far from being an "incredible job-creating machine," the trickle-down approach turns out to have created a smaller percentage increase in jobs than those of any of a series of Republican and Democrat non-trickle-down systems. We are not exactly sure why that is, but apparently there is something wrong with one of the premises of the syllogism. Either it is not true that people with more money invest more of it, or it is not true that investments create jobs. Perhaps both premises are wrong; or maybe each is partially right, partially wrong. All we know is that there is somewhere a "lack of fit" between the premises and reality.

And that, ultimately, is the problem with relying on "pure" logic to determine "what we know." So are there other, better epistemologies? Well, there indeed are others, though none are demonstrably better.

Rather than relying on logic, some people use a motivation-based epistemology. A motivation-based approach to knowledge assumes that the more noble the motive, the more truth there must be to support it. That is why our leaders always emphasize the nobility of any foreign involvement. If we are going into any conflict-filled situation, in Iran or Bosnia or wherever, we always are told that we are doing so for the noblest of reasons—to preserve democracy, to fight aggression, and so forth—*not* because *we* want anything for ourselves, such as land or oil, and certainly not because of any small-minded perceived slight, such as that a Saddam Hussein seemed to be thumbing his nose at us derisively.

A third epistemology might be called the faith-based approach to truth. Here the assumption is that our beliefs, both religious and secular, are true. Hence, if the preacher, rabbi, priest, or other "holy personage" says it, it must be true. If it is in our own personal "bible," it must be true. If I learned it at my father's knee, it must be true. The problem, of course, is that there are many false prophets, and if we have no epistemological system other than faith, we have no way of evaluating which prophets are the false ones. The history of the world is, among other things, a history of the ugly things we have done to each other in the name of some "higher" truth accepted on faith, from the burning of "witches" to the killing of "heathens," from the Nazis' eradication of Jews to the "ethnic cleansing" in Bosnia in the 1990s.

The fourth alternative is history-based epistemology. How often have we heard someone repeat the old canard about people who don't know history being doomed to repeat it? While there undoubtedly is *some* truth in the assertion, we should recognize that the major assumption on which a history-based epistemology relies is that the future will be like the past. But that is not always true. For instance, Clinton in the 1992 campaign made much of the argument that, since Bush had broken his promise not to raise taxes in the past, if reelected he would break that (or other) promises again. But that was not necessarily true. It may well have been, as Bush argued, that Bush had learned his lesson and would never again have bowed to tax-raising pressures. We all are capable of learning, changing, growing, and not making the same mistake again.

But history-based epistemologies do not recognize the possibility of such changes. And they *are* persuasive, for it is often enough the case that the same cause leads to the same effect that the generalization that the future will be like the past seems reasonable. To see the persuasiveness of such a position in action, I recommend you read an excellent analysis of Nixon's argumentation, based on the historic lessons from World War II, about why we should have been involved in Vietnam, as presented by one of our leading Aristotelian rhetorical critics, Forbes Hill.[24]

We also should recognize that in a heterogeneous society such as the United States, history provides the identity that clan once provided. And celebrations of that identity at historic points, such as the Fourth of July, provide a metaphoric unity . . . as well as a metaphoric reinforcement of history-based epistemologies.

Another epistemology is based on importance. Importance-based epistemology assumes a relationship between importance and truth; that is, the more important some assertion is, the more likely it is to be true.

A few years ago when I was handing out papers in a class, one student looked at her returned paper, an "F," and burst into tears. I dismissed the rest of the class and sat down by the sobbing student. When her crying subsided sufficiently, she blurted out "what must you think of me?" For this student, grades were so important that she had come to measure herself by them, to assume that whatever grade she got was a judgment of her as a human being; thus, she believed that if I had given her an "F" I must think she was a failure as a human. I think she was a little taken aback when I replied, "Oh, you . . . I *like* you, I just didn't like this last piece of work you submitted." She somehow had not yet tumbled to the fact that who we are and what we do on any given day are not absolutely correlated on any one-to-one basis, that *any* of us can have an "off" day without our whole world crumbling. Those with importance-based epistemologies find that lesson an especially difficult one to learn.

The final epistemology to be mentioned here is fact-based epistemology, which assumes that the gathering of verifiable facts ineluctably leads to the truth. What is overlooked in this epistemology is that facts do not "mean" on their own; they are interpreted, and the same facts, in different hands, lead to quite different conclusions. Examine nearly any controversy, and you discover that both sides have plenty of facts. Sometimes the facts are different, as the sides "count" different facts as relevant to the question, sometimes the facts are the same, but the interpretations differ. Sometimes a person isn't even "open" to the facts. For instance, George Bush once was asked how he would respond to a report under preparation on the relation between taxes and the deficit. He said, "I'm open-minded in terms of hearing from all these people as to what the situation is, what we do about it. But I'm not going to change my view as to how we get this deficit down."[25] In short, "gosh, I'm glad you're looking at this problem, but I already know what's wrong," or, as we're most accustomed to summarizing this response, "My mind's made up; don't confuse me with the facts."

In short, then, just as a logic-based epistemology can lead us astray, so can the others. Motivation-based, faith-based, history-based, importance-based, and fact-based epistemologies are just as unreliable. If fact, there is *no* foolproof and reliable way to "know" the truth. That's why we disagree so much, why we have so many arguments, why nobody ever finally and for all time wins the liberal-conservative battle. Henry Kissinger is said to have claimed that nobody would ever win the battle of the sexes because there's too much consorting with the enemy. Funny, but wrong. Nobody will ever win that battle or any of the other long-standing disagreements in society because nobody has a monopoly on truth . . . and even if they did, we wouldn't recognize it, because we have no foolproof way of determining truth.

## ▶ Axiology

Another of those words from a basic philosophy course! But this one is somewhat simpler. Axiology merely means "value structure," or how a person values (thus, evaluates) the various things, people, and events in the world.

To value something is to break from the norm of indifference. That is, of all the "things" in the world, each of us values only a miniscule portion, most often that cache of things we have accumulated. Of all the people in the world, each of us *values* only a few, most often those we know and like and a few we don't know but like and respect anyway. Of all the events in the world each day, each of us values only a very few, most often those that somehow impinge on our own lives. About the rest of the things, people, and events in the world we feel mostly indifference. We don't care that some Chinese person dropped and broke a favorite vase today; we don't care that some Indonesian couple is going through the agony of divorce today; we don't care that a flooding river is threatening the lives of some Germans today. These things, people, and events are nothing to us; we are indifferent to them.

Maybe the world should be different. Maybe it would be different if we cared more. Maybe we should feel some degree of remorse about our indifference. On the other hand, could we handle life if we broke down and cried whenever a pretty vase broke, if we shared the pain of every divorce, if we felt the need to make a contribution every time nature dealt anybody a cruel blow? No, probably not.

So if we think of our own lives, and of the lives of people we know, we recognize that we respond differently to the things we value and those to which we are indifferent. For one thing, we talk about the things we value (whether we like them or hate them, we have assessed a value, and we talk about them); we don't talk about those we don't value. And that recognition gives us our first clue for "getting at" the value structure of candidates. We can assume that they value positively the things they speak about affirmatively; that they devalue things they speak about negatively, and that they *might* be indifferent to what they don't mention. (I say "might" because other possibilities exist—such as their fear that their valuation might not match ours or their belief that no good solutions to the problem exist.)

We also want to know about candidates' hierarchies of values. That is, if we know from examining the speeches that a candidate values twenty-seven things, we still want to know whether number twelve is valued more or less than number twenty-three. To discover the hierarchy we can look at how often candidates mention the various valued items (on the assumption that they, like us, talk more about the things that are more important to them). We also can look at the intensity of language when speaking of various valued items. There is, after all, a clear difference between saying "The most important thing to be accomplished in the next four years is . . ." and "It would be nice if we could . . ." We also can attempt to determine which way a candidate would "opt" when several valued items are in conflict. With George Bush, for instance, we knew that if he had a chance to solve a world problem or a domestic problem, he would opt for the world stage. With Clinton, the opposite was the case; world affairs took a back seat to domestic problems. With both Dole and Clinton we knew that, given a choice between getting some of what they wanted through compromise or taking the all-or-nothing route, they both would opt to compromise.

We also want to know what the candidates' major beliefs about values are. The two major beliefs are called "objective" and "subjective." The "objective" belief, which tends to be conservative, says values are good or bad for all time and everywhere, that citizens should all hold the same values, that concurrence on values is necessary for a stable and moral society. The more liberal belief, called "subjective," says that what is valuable at one time and place may not be valuable at other times and in other places, that it is expected and okay for people to hold differing values, that we can disagree on the importance of various matters and still build a sustainable and excellent society.

Clearly, we will want to determine where the candidates stand on the major values in U.S. politics—freedom, justice, individualism, community, responsibility, and morality. And again, when those values are in conflict, we want to know which way the candidates will opt. For instance, when freedom of speech is in conflict with responsibility to the community (as in debates about so-called "hate radio" or the morality of films) which candidate stresses freedom, which supports responsibility? Are they consistent, or does one support freedom for hate ratio and censorship for Hollywood?

How are the candidates' value stances related to power issues? Do the candidates seem to want to win the power of the White House for "instrumental" reasons, i.e., to *do* things, or do they seem to seek power for "consummatory" reasons, for instance to prove self-worth? In 1980, for example, Ted Kennedy did poorly in his attempt to wrest the Democrat nomination away from Jimmy Carter; he was perceived to want the office just because it was "his turn."

What kinds of power do candidates value—military power, reward power, expert power? When faced with a situation that cannot be solved by the application of power, is the candidate's rhetoric tinged with frustration? In 1992, for instance, I had the distinct impression that Ross Perot was frustrated that everybody didn't just roll over and play dead when he, with all his economic power, entered the race; that he thought he was such a logical candidate that he couldn't understand why the others didn't just withdraw and leave the field to him.

Most citizens want to know the role of religion in the candidates' value structures. Although difficult to determine, what one should look for is whether, when candidates introduce religion, it is a gloss over secularly determined positions or interwoven in the discussion of the issues, suggesting that it was a factor in the decision-making process. We probably also will want to determine *which* religious motifs permeate candidates' rhetoric. There is, after all, a tremendous difference between the candidate who uses the "eye for an eye" formulation and the one who stresses the "turn the other cheek" prescription.

All candidates speak affirmatively about "the American dream." But we should dig a little deeper. *Which* American dream permeates the rhetoric? The dream of freedom? The dream of material wealth? Do you care? That is, is one of those dreams more important to you than the other?

The final axiological question to be addressed is the one with which this book started, *the* basic value controversy in the United States: How much freedom versus how much order? Where does the candidate stand on that question? Where do you?

## CONCLUSION

▶ In the preceding pages, we have raised an enormous number of questions that any of us can "put to" the candidates by carefully examining primary sources—speeches, interviews, and debates. I have attempted to demonstrate the centrality of personality, leadership ideal, ideology, epistemology, and axiology to the evaluation of candidates, and to provide some methods for "getting at" those evaluations.

▶ I recognize that declaring our independence from the interpretations of the media, thereby making our own contributions to the societal dialogue, is not easy. But then, nobody ever said the citizenship role was a walk in the park. As Stephen Carter, the William Nelson Cromwell Professor of Law at Yale University, put it: "If we are too busy or too cynical to go out and do the hard work of democracy . . . then we can hardly complain when others take advantage of our political laziness or incompetence."[26] And yet, it is probably the case that not all of us need to follow all the strictures in this chapter. Which we adopt will depend upon our own value structures. If you don't care about issues but are concerned about personalities, you might want to ignore ideological concerns and concentrate on the methods for examining the personality of each candidate. The next person will take exactly the opposite tack. And each of you will have something to offer the other as you take part in the societal dialogue, something uniquely your own rather than merely derived from the media.

▶ As difficult as the analytic approaches set forth in this chapter may be, the most difficult task is the first to be undertaken: we first must decide our own evaluative criteria. After we do that, evaluating the candidates is, by comparison, a piece of cake. It becomes nearly automatic, almost as easy as evaluating the "candidates" for boss, date, and neighbor.

## FOR FURTHER CONSIDERATION

**1.** Select one of the five criteria presented in this chapter (personality orientation, leadership ideal, ideology, epistemology, axiology) and apply it to one of the two presidential candidates in the last campaign, using *only* primary sources (their own words and actions) rather than what was reported in the media. Then, using only secondary sources (media commentary), analyze the same person by the same criterion. Compare the two analyses to see how much distortion was introduced by the media.

**2.** In 1996 both Dole and Clinton advocated tax cuts. Dole proposed a 15 percent across-the-board cut, while Clinton opted for a series of smaller targeted cuts. Using each of the five criteria, examine the proposals as set forth by the candidates (not as "chewed over" by the media) to see what their words tell you about how their respective cuts reflected their personalities, ideologies, and so forth.

## NOTES

1. R. Schmuhl, "The Rhetorical Presidency in an Age of Hyperdemocracy and Hypercommunication," *Brigance Forum,* April 1995, 19.
2. D. Watson, "Against Forgetting," *Utne Reader,* March/April 1984, 114.
3. R. M. Gonchar Brennan and D. F. Hahn, *Listening for a President: A Citizen's Campaign Methodology* (New York: Praeger, 1990), 45–179.
4. W. Anderson, "Looking for Mr. Active-Positive," *Human Behavior,* October 1976, 18.
5. J. D. Barber, "Adult Identity and Presidential Style: The Rhetorical Emphasis," *Daedalus* 97 (Summer 1968): 939.
6. G. A. Hauser, *Introduction to Rhetorical Theory* (Prospect Heights, IL: Waveland Press, 1986), 96.

7. H. Sidey, "Presidential Character," *Miller Center Journal* 1 (Spring 1994): 129.

8. *Ibid.*, 129.

9. *Ibid.*, 130.

10. R. A. Heifetz, "We're to Blame," *New York Times,* 8 November 1994, p. A15.

11. Gonchar Brennan and Hahn, *op. cit.*, 73.

12. R. B. Hirschfield, *The Power of the Presidency: Concepts and Controversy* (New York: Atherton Press, 1968), 5.

13. *Ibid.*, 5.

14. L. H. Lapham, "Democracy in America?" *Harper's,* November 1990, 54.

15. Hirschfield, *op. cit.*, 85.

16. *Ibid.*, 82.

17. W. C. Pool, E. Craddock and E. D. Conrad, *Lyndon Johnson: The Formative Years* (San Marcos: Southwest Texas State College Press, 1965), 79.

18. Gonchar Brennan and Hahn, *op. cit.*, 93.

19. J. Carter, "Transcript of President's Address to Country on Energy Problems," *New York Times,* 16 July 1979, p. A10.

20. S. Chatman, "Stylistics: Quantitative and Qualitative," *Style* 1 (Winter 1967): 33.

21. Sidey, *op. cit.*, 128.

22. M. Ivins, "Coming to the Aid of GOP Brethren," *Liberal Opinion Week,* 26 February 1996, 9.

23. *Ibid.*, 9.

24. F. I. Hill, "Conventional Wisdom—Traditional Form: The President's Message of November 3, 1969," *Quarterly Journal of Speech* 53 (December 1972): 373–386.

25. Gonchar Brennan and Hahn, *op. cit.*, 156.

26. S. L. Carter, *Integrity* (New York: Basic Books, 1996).

# Selected Readings

Alexander, M. S. "Defining the Abortion Debate." *ETC., A Review of General Semantics* 50 (fall 1993): 271–275.

Anastaplo, G. "Education, Television, and Political Discourse in America." *Center Magazine* 19 (July/August 1986): 18–26.

Anderson, W. "Looking for Mr. Active-Positive." *Human Behavior*, October 1976, 16–21.

Bailey, F. G. *The Tactical Uses of Passion: An Essay on Power, Reason, and Reality.* Ithaca, NY: Cornell University Press, 1983.

Barber, J. D. "Adult Identity and Presidential Style: The Rhetorical Emphasis." *Daedalus* 97 (summer 1968): 938–968.

Barber, J. D. "The Journalist's Responsibility: Make Reality Interesting." *Center Magazine* 18 (May/June 1985): 11–15.

Barber, J. D. *The Presidential Character: Predicting Performance in the White House.* Englewood Cliffs, NJ: Prentice-Hall, 1972.

Bartels, L. M. "Messages Received: The Political Impact of Media Exposure." *American Political Science Review* 87 (June 1993): 267–285.

Benjamin, G., ed. *The Communication Revolution in Politics: Proceedings of the Academy of Political Science* 34 (Number 4, 1982): 131–142.

Bennett, W. L. "White Noise: The Perils of Mass Mediated Democracy." *Communication Monographs* 59 (December 1992): 401–406.

Bennett, W. L., and M. Edelman. "Toward a New Political Narrative." *Journal of Communication* 34 (autumn 1985): 156–171.

Benoit, W. L., and W. T. Wells. *Candidates in Conflict: Persuasive Attack and Defense in the 1992 Presidential Debates.* Tuscaloosa: University of Alabama Press, 1996.

Benson, T. W. "Poisoned Minds." *Southern Speech Journal* 34 (fall 1968): 54–60.

Beres, L. R. "Embracing Omnicide: President Reagan and the Strategic Mythmakers." *Hudson Review* 36 (spring 1983): 17–29.

Berger, A. "Hot Language and Cool Lives." *In Language Awareness,* edited by P. A. Eschholz, A. F. Rosa, and V. P. Clark, 239–241. New York: St. Martin's, 1974.

Bernard, J. *The Female World.* New York: Free Press, 1981.

Berthold, C. "Kenneth Burke's Cluster-agon Method: Its Development and Application." *Central States Speech Journal* 27 (winter 1976): 302–309.

Bierstedt, R. "The Ethics of Cognitive Communication." *Journal of Communication* 13 (September 1963): 199–203.

Billig, M. *Ideology and Opinions: Studies in Rhetorical Psychology.* London: Sage, 1991.

Bineham, J. "Some Ethical Implications of Team Sports Metaphors in Politics." *Communication Reports* 4 (winter 1991): 34–43.

Bishop, G. F., R. G. Meadow, and M. Jackson-Beeck, eds. *The Presidential Debates: Media, Electoral, and Policy Perspectives.* New York: Praeger, 1978.

Black, E. "Ideological Justifications." *Quarterly Journal of Speech* 70 (1984): 144–150.

Black, E. "The Second Persona." *Quarterly Journal of Speech* 56 (April 1970): 109–119.

Black, E. "Secrecy and Disclosure as Rhetorical Forms." *Quarterly Journal of Speech* 74 (May 1988): 133–150.

Black, M. *The Labyrinth of Language.* New York: Praeger, 1968.

Blair, C., and M. Cooper. "The Humanist Turn in Foucault's Rhetoric of Inquiry." *Quarterly Journal of Speech* 73 (May 1987): 151–171.

Blonsky, M. *American Mythologies.* New York: Oxford University Press, 1992.

Blonsky, M., ed. *On Signs.* Baltimore: Johns Hopkins University Press, 1985.

Boorstin, D. J. *The Image: A Guide to Pseudo-Events in America.* New York: Harper and Row, 1961.

Borisoff, D., and D. F. Hahn. "Gender Power in Context: A Reevaluation of Communication in Professional Relationships." *New Dimensions in Communications: Proceedings of the 52nd Annual Conference* 8 (fall 1995): 11–27.

Borisoff, D., and D. F. Hahn. "The Mirror in the Window: Displaying Our Gender Biases." In *Voices in the Street: Explorations in Gender, Media, and Public Space,* edited by S. J. Drucker and G. Gumpert, 101–117. Creskill, NJ: Hampton Press, 1997.

Borisoff, D., and D. F. Hahn. "Thinking with the Body: Sexual Metaphors." *Communication Quarterly* 41 (summer 1993): 253–260.

Bormann, E. G. "A Fantasy Theme Analysis of the Television Coverage of the Hostage Release and the Reagan Inaugural." *Quarterly Journal of Speech* 68 (May 1982): 133–145.

Bowlby, R. *Just Looking: Consumer Culture in Dreiser, Gissing, and Zola.* New York: Methuen, 1985.

Brasch, W. M., and D. R. Ulloth, eds. *The Press and the State: Sociohistorical and Contemporary Studies.* Lanham, MD: University Press of America, 1986.

Broder, D. S. "Of Presidents and Parties." *Wilson Quarterly* 2 (winter 1978): 105–114.

Brown, G. "The Conclusion of Ronald Reagan's Narrative: The Rest of the Story." Paper presented at the annual convention of the Southern States Communication Association, Lexington, KY, 1989.

Brydon, S. R. "Outsider vs. Insider: The Two Faces of Jimmy Carter." Paper presented at Central States Speech Association Convention, Chicago, IL, February 1981.

Buller, D. B., K. D. Strzyzrewski, and F. C. Hunsaker. "Interpersonal Deception: II. The Inferiority of Conversational Participants as Deception Detectors." *Communication Monographs* 58 (March 1991): 25–40.

Burke, K. *Language as Symbolic Action: Essays on Life, Literature, and Method.* Berkeley: University of California Press, 1966.

Burke, K. *The Philosophy of Literary Form: Studies in Symbolic Action,* 3d ed. Berkeley: University of California Press, 1973.

Campbell, K. K., and K. H. Jamieson. *Deeds Done in Words: Presidential Rhetoric and the Genres of Governance.* Chicago: University of Chicago Press, 1990.

Canto, M. "The Politics of Women's Bodies: Reflections on Plato." In *The Female Body in Modern Culture: Contemporary Perspectives,* translated by A. Goldhammer, edited by S. R. Sulieman. Cambridge, MA: Harvard University Press, 1985.

Carpenter, R. H. "The Symbolic Substance of Style in Presidential Discourse." *Style* 16 (winter 1982): 38–49.

Carter, S. L. *Integrity.* New York: Basic Books, 1996.

Cassell, C. *Swept Away: Why Women Confuse Love and Sex.* New York: Fireside Press, 1984.

Charland, M. "Constitutive Rhetoric: The Case of the Peuple Québécois," *Quarterly Journal of Speech* 73 (May 1987): 133–150.

Chatman, S. "Stylistics: Quantitative and Qualitative." *Style* 1 (winter 1967): 29–43.

Chen, K. H. "Beyond Truth and Method: On Misreading Gadamer's Praxical Hermeneutics." *Quarterly Journal of Speech* 73 (May 1987): 183–199.

Cheney, G. "'Talking War': Symbols, Strategies, and Images." *Studies on the Left* 14 (1990–1991): 8–16.

Clark, R. "The Case Against All Forms of Government Secrecy." *Center Magazine* 11 (January/February 1978): 70–72.

Clayman, S. E. "Defining Moments, Presidential Debates, and the Dynamics of Quotability." *Journal of Communication* 45 (summer 1995): 118–146.

Condit, C. M. "Crafting Virtue: The Rhetorical Construction of Public Morality." *Quarterly Journal of Speech* 73 (1987): 79–97.

Connolly, W. E. *The Terms of Political Discourse*. Princeton, NJ: Princeton University Press, 1983.

Corcoran, P. E. *Political Language and Rhetoric*. Austin: University of Texas Press, 1979.

Cornfield, M. B. "The Press and Political Controversy: The Case for Narrative Analysis." Paper presented at convention of the American Political Science Association, Washington, DC, April 1991.

Cornwall, E. E., Jr. "The President and the Press: Phases in the Relationship." *Annals of the American Academy of Political and Social Sciences* 427 (September 1976): 53–64.

Davis, D. K., and T. F. N. Puckett. "Mass Entertainment and Community: Toward a Culture-Centered Paradigm for Mass Communication Research." *Communication Yearbook* 15 (1992): 3–34.

Davis, F. *Fashion, Culture, and Identity*. Chicago: University of Chicago Press, 1992.

de Beauvoir, S. *The Second Sex*. Translated and edited by H. M. Parshley. New York: Vintage Books, 1952.

deMause, L., and H. Ebel. *Jimmy Carter and American Fantasy: Psychohistorical Explorations*. New York: Two Continents/Psychohistory Press, 1977.

deMause, L. *Reagan's America*. New York: Creative Roots, 1984.

Denton, R. E., Jr., and D. F. Hahn. *Presidential Communication: Description and Analysis*. New York: Praeger, 1986.

Denton, R. E., Jr., and R. L. Holloway. *The Clinton Presidency: Images, Issues, and Communication Strategies*. Westport, CT: Praeger, 1996.

Denton, R. E., Jr., and M. Stuckey, "Presidential Speech as Mediated Conversation." Paper presented at the annual meeting of the Speech Communication Association, New York, November 1980.

DeWine, S. "Female Leadership in Male Dominated Organizations." *ACA Bulletin* 61 (August 1987): 19–29.

Dow, B. J. "Feminism, Difference(s), and Rhetorical Studies." *Communication Studies* 46 (spring 1995): 106–117.

Drucker, S. J., and G. Gumpert, "The Mediation of Political Talk." Paper presented at the annual convention of the International Communication Association, Miami, May 1992.

Duby, G., ed. *A History of Private Life, II. Revelations of the Medieval World*. Cambridge, MA: Belknap Press of Harvard University Press, 1988.

Eckhardt, K. W. "Exchange in Sexual Permissiveness." *Behavioral Science* Notes 1 (1971): 1–86.

Edelman, M. *Constructing the Political Spectacle*. Chicago: University of Chicago Press, 1988.

Edelman, M. "Myths, Metaphors, and Political Conformity." *Psychiatry* 30 (August 1967): 217–228.

Edelman, M. "On Policies that Fail." *Progressive*, May 1975, 22–23.

Edelman, M. *The Symbolic Uses of Politics*. Urbana: University of Illinois Press, 1967.

Edwards, G. C., III, and S. J. Wayne. *Presidential Leadership: Politics and Policy Making*. New York: St. Martin's, 1985.

Elder, C. D., and R. W. Cobb. *The Political Uses of Symbols*. New York: Longman, 1983.

Emerson, T. I. "The Danger of State Secrecy." *Nation*, 30 March 1974, 395–399.

Entman, R. M. *Democracy Without Citizens: Media and the Decay of American Politics*. New York: Oxford University Press, 1989.

Entman, R. M. "Reporting Environmental Policy Debate: The Real Media Biases." *Press/Politics* 1 (summer 1996): 77–92.

Epstein, E. J. *News from Nowhere.* New York: Random House, 1973.

Erickson, P. D. *Reagan Speaks: The Making of an American Myth.* New York: New York University Press, 1985.

Ericson, J. L., and R. F. Forston, eds. *Public Speaking as Dialogue: Readings and Essays.* Baton Rouge: Louisiana State University Press, 1970.

Eschholz, P. A., A. F. Rosa, and V. P. Clark, eds. *Language Awareness.* New York: St. Martin's, 1974.

Etzold, T. H., and J. L. Gaddis, eds. *Containment: Documents on American Policy and Strategy, 1945–1950.* New York: Columbia University Press, 1978.

Fallows, J. "Why Americans Hate the Media." *Atlantic Monthly,* February 1996, 45–64.

Fenno, R. *Home Style: House Members in Their Districts.* Boston: Little, Brown, 1978.

Fishkin, J. S. "Talk of the Tube: How to Get Teledemocracy Right." *American Prospect,* fall 1992, 46–52.

Fitzgerald, V. M. "Public Opinion Polls and Network News Coverage of Presidential Campaigns." Paper presented at the annual convention of the Speech Communication Association, San Antonio, TX, November 1995.

Freedman, R. *Beauty Bound.* Lexington, MA: D. C. Heath, 1986.

Friedberg, A. "*Les Flaneurs du Mal* (1): Cinema and the Postmodern Condition." *PMLA,* May 1991, 419–431.

Friedenberg, R. V., ed. *Rhetorical Studies of National Political Debates, 1960–1992.* New York: Praeger, 1993.

Friedrich, C. J. *The Pathology of Politics: Violence, Betrayal, Corruption, Secrecy, and Propaganda.* New York: Harper and Row, 1972.

Fromm, E. *The Dogma of Christ and Other Essays on Religion, Psychology, and Culture.* Greenwich, CT: Fawcett, 1955.

Galbraith, J. K. "Who Needs the Democrats?" *Harper's,* July 1970, 43–62.

Gandy, O. H. "The Surveillance Society: Information Technology and Bureaucratic Social Control." *Journal of Communication* 39 (summer 1989): 61–76.

Gardner, G. *The Mocking of the President: A History of Campaign Humor from Ike to Ronnie.* Detroit: Wayne State University Press, 1988.

Garver, E. "Ancient Rhetoric and Modern Problems." In *Rhetoric 78: Proceedings of Theory of Rhetoric, An Interdisciplinary Conference,* edited by R. L. Brown, Jr. and M. Steinmann, Jr., 77–89. Minneapolis: University of Minnesota Center for Advanced Studies in Language, Style, and Literary Theory, 1979.

Gibson, W. *Euphemism.* Harper Studies in Language and Literature pamphlet. New York: Harper and Row, 1974.

Glasser, T. L., and C. T. Salmon. *Public Opinion and the Communication of Consent.* New York: Guilford, 1995.

Glendon, M. A. *Rights Talk: The Impoverishment of Political Discourse.* New York: Free Press, 1991.

Golding, P., G. Murdock and P. Schlesinger. *Communicating Politics: Mass Communications and the Political Process.* New York: Holmes and Meier, 1986.

Goldman, E. F. "Party of One: On Presidential Prose." *Holiday,* April 1963, 11–19.

Gonchar Brennan, R. M., and D. F. Hahn. *Listening for a President: A Citizen's Campaign Methodology.* New York: Praeger, 1990.

Gonchar, R. M., and D. F. Hahn. "Political Myth: The Image and the Issue." *Today's Speech* 20 (summer 1972): 57–65.

Gonchar, R. M., and D. F. Hahn. "The Rhetorical Predictability of Richard M. Nixon." *Today's Speech* 19 (fall 1971): 3–13.

Graber, D. A. "Television Coverage of the 1984 Campaign." Paper presented at the annual convention of the International Communication Association, Montreal, June 1987.

Graff, H. F. "The 'Ordinary Man' as President." *New Leader*, 2 September 1974, 7–9.

Grainger, R. *The Language of the Rite*. London: Darton, Longman and Todd, 1974.

Greene, J. R. *The Crusade: The Presidential Election of 1952*. Lanham, MD: University Press of America, 1985.

Greenstein, F. I. *Leadership in the Modern Presidency*. Cambridge, MA: Harvard University Press, 1988.

Grimes, R. L. *Marrying and Burying: Rites of Passage in a Man's Life*. Boulder, CO: Westview Press, 1995.

Grossman, M. B., and M. J. Kumar. "The White House and the News Media: The Phases of Their Relationship." *Political Science Quarterly* 93 (spring 1979): 37–53.

Gurevitch, M., and A. P. Kavoori. "Television Spectacles as Politics." *Communication Monographs* 59 (December 1992): 415–420.

Hahn, D. F. "Corrupt Rhetoric: President Ford and the Mayaguez Affair." *Communication Quarterly* 28 (spring 1980): 38–43.

Hahn, D. F. "The Effect of Television on Presidential Campaigns." *Today's Speech* 18 (spring 1970): 4–17.

Hahn, D. F. "Flailing the Profligate: Carter's Energy Sermon of 1979." *Presidential Studies Quarterly* 10 (fall 1980): 583–587.

Hahn, D. F. "Myths, Metaphors, and American Politics." *Et Cetera* 35 (September 1978): 254–264.

Hahn, D. F. "Nixon's Second (Hortatory) Inaugural." *Speaker and Gavel* 10 (May 1973): 111–113.

Hahn, D. F. "Old Rhetoric in Old Bottles." *Speaker and Gavel* 8 (March 1971): 70–72.

Hahn, D. F. "Political Language: The Art of Saying Nothing." *In Beyond 1984: The English Language in an Orwellian Age*, edited by William Lutz, 111–120. Chicago: National Council of Teachers of English, 1989.

Hahn, D. F. "Romantic and Sexual Symbolism in Presidential Politics." Paper presented at the annual convention of the Speech Communication Association, Miami, November 1993.

Hahn, D. F., and D. Borisoff. "Gender and the Binary Discourse System." *Speech Communication Annual* 9 (spring 1995): 33–50.

Hahn, D. F., and R. L. Ivie. "'Sex' as Rhetorical Invitation to War." *Et Cetera* 45 (spring 1988): 15–21.

Hahn, D. F., and S. Mackey-Kallis. "The Passionless Honeymoon: Bush in the White House." Paper presented at the annual convention of the Eastern Communication Association, Philadelphia, April 1990.

Hahn, D. F., and M. Stuckey. "From Courtship to Date-Rape: False Intimacy in the White House." Paper presented at the annual convention of the Eastern Communication Association, Portland, ME, April 1992.

Hallin, D. C. "The Passing of the High Modernism of American Journalism." *Journal of Communication* 42 (summer 1992): 14–25.

Halverson, J. "The Psycho-Pathology of Style: The Case of Right-Wing Rhetoric." *Antioch Review* 31 (spring 1971): 97–108.

Hankins, G. A. "Western Media Coverage of Conflicts in Their Own Backyard: An Analysis of News Media Coverage of the African-American Community." Paper presented at the annual convention of the Speech Communication Association, Chicago, November 1990.

Hart, R. P. *The Sound of Leadership: Presidential Communication in the Modern Age*. Chicago: University of Chicago Press, 1987.

Hart, R. P. *Verbal Style and the Presidency: A Computer-Based Analysis*. Orlando, FL: Academic Press (Harcourt Brace Jovanovich), 1984.

Hatfield, E., and S. Sprecher. *Mirror, Mirror: The Importance of Looks in Everyday Life*. Albany: State University of New York Press, 1986.

Hauser, G. A. *Introduction to Rhetorical Theory.* Prospect Heights, IL: Waveland Press, 1986.

Heer, F. "Man's Three Languages." *Center Magazine* 4 (November/December 1971): 66–70.

Henley, N. M. *Body Politics: Power, Sex, and Nonverbal Communication.* Englewood Cliffs, NJ: Prentice-Hall, 1977.

Higonnet, M. R., J. Jenson, S. Michel, and M. C. Weitz, eds. *Behind the Lines: Gender and the Two World Wars.* New Haven: Yale University Press, 1987.

Hill, F. I. "Conventional Wisdom—Traditional Form: The President's Message of November 3, 1969." *Quarterly Journal of Speech* 58 (December 1972): 373–386.

Hillbruner, A. "Born Again: Carter's Inaugural Sermon." Paper presented at Speech Communication Association Convention, Washington, DC, December 1977.

Hirschfield, R. B. *The Power of the Presidency: Concepts and Controversy.* New York: Atherton Press, 1968.

Hirschman, A. O. *The Rhetoric of Reaction: Perversity, Futility, Jeopardy.* Cambridge, MA: Belknap Press of Harvard University Press, 1991.

Hocking, J. E., and D. C. Leathers. "Nonverbal Indicators of Deception: A New Theoretical Perspective." *Communication Monographs* 47 (June 1980): 119–131.

Hopper, R., and R. A. Bell. "Broadening the Deception Construct." *Quarterly Journal of Speech* 70 ( August 1984): 288–302.

Irigaray, L. *An Ethics of Sexual Difference.* Ithaca, NY: Cornell University Press, 1993.

Ivie, R. L. "Images of Savagery in American Justifications for War." *Communication Monographs* 47 ( November 1980): 279–294.

Ivie, R. L. "The Metaphor of Force in Prowar Discourse: The Case of 1812." *Quarterly Journal of Speech* 68 (August 1982): 240–253.

Jack, E.T. "A Community's Public Talk." *PS: Political Science and Politics,* December 1993, 722–725.

Jamieson, K. H. *Eloquence in an Electronic Age: The Transformation of Political Speechmaking.* New York: Oxford University Press, 1988 .

Jamieson, K. H. *Packaging the Presidency: A History and Criticism of Presidential Campaign Advertising.* New York: Oxford University Press, 1984.

Jamieson, K. H., and D. S. Birdsell. *Presidential Debates: The Challenge of Creating an Informed Electorate.* New York: Oxford University Press, 1988.

Jamieson, K. H., and K. K. Campbell. *The Interplay of Influence: Mass Media and Their Publics in News, Advertising, Politics.* Belmont: Wadsworth, 1992.

Johnson, M. *The Body in the Mind: The Bodily Basis of Meaning, Imagination, and Reason.* Chicago: University of Chicago Press, 1987.

Johnstone, C. L. "Illuminating the Logos: Speech, Thought, and Being in the Philosophy of Heraclitus." Paper presented at the Eastern Communication Association annual convention, Ocean City, MD, May 1989.

Johnstone, C. L. "Thoreau and Civil Disobedience: A Rhetorical Paradox." *Quarterly Journal of Speech* 60 (October 1974): 313–322.

Kearns, D. *Lyndon Johnson and the American Dream.* New York: New American Library, 1976.

Keen, S. *Faces of the Enemy: Reflections of the Hostile Imagination.* San Francisco: Harper and Row, 1986.

Keen, S. *Fire in the Belly: On Being a Man.* New York: Bantam Books, 1991.

Kernell, S. *Going Public: New Strategies of Presidential Leadership.* Washington, DC: Congressional Quarterly Press, 1986.

Kiewe, A. *The Modern Presidency and Crisis Rhetoric.* Westport, CT: Praeger, 1994.

Kornbluh, F. A. "The New Literature on Gender and the Welfare State: The U.S. Case." *Feminist Studies* 22 (spring 1996): 171–197.

Kraus, S., ed. *The Great Debates: Background, Perspective, Effects.* Bloomington: Indiana University Press, 1962.

Kraus, S., ed. *The Great Debates: Carter vs. Ford, 1976.* Bloomington: Indiana University Press, 1979.

Kraus, S. *Televised Political Debates and Public Policy.* Hillsdale, NJ: Lawrence Erlbaum, 1988.

Kruger, H. N. "The Access to Federal Records Law." *Freedom of Information Center Report No. 186,* September 1967, 1–7.

LaFeber, W. *Inevitable Revolutions: The United States in Central America.* New York: Norton, 1984.

Lakoff, G., and M. Johnson. *Metaphors We Live By.* Chicago: University of Chicago Press, 1980.

Lerner, M. "Clinton's Hypocrisy Factor." *Tikkun* 9 (May/June 1994): 8–10.

Lowi, T. *The Personal President: Power Invested, Promise Unfulfilled.* Ithaca, NY: Cornell University Press, 1985.

Lutz, W. "Doublespeak Here and There." *Quarterly Review of Doublespeak* 15 (January 1989): 4–10.

Lyford, J. P. "Journalism in Government." *Center Magazine* 7 (July/August 1974): 2–7.

Martel, M. *Political Campaign Debates: Images, Strategies, and Tactics.* New York: Longman, 1983.

McClosky, H. "Consensus and Ideology in American Politics." *American Political Science Review* 58 (June 1964), 361–382.

McConnell, F. D. "Toward a Lexicon of Slogans." *Midwest Quarterly* 13 (October 1971): 69–90.

McGee, M. C. "The 'Ideograph': A Link Between Rhetoric and Ideology." *Quarterly Journal of Speech* 66 (February 1980): 1–16.

McGee, M. C. "The Origins of 'Liberty': A Feminization of Power." *Communication Monographs* 47 ( March 1980): 23–45.

Meadow, R. G. *Politics as Communication.* Norwood, NJ: Ablex, 1980.

Meyrowitz, J. *No Sense of Place: The Impact of Electronic Media on Social Behavior.* New York: Oxford University Press, 1985.

Meyrowitz, J. "The Rise of 'Middle Region' Politics." *Et Cetera* 34 ( June 1977): 133–140.

Miles, M. R. *Carnal Knowing: Female Nakedness and Religious Meaning in the Christian West.* New York: Vintage Books, 1989.

Miller, J. H. "The Still Heart: Poetic Form in Wordsworth." *New Literary History* 2 (winter 1971): 297–310.

Mitchell, L. D. *With the Nation Watching.* Lexington, MA: Lexington Books, 1979.

Mumby, D. K. "Ideology and the Social Construction of Meaning: A Communication Perspective." *Communication Quarterly* 37 (fall 1989): 291–304.

Murray, H. A., ed. *Myth and Mythmaking.* Boston: Beacon Press, 1960.

Nicolson, N., and J. Trautman, eds. *The Letters of Virginia Woolf: Volume II, 1912–1922.* New York: Harcourt Brace Jovanovich, 1976.

Nimmo, D. D., and K. R. Sanders, eds. *Handbook of Political Communication.* Beverly Hills, CA: Sage, 1981.

Opfer, J., and P. A. Andersen. "Explaining the Sound Bite: A Text of a Theory of Metaphor and Assonance." Paper presented at the annual convention of the Western Speech Communication Association, Boise, ID, February 1992.

Osborn, M. "The Rhetorical Metaphor in Criticism." Unpublished and undated manuscript, Memphis State University.

Paletz, D. L., and R. M. Entman. *Media, Power, Politics.* New York: Free Press, 1981.

Parenti, M. *Land of Idols: Political Mythology in America.* New York: St. Martin's, 1994.

Pathey-Chavez, G. G., L. Clare, and M. Youmans. "Watery Passion: The Struggle Between Hegemony and Sexual Liberation in Erotic Fiction for Women." *Discourse and Society* 7 (January 1996): 77–106.

Patterson, T. E. *Out of Order.* New York: Knopf, 1993.

Patterson, T. G., ed. *The Origins of the Cold War.* Lexington, MA: D.C. Heath, 1974.

Pitkin, H. F. *Fortune is a Woman: Gender and Politics in the Thought of Niccolo Machiavelli.* Berkeley: University of California Press, 1984.

Pool, W. C., E. Craddock, and E. D. Conrad. *Lyndon Johnson: The Formative Years*. San Marcos: Southwest Texas State College Press, 1965.

Press, C., and K. VerBurg. *American Politicians and Journalists*. Glenview, IL: Scott, Foresman, 1988.

Pyle, C. H. "Spies Without Masters: The Army Still Watches Civilian Politics." *Civil Liberties Review* 1 (summer 1974): 38–49.

Ranney, A., ed. *The Past and Future of Presidential Debates*. Washington, DC: American Enterprise Institute for Public Policy Research, 1979.

Reich, D. R., and P. A. Dawson. *Political Images and Realities: Essays and Readings on the Concepts and Substance of American Politics*. North Scituate, MA: Duxbury Press, 1972.

Ritter, K. W., ed. *The 1980 Presidential Debates*. Lawrence, KS: Allen Press, 1981. (Special issue of *Speaker and Gavel* 18:2.)

Ritter, K. W., and J. R. Andrews. *The American Ideology: Reflections on the Revolution in American Rhetoric*. Annandale, VA: Speech Communication Association, 1978.

Rockman, B. *The Leadership Question: The Presidency and the American System*. New York: Praeger, 1984.

Rubin, L. B. *Intimate Strangers: Men and Women Together*. New York: Harper & Row, 1983.

Rushing, J. H. "Evolution of 'The New Frontier' in *Alien* and *Aliens:* Patriarchal Co-optation of the Feminine Archetype." *Quarterly Journal of Speech* 75 (February 1989): 1–24.

Ryan, H., ed. *U.S. Presidents as Orators: A Bio-Critical Sourcebook*. Westport, CT: Greenwood, 1995.

Saloma, J. S., III. *Ominous Politics*. New York: Hill and Wang, 1984.

Schiappa, E. "Interdisciplinarity and Social Practice: Reflections on Dow, Condit, and Swartz." *Communication Studies* 46 (spring–summer 1995): 140–147.

Schmuhl, R. "The Rhetorical Presidency in an Age of Hyperdemocracy and Hypercommunication." *Brigance Forum*, April 1995, 13–19.

Scholes, R. *Uncoding Mama: The Female Body as Text*. New Haven, CT: Yale University Press, 1982.

Schudson, M. "The Limits of Teledemocracy." *American Prospect*, fall 1992, 41–45.

Selnow, G. W. "Values in Prime-Time Television." *Journal of Communication* 40 (spring 1990): 64–74.

Sennett, R. *The Fall of Public Man*. New York: Knopf, 1977.

Shapiro, M. J. *Language and Politics*. New York: New York University Press, 1984.

Sidey, H. "Presidential Character." *Miller Center Journal* 1 (spring 1994): 127–131.

Simons, H. W., and A. A. Aghazarian, eds. *Form, Genre, and the Study of Political Discourse*. Columbia: University of South Carolina Press, 1986.

Singer, M. G. "The Pragmatic Use of Language and the Will to Believe." *American Philosophical Quarterly* 8 (January 1971): 24–34.

Smith, C. A. *Political Communication*. San Diego, CA: Harcourt Brace Jovanovich, 1990.

Smith, S. A., ed. *Bill Clinton on Stump, State, and Stage: The Rhetorical Road to the White House*. Fayetteville: University of Arkansas Press, 1994.

Snow, R. P. *Creating Media Culture*. Beverly Hills: Sage, 1983.

Sorkin, M. C., ed. *Variations on a Theme Park: The New American City and the End of Public Space*. New York: Hill and Wang, 1992.

Spero, R. *The Duping of the American Voter: Dishonesty and Deception in Presidential Television Advertising*. New York: Lippincott and Crowell, 1980.

Springer, M., ed. *What Manner of Women: Essays on English and American Life and Literature*. New York: New York University Press, 1977.

Sproule, J. M. "Propaganda. The Ideological Rhetoric." Paper presented at the Conference of the Rhetoric Society of America, University of Texas at Arlington, May 1988.

Steamer, R. J. "A Self-Evident Assumption." *Freedom of Information Center Publication No. 32,* July 1960, 1–3.

Stelzner, H. "Humphrey and Kennedy Court West Virginia, May 3, 1960." *Southern Speech Communication Journal* 37 (fall 1971): 21–33.

Stewart, L. P., and S. Ting-Toomey, eds. *Communication, Gender, and Sex Roles in Diverse Interaction Contexts.* Norwood, NJ: Ablex, 1987.

Stuckey, M. E. *Playing the Game: The Presidential Rhetoric of Ronald Reagan.* New York: Praeger, 1990.

Stuckey, M. E. *The President as Interpreter-in-Chief.* Chatham, NJ: Chatham House, 1991.

Swanson, D. L. "And That's the Way it Was? Television Covers the 1976 Presidential Campaign." *Quarterly Journal of Speech* 63 (October 1977): 239–248.

Swanson, D. L., and D. Nimmo. *New Directions in Political Communication: A Resource Book.* Newbury Park: Sage, 1990.

Swerdlow, J. L. *Beyond Debate: A Paper on Televised Presidential Debates.* New York: Twentieth Century Fund, 1984.

Swerdlow, J. L., ed. *Presidential Debates: 1988 and Beyond.* Washington, DC: Congressional Quarterly Press, 1988.

Szasz, T.S. "Language and Humanism." *Humanist,* January/February 1974, 25–30.

Tavris, C. *The Mismeasure of Woman.* New York: Simon & Schuster, 1992.

Thass-Thienemann, T. *The Interpretation of Language, Vol. II: Understanding the Unconscious Meaning of Language.* New York: Jason Aronson, 1968.

Thompson, K. W., ed. *The White House Press on the Presidency.* Lanham, MD: University Press of America, 1983.

Trent, J. S., and R. V. Friedenberg. *Political Campaign Communication: Principles and Practices,* 2d ed. New York: Praeger, 1991.

Turner, S. "Intelligence and Secrecy in an Open Society." *Center Magazine* 19 (March/April 1986): 2–5.

Underhill, R. *The Bully Pulpit: From Franklin Roosevelt to Ronald Reagan.* New York: Vantage Press, 1988.

van Dijk, T. A. "Discourse Semantics and Ideology." *Discourse and Society* 6 (April 1995): 243–289.

Veyne, P., ed. *A History of Private Life, I: From Pagan Rome to Byzantium.* Cambridge, MA: Belknap Press of Harvard University Press, 1987.

Wadsworth, A. J., and L. L. Kaid. "Incumbent and Challenger Styles in Presidential Advertising." Paper presented at the annual convention of the International Communication Association, Montreal, June 1987.

Weaver, R. M. *The Ethics of Rhetoric.* Chicago: Regnery, 1953.

Weaver, R. M. *Visions of Order: The Cultural Crisis of Our Time.* Baton Rouge: Louisiana State University Press, 1964.

Weiler, M., and W. B. Pearce. *Reagan and Public Discourse in America.* Tuscaloosa: University of Alabama Press, 1992.

Weinberger, C. W. *Soviet Military Power.* Washington: GOP, 1983.

Weisbord, M. R. *Campaigning for President: A New Look at the Road to the White House.* Washington, DC: Public Affairs Press, 1964.

White, T. H. *The Making of the President 1964.* New York: Atheneum, 1965.

Wilkinson, R. *American Tough: The Tough-Guy Tradition and American Character.* New York: Harper and Row (Perennial Library), 1984.

Wilson, J. *Politically Speaking: The Pragmatic Analysis of Political Language.* Oxford: Basil Blackwell, 1990.

Windt, T. O., Jr. *Presidents and Protesters: Political Rhetoric in the 1960s.* Tuscaloosa: University of Alabama Press, 1990.

Windt, T., and B. Ingold. *Essays in Presidential Rhetoric.* Dubuque, IA: Kendall/Hunt, 1983.

Wolf, N. *The Beauty Myth: How Images of Beauty Are Used against Women.* New York: Morrow, 1991.

Woodward, G. C. *Perspectives on American Political Media.* Boston: Allyn and Bacon, 1997.

Woodward, G. C. "Toward a Model of Recurring Form in Presidential Rhetoric: An Overview." Paper presented at Central States Speech Association Convention, Lincoln, NE, April 1983.

Yudof, M. G. *When Government Speaks: Politics, Law, and Government Expression in America.* Berkeley: University of California Press, 1983.

Zacharius, D. W. "Communication and Social Change." *Quarterly Journal of Speech* 58 (April 1972): 217–223.

Zarefsky, D. *President Johnson's War on Poverty: Rhetoric and History.* University: University of Alabama Press, 1986.

Zarefsky, D. "The Roots of American Community." The Carroll C. Arnold Distinguished Lecture Presented at the Annual Convention of the Speech Communication Association, San Antonio, Texas, 17 November 1995. Boston: Allyn and Bacon, 1996.

# Index

# About the Author

**DAN F. HAHN** is a Visiting Professor in the Department of Culture and Communication at New York University. Educated at Kansas State University (B.S.), the University of Kansas (M.A.), and the University of Arizona (Ph.D.), he is the author of more than 150 articles and papers that explore aspects of political communication. He is also the coauthor of two books, *Presidential Communication: Description and Analysis* (with Robert E. Denton, Jr.) and *Listening for a President: A Citizen's Campaign Methodology* (with Ruth Gonchar Brennan).

Dr. Hahn has chaired the departments of communication at Queens College and Florida Atlantic University. He has served as president of the Eastern Communication Association. His recent honors include the National Speakers Association's Outstanding Professor Award (1994), the Florida Communication Association's Scholar of the Year Award (1995), selection for *Who's Who Among America's Teachers* (1996), the Eastern Communication Association's Distinguished Service Award for lifetime contributions to the field (1996), and election as an Eastern Communication Association Research Fellow (1996) and Teaching Fellow (1997).